Bankruptcy: The Law and Practice

Fourmat Publishing

Bankruptcy: The Law and Practice

by Clive Grenville

London
Fourmat Publishing
1987

ISBN 1 85190 032 2

First published 1987

Fourmat Publishing
27 & 28 St Albans Place, Islington Green, London N1 ONX
Printed in Great Britain

Preface

Bankruptcy is an artificial system, the creation of successive statutes, which does not originate from common law. It applies to individuals not corporations, and in 1976 the legislation started to be contained within the generic expression "insolvency", so that now the words "individual insolvency" and "bankruptcy" are interchangeable.

The law on bankruptcy, which had been generally set in its modern form for over one hundred years, starting with the Bankruptcy Act 1883, was amended by Part III of the Insolvency Act 1985. This has now been consolidated in Parts VIII to XI of the Insolvency Act 1986, otherwise identified by that curious amalgam, "the second group of Parts", to which all references in this book relate unless otherwise stated.

The following provisions of the 1985 Act have not been consolidated as they affect amendments to both Acts: s 215 (land registration), s 218 (employment), s 219 (banking), and s 220 (administration orders). Both Acts came fully into force on 29 December 1986 and have to be read together in regard to the consequential provisions. Likewise, minor parts of the Bankruptcy Act 1883 and the Insolvency Act 1976 still apply, and reference to these is made in the text where appropriate.

Before any proceedings may be commenced in bankruptcy, the creditor had previously to answer the following questions:

1. Is the individual legally capable of being made bankrupt?
2. Has he committed an act of bankruptcy?
3. Is the individual who proposes to initiate the proceedings legally competent to do so?
4. Has the debtor presented his own petition in bankruptcy?

To which he must now add:

5. Is there an interim order?

Question 2, however, is obsolete, for there is now no requirement for the "act of bankruptcy"; it is replaced by the catch-all "no reasonable prospect of paying", to which conditions apply, and there is now no formal receivership, merely an order. All matters previously referred to either as "acts" or "avoidable acts" of bankruptcy, together with the date of the receiving order, have therefore been swept aside and are not revived in this book unless the context so permits.

Of immediate importance is the need for the debtor to understand the new alternative procedures; and for the creditor to recognise the potential advantage of the new code as a businesslike way for debt recovery, whilst not necessarily reducing the bankrupt and his family to penury.

For the debtor, the advantage of presenting his own petition could now be immense. He should quickly identify his present and projected level of indebtedness, and ask himself the following questions:

1. Do my unsecured debts amount to more or less than £20,000?
2. What is the value of my assets?
3. Have I a proposal to make to my creditors?
4. Have I something to hide?
5. Does the prospect of a discharge in two years rather than three years or even later appeal?

A debtor's petition does not inevitably lead to a bankruptcy order and a significant helping hand is now available to those willing to grasp it. I refer, of course, to that new breed of professional in private practice, the licensed insolvency practitioner. Such a practitioner may be "nominated"; he may "supervise" and he may be "trustee". He will be there to advise the court, the creditors and especially the debtor. He will also be the official receiver. Never again will he be that unlicensed fellow in the small ads column of the press, out for a quick buck at the expense of those in debt grabbing at any straw offered. This implements government policy of encouraging competition, both as a means of widening the choice for the consumer creditor and debtor, and as an essential discipline for the insolvency practitioner, for he used to be released when his trusteeship was concluded; now the effect of his "release" is somewhat misleading as he continues to remain exposed to personal liability under s 304 whether or not there is, or is likely to be, a surplus for the bankrupt.

The legal principles applied in bankruptcy scan many facets of law, valuation, management and accountancy. The insolvency practitioner finds stimulation in an interweaving of several topics to get a composite feel for the legal implications of the various situations that may confront him. For that the new procedures look good.

It is also good that in a sense the totality of the legislation package now before the debtor for the first time provides a stark choice by virtue of clear bench-marks of potential liability. The depths of brinkmanship are graded for the debtor, who in a sense can be master of his own destiny with bankruptcy remaining the worst scenario, either because of size, or through repeat failures, or by the simple device of doing nothing and letting all the creditors go hang - in other words, the dishonest debtor. Whether that will work out in practice only time can tell, for as yet no-one has determined a fairer system for everyone involved. The onus on the debtor to seek early professional advice is now more important than ever for all concerned.

Thus the major change in procedure introduced by the Act is five-fold: first, effect is given to the abolition of the receiving and adjudication orders by the introduction of the singular bankruptcy order in an attempt to simplify that procedure. Second, the moratorium is introduced during which no petition relating to the debtor may be presented or proceeded with where he intends to make a proposal to his creditors which leads to an interim order. Third, the ability of the debtor to have his affairs managed by the simplified small bankruptcies, or "summary" procedure, is vastly widened to take in the whole of the first tranche of £750 to £20,000, provided that bankruptcy is not a recurrent option in the particular case. Fourth, more than ever before there is an emphasis on humanity to the family: the supervening right of the trustee to take the family home and income is postponed to the interest of the spouse, and the debtor is allowed the opportunity of *continuing* to make a living so as to provide for himself and his family. In return he may make a contribution from his future income for up to three years beyond discharge towards the payment of his creditors Fifth, the Insolvent Partnerships Order 1986 provides that a partnership may now be wound up as an unregistered company, that is, without involving the insolvency of the partners.

On current statistics, either the voluntary or summary procedures could be the effective way through for up to 98% of bankrupts if they are properly advised. Primarily to give effect to this particular form of privatisation, summary procedures lie in bankruptcy. It is available to help those creditors and debtors who seek to help themselves, but of necessity under official constraint. This trivial pursuit of the smaller debtor has been quietly forged under the new Act into a major force for change. Surprisingly it is subject to muddled rules which subtly put the reform back to the so-called "straightforward" procedures that lay behind the much criticised government thinking in 1980 (*A Consultative Document: HMSO Cmnd 7967*) to withdraw the official receiver from his responsibilities.

Summary administration was previously an admirable way through bankruptcy for the smaller debtor (then under £4,000). Even so, this accounted for half the number of receiving orders made in the last full year before the new Act; in 1985, out of 6,716 receiving orders, 3,280 were handled summarily by official receivers, and 103 by non-official trustees - making 50.4% of the total. The issue now of a certificate for the estate to be administered summarily is based on the bankruptcy order, with the certificate, so to speak, "riding on its back".

There still remains on the statute book, as part of the alternative package and without financial limits, the under-used and basically unchanged deed of arrangement. This remains an alternative way through for the debtor in those cases where creditors are minded to agree that an arrangement of assets and income or assignment of property may provide the best form of recovery. The sharp difference now is that whereas in itself it used to trigger the bankruptcy process, with the demise of the "act of bankruptcy" it no longer can: prospects for its revival look good if the professions grasp the nettle.

The deed had to all intents and purposes become obsolete as limited liability became almost universally adopted by the owner of the family firm. The fact that the director is now no longer safe from enquiry and personal liability by virtue of the first group of Parts of the new Act (not covered by this volume other than in reference to partnerships), the popularity of incorporation could wain as its effect strikes home. That would most likely be in favour of the unincorporated association and consequently give rise to a welcome resurgence in the use of the formal assignment or other arrangement for those firms which unfortunately fail.

Likewise, the existing administration order procedure in the county court is now still available for the smaller debtor whose debts do not exceed £5,000, particularly on application by a creditor for an attachment of earnings order. Together with the deed of arrangement and the interim order, this certainly provides a choice of rescue strategy to avoid the full implication of bankruptcy.

But this is not all, for few remaining parts of the old legislation escape a swath of editing by the Insolvency Service, except that there is unhappily a vast increase in secondary legislation which creates a formidable new web of consumer law created by civil servants, not Parliament.

How then do the original tenets of bankruptcy law hold true under this new code? The primary purpose of bankruptcy is to secure equality among the creditors and to prevent one creditor obtaining an unfair advantage over the others, although statute does not always allow this and introduces the preferred claim. Second, bankruptcy law allows a mirror on antecedent transactions and for the trustee to claw these back to the estate so as to protect the creditors from a dishonest debtor; conversely he may disclaim onerous contracts Third, the basic policy is to protect the debtor from the extreme enforcement of legal rights by his creditors.

Those who receive only a proportion of their debts naturally consider that the debtor should not be excused payment of the balance of them. However, the legislature now more than ever rejects that view and says that it is in the interests of the public at large that the debtor should be initially taken in hand, soon encouraged to make a fresh start to earn a living, and that his family be protected. In 1976, when there was said to be a mass of some 60,000 undischarged bankrupts overloading the system, the then government reduced the previously uncertain period for discharge basically to a fixed automatic discharge after only five years.

Now the period has been further reduced to just two or three years; all this is clearly light years away from the Fleet debtors' prison of the last century, and can make the new Act appear attractive as a more satisfactory way of enforcing debts than was previously the case. Otherwise, the basic aims of the creditor and the bankrupt appear to be well satisfied by the new Act.

Nevertheless, it is often overlooked that costs can still be expected to take a substantial portion of the estate; in 1984, for example, out of every £1 of net assets realised, 64.5p was spent on administration where the official trustee was trustee, and 52.9p where there was a non-official trustee, with unsecured creditors getting just under 30p in the £. The new scale of fees and remuneration is set out in Appendix 5 and creditors should be encouraged to consider carefully their full effect before waving the axe; above all they should take independent professional advice.

In 1985 the estimated liabilities in 6,358 bankruptcy cases and 48 deeds of arrangement amounted in total to £341m and the estimated value of the assets was £86m, leaving an overall estimated deficit of some £256m. The largest bankruptcy case had estimated liabilities of some £30m and there were three other cases each with liabilities over £10m, the largest deed of arrangement having liabilities of £567,000. The position in the last ten years is shown in the table below (using estimates by the respective debtors):

Amount of insolvency 1977 - 1986

Year	*No of Receiving Orders*	*Liabilities '000s*	*Assets '000s*
1977	4,095	105,459	16,156
1978	3,540	206,236	20,239
1979	3,170	66,355	21,900
1980	3,652	69,117	39,557
1981	4,744	170,227	39,662
1982	5,319	211,034	34,642
1983	6,576	227,067	54,389
1984	7,726	558,932	103,658
1985	6,358	337,481	84,173
1986	6,700	452,000	90,000

Source: Bankruptcy Annual Reports (under s 379 of the Act), except for the 1986 figures, which are provisional (and include two bankruptcy orders).

To keep the book to a readable size and a ready reference for the practitioner, the law as stated does not dwell on the anomalous criminal bankruptcy order - of which one learned judge said "of itself it has no practical effect at all" (Mr Justice Hodgson in *R* v *Garner, Bullen & Howard* [1986] 1 All ER 78, [1986] 1 WLR 73). Hodgson J went on to point out that all it did in his view was to provide conclusive proof of (an act of) bankruptcy on which the official petitioner - the Director of Public Prosecutions - or one of the creditors named could petition, ie under s 264(1)(d) of the Act for a criminal bankruptcy order under s 39(1) of the Powers of Criminal Courts Act 1973. Better alternatives are, however, now expected from Parliament. Nor does this book fully cover specialised court administration; it applies to the bankruptcy of individuals whether male or female (although the former only are generally referred to) and to non-corporate partnerships in England and Wales only.

In the all too few areas where the law is basically unaltered and yet still requires explanation, references to the many older authoritative cases are included. In the interests of a coherent text, liberal references are made to the Act, the Rules and the Regulations, which are also listed in Appendix 4.

It must be pointed out that many areas of uncertainty have surfaced, ripe for a rich harvest of argument by the insolvency practitioner and pickings for the lawyer, and crying out for clarification by the courts. All this in what was euphemistically described by government as a "simplified code for bankruptcy" - maybe therein hides a message for the debtor, the creditor - and insolvency practitioner - alike! So far as this book is concerned, I hope that whatever its demerits, it will at least be easier to find one's way about this compact volume than the Act with its burdensome secondary legislation.

The law as stated applies to all petitions presented from 29 December 1986 and attempts to be correct to 1 September 1987.

Clive Grenville
September 1987

Contents

Table of cases

Insolvency Act 1986: Table of sections

Chapter 1

The moratorium and interim order

1. Introduction

The aim of the new Act is to reduce the considerable number of debtors who, under the old legislation, would have been subject to the full rigour of bankruptcy; thereby to reduce the costs of the administration and consequently make more of the realisations available for the creditors, leaving the more serious cases for full investigation by the Insolvency Service. For the first time in bankruptcy law the Act therefore considerably extends the procedures previously only open to the very small judgment debtor in the county court with the administration order, by giving the larger debtor a reasonable opportunity of a moratorium that should prove effective.

The effect of an interim order is that no bankruptcy petition may be presented or other proceedings commenced or continued. It attempts to do this by going on the one hand along the road previously the reserve of company law and its provision for an administration order, and on the other by eliminating the unsatisfactory features of the Bankruptcy Act 1914 in relation to compositions and schemes of arrangement that were so often stillborn because of the onerous conditions that had to be satisfied at the outset.

All is now embraced in the "voluntary arrangement" which may be approached from two principle directions: firstly and without limit, by direct application to the court, and secondly via a debtor's petition in bankruptcy, when the debtor may, so to speak, be saved from himself provided the level of unsecured debt is less than £20,000 and that he has assets worth at least £2,000. Under the Act, therefore, a debtor who enters into a successful voluntary arrangement with his creditors will not become a bankrupt provided he does not default on the terms of the arrangement.

(a) By direct application

An application may not be made where the court has appointed an insolvency practitioner to inquire into the debtor's affairs and report to the court following a debtor's petition. Direct application to the court clearly presupposes the debtor's desire for an arrangement and may follow the making of a bankruptcy order on a creditor's petition. This is given legal effect when the court grants a stay from the onslaught of creditors, for just fourteen days, by the issue of an interim order. The debtor has to satisfy the court of his intention and in particular that he was competent to petition for his own bankruptcy, although in this instance there are no minimum or maximum levels of debt or assets.

During the fourteen days, and indeed whilst awaiting the appointment at the court, it is up to the debtor to get his proposals together and give them to the nominee who has been appointed by the court to handle the arrangement, and who then reports to the court whether or not to summon a meeting of the creditors.

If so, the creditors then have up to 28 days to approve or reject the proposals. The chief considerations are likely to be the return they can reasonably expect on their, albeit unwilling, investment in the debtor compared with the likely costs of a fully fledged bankruptcy. An eye cast over the new fee scales will soon caution the creditor against expecting a handsome dividend even in the most propitious circumstances. He will realise that dividends in excess of 50p in the £ are now likely to be the exception rather than the rule.

If the creditors approve the arrangement a supervisor is appointed to conduct the administration; if they do not the court may discharge the interim order. What then for the debtor?

Should the creditors proceed along the lines of presenting their own petition (deposit £200), such a finite move would severely limit the debtor's scope for alleviation, either by any unexpected improvement in his finances through the moratorium, or alternatively in respect of the summary procedure for small bankruptcies where the amount owed to unsecured creditors is less than £20,000. On the other hand, he could either agree to enter into a deed of arrangement, which must be duly registered for otherwise it will be null and void (see page 329), or present his own bankruptcy petition to the court.

(b) Debtor's petition in bankruptcy

Should he proceed with his own petition this might just give him such an opportunity to shrink back from the precipice no matter how obscure such a prospect might seem at the time. For this purpose he needs to have saved his last £100 for the deposit and the fee of £15, plus VAT.

A debtor's petition also provides a specific opportunity to mount a voluntary arrangement because the court is bound, subject to conditions precedent, to refer the matter to an insolvency practitioner for review outside the bankruptcy processes and to prepare a report for the court stating whether the debtor is willing to make a proposal for a voluntary arrangement. He also tells the court whether, in his opinion, a meeting of the debtor's creditors should be summoned, and if so the date, time and place.

The court then has to decide whether it is inappropriate to make a bankruptcy order, and instead make an interim order. This can only be effected where the level of unsecured debts is under £20,000 and provided that the value of the debtor's assets is at least £2,000; if so the petition is then discontinued. If the level of debt is under £20,000 but the level of assets is less than £2,000, then a certificate for summary administration may be issued. Where the level of debt is not higher than £5,000 and irrespective of the value of assets, the administration order procedure may be available (in the county court only following a judgment). Where debts are in excess of £20,000, a bankruptcy order is made irrespective of assets, and bankruptcy commences on that day and continues until it is discharged or it is annulled. It is felt that a bottom line of £2,000 value of assets makes it feasible for the arrangement to be administered and still allow sufficient moneys to be in hand for the supervisor's fee and other expenses, except that such a consideration does not apply for a debtor's direct application ((a) above) to the court.

2. The debtor's proposal

In a Case 2, the debtor (who is not a bankrupt) initially serves notice on the intended nominee, a licensed insolvency practitioner, of his proposal and gives him, or his authorised representative, a copy inviting him to act as his nominee. In a Case 1 (an undischarged bankrupt) the debtor prepares a proposal for the official receiver or trustee if there is one, which provides a short explanation as to why a voluntary arrangement under Part VIII is desirable and notifies them of the nominee's name and address. Acceptance by the nominee is by way of endorsing a copy of the notice, and returning it straightaway (Rule 5.4).

So as to enable the nominee to prepare his report the debtor gives him a document setting out the terms of the voluntary arrangement which he is proposing to submit to the court, a statement of his affairs (see page 9) and the reasons why his creditors may be expected to concur in such an arrangement.

By Rule 5.3, the following matters should be stated or dealt with in the proposal:

- (a) so far as within the debtor's immediate knowledge:
  - (i) his assets, with an estimate of their respective values,
  - (ii) the extent (if any) to which the assets are charged in favour of creditors,
  - (iii) the extent (if any) to which particular assets are to be excluded from the voluntary arrangement;
- (b) particulars of any property, other than assets of the debtor himself, proposed to be included in the arrangement, the source of such property and the terms on which it is to be made available for inclusion;
- (c) the nature and amount of the debtor's liabilities (so far as within his immediate knowledge), and the manner in which it is proposed those liabilities are to be met, modified, postponed or otherwise dealt with, and:
  - (i) how it is proposed to deal with preferential creditors and creditors who are, or claim to be, secured,
  - (ii) how creditors who are associates of the debtor (being creditors of his) are proposed to be treated under the arrangement, and
  - (iii) (Case 2 only) whether there are, to the debtor's knowledge, any circumstances raising the possibility, in the event that he should be

adjudged bankrupt, of claims under -
s 339 (transactions at an undervalue);
s 340 (preferences); or
s 343 (extortionate credit transactions), (see page 169).
If so, whether, and how, it is proposed under the voluntary arrangement to provide wholly or partly for indemnifying the insolvent estate in respect of such claims;

(d) whether any, and if so what, guarantees have been given of the debtor's debts by other persons, specifying which (if any) of the guarantors are associates of his;
(e) the proposed duration of the voluntary arrangement;
(f) the proposed dates of distributions to creditors, with estimates of their amounts;
(g) the amount proposed to be paid to the nominee (as such) by way of remuneration and expenses;
(h) the manner in which it is proposed that the supervisor of the arrangement should be remunerated, and his expenses defrayed;
(j) whether, for the purposes of the arrangement, any guarantees are to be offered by any persons other than the debtor, and whether (if so) any security is to be given or sought;
(k) the manner in which funds held for the purposes of the arrangement are to be banked, invested or otherwise dealt with pending distribution to creditors;
(l) the manner in which funds held for the purpose of payment to creditors, and not so paid on the termination of the arrangement, are to be dealt with;
(m) if the debtor has a business, the manner in which it is proposed to be conducted during the course of the arrangement;
(n) details of any further credit facilities which it is intended to arrange for the debtor, and how the debts so arising are to be paid;
(o) the functions which are to be undertaken by the supervisor of the arrangement;
(p) the name, address and qualification of the person proposed as supervisor of the voluntary arrangement, and confirmation that he is (so far as the debtor is aware) qualified to act as an insolvency practitioner in relation to him.

With the nominee's written agreement, the proposal may be amended at any time up to the delivery of the nominee's report to the court under s 256.

3. Debtor's application to the court for an interim order

There is no set form of order; in line with corporate arrangements it was felt that this was best left to the insolvency practitioner to arrange so as to keep the order simple.

(a) Circumstances in which an order may be made

Application to the court for an interim order may be made under s 253 where the debtor intends to make a proposal to his creditors for a composition in satisfaction of his debts, or a scheme of arrangement of his affairs, and where he has nominated an insolvency practitioner to supervise its implementation.

(b) Who may apply

Application for an interim order may be made by the debtor (under s 253(3)) provided that he has not already presented a bankruptcy petition and had an insolvency practitioner appointed. If he is an undischarged bankrupt, a "Case 1" (which may also be a second or subsequent bankruptcy), then the application may alternatively be made by the trustee of his estate or the official receiver; if it is not then the debtor must give notice to them. In the more usual case where the debtor is not an undischarged bankrupt then it is known as "Case 2" and the nominee acts as supervisor. One is bound to wonder at this ordering of the numbering, which defies logic. An application from a Case 1 debtor will be made directly to the court following the making of a bankruptcy order on a creditor's petition. A Case 2 application will arise either from the decision of the court on a debtor's petition, and without previous reference to the bankruptcy court, will be made by direct application.

(c) Effect of the application

At any time when the application is pending, the court may stay any action, execution or other legal process against the property or person of the debtor. Any court in which proceedings are pending against an individual may, on proof that an application under s 253 has been made in respect of that individual, either stay the proceedings or allow them to continue on such terms as it thinks fit (s 254).

(d) Application to the court

An application to the court under s 253 for an interim order must be accompanied by a copy of the notice to the intended nominee endorsed to the effect that he agrees so to act, and an affidavit of the following matters (Rule 5.5(1)):

- (i) the reasons for making the application;
- (ii) particulars of any execution or other legal process which, to the debtor's knowledge, has been commenced against him;
- (iii) that he is an undischarged bankrupt or (as the case may be) that he is able to petition for his own bankruptcy;
- (iv) that no previous application for an interim order has been made by or in respect of the debtor in the period of twelve months ending with the date of the affidavit; and
- (v) that the nominee under the proposal (naming him) is a person who is qualified to act as an insolvency practitioner in relation to the debtor, and is willing to act in relation to the proposal.

On receiving the application and affidavit, the court fixes a venue for the hearing and the applicant must give at least two days' notice of the hearing in Case 1 to the bankrupt, the official receiver and trustee; in Case 2 to any creditor who to the debtor's knowledge has presented a bankruptcy petition against him; and in either case, to the nominee who has agreed to act in relation to the debtor's proposal (Rule 5.5(4)).

(e) The hearing

Rule 5.6 provides that anyone who had notice under Rule 5.5(4) may appear or be represented at the hearing of the application. In deciding whether to make an interim order, the court must take into account any representations made by or on behalf of any of those persons; in particular, the court must takc note of representations as to whether an order should be made containing such provision as is referred to in s 255(3) and (4) as to staying bankruptcy proceedings and administration of the estate.

If the court makes an interim order, it fixes a venue for consideration of the nominee's report. The date for that consideration may not be later than the date on which the interim order ceases to have effect under s 255(6) However, if, under s 256(4) an extension of time is granted for filing the nominee's report, the court shall, unless there appear to be good reasons against it, extend the period for which the interim order has effect by the corresponding length of time. Anybody who has been given notice under Rule 5.5(4) may appear or be represented at the hearing.

(f) When the order can be made

The order is made by the court if it thinks that it would be appropriate to do so to facilitate the consideration and implementation of the debtor's proposal. By s 255, it has to be satisfied as to the following matters:

(i) that the debtor intends to make the proposal;
(ii) that on the day of making the application he was an undischarged bankrupt or was able to petition for his own bankruptcy;
(iii) that no previous application has been made by him within the previous twelve months; and
(iv) that the nominee is a licensed insolvency practitioner and is willing to act in relation to the proposal.

(g) When the order cannot be made

The court cannot hear the application while a bankruptcy petition presented by the debtor is pending where the court has already appointed an insolvency practitioner to inquire into his affairs and report to the court.

4. The interim order

(a) Following the making of an order

Rule 5.7 requires that where an interim order is made, at least two sealed copies of the order must be sent by the court forthwith to the person who applied for it; that person must serve one of the copies on the nominee under the debtor's proposal. The applicant must also forthwith give notice of the making of the order to any person who had notice of the hearing under Rule 5.5(4) and was not present or represented at the meeting. Rule 5.7 applies to any order made by the court at the hearing.

(b) Effect

The effect of an interim order is that no bankruptcy petition relating to the debtor may be presented or proceeded with, and no other proceedings, execution or other legal process may be commenced or continued against the debtor or his property except with the leave of the court (s 252(2)). In other words, it provides a moratorium for the insolvent debtor.

(c) Contents

In a Case 2, the order may contain provisions staying proceedings in the bankruptcy or modifying any provision in the Act or rules in its application to the debtor's bankruptcy.

In a Case 1, the order may contain provisions staying proceedings in bankruptcy or modifications to the Act or any of the Rules in their application to the debtor's bankruptcy. In respect of a bankrupt it should not relax or remove any of the requirements unless the court is satisfied that the provision is unlikely to result in any significant diminution in value of the estate for the purposes of the bankruptcy.

(d) Time limits

An interim order ceases to have effect at the end of fourteen days beginning with the day after the making of the order, unless the court, on the application of the nominee, extends the period to enable him to have more time to prepare his report.

5. The nominee

(a) Notice to intended nominee

To enable the intended nominee to prepare his report within the fourteen days following the interim order, the debtor has to give him a document setting out the terms of the voluntary arrangement he proposes, as well as a statement of his affairs, within seven days after his proposal is delivered.

Under Rule 5.4, the notice, accompanied by a copy of the proposal (see page 3), must be delivered to the nominee himself, or to a person authorised to take delivery of documents on his behalf. If the intended nominee agrees to act, he must endorse a copy of the notice to the effect that it has been received by him, and the date of receipt. That copy notice must be returned by the nominee forthwith to the debtor at an address specified by him in the notice for that purpose. In Case 1, where the bankrupt gives notice of his proposal to the official receiver and the trustee (if any), the notice must contain the name and address of the insolvency practitioner who has agreed to act as nominee.

(b) Additional disclosure for the assistance of the nominee

If the nominee feels he cannot properly prepare his report on the basis of the information contained in the debtor's proposals and statement of affairs, he may require from the debtor:

- (i) further and better particulars of the circumstances in which, and the reasons why, he is insolvent or threatened with insolvency;
- (ii) particulars of any previous proposals which have been made by him under Part VIII of the Act;
- (iii) any further information about his affairs which the nominee thinks necessary for the purposes of his report.

The nominee may also call on the debtor to inform him whether and in what circumstances he has at any time been concerned in the affairs of any company (whether or not incorporated in England and Wales) which has become insolvent; or been adjudged bankrupt or entered into an arrangement with his creditors.

To enable the nominee to consider the debtor's proposal and prepare his report on it, the debtor must give him access to his accounts and records. (Rule 5.9)

(c) The statement of affairs

The statement of affairs is made up to a date not earlier than two weeks before the date of the notice to the nominee, and will normally be delivered by the debtor to the nominee within seven days after his proposal. There is no special form, but for particulars see page 119 - Statement of Affairs.

Where a Statement has previously been delivered with the debtor's petition (see above), or following a creditor's petition (Case 1), then the debtor need not deliver a further statement unless the nominee requires him to do so. This would normally be with a view to supplementing or amplifying the former one; for example, the listing of preferred creditors as such is an additional requirement here, as is a requirement to distinguish debts owed to associates.

(d) The nominee's report on the proposal

Before the order ceases to have effect, the nominee submits his report to the court. If the court is satisfied that a meeting of the debtor's creditors should be summoned to consider the debtor's proposal, the court then directs that the period for which the interim order has effect be extended for a specified period to enable the creditors to consider it.

The nominee's report is governed by Rule 5.10 under s 256. He must deliver it to the court not less than two days before the interim order ceases to have effect. It must be accompanied by a copy of the debtor's proposal (with amendments, if any, authorised under Rule 5.3(3)); and a copy or summary of any statement of affairs provided by the debtor.

If the nominee states that in his opinion a meeting of the debtor's creditors should be summoned under s 257, his comments on the debtor's proposal must be annexed to his report. If his opinion is otherwise, he must give his reasons.

The court endorses the nominee's report with the date on which it is filed in court. Any creditor of the debtor is entitled, at all reasonable times on any business day, to inspect the file.

In Case 1, the nominee must send to the official receiver:

(i) a copy of the debtor's proposal,
(ii) a copy of his (the nominee's) report and his comments accompanying it (if any); and
(iii) a copy or summary of the debtor's statement of affairs.

In Case 2, the nominee sends a copy of each of those documents to any person who has presented a bankruptcy petition against the debtor.

(e) Debtor's replacement of nominee

Where the nominee has failed to submit the report, the debtor may apply to the court to replace the nominee by another insolvency practitioner, and/or direct that the interim order be renewed (where it has expired) or continued for such further period as the court may specify. By Rule 5.11 the debtor must give the nominee at least seven days notice of his application.

(f) Discharging the interim order

The court may discharge the order if it is satisfied, on the application of the nominee, that the debtor has failed to comply with his obligations, or that for any other reason it would be inappropriate for a meeting of the debtor's creditors to be summoned to consider the debtor's proposal.

6. The meeting of creditors

For this purpose the "creditors" of a debtor or undischarged bankrupt include every person who is a creditor of the bankrupt in respect of a bankruptcy debt, and every person who would be such a creditor if the bankruptcy had commenced on the day on which notice of the meeting is given. A meeting of all creditors is summoned by the nominee unless the court otherwise directs, to decide whether to approve the proposed voluntary arrangement (s 257).

(a) Duty of nominee to summon a creditors' meeting

Where the nominee, or his replacement, has reported to the court that a meeting of the debtor's creditors should be summoned, then he should summon the meeting for the time, date and place proposed in his report. The meeting must be held not less than fourteen days nor more than 28 days from the date on which the nominee's report was filed in court (see page 201). Notices are sent at least fourteen days before the hearing to all creditors specified in the debtor's statement of affairs and any other creditors of whom the nominee is otherwise aware. With the notice are sent:

(i) a copy of the proposal (stating the court in which it has been filed);
(ii) a copy of the statement of affairs (or a summary including a list of creditors and the amounts of their debts);
(iii) the nominee's comments on the proposal;
(iv) forms of proxy (Form 8.1);
(v) a statement of the effect of Rule 5.18(1), (3) and (4) (requisite majorities - see page 203).

The meeting must be held between 10 am and 4 pm on a business day at a venue convenient to creditors.

(b) Conduct of the meeting

The conduct of the creditors' meeting is in accordance with the rules as set out at page 201. Voting is calculated according to the value of the creditor's debt. A majority of at least 75% of value of debt owed to the creditors present (or voting by proxy) is needed for the proposal to be binding on all creditors who were notified of it.

(c) Modifying the proposals

The modifications may include one conferring the functions proposed to be conferred on the nominee on another person qualified to act as an insolvency practitioner in relation to the debtor. But they may not include any modification by virtue of which the proposal ceases to be a proposal such as is mentioned in s 253, or approve any modification unless the debtor consents to each modification.

(d) Decision of the meeting

The result is to bind everyone who had notice of the meeting; and the supervisor(s), who may be the original nominee, implements the scheme, applying to the court for directions as necessary. The meeting may not approve any proposal or modification which affects the right of a secured creditor of the debtor to enforce his security, except with the concurrence of the creditor concerned. Nor may it approve any proposal or modification which purports to upset the existing rights of preferential creditors (if any) without the concurrence of the preferential creditor concerned. All such priority debts are paid *pari passu* in themselves. A preferential debt as defined by s 258(7) has the same meaning as given to it under s 386 (see page 234).

7. Action to be taken following creditors' meeting

(a) Reporting back to the court

After the conclusion of the meeting, the Chairman reports the result of it to the court within four days, by filing a copy of his report in court; that copy is then endorsed with the date of filing. Immediately after so reporting he gives notice of the result of the meeting to all those who were sent notice of the meeting. The period of 28 days within which the creditors and other persons can challenge the decision of the meeting, for example in the event of some material irregularity, commences with the day the chairman of the meeting reports to the court, and not the date of giving notice to the creditors.

The report, prepared by the chairman of the meeting, must:

"(a) state whether the proposal for a voluntary arrangement was approved or rejected and, if approved, with what (if any) modifications;

(b) set out the resolutions which were taken at the meeting, and the decision on each one;

(c) list the creditors (with their respective values) who were present or represented at the meeting, and how they voted on each resolution; and

(d) include such further information (if any) as the chairman thinks it appropriate to make known to the court." (Rule 5.22(2))

(b) Continuation of interim order

The order ceases to have effect 28 days after the report was made to the court. This period allows time for a challenge to the decision of the creditors' meeting, in which event the court may give a direction under s 262(6) continuing or renewing the order for such period as may be specified.

(c) Reports to the Secretary of State

Voluntary arrangements are subject to a system of registration provided for in rules 5.23 and 5.24. The Secretary of State maintains a register of individual voluntary arrangements, which is open to public inspection. Immediately after the chairman of the creditors' meeting has filed in court a report that the meeting has approved the voluntary arrangement, he must report the following details to the Secretary of State, which are recorded in the register:

(i) the name and address of the debtor;

(ii) the date on which the arrangement was approved by the creditors;

(iii) the name and address of the supervisor; and

(iv) the court in which the chairman's report has been filed.

(d) Approval of interim order

The approved arrangement takes effect as if made by the debtor at the meeting, and binds every person who, in accordance with the rules, had notice of, and was entitled to vote at, the meeting whether or not he was present or represented at it, as if he were a party to the arrangement.

(e) Discharge of interim order

If the report is that the meeting has declined, with or without modifications, to approve the debtor's proposal, the court may discharge any interim order which is in force in relation to the debtor.

(f) Deeds of arrangement

The requirements of the Deeds of Arrangement Act, for registration of deeds and the like, do not apply to the approved voluntary arrangement.

(g) False representation

The debtor commits an offence if he makes any false representation or commits any other fraud for the purpose of obtaining the approval of his creditors to a proposal for a voluntary arrangement under Part VIII of the Act. A person guilty of this offence is liable to imprisonment or a fine, or both. (Rule 5.30)

8. Effect of approval of voluntary arrangement

(a) Effect of creditors' approval on a Case 1 debtor

If the debtor has been an undischarged bankrupt the court may do one or both of the following:

- annul the bankruptcy;
- give such directions with respect to the conduct of the bankruptcy and the administration of the estate as it thinks appropriate for facilitating the implementation of the approved voluntary arrangement (s 261),

except that court may not annul a bankruptcy order at any time within 28 days from the day on which the report of the creditors' meeting was made to the court; or at any time when an application to challenge the decision of the meeting has been made or an appeal in respect of such an application is pending; or at any time in the period within which such an appeal may be brought. As to the effect of a voluntary arrangement on a bankruptcy order, see page 291.

(b) Effect of creditors' approval on a Case 2 debtor

The effect of a successful application by a Case 2 debtor for a voluntary arrangement is the same as if he had been a discharged bankrupt. Where proceedings on a bankruptcy petition have been stayed by an interim order which ceases to have effect, that petition is deemed (unless the court otherwise orders) to have been dismissed.

If the debtor is dissatisfied by any act, omission or decision of the supervisor he may apply to the court, and on such application the court may confirm, reverse or modify any act or decision of the supervisor, give him directions or make such other order as it thinks fit.

Any interim order in force in relation to the debtor immediately before the end of 28 days beginning with the day on which the report was made to the court ceases to have effect at the end of that period, unless the court otherwise directs if the meeting's decision is challenged.

(c) Filling a vacancy

The court may make an order substituting a new insolvency practitioner for the existing supervisor or to fill a vacancy where it is expedient to appoint a person or persons to carry out the functions of the supervisor, and it is inexpedient, difficult or impracticable for an appointment to be made without the assistance of the court. This power is exercisable by the court so as to increase the number of persons exercising the functions of the supervisor, or, where there is more than one person exercising those functions, so as to replace one or more of them.

(d) Effect of irregularity

An approval given at a creditors' meeting is not invalidated by any irregularity at or in relation to the meeting, other than under s 262 which provides for challenging the meeting's decision (see page 17).

(e) Resolutions to follow approval

Where two or more insolvency practitioners are appointed to act as supervisor, the creditors may resolve that acts in connection with the arrangement may be performed by one of them alone, by both or by all. If at the creditors' meeting a resolution is moved for the appointment of some person other than the nominee to be supervisor then at or before the meeting that person must consent in writing to act (unless he is present and signifies his consent), and confirm in writing that he is qualified to act as an insolvency practitioner in relation to the debtor.

(f) Public utilities

The effect on supplies of gas, water, electricity and telephone when a voluntary arrangement is approved is that payment of any charges for supplies may be guaranteed by the supervisor. Public utilities cannot withhold supplies, or make it a condition of supply that any charges outstanding before the relevant day are paid.

9. The supervisor

At this stage the supervisor - who most probably is the nominee in new clothes - takes over and is put in possession of the assets included in the arrangement. He is formally known as the "supervisor of the voluntary arrangement". His role is to supervise the carrying out of the voluntary arrangement approved under s 258(3). The person appointed immediately gives the Secretary of State written notice of his appointment, whether he is the first appointee or has been appointed to replace another. If he vacates office he likewise gives written notice.

After the chairman of the creditors' meeting makes his report to the court, the Case 2 debtor and the official receiver or trustee in Case 1, must do all that is required for putting the supervisor into possession of the assets.

(a) Duties of supervisor

Rule 5.21 deals with the payments to the official receiver following the handover of assets to the supervisor:

"5.21 ......

(2) On taking possession of the assets in Case 1, the supervisor shall discharge any balance due to the official receiver and (if other) the trustee by way of remuneration or on account of -

(a) fees, costs, charges and expenses properly incurred and payable under the Act or the Rules, and

(b) any advances made in respect of the insolvent estate, together with interest on such advances at the rate specified in section 17 of the Judgments Act 1838 at the date of the bankruptcy order.

(3) Alternatively in Case 1, the supervisor must, before taking possession, give the official receiver or the trustee a written undertaking to discharge any such balance out of the first realisation of assets.

(4) The official receiver and (if other) the trustee has in Case 1 a charge on the assets included in the voluntary arrangement in respect of any sums due as above until they have been discharged, subject only to the deduction from realisations by the supervisor of the proper costs and expenses of realisation.

Any sums due to the official receiver take priority over those due to a trustee.

(5) The supervisor shall from time to time out of the realisation of assets discharge all guarantees properly given by the official receiver or the trustee for the benefit of the estate, and shall pay all their expenses "

Rules 5.26 and 5.27 go on to provide for the further duties of the supervisor:

(b) Supervisor's accounts and reports

"5.26 - (1) Where the voluntary arrangement authorises or requires the supervisor -

(a) to carry on the debtor's business or to trade on his behalf or in his name, or

(b) to realise assets of the debtor or (in Case 1) belonging to the estate, or

(c) otherwise to administer or dispose of any funds of the debtor or the estate,

he shall keep accounts and records of his acts and dealings in and in connection with the arrangement, including in particular records of all receipts and payments of money.

(2) The supervisor shall, not less often than once in every 12 months beginning with the date of his appointment, prepare an abstract of all receipts and payments of money, and send copies of it, accompanied by his comments on the progress and efficacy of the arrangement, to -

(a) the court,

(b) the debtor, and

(c) all those of the debtor's creditors who are bound by the arrangement.

If in any period of 12 months he has made no payments and had no receipts, he shall at the end of that period send a statement to that effect to all who are specified in sub-paragraphs (a) to (c) above.

(3) An abstract provided under paragraph (2) shall relate to a period beginning with the date of the supervisor's appointment or (as the case may be) the day following the end of the last period for which an abstract was prepared under this Rule; and copies of the abstract shall be sent out, as required by paragraph (2), within the 2 months following the end of the period to which the abstract relates.

(4) If the supervisor is not authorised as mentioned in paragraph (1), he shall, not less often than once in every 12 months beginning with the date of his appointment, send to all those specified in paragraph 2(a) to (c) a report on the progress and efficacy of the voluntary arrangement.

(5) The court may, on application by the supervisor, vary the date on which the obligation to send abstracts or reports arises.

(c) Production of accounts and records to Secretary of State

5.27 - (1) The Secretary of State may at any time during the course of the voluntary arrangement or after its completion require the supervisor to produce for inspection -

(a) his records and accounts in respect of the arrangement; and

(b) copies of abstracts and reports prepared in compliance with Rule 5.26.

(2) The Secretary of State may require production either at the premises of the supervisor or elsewhere; and it is the duty of the supervisor to comply with any requirement imposed on him under this Rule.

(3) The Secretary of State may cause any accounts and records produced by him under this Rule to be audited; and the supervisor shall give to the Secretary of State such further information and assistance as he needs for the purposes of his audit."

The supervisor may apply to the court for directions in relation to any matter arising.

(d) Fees and costs

The charges that may be incurred for these arrangements comprise any disbursements made by the nominee prior to the approval of the arrangement together with any remuneration for his services as such agreed between himself and the debtor, the official receiver or the trustee. In addition are those charges which are either sanctioned by the terms of the arrangement or would be payable (or correspond to those which would be payable) in the debtor's bankruptcy (see Appendix 5 and Rule 5.28).

10. Transitional arrangements

Where before the appointed day, 29 December 1986, either a petition in bankruptcy was presented or a receiving order or adjudication in bankruptcy was made, then the petition, order or other matter which is provided for under the Bankruptcy Act 1914 continues on and after the appointed day to have the same effect; effectively it replaces the provisions in the new Act. It is thus not possible to slip from adjudication in bankruptcy under the old Act into the new voluntary arrangements on a petition presented before 29 December 1986. The new legislation therefore specifically allows for the old procedure not to be set aside in such cases.

In *Re Woodman & Sullivan* (High Court, 2 April 1987, unreported), a partnership petitioned in bankruptcy on 8 September 1986. The receiving order was made on 6 January 1987. The petition therefore was under the old legislation, but the debtors contended that the voluntary arrangements were available to them by virtue of the new legislation. The court held that the voluntary arrangements were not available to them and accordingly they were adjudged bankrupt. The proper course of action was for them to proceed with a scheme of arrangement following the bankruptcy, under s 21 of the Act of 1914.

11. Conclusion of the voluntary arrangement

Not more than 28 days after the final completion of the voluntary arrangement, the supervisor must send to all creditors who are bound by the arrangement, and to the debtor, a notice that the arrangement has been fully implemented. The notice must be accompanied by a copy of a report by the supervisor summarising all receipts and payments made by him in pursuance of the arrangement, and explaining any difference in the actual implementation of it compared with the proposal approved by the creditors' meeting. Within the same time limit, the supervisor must send to the Secretary of State and to the court a copy of the notice and report. The court may, on application by the supervisor, extend this 28 day period.

Where the debtor has failed to comply with his obligations, or the court was misled by false information in any material particular which led to the making of the arrangement, the court may make a bankruptcy order on a petition by the supervisor or by a creditor bound by the arrangement under s 264(1)(c), which cancels the arrangement. However, there appears to be nothing to prevent the supervisor trying again once the dust has settled, or accepting appointment as trustee in bankruptcy under s 297(5) (see Gudiance Notes, para (12), page 27). As to the supervisor's expenses in the voluntary arrangement, see page 231.

The court is bound to have regard to the special rules in the Administration of Insolvent Estates of Deceased Persons Order 1986 which, by art 3, apply to s 252 of the Act (interim order) and are discussed at page 313.

12. Appeal to the court

(a) Replacement of supervisor

If the debtor, any of his creditors or any other person is dissatisfied by an act, omission or decision of the supervisor, he may apply to the court, and on such application the court may confirm, reverse or modify any act or decision of the supervisor, give him directions, or make such order as it thinks fit (s 263(3)).

(b) By supervisor

The supervisor may apply to the court for directions in relation to any particular matter arising under the voluntary arrangement (s 263(4)).

(c) Challenging the decision of the meeting of creditors

The following may, under s 262, challenge the meeting of creditors within 28 days beginning with the day on which the report of the creditors' meeting was made to the court:

- (i) the debtor (Case 2);
- (ii) a person entitled to vote in accordance with the rules;
- (iii) the nominee (or his replacement); and
- (iv) the trustee or the official receiver (Case 1).

The grounds of application are that a voluntary arrangement approved unfairly prejudices the interests of a creditor of the debtor, and/or that there has been some material irregularity at or in relation to such a meeting. If the creditors' meeting has declined (with or without modifications) to approve the debtor's proposal, the court may discharge any interim order which is in force in relation to the debtor. This would normally be sufficient to give effect to the application of the official receiver to proceed to bankruptcy; see *Re a Debtor* (1910) 130 LTJo 176.

However, the section says that the court *may* discharge the order, not that it *shall*, and in a decision under the old law where, *inter alia*, non-approval of a scheme of arrangement was a ground for bankruptcy, the court was not bound to proceed to the bankruptcy forthwith but might adjourn the application for good reason; see *Re Thurlow (Lord), ex parte Official Receiver* [1895] 1 QB 724, where it was held that this discretion is rightly exercised where it will be to the advantage of the creditors to have the (adjudication) postponed.

The court has a general power under s 266(3) if it appears to it appropriate to do so, on the grounds that there has been a contravention of the rules, or for any other reason likely to provide an effective challenge to the decision of the creditors' meeting under s 262, to dismiss a bankruptcy petition or to stay proceedings on such a petition. Where it stays a petition it may do so on such terms and conditions as it thinks fit. Likewise, an appeal may be made to a single judge of the High Court, and an appeal from a decision of that judge on such an appeal lies, with leave, to the Court of Appeal.

(d) Revocation and suspension

If the court accepts this, then it may revoke or suspend any approval given by the meeting, and/or give a direction to any person for summoning a further meeting of the debtor's creditors to consider any revised proposal he may make, or if there has been some material irregularity, to reconsider his original proposal. Where the court gives a direction, it may likewise continue or renew the interim order as the case may be. If the debtor does not intend to submit such a proposal, the court revokes the direction it has given and revokes or suspends any approval given at the previous meeting.

Where the court makes an order under s 262 on such an application to revoke or suspend the arrangement, it has the discretion to give supplemental directions, in particular with respect to things done since the meeting under any voluntary arrangement approved by the meeting, and such things done since then as could not have been done if an interim order had been in force when they were done.

Rule 5.25 provides that when the order has been made, the person who applied for it must serve sealed copies of it -

(i) in Case 1, on the debtor, the official receiver and the trustee;
(ii) in Case 2, on the debtor; and
(iii) in either case on the supervisor of the voluntary arrangement.

If the order includes a direction by the court under s 262(4)(b) for any further creditors' meeting to be summoned, notice must also be given (by the person who applied for the order) to whoever is, in accordance with the direction, required to summon the meeting.

In Case 2 the debtor, or in Case 1 the official receiver or trustee is required to:

(i) forthwith after receiving a copy of the order, give notice of it to all persons who had notice of the creditors' meeting which approved the voluntary arrangement or who otherwise appear to be affected by the order;
(ii) within seven days of their receiving a copy of the order (or within such longer period as the court may allow), give notice to the court whether it is intended to make a revised proposal to creditors, or to invite re-consideration of the original proposal.

The person on whose application the order of revocation or suspension was made must, within seven days after the making of the order, give written notice of it to the Secretary of State.

An approval given at a creditors' meeting summoned under s 257 is not invalidated by any irregularity at or in relation to the meeting except in pursuance of a challenge under s 262.

Chapter 2

The insolvency practitioner

1. Introduction

Authorisation to act in insolvency matters is now a statutory requirement following the recommendations of the Report of the Review Committee in 1982 (Cmnd 8558) prompted by a spate of fraud committed on those most at risk by unqualified practitioners, and now adopted by the government.

Part I of the 1985 Act introduced for the first time the licensing as insolvency practitioners of those considered suitable for the role of trustee and other such office holders under the Act, coupled with such safeguards as security bonding. Part XIII of the 1986 Act now restricts *unqualified* persons (ie those without formal professional qualification) from acting as trustees in bankruptcy etc to those with at least ten years experience and whom a competent authority (the Secretary of State) may determine to be fit and proper. It does not apply to official receivers although they are likewise appointed directly by the Secretary of State under s 399.

In many ways this was what remained of an earlicr government attempt in a Consultative Document 1980 (Cmnd 7967) to generate interest in an almost totally private insolvency service, and to get over the problem later referred to by the Review Committee that the manner in which some insolvent estates were then being administered gave cause for concern (para 735). The 1986 Act has already changed the name of the licensing authority for the unqualified practitioner from "relevant" authority to "competent" authority, but seemingly without alteration to its meaning.

2. A licence to practise

By s 419 of the Act, detailed regulations (The Insolvency Practitioners Regulations 1986, SI 1986 No 1995) set out positively the matters for the competent authority to consider in determining whether an unqualified applicant for authorisation is a fit and proper person to act as an insolvency practitioner. The Act lays down the minimum qualification by reference to education, practical training and work experience. For everyone (including qualified practitioners) the Regulations lay down requirements for security and record-keeping.

(a) When necessary

A person acts as an insolvency practitioner, and must therefore be licensed by an authorising body, when he acts as a trustee in bankruptcy (Chapter 7); or interim receiver (Chapter 6); as trustee under a deed of arrangement made for the benefit of creditors (Chapter 23); as a supervisor of a voluntary arrangement proposed for him (Chapter 1); or, in the case of an insolvent deceased individual, as the administrator of that estate (Chapter 21).

The requirement does not, however, apply, for example, to a chartered surveyor appointed as a receiver of the rents and profits by a mortgagee under s 110 of the Law of Property Act 1925 by reason of the mortgagor being adjudged bankrupt, or to the appointment of a special manager under s 370 of the Act (see page 89).

(b) Authorising bodies

A person is licensed to act as an insolvency practitioner either:

(i) by the recognised professional body of which he is a member; or
(ii) when he holds an authorisation to act as an insolvency practitioner granted by a competent authority under s 393 of the Act.

"Recognised professional bodies" in England and Wales, membership of which will entitle an individual to apply for a licence, are the Chartered Association of Certified Accountants, the Insolvency Practitioners Association, the Institute of Chartered Accountants, and The Law Society (art 2 Insolvency Practitioners (Recognised Approved Bodies) Order 1986). Any other body may be recognised by order made under s 391(1) if it regulates the practice of a profession and:

(i) enforces rules in accordance with s 391(2) for securing that members permitted by or under the rules to act as insolvency practitioners are fit and proper persons so to act; and
(ii) it meets acceptable requirements as to education, practical training and experience.

The requirement that insolvency practitioners be fit and proper persons will not, of course, automatically be met by being a solicitor or member of a recognised accountancy body, for by s 391(2) the licensing procedures will be self-regulating and members will be subject to the rules of the professional body in the practice of the profession in question (s 391(3)).

The order recognising the body may be revoked under s 391(4) if it appears to the Secretary of State that it no longer falls within subs (2); in this eventuality provision may be made to protect practising members for a specified period after the revocation takes effect.

References in s 391 to members of a recognised professional body are to persons who, whether members of that body or not, are subject to its rules in the practice of the profession in question (see also the *Guidance Notes* at para 7 below).

A "competent authority" is defined by s 392(2) as the body or person so specified in directions given by the Secretary of State in relation to cases of that description; and in relation to a case not falling within that definition, the Secretary of State. No such direction has yet been given and there are no immediate proposals to appoint anyone besides the Secretary of State.

(c) Persons not qualified to act as insolvency practitioners

A person is not qualified to act as an insolvency practitioner by s 390(4) if at that time:

- (i) he has been adjudged bankrupt or sequestration of his estate has been awarded and he has not been discharged;
- (ii) he is subject to a disqualification order under the Company Directors Disqualification Act 1986;
- (iii) he is a patient within the meaning of Part 7 of the Mental Health Act 1983;
- (iv) he is not an individual; or
- (v) there is no security in force.

A person who acts as an insolvency practitioner in relation to a company or an individual while unlicensed to do so is liable to imprisonment, a fine, or both.

(d) Loss of qualification as insolvency practitioner

If a trustee ceases to be qualified he loses his licence and must vacate any office he is holding.

3. Requirements for authorisation of the unqualified practitioner

(a) Role of the competent authority

The main role of the competent authority lies in considering the flush of applications for licences to practise as an insolvency practitioner from those qualified by experience only. Thereafter it appears that it will be reduced to a watchdog role by virtue of its power to withdraw a practising licence.

(b) Matters determining whether an applicant is fit and proper

The applicant must establish that he has been (or, where he has been employed for the last ten years but is not yet carrying on his own practice, will be), conducting his insolvency practice with the independence, integrity and professional skills appropriate to the range and scale of the practice and the proper performance of the duties of an insolvency practitioner.

By Reg 4, other matters to be taken into account include whether he has been convicted of any offence involving fraud, dishonesty or violence; contravened any insolvency or subordinate legislation; engaged in deceitful, oppressive or otherwise unfair or improper practices; established adequate systems of control and accounting; whether in any case where he has acted as an insolvency practitioner has failed to disclose a conflict of interest between his so acting and any interest of his own whether personal, financial or otherwise, without having received such consent.

(c) Education and training

The requirements for the education and training of insolvency practitioners are contained in Regulation 5 of the Insolvency Practitioners Regulations 1986. Regulation 5 and Sch 1 require that an applicant under the age of 35 on 15 December 1986 and who has not held an authorisation under s 393 of the 1986 Act or s 5 of the 1985 Act must have one or more of the educational attainments set out in Part I of Sch 1, or their equivalent. Schedule 1 is reproduced in Appendix 1. Part II of the Schedule lists 12 examining boards and Part III, the nineteen acceptable subjects referred to above.

There is no academic requirement for this aged 35 years or over on 15 December 1986, for whom the emphasis is on experience; or for those who had already been granted an authorisation by the "relevant" (now known as the "competent") authority under the 1985 Act. However, in the latter case, the practitioner must, for these purposes, have been appointed in at least one case under the law of England and Wales within the period from the commencement of that authorisation to the making of the application.

(d) Practical training

The requirements as to practical training and work experience prescribed by Reg 6 for the purposes of s 393(2)(b) are either that:

".......

(2) (a) the applicant has been appointed an office-holder in not less than 30 cases within the period of 10 years immediately prior to the making of his application; or

(b) the applicant -

(i) was first employed by a person carrying on insolvency practice in that practice not later than 10 years prior to the making of his application; and

(ii) within the period of 10 years referred to in sub-paragraph (a) above has acquired not less than 7,000 hours of insolvency work experience whether in the employment of a person carrying on an insolvency practice or as an office-holder; and

(iii) satisfies the condition set out in sub-paragraph (c) below.

(c) The condition referred to [immediately above] is that the applicant must show he satisfies one of the following three requirements:-

(i) he has been appointed an office-holder in at least 5 cases within the period of 5 years immediately prior to the making of his application; or

(ii) he has acquired 1,000 hours or more of higher insolvency work experience within such period; or

(iii) he can show that within such period he has achieved one of the following combinations of appointments as an office-holder and hours acquired of higher insolvency work experience:-

(a) not less than 4 cases and 200 hours
(b) not less than 3 cases and 400 hours
(c) not less than 2 cases and 600 hours
(d) not less than 1 case and 800 hours."

An "office-holder" in the Regulations means a person who acts or has acted as an insolvency practitioner, a trustee in sequestration, or a judicial factor on the bankrupt estate of a deceased person, or in an equivalent capacity outside Great Britain. "A person carrying on ...." includes a firm or partnership. "Employment by a person carrying on ......" includes Crown employment in the Insolvency Service of the Department of Trade and Industry.

(e) Overseas practitioners

Those experienced under the laws of a country or territory outside Great Britain must demonstrate that they have no less than 1,400 hours of insolvency work experience or higher insolvency work experience in cases under English and Welsh or Scottish law, acquired within two years immediately prior to their making the application, together with a good command of the English language.

(f) Acting for associates

No account is taken of cases in which the practitioner was appointed receiver by or on behalf of a creditor who was an associate of his either inside or outside Great Britain, or liquidator in a member's voluntary winding-up where his associates were entitled to exercise, or control the exercise of, one third or more of the voting power at that meeting.

Where the applicant has been an office-holder in relation to two or more individuals who were carrying on business in partnership with each other then that is counted as a single office only for the purpose of Rule 2(c)(i) above.

Note the extended meaning of "associate", including "relative", under s 435 of the Act.

4. Transitional arrangements

Where an individual began to act as an insolvency practitioner in relation to any person before 29 December 1986, he is not prevented from continuing to act whether or not he holds an authorisation under s 3 or s 5 of that Act of 1985, or a security bond is in force. This is provided that:

(i) under the 1985 Act, he was a member of one of the recognised professional bodies and was permitted to act as an insolvency practitioner by or under the rules of that body:

(ii) where he is unqualified, the former regulations (SI 1986 No 951) continue to apply, whereby a relevant authority (the Secretary of State) licensed the practitioner. This has effect in relation to any application made before 29 December 1986 where no authorisation was granted, decision of the Tribunal handed down (s 8(4) 1985 Act), or written notice of a proposed refusal or withdrawal of authorisation has been given before the appointed day under s 9 of the 1985 Act.

The rules as to costs and taxation (see page 257) also apply to bankruptcy proceedings commenced before the appointed day.

5. Security bonding

By s 390(3) no person is qualified to act as an insolvency practitioner unless there is in force at that time security for the proper performance of his duties and obligations, which meets the prescribed requirements. By Regulation 10 and Sch 2 of the Regulations, there are two elements to the requirements for security - the general bond and the certificate of specific penalty.

(a) General bond

Under the general bond the surety is jointly and severally liable in the general penalty sum of £25,000. The bond is retained by the recognised professional body or the competent authority by which the practitioner has been authorised to act, as the case may be.

(b) Certificate of specific penalty

A certificate of specific penalty is issued under that bond in respect of the practitioner acting in relation to a particular person or company; the specific penalty sum under the certificate must not be less than the value of that person's assets. The maximum amount of the specific penalty sum under any bond entered into by an insolvency practitioner is £5m.

(c) Value of the debtor's estate

The value of a person's assets for the purposes of *(b)* above is the value at the date of the appointment of the practitioner, estimated by him having regard (where appropriate) to the estimated value of those assets disclosed in any statement of affairs and any comments of creditors or the official receiver on that statement. Where the value is less than £5,000 the value of those assets is deemed to be £5,000. Where the value is more than £5m, the value is deemed to be £5m.

(d) Duty of the creditors

It is the duty of the creditors' committee (or any committee of the creditors established for the purposes of a Part VIII voluntary arrangement) to review the adequacy of this security from time to time. By Rule 12.8(1), where any person has to appoint, or certify the appointment of, an insolvency practitioner to any office, he is under a duty to satisfy himself that the person appointed or to be appointed has security for the proper performance of his functions.

(e) Costs

The cost of the security is defrayed as an expense of the proceedings in an insolvency.

6. Records to be kept

For the estate of each person for whom the insolvency practitioner acts he must, by Reg 15 and as part of the licensing procedure, maintain a record in the form set out in Appendix 1 (see "Form of Record"), keep it up to date and preserve it for a period of ten years from the date on which the practitioner is granted his release or discharge in respect of that estate, or the date on which any security or caution maintained in respect of that estate expired or otherwise ceased to have effect, whichever is the later date. (Individual administrative records are maintained for six years.)

The records are then available for production to the Secretary of State, the authorising body or any duly appointed representative of such a body on giving reasonable notice to the practitioner, the authorising body being either the professional body of which he is a member or the competent authority which granted his authorisation. The practitioner then notifies the authorising body of the place where the records are maintained and the place (if different) where, and the manner in which, they are to be produced. As to needs of the creditors' committee, see page 225.

Where the records are maintained in non-documentary form, references to their production include references to producing a copy of the records in legible form.

7. Insolvency practice - ethical statement

The following passages are quoted from guidance notes issued by the accountancy professional bodies recognised under s 391(1), and apply to all their members practising in bankruptcy:

> "*Introductory note*
>
> 1. The Insolvency Acts 1985 and 1986 together with the associated rules make sweeping changes in the law of insolvency practice and introduce new roles for insolvency practitioners such as administrator and supervisor of voluntary arrangements. Council considers that there is a need for ethical advice to be available to members on the situations created by the new measures at an early stage in their life and has therefore approved issue of the following guidance with immediate effect.
>
> It is anticipated that there may be a need for further, more extensive

guidance to be issued in due course after the full implications of the new measures have been assessed in practice ......

Obtaining insolvency work

2. The offer or payment of commission to a member's employee or to another public accountant in return for the introduction of a client is generally permitted. However the special nature of insolvency appointments makes the payment or offer of any commission for, or the furnishing of any valuable consideration toward the introduction of insolvency appointments inappropriate.

The attention of members is also drawn to ...... the Insolvency Rules 1986, which provide for remuneration to be disallowed to a ...... trustee (r 6.148) whose appointment has been procured by improper solicitation.

[The point is that an order of the court under this rule effectively overrides the creditors' meeting in committee or in open meeting and any resolution carried to ameliorate the situation would be overruled.]

Professional independence and the acceptance of insolvency appointments

3. The following paragraphs refer to specific situations in which a member may not properly accept appointment. In situations other than those dealt with a member should only accept office in any insolvency role sequential to one in which he or his practice or a person at that time in the employment of his practice has previously acted after giving careful consideration to the implications of acceptance in all the circumstances of the case, and satisfying himself that his independence is unlikely to be compromised, by a prospective conflict of interest or otherwise. If he remains in doubt as to his position he should seek advice from Membership Committee via the legal department.

A member who is invited to accept an insolvency appointment jointly with another practitioner should be guided by similar principles to those set out in relation to sole appointments.

The attention of members is drawn to the statutory disqualification on acting as an insolvency practitioner, in particular s 390 Insolvency Act 1986. [See 2(c) below] ......

5. Where a practice or a partner in or a person at that time in the employment of a practice has, or during the previous three years has had, a continuing professional relationship (as to which see paragraph 7) with a client, no partner or employee of the practice should accept appointment as supervisor of a voluntary arrangement or as trustee in bankruptcy or as a trustee under a deed registered under the Deeds of Arrangements Act 1914 in relation to that client see also paragraph 19 (below)). ......

7. Such 'continuing professional relationship' as is referred to in paragraph ...... (5) ...... above commences at the date of appointment of a practice by a client, at the date of issue of letters of engagement or at the commencement of work whichever is the earliest.

8. A continuing professional relationship would not normally arise where the relationship is one which springs from the appointment of the practice by, or at the instigation of, a creditor or other party having an actual or potential financial interest in a company or business to investigate, monitor or advise on its affairs, unless there has been a direct involvement in the management of the company or business. ......

Bankruptcy following appointment as supervisor of individual voluntary arrangements [see page 86]
12. A member who has been, or whose partner or a person at that time in the employment of whose practice has been, supervisor of a voluntary arrangement in relation to a debtor may, provided the considerations indicated in paragraph 3 (above) are satisfied, accept appointment as trustee in bankruptcy of that debtor provided that is by a general meeting of the creditors under the provisions of s 292(1)(a) Insolvency Act 1986 or if the member has been appointed by the court under s 297(5) of the Act. [It should, however, be observed that appointment of the trustee in these circumstances is a special case reserved by s 297(5) for the court. It therefore appears that s 292(1)(c) does not give the creditors the authority suggested by this note, and they would, with respect, be acting *ultra vires* should they attempt to authorise appointment in these circumstances.] ......
Practice merger: transfer of partners and employees
18. When two practices merge, partners of the merged practice become subject to common ethical constraints in relation to accepting new insolvency appointments to clients of either of the former practices. However existing appointments which are rendered in apparent breach of the guidance by such merger need not be determined automatically, provided that a considered review of the situation by the practice discloses no obvious and immediate conflict such as the need to sue a new colleague.
19. Where a partner or an employee of a practice has, in any former practice, undertaken work upon the affairs of a company or debtor in a capacity which is incompatible with an insolvency assignment of his new practice, he should not personally work or be employed on that assignment, save in the case of an employee of such junior status that his duties in the former practice did not involve the exercise of any professional judgement or discretion. ......
Purchase of assets of any insolvent company or debtor [see page 220]
22. The Insolvency Rules 1986 contain prohibitions on members of a ...... creditors' committee acquiring any asset in the estate of an insolvent ...... debtor (save with leave of the court or the committee). [It should be noted that while permission is generally given *before* the transaction is entered into, the authority of the committee cannot be refused *afterwards*; see page 220.] Save in circumstances which clearly do not impair his objectivity a member appointed to any insolvency appointment in relation to a ...... debtor should not himself acquire directly or indirectly any of the assets of the ...... debtor nor knowingly permit any partner or employee of his practice or any close relative of himself, or of a partner or employee directly or indirectly to do so.

Where a contract is already in existence between the insolvent ...... debtor and a partner or an employee of his practice the member should seek guidance from the legal department as to the propriety of his accepting the appointment." (June 1987)

8. Insolvency Court Users' Committee

This committee of practitioners, which includes representation from The Law

Society, Insolvency Practitioners' Association, Chancery Bar, Department of Trade and Industry, the Lord Chancellor's Department, as well as judges and registrars, is designed to operate as a clearing house through which practical difficulties encountered by practitioners and the general public in the course of using the insolvency courts can be aired and which it is hoped can put in train any necessary remedial action. Members of the professional bodies represented should communicate with their professional bodies, and others should communicate directly with the Secretary of the committee in the Chancery Chambers of the Royal Courts of Justice in London.

9. The application for authorisation by the unqualified practitioner

(a) Applying for authorisation

Application is made to the "competent authority" under s 392 for authorisation to act as an insolvency practitioner, in such manner as the authority may direct. Notice of the application is published. It will contain or be accompanied by such information as the authority may reasonably require for the purpose of determining the application, together with a fee of £200 plus VAT. At any time after receiving the application and before determining it, the authority may ask for additional information; such directions and requirements may differ between applications and the information provided will be in such form or verified in such manner as the authority may specify.

An application may be withdrawn before it is granted or refused. Any moneys received on an application to a competent authority other than the Secretary of State may be retained by it, and sums received by the Secretary of State are paid into the Consolidated Fund.

(b) When the application will be approved

By s 393(2) the application will be granted if it appears that the applicant is, firstly, a fit and proper person to act as an insolvency practitioner; and, secondly, that he meets the prescribed requirements with respect to education, practical training and experience (see above).

Where a competent authority grants an authorisation under s 393 it is required to give written notice of that fact to the applicant, specifying the date on which the authorisation takes effect.

An authorisation, if not previously withdrawn, continues in force for such period not exceeding the prescribed maximum as may be specified in the authorisation. No authorisation granted pursuant to an application may continue in force for more than three years from the date on which it is granted.

(c) Notice of refusal of application

Where the authority proposes to refuse an application it must first give the applicant written notice of its intention to do so, setting out particulars of the grounds on which it proposes to act, together with particulars of the rights exercisable by the refused applicant, namely the right to make representations and to refer to the Tribunal.

A person on whom notice is served has fourteen days within which to make written representation to the competent authority, who then must have regard to any representations in determining whether to refuse the application. The procedure for reference to the Tribunal following refusal is as for a notice to withdraw authorisation; see *(e)* below.

(d) Withdrawal of authorisation

The authorisation may be withdrawn under s 393(4) if it appears either that the holder is no longer a fit and proper person or that he has failed to comply with any provisions of the Act or Regulations, or, in purported compliance with any such provision, has furnished the competent authority with false, inaccurate or misleading information. It may also be withdrawn by the competent authority at the request of, or with the consent of, the licensee. The competent authority must first give him written notice of its intention to do so, setting out particulars of the grounds on which it proposes to act, and the date on which it is proposed that the withdrawal should take effect. The notice will also give particulars of the rights exercisable by a person on whom the notice is served, who then has fourteen days to make written representation to the competent authority which, having regard to any representations, must determine whether or not to withdraw the authorisation.

(e) Reference to the Tribunal

Where a person is served with a notice to refuse an application or to withdraw an authorisation, the practitioner may give written notice to the competent authority requiring the case to be referred to the Insolvency Practitioners Tribunal. Under s 396(2)(a) this must be given at any time within 28 days after the date of service of the notice that the authority does not propose to alter its decision. The authority then has a further seven days to decide whether or not to reverse its decision; if not it must refer the case to the Tribunal.

The Tribunal must investigate the case and make a report to the competent authority, with a copy to the applicant, stating what would in their opinion be the appropriate decision in the matter, and the reasons for that opinion. It is the duty of that authority, with the report in front of them, to re-open the matter and decide whether or not to alter their decision; they also have a discretion whether or not to publish the report.

(f) Refusal or withdrawal of an authorisation without reference to Tribunal

Where the period of 28 days has expired without the applicant making any requirement under s 396(2)(a), or any representations under s 395, or the competent authority has given notice that it does not propose to alter its decision such as is mentioned in s 396(2)(b) and the period of 28 days has expired without the making of any such requirement, the competent authority may give written notice of the refusal or withdrawal to the person concerned in accordance with the proposal in the notice (ie to refuse an application or withdraw an authorisation, as the case may be) (s 398).

(g) Judicial review

It appears it would not be possible for the applicant to go straight to the courts to seek judicial review of the decision of the competent authority:

> "The normal remedy sought in such circumstances is *certiorari*, and RSC O.53 r 3 appears to be wide enough in terms to limit direct application in these circumstances as the court is empowered to adjourn the application for leave to seek judicial review until an appeal is determined. The recent trend in judicial decisions also supports this view and seeks to limit the availability of judicial review in circumstances where an alternative avenue of challenge exists; for example in *R* v *Home Secretary ex parte Swati* [1986] 1 All ER 717 (which concerned immigration) the Court of Appeal repeated an old approach, that judicial review would only be granted in exceptional circumstances if there was an alternative remedy. Here too the alternative was an appeal to a Tribunal." (3 *Insolvency Law & Practice* 36)

10. Insolvency Practitioners Tribunal

An unqualified practitioner served by the competent authority with a notice under s 394(2) to refuse an application, or to withdraw a previous authorisation to practice as an insolvency practitioner may give written notice to the competent authority requiring the case to be referred to the Tribunal, which then investigates the case and reports to the competent authority.

There is no appeal to the Tribunal for a member of a professional body recognised under s 391, who is subject to the disciplinary and appeal procedures of his own association, institute or society.

By s 396, Sch 7 of the Act applies. The Insolvency Practitioners Tribunal (Conduct of Investigation) Rules 1986 (amended, SI 1986 No 952) and s 397 set out the procedure under which the Tribunal conducts its investigations.

(a) Panel of members

Schedule 7 of the 1986 Act provides that members of the Tribunal shall be selected from panels drawn up and revised by the Secretary of State from:

"(a) ...... persons who are barristers, advocates or solicitors, in each case of not less than 7 years' standing, and are nominated for the purpose by the Lord Chancellor or the Lord President of the Court of Session, and

(b) ...... persons who are experienced in insolvency matters".

The Tribunal may sit as a single panel or in two or more divisions. It exercises its functions by three members consisting of a chairman and two others.

(b) Reference to the Tribunal

The authority sends the Tribunal a copy of the written notice served by it on the applicant under s 394(2), together with a copy of his notification that he wishes the case to be referred. They give notice to the applicant of the date on which the case has been referred to the Tribunal and of the address to which any statement, notice or other document required by the rules to be given or sent to the Tribunal is to be given or sent.

(c) Further information

Within 21 days of the referral, the authority sends to the Tribunal such further information and copies of documents and records as it considers would be of assistance, with copies to the applicant. Otherwise they notify the Tribunal and the applicant if there is no such information or copies available.

(d) Statement of the applicant

Within 21 days thereafter the applicant sends to the Tribunal, with a copy to the authority, a statement of his grounds for requiring the case to be investigated, specifying which matters of fact (if any) contained in the written notice he disputes, any other matters he considers should be drawn to their attention and the names and addresses of any witnesses whose evidence he wishes the Tribunal to hear.

(e) Investigation by the Tribunal

As soon as the Tribunal has considered the matter, it notifies the authority and the applicant of the manner in which it proposes to conduct its inquiries, and in particular whether oral evidence is to be taken, upon which the authority and the applicant may make their respective representations. The Tribunal then investigates the case and makes a report by carrying out such inquiries as it thinks appropriate into and concerning the information, documents, records and matters placed before it.

(f) Taking of evidence

Any investigation by the Tribunal must be in private and conducted so as to afford a reasonable opportunity for representations to be made to them by or on behalf of the applicant. The authority and the applicant may both be represented by Counsel, a solicitor, or any other person allowed to appear by the Tribunal.

For the purposes of any such investigation, by Sch 7, para 4, the Tribunal:

"(2) (a) may by summons require any person to attend, at such time and place as is specified in the summons, to give evidence or to produce any books, papers and other records in his possession or under his control which the Tribunal consider it necessary for the purposes of the investigation to examine, and

(b) may take evidence on oath, and for the purposes administer oaths, or may, instead of administering an oath, require the person examined to make and subscribe a declaration of the truth of the matter respecting which he is examined.

but no person shall be required, in obedience to such a summons, to go more than ten miles from his place of residence, unless the necessary expenses of his attendance are paid or tendered to him.

(3) Every person who -

(a) without reasonable excuse fails to attend in obedience to a summons issued under this paragraph, or refuses to give evidence, or

(b) intentionally alters, suppresses, conceals or destroys or refuses to produce any document which he may be required to produce for the purpose of an investigation by the Tribunal,

is liable to a fine".

The applicant and the authority are entitled to be present and to put such additional questions as may appear to be relevant, and also to take copies of any evidence such as computer or other non-documentary records not previously placed before the Tribunal. "It would seem therefore that the Tribunal can consider evidence that comes from neither the applicant nor the competent authority, but this could well lead to potential problems of *ultra vires*, and, perhaps, breach of natural justice." (3 *Insolvency Law & Practice* 37).

(g) Final representations

After it has completed the taking of evidence the Tribunal gives the applicant and the authority a reasonable opportunity of making either oral or written representations on the evidence, and subject matter of the investigation generally.

(h) Tribunal's report

The Tribunal is required to make its report to the authority no later than four months after the date on which the case was referred to it, unless the authority, on the application of the Tribunal, in exceptional circumstances, permits the report to be made within such further period as it may notify to the Tribunal in writing.

(i) Powers of chairman

Anything required or authorised to be done by the Tribunal may be done by the chairman, with the exception of the settling of the manner in which it is to conduct its investigation, the hearing or consideration of representations and the taking of evidence.

Chapter 3

The debtor's petition in bankruptcy

1. Introduction

A debtor may become bankrupt on his own initiative and receive the protection of the law from his creditors by presenting his own petition. Alternatively, by so doing, he may initiate the possibility of an interim order leading to a voluntary arrangement (s 385). In order to obtain an adjudication in bankruptcy a petition must be presented asking that a bankruptcy order be made in respect of the debtor's estate. The petition may be, wisely, presented by the debtor himself; by a creditor, or by the disillusioned supervisor under an interim order.

It is more than ever up to the individual to present his or her own petition (Form 6.27) when he or she is unable to pay his/her debts (Rule 5.272(1)). It is inconceivable that, except for the foolish and those covered by the situations outlined below, he should sit back and allow the creditors to go ahead with their own petition; likewise the rules relating to the presentation of the petition are straightforward and facilitate immediate action by the courts.

The deposit payable before presentation is £100 and the fee is £15 plus VAT. If the bankrupt's estate is sufficient to pay the whole or part of the relevant administration fee then the deposit is repaid to the extent that it is not required for payment of that fee. The petition must be accompanied by a statement of affairs in Form 6.28 (see page 119) which contains full particulars of the debtor's creditors and of his debts, other liabilities, assets and other information. The cynic, baulking at the costs of a creditors' petition, might consider that it would be a good investment to give the money to the debtor; the canny debtor would accept.

The presentation of his own petition by the debtor triggers two alternative procedures which are available to him and which would *not* be available at the same time as a petition presented against him by a creditor. They are:

(a) the possibility of a moratorium leading to an interim order with a view to the formal re-arrangement of his affairs but outside bankruptcy (see Chapter 1); or

(b) a certificate for the summary administration of his estate leading to less onerous investigation and procedures and culminating in automatic discharge in two, rather than three, years (see page 43).

It also has the effect of staying any action, execution or other legal process against the property or person of the debtor, or allowing them to continue but only on such terms as the court thinks fit. Improper use of the presentation of his own petition is a matter of which the court is bound to take notice and if appropriate will rescind an order made or annul the bankruptcy; see *Re Hancock ex parte Hillearys* [1904] 1 KB 585.

2. The petition

(a) Admission of insolvency

A debtor's petition (Form 6.27) may be presented to the court only on the grounds (s 272(1)) that the debtor is unable to pay his debts, requesting that a bankruptcy order be made against him, and without regard to a minimum "bankruptcy level".

(b) Identification of debtor

The petition is required to state the following matters with respect to the debtor, particulars of which determine the full title of the proceedings:

"(a) his name, place of residence and occupation (if any). [If the debtor has used a name other than the one given under this paragraph, that fact must be stated in the petition];

(b) the name or names in which he carries on business, if other than his true name, and whether, in the case of any business of a specified nature, he carries it on alone or with others;

(c) the nature of his business, and the address or addresses at which he carries it on;

(d) any name or names, other than his true name, in which he has carried on business in the period in which any of his bankruptcy debts were incurred and, in the case of any such business, whether he has carried it on alone or with others; and

(e) any address or addresses at which he has resided or carried on business during that period, and the nature of that business." (Rule 6.38(1))

(c) Statement of affairs

By s 272(2), the petition is accompanied by a statement of the debtor's affairs verified by affidavit in Form 6.28 (see page 95), containing basic particulars of the debtor's creditors, of his debts, other liabilities, assets and other information as detailed and discussed in Chapters 8 and 9. Further particulars may be sought by the official receiver. The affidavit may be sworn before an officer of the court duly authorised in that behalf.

(d) Requirement to submit accounts

Under Rule 6.69 the bankrupt must, at the request of the official receiver, supply to him accounts relating to his affairs of such nature, as at such date and for such period as the official receiver may specify. The period specified may begin from a date up to three years preceding the date of the presentation of the bankruptcy petition. However, on the application of the official receiver, the court may require accounts relating to an earlier period.

The accounts must, if the official receiver so requires, be verified by affidavit, and in any event must be delivered by the bankrupt to the official receiver within 21 days of the request, or such longer period as the official receiver may allow. Two copies of the accounts (and affidavit if it has been required) are to be delivered; and the official receiver files one set of copies in court.

(e) Declaration

If, within five years preceding the date of the petition:

- (i) the petitioner has been adjudged bankrupt; or
- (ii) has made a composition with his creditors or a scheme of arrangement; or
- (iii) has entered into any voluntary arrangement; or
- (iv) has been subject to an administration order under Part VI County Courts Act 1984,

particulars must be included in the petition (Rule 6.39(2)).

(f) Further disclosure

Under Rule 6.72, the official receiver may at any time require the bankrupt to submit (in writing) further information amplifying, modifying or explaining anything contained in his statement of affairs, or in accounts submitted in pursuance of the Act or the Rules. Again, such information shall, if the official receiver so directs, be verified by affidavit, and, whether or not so verified, it must be delivered to him within 21 days from the date of the requirement, or such longer period as he may allow. Two copies of the information, and any affidavit required, must be submitted; the official receiver files one set of copies in court.

3. Application to the court

(a) Procedure for presentation and filing

Rule 6.42 requires that the petition (Form 6.37) and the statement of affairs (Form 6.28) be filed in court, together with three copies of the petition, and two copies of the statement. A receipt for the deposit payable on presentation must be produced before the petition can be filed. Of the three copies of the petition delivered :

- (i) one is returned to the petitioner, endorsed with any venue fixed;
- (ii) another, so endorsed, is retained by the court, to be sent to the official receiver if he is appointed interim receiver or a bankruptcy order is made; and
- (iii) the remaining copy is retained by the court, to be sent to an insolvency practitioner (if appointed under s 273(2)).

Of the two copies of the statement of affairs :

(i) one is retained by the court, to be sent to the official receiver if he is appointed interim receiver or a bankruptcy order is made; and

(ii) the other is retained by the court to be sent to the insolvency practitioner (if appointed).

The affidavit verifying the debtor's statement of affairs may be sworn before an officer of the court duly authorised in that behalf.

(b) Notice to Chief Land Registrar

The court sends notice of the petition (Form 6.14) to the Chief Land Registrar for registration in the register of pending actions (Rule 6.43; see page 143).

(c) Venue

The petition is presented to either the High Court or the county court by virtue of s 373. It is presented to the High Court:

"(a) if the debtor has resided or carried on business in the London insolvency district for the greater part of 6 months immediately preceding the presentation of the petition, or for a longer period in those 6 months than in any other insolvency district; or

(b) the debtor is not resident in England and Wales." (Rule 6.40(1))

Otherwise it is presented to the debtor's own county court, which is:

"(a) the county court for the insolvency district in which he has resided or carried on business for the longest period in those 6 months, or

(b) if he has for the greater part of those 6 months carried on business in one insolvency district and resided in another, the county court for that in which he has carried on business, or

(c) if he has during those 6 months carried on business in more than one insolvency district, the county court for that in which is, or has been for the longest period in those 6 months, his principal place of business".

(Rule 6.40(2))

In a county court case, if it is more expedient for the debtor, with a view to expediting his petition, the petition may be presented to the nearest full time court to the debtor's own county court. See Appendix 3 for a full list of alternative courts.

(d) Domicile

A bankruptcy petition may not be presented to the court unless by s 265 the debtor is domiciled in England and Wales, is personally present in England and Wales on the day on which the petition is presented or, at any time in the period of three years ending with that day, has been ordinarily resident, or has had a place of residence or *has been carrying on business* in England and Wales. "Carrying on business" includes the carrying on of business by a firm or partnership of which the individual is a member, and the carrying on of business by an agent or manager for the individual or for such a firm or partnership.

(e) Withdrawal of petition

A bankruptcy petition may not be withdrawn without the leave of the court.

4. Hearing the petition

By Rule 6.42(2) the court may hear the petition as soon as it is filed in court. If it does not do so immediate referral may be made to an alternative county court (see Appendix 3) which may then be sitting. This enables a debtor to present his petition and have it heard expeditiously, thus gaining the "protection" afforded by the Act from creditors (s 374 and Rule 6.40(3)).

When the debtor's petition is before the court (and only in the case of a debtor), the court is bound by s 273 to consider *not* making a bankruptcy order, but to consider the four alternative procedures available as set out below, ie to:

(a) issue a certificate for summary administration; or
(b) appoint an insolvency practitioner to submit a report stating whether or not the debtor is willing to make a proposal for a voluntary arrangement; and/or in any event to
(c) appoint an interim receiver; or
(d) stay proceedings.

To put it another way, following the issue of a debtor's petition, the court, except in the case of the obviously dishonest debtor, has to make up its mind on the facts before it which course it can follow, failing which it is bound to make a bankruptcy order (see page 70).

(a) Summary administration

Should the unsecured debts not exceed the small bankruptcies level of £20,000 and other conditions are satisfied then the court may issue a certificate for the estate to be administered summarily (see page 45). However, by Rule 6.48 the certificate may or may not be included in the bankruptcy order (Form 6.30).

(b) Appointment of an insolvency practitioner under s 273(1)(d)

Where the court considers that it would be appropriate, it appoints an insolvency practitioner to act in the debtor's case under s 273(2). His fee is set at £100 (inclusive of VAT) and the court must immediately (Rule 6.44(1)):

(i) send to the person appointed -
- a sealed copy of the order of appointment, and
- copies of the petition and statement of affairs,

(ii) fix a venue for the insolvency practitioner's report to be considered, and
(iii) send notice of the venue to the insolvency practitioner and the debtor.

By s 274(1) the person appointed inquires into the debtor's affairs and within the time allowed by the court, submits his report to it. The report must indicate:

(i) whether the debtor is willing, for the purposes of Part VIII to make a proposal for a voluntary arrangement;
(ii) subject to s 258(3), whether the practitioner is prepared to act in relation to any voluntary arrangement to which the report relates either as trustee or otherwise for the purpose of supervising its implementation;
(iii) whether in his opinion a meeting of creditors should be summoned;
(iv) the date, time and place at which he proposes any such meeting should be held.

If the petitioner has in fact already entered into a Part VIII voluntary arrangement, it would still be appropriate for the court to appoint an insolvency practitioner to prepare a report under s 274 and to act in relation to any voluntary arrangement to which the report relates, either as trustee or supervisor (see page 12 *et seq*).

(c) Appointment of an interim receiver

Where the court has referred the debtor to an insolvency practitioner for a report, the court may under s 286(2) and without making a bankruptcy order, when it is shown to be necessary for the protection of the debtor's property, appoint that practitioner (instead of the official receiver) to be interim receiver of the debtor's property (see page 67). Alternatively and without relation to the referral, the official receiver may be appointed to be interim receiver before making a bankruptcy order, so as to avoid the need to make an immediate interim order.

(d) Staying proceedings

By s 266(3) the court has a general power, if it appears to it appropriate to do so on the grounds that there has been a contravention of the rules or for any other reason, to dismiss a bankruptcy petition or to stay proceedings on such a petition, on such terms and conditions as it thinks fit.

5. Report to the court by the insolvency practitioner

By s 274(1) the insolvency practitioner submits his report within the time allowed, stating whether the debtor is willing to make a proposal for a voluntary arrangement, known as a Part VIII arrangement. The object is to make an interim order as soon as the proposals seem feasible so that a bankruptcy order is immediately avoided, and other legal processes are likewise stayed. It is appropriate for the smaller debtor who is prepared to enter into a sensible arrangement of his affairs where his creditors can be persuaded to agree.

The proposal under s 253, known as a "composition" or "scheme of arrangement" provides for some person, "the nominee", to act as trustee or otherwise in relation to the voluntary arrangement, but only for the purpose of supervising its implementation. In the meanwhile the court grants an "interim order" if and until the creditors agree at a formal meeting. If they do, a supervisor is appointed to implement and supervise the approved voluntary arrangement. If they do not, then a bankruptcy petition may be presented against the debtor.

On considering the report the court may either:

(i) make an interim order under s 252 so as to give the creditors time to meet to consider the proposals; or, if it thinks that inappropriate

(ii) make a bankruptcy order under s 274(3) (see page 70).

A report which states that the debtor is willing to enter into a Part VIII arrangement should also state whether, in the opinion of the person making the report, a meeting of the debtor's creditors should be summoned to consider the proposal. If so, he should state the date on which, and time and place at which he proposes the meeting should be held. He proceeds to arrange the meeting unless the court otherwise directs (Rule 6.44(2) and (3); see page 201).

Rule 6.44 requires the insolvency practitioner to file his report in court with one copy, and send one copy of it to the debtor, so as to be in his hands not less than three days before the date fixed for consideration of the report. The debtor is entitled to attend when the report is considered, and must attend if so directed by the court. If he attends, the court must hear any representations which he makes concerning matters dealt with in the report. If the official receiver is appointed interim receiver or a bankruptcy order is made, a copy of the insolvency practitioner's report, the debtor's petition and his statement of affairs is sent by the court to the official receiver.

An interim order made by virtue of the above ceases to have effect at the end of such period as the court may specify.

6. Meeting of creditors

The insolvency practitioner summons the meeting of creditors for the time, date and place proposed in his report. The meeting is then deemed to have been summoned under s 257 and the procedures relating thereto under Part VIII voluntary arrangements (see page 11 *et seq*) and as to creditors' meetings (Chapter 14) apply.

The meeting may approve or decline to approve the proposed voluntary arrangement, or approve it with modifications to which the debtor must assent. If he does not, then the proposal cannot be approved. He and all persons attending have a right to challenge the creditors' meeting before the courts on the grounds that there has been some material irregularity or that the approved arrangement unfairly prejudices the interests of a creditor or of the debtor. The court may suspend or revoke approval or give directions. If the arrangement is not approved or suspended then a bankruptcy order is made.

7. Valuation requirements following a debtor's petition for a bankruptcy order

By s 273(1)(a) the court is bound not to make a bankruptcy order on a debtor's petition if he is classed as a "small bankrupt", that is where is appears to the court that if an order were made the *aggregate* amount of the bankruptcy debts, so far as liquidated and unsecured, would be less than the *small bankruptcies level,* and that the value of the estate would be equal to no more than the *minimum amount.*

"Aggregate" means the sum total of those debts remaining after the value of any security relevant to the property has been deducted from the gross amount.

"Small bankruptcies level" means the level of unsecured debt above which a bankruptcy order is inevitable, set at £20,000.

"Minimum amount": It appears that the "value of the bankrupt's estate" refers (if an order were made) to all the property that is available to the estate, and which might contribute to lifting it above the minimum bankruptcy threshold of £2,000.

"Property" includes money, goods, things in action, land and every description of interest, whether present or future or vested or contingent, arising out of, or incidental to, property. For a detailed consideration of those assets capable of inclusion in the estate of a bankrupt, see page 107 *et seq*.

It is therefore immaterial whether or not the debts or liabilities in respect of which the petition is presented are present or future, and consequently it is the sum of all the parts which makes up the total indebtedness that is required to form the aggregate sum which the insolvency practitioner will need to assess. Note that by Rule 6.114 a creditor may prove for a *debt*, payment of which was not due at the date of the bankruptcy order but was due later, even after discharge. The "debt" is usually for all practical purposes based on the amount of the estimated sum that is provable in the bankruptcy. Otherwise it is based on the estimated amount that is accepted by the court under s 322(4) at that time. By s 382, it includes any debt or liability to which the bankrupt is subject at the commencement of the bankruptcy together with any debt or liability to which he may become subject by reason of any obligation incurred before the commencement of the bankruptcy.

If either the debtor or creditor is dissatisfied then he may may appeal under s 303.

Other matters to be taken into account in arriving at the small bankruptcies level of debts or minimum amount of assets mainly concern the effect of security, interest and costs incurred by the debtor before the petition:

(a) The effect of security

By Rule 6.115, a secured creditor may alter the value which he has put upon his security in his proof of debt only with the leave of the court, and that amount is treated in all respects as an amended valuation by Rule 6.119. This may, of course, be material to the initial value placed on the estate by the court before being satisfied as to the correctness of the issue of a certificate. See also Chapter 13.

Where the creditor is relying on security which is incapable of valuation initially, but the debt turns out to be more than anticipated, it has been held that while the creditor was to be allowed to re-adjust his claim (a situation reinforced by Rule 6.115), he was not thereby to create any injustice to the other parties in a bankruptcy, and could not do so in a way which would interfere with anything that has been done prior to the change of his proof; see *Re McMurdo, Penfield* v *McMurdo* [1902] 2 Ch 684.

(b) Interest

Where a debt bears interest, that interest is provable under s 322(2) as part of the debt (but not in respect of any period after the commencement of the bankruptcy) and that sum is added to the debt so as to comprise its total value. The rate of interest is the greater of the rate specified in s 17 of the Judgments Act 1838 at the commencement of the bankruptcy, and the rate applicable to that debt apart from the bankruptcy.

(c) Judgment debt

Where a debt is in respect of a judgment, then in estimating it, the costs of the action are brought into account; see *Re Hoffman, ex parte Carr* (1879) 11 ChD 62. But note that any fine imposed for an offence and any obligation arising under an order made in family or domestic proceedings are not provable and therefore may not be added to the aggregate sum of the debts.

(d) Costs of proving the bankruptcy debt

The cost of proving (other than trustee's costs) is born by the creditor including the cost of providing documents and evidence, eg for substantiating his claim, unless the court otherwise orders.

One method of valuation and other matters relating to debts and assets is discussed in the context of the statement of affairs in Chapter 8.

8. Costs and expenses

(a) Solicitor's costs

In any case where a petition is presented by an individual against himself, any solicitor acting for him may give credit in his bill of costs for any sum or security received from him as a deposit on account of the costs and expenses to be incurred for the filing and prosecution of the petition. The deposit will be noted by the taxing officer on the taxing certificate.

If a debtor's petition is presented and heard before a creditor's petition which was presented first, and an order is made, then Rule 7.37 provides that, unless the court considers that the insolvent estate has benefited by the insolvent's conduct, or that there are otherwise special circumstances justifying the allowance of costs, no costs may be allowed to the insolvent or his solicitor out of the insolvent estate.

The solicitor's privilege in matters of bankruptcy includes the right to refuse to disclose confidential information from a third party; see *Re Sarah C Getty Trust Ltd* [1985] 1 QB 956.

(b) Expenses of preparing accounts

Rule 6.71 provides that:

"(1) If the bankrupt cannot himself prepare proper accounts under Rule 6.69, the official receiver may, at the expense of the estate, employ some person or persons to assist in their preparation.

(2) At the request of the bankrupt, made on the grounds that he cannot himself prepare the accounts, the official receiver may authorise an allowance payable out of the estate (in accordance with the prescribed order of priority) towards expenses to be incurred by the bankrupt in employing some person or persons to assist him in their preparation.

(3) Any such request by the bankrupt shall be accompanied by an estimate of the expenses involved; and the official receiver shall only authorise the employment of a named person or a named firm, being in either case approved by him.

(4) An authorisation given by the official receiver under this Rule shall be subject to such conditions (if any) as he thinks fit to impose with respect to the manner in which any person may obtain access to relevant books and papers.

(5) Nothing in this Rule relieves the bankrupt from any obligation with respect to the preparation and submission of accounts, or to the provision of information to the official receiver or the trustee."

(c) Repayment of deposit

The deposit paid by the debtor is to be repaid in full where a bankruptcy petition is dismissed, withdrawn or annulled, unless a fee has become payable to the insolvency practitioner (see page 37). Where the assets of the estate are sufficient to pay the whole or part of that fee, then the deposit is repaid.

(d) Court costs

The general rule as to costs of and incidental to any proceeedings in the Cvil Division of the Court of Appeal and in the High Court under s 51(1) Supreme Court Act 1981 is that they are in the discretion of the court, except that nothing in that subsection overrides the practice in bankruptcy laid down in the Insolvency Rules or Regulations, which may differ. Thus under Rule 12.2, all fees, costs, charges and other expenses incurred in the course of bankruptcy proceedings are to be regarded as expenses of the bankruptcy.

Chapter 4

Summary administration

1. Introduction

The certificate for the summary administration of a bankrupt's estate is intended primarily to cover what is sometimes known as the "consumer debtor" and also the "small businessman debtor". "Summary" means "small"; it is not actually defined in the Act, but this common sense interpretation is appropriate because summary administration is relevant only where the aggregate amount of the debts is less than £20,000 in respect of unsecured liabilities only.

This alternative procedure to a more stringent bankruptcy can now be expected to govern the majority of cases of debt following those debtors' petitions described as "small". In the past up to 98% of all receiving orders (following petitions by both creditors and debtors) were made where debts did not exceed £20,000 - the level at which the new procedure applies. The new summary administration has little relationship to that known in the old legislation by the same title. The Act scatters the provisions throughout the legislation. Section 275 of the Act is now read with the hybrid s 273 (which also and separately applies to voluntary arrangements) in the section of Part IX of the Act headed "Debtor's Petition", together with Rule 6.48.

The three most important features for the debtor are that the official receiver only has a discretionary duty rather than a mandatory duty to enquire fully into his conduct and affairs (s 289(5)); secondly automatic discharge follows in two years rather than the three years of a full bankruptcy; thirdly, there is exemption from criminal liability for failure to keep proper accounts records provided that the outstanding liabilities are not more than the minimum of £20,000 presently prescribed.

The debtor should remember that the benefits of summary procedures are not available following the issue of a petition by a creditor, but only on the hearing of a debtor's petition.

2. Conditions for issuing the certficate

Providing that the petition is presented by the debtor and the court is satisfied by affidavit verifying the debtor's statement of affairs as to the following matters, it is bound to issue a certificate for the summary administration of the bankrupt's estate under s 275:

(a) that if a bankruptcy order were made, the aggregate amount of unsecured bankruptcy debts would be less than the small bankruptcies level, presently £20,000; and
(b) the debtor has neither been adjudged bankrupt within five years ending with the presentation of the petition nor made a composition with his creditors in satisfaction of his debts or a scheme of arrangement of his affairs within five years; and
(c) that it would not be appropriate to appoint a person to prepare a report under s 274 for a proposed voluntary arrangement (for example, because he has no proposals to make, or where there are only one or two creditors, and/or the creditor(s) are without statutory power to come to terms); and
(d) that it would be inappropriate to make an interim order under Part VIII because the value of the assets would be less than the minimum amount (thus providing, for example, insufficient assets to support a supervisor's fee).

Once these conditions have been satisfied then neither an interim order nor a bankruptcy order will be made; the full impediment of bankruptcy will thereby be avoided, although it appears the certificate may nevertheless be contained within the bankruptcy order on the debtor's petition (Form 6.30; Rule 6.48). If the certificate is not so included, the court immediately sends copies of it to both the official receiver and to the bankrupt. However, there is no published form separate from the bankruptcy order.

A certificate is *not* available:

(a) where the aggregate amount of the unsecured bankruptcy debts is more than the small bankruptcy level; or
(b) for bankrupt partnerships (as distinct from the individual member partners); or
(c) for insolvent estates of deceased persons; or
(d) for second bankruptcies within the period of five years ending with the presentation of the petition; or
(e) for those debtors who made a composition with their creditors in satisfaction of their debts, or a scheme of arrangement of their affairs within the same five year period.

Where the debtor cannot satisfy the requirements, or if the certificate is revoked (see below), then the matter proceeds outside the summary process by the issue of a bankruptcy order for full administration in bankruptcy.

3. Relationship to Part VIII voluntary arrangements

The summary procedure is effected only after the court decides that it would be inappropriate to make an interim order under s 252, ie where the debtor intended to make a proposal for a voluntary arrangement and it has not been accepted by the court. In that event, it is not appropriate for the case to be referred to an insolvency practitioner to report further on the case (or at all).

It is coincidental that the maximum level of unsecured bankruptcy debts qualifying a case for referral to an insolvency practitioner to assess the possibility of a voluntary arrangement with his creditors is the same, at £20,000 (by the Insolvency Proceedings (Monetary Limits) Order SI 1986 No 1996). However, logically it would seem that this does facilitate its consideration without the confusion of further overlapping procedures.

4. The effect of the certificate

The effect of the issue of the certificate is that the provisions of the Act relating to full bankruptcy following a debtor's petition are subject to the following modifications:

- (a) the duty of the official receiver to carry out an investigation into the conduct and affairs of the bankrupt is discretionary only, not mandatory;
- (b) an application cannot be made for an interim order so as to present proposals for a voluntary arrangement;
- (c) no general meeting of creditors is summoned to appoint a trustee;
- (d) within twelve weeks after the issue of the certificate the official receiver gives notice to creditors of the making of the bankruptcy order if he has not already done so previously;
- (e) where the official receiver is trustee no creditor's committee will be set up. At any such time the functions of the committee are vested in the Secretary of State (see page 228);
- (f) the bankrupt remains personally subject to the full impediment of his bankruptcy;
- (g) discharge is automatic for the bankrupt in two years not three years beginning with the commencement of the bankruptcy (see page 46).

5. Trustee for the certificate

The official receiver is the trustee with effect from the issue of the certificate, although the court has a discretion to appoint a person other than the official receiver as trustee.

Where a trustee has been appointed, the official receiver sends a copy of the certificate of summary administration to him, whether or not it is included in the bankruptcy order (Rule 6.49). In that case the duty of the bankrupt to deliver possession of his estate, and to attend on the official receiver, does not apply.

In the event of a vacancy, the official receiver may refer to the court the need to fill it. If the vacancy arises because a person appointed by the Secretary of State has ceased to hold office, then the official receiver refers the matter to the court, or the Secretary of State who may either make an appointment or decline to make one. If no appointment is made the official receiver continues to be trustee but without prejudice to his power to make a further reference. It is submitted that as the Secretary of State has a dual role of appointment, namely to the Insolvency Service and also as the "competent authority" for the appointment of insolvency practitioners (see page 20), the apparent narrowness of the section is justified.

6. Revocation

The court may at any time under s 275(3) revoke a certificate for summary administration either of its own motion or on the application of the official receiver, in which case he gives fourteen days notice of the application to the bankrupt. The ground on which the court may act is that it appears to it that the certificate ought not to have been issued. If the court revokes the certificate it forthwith gives notice to the official receiver, the bankrupt, and the trustee if there is one, by Form 6.31.

7. Automatic discharge

Where the certificate for the summary administration of the bankrupt's estate has not been revoked before the bankrupt's discharge, he is automatically discharged in two years under s 279(2)(a) provided that he has not been an undischarged bankrupt in the period of fifteen years ending with the commencement of the bankruptcy. The period for automatic discharge runs from the commencement of the bankruptcy unless the official receiver reports to the court that the bankrupt has failed or is failing to comply with the obligations which follow a bankruptcy, in which case the court may order that the relevant period shall cease to run for such period, or until the fulfilment of such conditions.

Where the court is satisfied on an application by the official receiver under s 279(3) that an undischarged bankrupt has failed or is failing to comply with any of his obligations then the automatic discharge of the bankrupt may be suspended. This is without prejudice to any power of the court to annul a bankruptcy order (see page 288).

Chapter 5

The creditor's petition in bankruptcy

1. Introduction

A "creditor" in relation to a bankrupt means a person to whom any of the bankruptcy debts is owed. In relation to an individual to whom a bankruptcy petition relates, it means a person who would be a creditor in the bankruptcy if a bankruptcy order were made on that petition, and the petitioning creditor or each of the petitioning creditors must be a person to whom the debt or at least one of the debts is owed. A "bankruptcy petition" means a petition to the court for a bankruptcy order.

In these proceedings a person who has been wronged by a debtor's default on his financial commitments sets the law in motion by issuing a "statutory demand" on the debtor. The proceedings differ substantially from those where a debtor presents his own petition.

A creditor's petition must be in respect of one or more debts owed by the debtor to a value of not less than the bankruptcy level, presently £750. The deposit required before the petition is presented is £200 and the fee payable is £45 plus VAT. The rules relating to the presentation are set out later in the chapter (at page 57); they are the same whether the petition is presented by a creditor or the supervisor under an interim order.

It is necessary to prove not simply that there is a debt owing to the petitioning creditor at the date of the hearing of the petition, but that there is a debt of at least £750 which the debtor has no reasonable prospect of being able to pay. The matter to be proved to the satisfaction of the court is not that the debtor *was* not so indebted at the date of presentation of the petition, but that he *is* so indebted at the date of the hearing: see *Re Patel (A debtor)* [1986] 1 All ER 522 and *Re A Debtor, Ex parte Debtor* v *Goacher* [1979] 1 All ER 870.

(a) Presentation by a creditor

Presentation by a creditor calls for a creditors' petition with a statutory demand. Before the court will hear a creditor's petition all the following conditions have to be satisfied at the time the petition is presented:

(i) the amount of the debt, or the aggregate amount of the debts, is equal to or exceeds the bankruptcy level of £750;

(ii) the debt, or each of the debts, is payable either immediately (Form 6.7 or 6.9 - unsatisfied execution) or at some certain future time (Form 6.8);
(iii) the debt(s) is unsecured;
(iv) the debtor appears to be "unable to pay" or to have "no reasonable prospect of being able to pay";
(v) there is no outstanding application to set aside a statutory demand served under s 268 in respect of the debt or any of the debts;
(vi) at least three weeks have elapsed since the statutory demand (where required) was served;
(vii) at least fourteen days have elapsed since the petition was served on the debtor.

(b) Presentation by a supervisor

In these circumstances the petition is a default petition (Form 6.10) (see page 60). Where the debtor, in a voluntary arrangement, fails to comply with his obligations under the order for a composition or scheme, then his supervisor(s) or any creditor bound by the arrangement may return to the court and present a default petition on the basis that the information given by the debtor was false or misleading in any material particular or contained material omissions (s 276) in the statement of affairs or other document supplied by him or otherwise made available to his creditors at or in connection with the creditors' meeting; or that he has failed to do such things as may have been reasonably required of him by his supervisor.

(c) Expedited petition

In the case of a creditor's petition presented wholly or partly in respect of a debt which is the subject of a statutory demand, the petition may be presented before the end of the three week period by virtue of s 270 if there is a serious possibility that the debtor's property or the value of any of his property will be significantly diminished during that period and the petition contains a statement to that effect. The court may not, however, make a bankruptcy order until at least three weeks have elapsed since the service of any statutory demand under s 268.

(d) Interim receiver

If it is shown to be necessary for the protection of the debtor's property, the court may appoint the official receiver to be interim receiver of the debtor's property at any time after the presentation of the petition (see page 69).

(e) Restriction on proceedings

At any time when proceedings on a bankruptcy petition are pending, the court may stay any action, execution or other legal process against the property or person of the debtor, or allow them to continue on such terms as it thinks fit.

2. The statutory demand

The debtor appears to be *unable to pay* a debt when the debt is due for payment but either:

(a) the petitioning creditor to whom the debt is owed has served on the debtor a demand known as a statutory demand (Form 6.1 or 6.2) requiring him to pay it or secure or compound for it to his satisfaction, and at least three weeks have elapsed since the demand was served and the demand has been neither complied with nor set aside in accordance with the rules; or

(b) execution or other process issued in respect of the debt on a judgment or order of any court in favour of the petitioning creditor (or one or more of the petitioning creditors to whom the debt is owed) has been returned unsatisfied in whole or in part.

He has *no reasonable prospect of being able to pay* only if the debt is *not* immediately payable and the petitioning creditor to whom it is owed has served on the debtor a demand (Form 6.3) requiring him to establish to the satisfaction of the creditor that there is a reasonable prospect that the debtor will be able to pay the debt when it falls due, and at least three weeks have elapsed during which time the demand has been neither complied with nor set aside in accordance with the rules. It is also assumed that the "prospect" given by the facts and other matters known to the creditor at the time he entered into the transaction resulting in the debt was a reasonable prospect:

> "A creditor pursuing bankruptcy proceedings for a future debt has to show that circumstances have materially altered since he entered into the matter and that in effect there was at that time a reasonable prospect that the debt would be paid on time but now there is not. This protects the debtor in circumstances where the procedure would otherwise be open to abuse by a creditor seeking unfairly to force early repayment of a debt" (Hansard: Standing Committee E 13/6/85 Col.359).

Transactions entered into before the appointed day have effect on and after that day as if references under the 1914 Act to "acts of bankruptcy" include failure to comply with a statutory demand served under s 268 of the Act (Sch 11 para 12).

(a) Form and content of the statutory demand

Rules 6.1 and 6.2 require that a statutory demand must:

(i) be dated;

(ii) be signed either by the creditor himself or by a person stating himself to be authorised to make the demand on the creditor's behalf;

(iii) specify whether it is made under s 268(1) (debt payable immediately - Form 6.1) or s 268(2) (debt not so payable - Form 6.3);

(iv) state the amount of the debt, and the consideration for it (or, if there is no consideration, the way in which it arises) and:

- if made under s 268(1) and founded on a judgment or order of a court, details of the judgment or order (Form 6.2); and
- if made under s 268(2), the grounds on which it is alleged that the

debtor appears to have no reasonable prospect of paying the debt.

(v) if the amount claimed in the demand includes:

- any charge by way of interest not previously notified to the debtor as a liability of his, or
- any other charge accruing from time to time,

identify the amount or rate of the charge and the grounds on which it is claimed, and in either case the amount claimed must be limited to the amount which has accrued due at the date of the demand;

(vi) include an explanation to the debtor of:

- the purpose of the demand and the fact that if the debtor does not comply with it bankruptcy proceedings may be commenced against him;
- the time within which the demand must be complied with if bankruptcy proceedings are to be avoided;
- the methods of compliance available;
- the debtor's right to apply to the court for the statutory demand to bc set aside;

(vii) specify one or more named individuals with whom the debtor may communicate with a view to securing or compounding for the debt to the satisfaction of the creditor or, as the case may be, establishing to the creditor's satisfaction that there is a reasonable prospect that the debt will be paid when it falls due. The address and telephone number (if any) of any such individual must also be included.

See *Re A Debtor (No 75N of 1982)* v *National Westminster Bank plc* [1983] 3 All ER 545 as to the effectiveness of a notice.

(b) Cases where the creditor holds security

If the creditor holds any security, the full amount of the debt must be specified together with the nature of the security and the value which the creditor puts on it as at the date of the statutory demand (s 269). The amount claimed is thus the full amount of the debt after deducting the amount specified as the value of the security.

(c) Service

The creditor is under an obligation to do all that is reasonable for the purposes of bringing the statutory demand to the debtor's attention and if practicable in the particular circumstances, to cause personal service of the demand to be effected and sworn on affidavit (Form 6.11).

(d) Substituted service

Under Rule 6.3(3):

"Where the statutory demand is for payment of a sum due under a judgment or order of any court and the creditor knows, or believes with reasonable cause -

(a) that the debtor has absconded or is keeping out of the way with a view to avoiding service, and

(b) there is no real prospect of the sum due being recovered by execution or other process,

the demand may be advertised in one or more newspapers; and the time limited for compliance with the demand runs from the date of the advertisement's appearance or (as the case may be) its first appearance."

Practice Direction Bankruptcy 4/86 [1987] 1 All ER 604 further provides:

"Statutory demands

1. The creditor is under an obligation to do all that is reasonable to bring the statutory demand to the debtor's attention and, if practicable, to cause personal service to be effected. Where it is not possible to effect prompt personal service, service may be effected by other means such as first class post or insertion through a letter box.

2. Advertisement can only be used as a means of substituted service where: (a) the demand is based on a judgment or order of any court; (b) the debtor has absconded or is keeping out of the way with a view to avoiding service; and (c) there is no real prospect of the sum due being recovered by execution or other process.

As there is no statutory form of advertisement, the court will accept an advertisement in the following form:

Statutory Demand

(Debt for liquidated sum payable immediately following a judgment or order of the court)

To (block letters) of

TAKE NOTICE that a statutory demand has been issued by

Name of Creditor

Address

The creditor demands payment of £ the amount now due on a judgment/order of the High Court of Justice Division [or County Court] dated the day of 19

The statutory demand is an important document and it is deemed to have been served on you on the date of the first appearance of this advertisement. You *must* deal with this demand within 21 days of the service on you or you could be made bankrupt and your property and goods taken away from you. If you are in any doubt as to your position, you should seek advice *immediately* from a solicitor or your nearest Citizens' Advice Bureau.

The statutory demand can be obtained or is available for inspection and collection from:

Name:

Address

[Solicitor for] the creditor

Tel No. Reference

You have only 21 days from the date of the first appearance of this advertisement before the creditor may present a bankruptcy petition'

3. In all cases where substituted service is effected, the creditor must have taken all those steps which would suffice to justify the court making an order for substituted service of a petition. The steps to be taken to obtain an order for substituted service are set out below. Practitioners are reminded that failure to comply with the requirements of this Practice Direction may result in the

court declining to file the petition (see r 6.11(5)(a)) [as to swearing affidavit of substituted service see Form 6.12.]"

For a discussion of the situation where a debtor departs out of the jurisdiction and *conceals* his whereabouts and the registrar refuses an order for substituted service, see *Re a Debtor (No 419 of 1939)* [1939] 3 All ER 429. As to *whether* the debtor is keeping out of the way, see *Re a Debtor (No 75 of 1982)* [1984] 1 WLR 353.

(e) Transitional arrangements

Rule 6.36 deals with old bankruptcy notices and provides that a person who, before 29 December 1986, served a bankruptcy notice under the Bankruptcy Act 1914 may proceed as though the notice were a statutory demand provided:

(i) the debt in respect of which the bankruptcy notice was served has not been paid, secured or compounded for in the terms of the notice and the Act of 1914;

(ii) the date by which compliance with the notice was required was not more than three months before the date of presentation of the petition; and

(iii) there has not, before the appointed day, been presented any bankruptcy petition with reference to an act of bankruptcy arising from non-compliance with the bankruptcy notice.

If application is made under the 1914 Act on or before 29 December 1986 to set aside the bankruptcy notice, that application is treated as an application duly made (on the date on which it was in fact made) to set aside a statutory demand duly served on the date on which the bankruptcy notice was in fact served.

3. Debtor's application to set aside statutory demand

(a) Application to the court

The debtor may apply to the appropriate court, in Form 6.4, for an order setting aside the statutory demand. The time limit for so doing is eighteen days from the date of service of the demand, or, where the demand was advertised under Rule 6.3, eighteen days from the date of the appearance of the advertisement or, as the case may be, its first appearance.

The "appropriate court" is normally that to which a debtor would present his own petition (see page 36). However, the appropriate court is the High Court where the demand is issued by a Minister of the Crown or a Government Department and (a) the debt or a part of it equals or exceeds the bankruptcy level and is the subject of a judgment or order of any court; and (b) the statutory demand specifies the date of the judgment or order and the court in which it was obtained, but indicates the creditor's intention to present a bankruptcy petition against the debtor in the High Court (Rule 6.4(2)). See *Re A Debtor (2A of 1980)* [1981] Ch 148 where a petition by the Inland Revenue was transferred from the High Court to the county court.

Rule 6.4(3) provides that:

> "as from (inclusive) the date on which the application is filed in court, the time limited for compliance with the statutory demand ceases to run, subject to any order of the court under Rule 6.5(6)."

Finally, the application to set aside must be supported by an affidavit (Form 6.5) specifying the date on which the statutory demand came into the debtor's hands, and the grounds on which he claims that it should be set aside. A copy of the statutory demand must have exhibited to it the affidavit.

Practice Direction Bankruptcy 1/87 [1987] 1 All ER 607 provides:

> "1. The application (Form 6.4) and affidavit in support (Form 6.5) exhibiting a copy of the statutory demand must be filed in court within 18 days of service of the statutory demand on the debtor. Where service is effected by advertisement in a newspaper the period of 18 days is calculated from the date of the first appearance of the advertisement: see *Practice Direction (Bankruptcy 4/86[page 51])*. Three copies of each document must be lodged with the application to enable the court to serve notice of the hearing date on the applicant, the creditor and the person named in Pt B of the statutory demand.
>
> 2. Where, to avoid expense, copies of the documents are not lodged with the application, any order of the registrar fixing a venue is conditional on copies of the documents being lodged on the next business day after the registrar's order, otherwise the application will be deemed to have been dismissed.
>
> 3. Where the statutory demand is based on a judgment or order, the court will not at this stage go behind the judgment or order and inquire into the validity of the debt nor as a general rule, will it adjourn the application to await the result of an application to set aside the judgment or order.
>
> 4. When the debtor (a) claims to have a counterclaim, set-off or cross demand (whether or not he could have raised it in the action in which the judgment or order was obtained) which equals or exceeds the amount of the debt or debts specified in the statutory demand or (b) disputes the debt (not being a debt subject to a judgment or order), the court will normally set aside the statutory demand if, in its opinion, on the evidence there is a genuine triable issue. ......"

(b) Grounds for setting aside

The court may set aside the statutory demand (Form 6.6) or dismiss the application to set the statutory demand aside if it is satisfied that the debtor is able to pay all his debts, or is satisfied:

- (i) that the debtor has made an offer to secure or compound for a debt in respect of which the petition is presented;
- (ii) that the acceptance of that offer would have required the dismissal of the petition; and
- (iii) that the offer has been unreasonably refused.

In determining whether the debtor is able to pay all his debts, the court takes into account his contingent and prospective liabilities. As from the date on which the application is dismissed, the time limit for compliance with the statutory demand runs again.

(c) Hearing the application

Rule 6.5(2) - (6) provides a procedure where the application is not dismissed under *(b)* above:

" (2) ...... the court shall fix a venue for it to be heard, and shall give at least 7 days' notice of it to -

(a) the debtor or, if the debtor's application was made by a solicitor acting for him, to the solicitor,

(b) the creditor, and

(c) whoever is named in the statutory demand as the person with whom the debtor may enter into communication with reference to the demand (or, if more than one person is so named, the first of them).

(3) On the hearing of the application, the court shall consider the evidence then available to it, and may summarily determine the application or adjourn it, giving such directions as it thinks appropriate.

(4) The court may grant the application if -

(a) the debtor appears to have a counterclaim, set-off or cross demand which equals or exceeds the amount of the debt or debts specified in the statutory demand; or

(b) the debt is disputed on grounds which appear to the court to be substantial; or

(c) it appears that the creditor holds some security in respect of the debt claimed by the demand, and either Rule 6.1(5) is not complied with in respect of it, or the court is satisfied that the value of the security equals or exceeds the full amount of the debt; or

(d) the court is satisfied, on other grounds, that the demand ought to be set aside.

(5) Where the creditor hold some security in respect of his debt, and Rule 6.1(5) is complied with in respect of it but the court is satisfied that the security is under-valued in the statutory demand, the creditor may be required to amend the demand accordingly (but without prejudice to his right to present a bankruptcy petition by reference to the original demand).

(6) If the court dismisses the application, it shall make an order authorising the creditor to present a bankruptcy petition either forthwth or on or after a date specified in the order.

A copy of the order shall be sent by the court forthwith to the creditor."

(d) Applications for an extension of time to apply to set aside a statutory demand

Practice Direction *Bankruptcy 1/87* [1987] 1 All ER 607 provides:

" ...... Each term two judges of the Chancery Division will sit to hear insolvency cases, one of whom (the bankruptcy judge) will be primarily concerned to hear cases affecting individual debtors.

After the expiration of 18 days from the date of service of the statutory demand, the debtor must apply for an extension of time if he wishes to apply to set aside the demand. The application for extension of time and (if necessary) to restrain the presentation of a bankruptcy petition should be made to the bankruptcy judge, but in cases of urgency and where the bankruptcy judge is not available the application may be made to the judge hearing ordinary motions. [See the Practice Direction in Appendix 2].

Paragraphs 1 and 2 of Form 6.5 (affidavit in support of application to set aside statutory demand) should be used in support of the application for extension of time with the following additional paragraphs:

3. That to the best of my knowledge and belief the creditor(s) named in the demand has/have not presented a petition against me.

4. That the reasons for my failure to apply to set aside the demand within 18 days after service are as follows ......

5. Unless restrained by injunction the creditor(s) may present a bankruptcy petition against me."

The fee on the application will be £15."

4. Contents of the creditor's petition

The requirements are set out in rules 6.7 to 6.32. The relevant forms are Forms 6.7 to 6.10. The following information about the debtor must be contained in the petition (Rule 6.7(1)):

(a) his name, place of residence and occupation (if any). If, to the petitioner's personal knowledge, the debtor has used any name other than the name specified, that fact must also be stated;
(b) the name(s) in which he carries on business, if other than his true name, and whether, in the case of any business of a specified nature, he carries it on alone or with others;
(c) the nature of his business, and the address(es) at which he carries it on;
(d) any name(s), other than his true name, in which he has carried on business at or after the time when the debt was incurred, and whether he has done so alone or with others;
(e) any address(es) at which he has resided or carried on business at or after that time, and the nature of that business.

The petition must identify the debt in question by stating (Rule 6.8(1)):

(a) the amount of the debt, the consideration for it (or, if there is no consideration, the way in which it arises) and the fact that it is owed to the petitioner;
(b) when the debt was incurred or became due;
(c) if the amount of the debt includes any interest charge not previously notified to the debtor or any other charge accruing from time to time, the amount or rate of the charge (separately identified) and the grounds on which it is claimed to form part of the debt;
(d) either -
    - that the debt is for a liquidated sum payable immediately, and the debtor appears to be unable to pay it, or
    - that the debt is for a liquidated sum payable at some specified future time and the debtor appears to have no reasonable prospect of being

able to pay it,

and in either case that the debt is unsecured, subject to s 269 (above).

Where the debt is one requiring a statutory demand, the petition must also state the date and manner of service of the statutory demand, that the demand has been neither complied with nor set aside, and that no application to set it aside is outstanding.

Where the debt arises under a court judgment or order and execution has been returned unsatisfied, the petition must state the court from which the execution or other process issued, and particulars of the return.

Further guidance is provided by Practice Direction *Bankruptcy 3/86* [1987] 1 All ER 602:

"1. The petition does not require dating, signing or witnessing.

2. In the title it is only necessary to recite the debtor's name, eg Re John William Smith or Re J W Smith (male). Any alias or trading name will appear in the body of the petition. This also applies to all other statutory forms other than those which require the "full title".

3. Where the petition is based on a statutory demand, only the debt claimed in the demand may be included in the petition, except that interest or other charges which have accrued since the date of the demand to the date of the petition may be added; see r 6.8(1)(c) of the 1986 Rules read with r 6.1(4).

4. When completing para 2 of the petition, attention is drawn to r 6.8(1)(a) to (c), particularly where the 'aggregate sum' is made up of a number of debts.

5. Date of service of the statutory demand (para 4 of the petition): (a) In the case of personal service, the date of service as set out in the affidavit of service [Form 6.11] should be recited and whether service is effected before/after 1600 hours on Monday to Friday or before/after 1200 hours on Saturdays; see RSC O 65 r 7. (b) In the case of substituted service [Form 6.12] (otherwise than by advertisement), the date alleged in the affidavit of service should be recited. (As to the date alleged see *Practice Direction (Bankruptcy 4/86)* [page 51]. (c) In the strictly limited case of substituted service by advertisement under r 6.3 of the 1986 Rules, the date to be alleged is the date of the advertisement's appearance or, as the case may be, its first appearance; see rr 6.3(3) and 6.11l(8).

6. There is no need to include in the preamble or at the end of the petition details of the person authorised to present the petition.

7. Certificates at the end of the petition: (a) the period of search for prior petitions has been reduced to *three* years; (b) where a statutory demand is based wholly or in part on a county court judgment the following certificate, which replaces the affidavit of county court search, is to be added:

> 'I/We certify that on the day of 19 I/we attended on the county court and was/were informed by an officer of the court that no money had been paid into court in the action or matter ...... v ...... Plaint No ...... pursuant to the statutory demand.'

This certificate will not be required when the demand also required payment of a separate debt, not based on a county court judgment, the amount of which exceeds the bankruptcy level (at present £750).

8. Deposit on petition. The deposit [£200] will now be taken by the court

and forwarded to the Official Receiver. The petition fee and deposit should be handed to the Supreme Court Accounts Office, Fee Stamping Rooms, who will record the receipt and will impress two entries on the original petition, one in respect of the court fee and the other in respect of the deposit. Cheque(s) for the whole amount should be made payable to 'HM Paymaster General'."

5. Procedure for presentation of the creditor's petition

(a) Presentation and filing

The petition and affidavit are filed in court on production of the receipt for the deposit payable on presentation. Copy petitions for service on the debtor and for exhibiting to the affidavit of service must be supplied to the court. The court will endorse the petition and copies with the date and time of filing, and a venue for the hearing.

When filed, the court notifies the Chief Land Registrar so that the petition may be registered in the register of pending actions (Form 6.14; see page 143).

For application to restrain presentation, see the Practice Direction in Appendix 2.

(b) Venue

The petition is presented to the High Court in the following cases:

"(a) if the petition is presented by a Minister of the Crown or a Government Department, and either in any statutory demand on which the petition is based the creditor has indicated the intention to present a bankruptcy petition to that Court, or the petition is presented under section 268 (1)(b) [execution unsatisfied], or

(b) if the debtor has resided or carried on business within the London insolvency district for the greater part of the 6 months immediately preceding the presentation of the petition, or for a longer period in those 6 months than in any other insolvency district; or

(c) if the debtor is not resident in England and Wales, or

(d) if the petitioner is unable to ascertain the residence of the debtor or his place of business." (Rule 6.9(1)).

Otherwise it is presented to the debtor's own county court (Rule 6.9(2) - (4) as under Rule 6.40(2) - debtor's own petition (see page 36)).

(c) Affidavit to verify petition

The petition must be verified by affidavit (Form 6.13), to which the petition is exhibited. If the petition relates to debts to different creditors, the debts to each creditor must be verified separately. The affidavit must be made by:

(i) the petitioner or, if more than one, by any one of them;

(ii) some person, such as a director of a company or a solicitor, who has been concerned in the matters giving rise to the petition; or

(iii) some responsible person duly authorised to make the affidavit and having the requisite knowledge of the matters giving rise to the petition.

In cases (ii) and (iii) the person making the affidavit must identify himself and state his capacity, authority, and means of knowledge of the matters sworn.

The affidavit is *prima facie* evidence of the truth of the statements in the petition to which it relates. If the petition is based on a statutory demand and more than four months have elapsed between service of the demand and presentation of the petition, the affidavit must also explain the delay.

(d) Amendment of petition

After presentation, the petition may be amended at any time, with the leave of the court and on such terms as the court may think fit, by the omission of any creditor or any debt.

(e) Proof of service of statutory demand

Where the petition must have been preceded by a statutory demand, ie in those cases where it was not in respect of an execution or other process on a judgment or order of any court, the petition must be accompanied by an affidavit proving service of the demand. A copy of the demand must be exhibited to the petition.

Where service was effected personally, the affidavit of service must be made by the person who effected service (Rule 6.11(3); Form 6.11). However, where service (in whatever manner) has been acknowledged in writing by the debtor himself or by some person stating in the acknowledgement that he is authorised to accept service on the debtor's behalf, the affidavit of service may be made by the creditor or the person acting on his behalf, and the acknowledgement of service must be exhibited to the affidavit (Rule 6.11(4)).

In any other case, the affidavit must be made by someone having direct personal knowledge of the means adopted for service of the demand, and must (by Rule 6.11(5), Form 6.12):

(i) give particulars of the steps taken to serve the demand. These steps must be of a nature sufficient to justify an order for substituted service of a petition;

(ii) where those steps were unsuccessful, state the means whereby it was sought to bring the demand to the debtor's attention; and

(iii) specify a date to which, to the best of the knowledge, information and belief of the person making the affidavit, the demand will have come to the debtor's attention. In this case, unless the court orders otherwise, the date is the date deemed to have been the date on which the statutory demand was served.

Practice Direction Bankruptcy 5/86[1987] 1 All ER 606 further provides:

"1. ...... Rule 6.11(3) provides that, if the statutory demand has been served personally, the affidavit of service must be made by the person who effected that service.

Rule 6.11(4) provides that, if service of the demand (however effected) has been acknowledged in writing, the affidavit of service must be made by the creditor or by a person acting on his behalf.

Rule 6.11(5) provides that, if neither r 6.11(3) nor r 6.11(4) applies, the affidavit must be made by a person having direct knowledge of the means adopted for serving the demand.

2. *Form 6.11 (affidavit of personal service of statutory demand)*
This form should only be used where the demand has been served personally and acknowledged in writing; see r 6.11(4).

If the demand has not been acknowledged in writing, the affidavit should be made by the process server and paras 2 and 3 (part) of Form 6.11 should be omitted; see r 6.11(3).

3. *Form 6.12 (affidavit of substituted service of statutory demand)*
This form can be used whether or not service of the demand has been acknowledged in writing. Paragraphs 4 and 5 (part) provide for the alternatives.

Practitioners are reminded, however, that the appropriate person to make the affidavit may not be the same in both cases.

If the demand has been acknowledged in writing, the appropriate person is the creditor or a person acting on his behalf. If the demand has not been acknowledged, that person must be someone having direct knowledge of the means adopted for serving the demand.

Practitioners may find it more convenient to allow process servers to carry out the necessary investigation whilst reserving to themselves the service of the demand. In these circumstances para 1 should be deleted and the following paragraph substituted:

'1. Attempts have been made to serve the demand, full details of which are set out in the accompanying affidavit of .....'".

Where the statutory demand was advertised (see page 51), the affidavit must be made by the creditor himself or by a person having direct knowledge of the circumstances, and the affidavit must state the means of the creditor's knowledge or belief and the date(s) on which, and the newspaper in which, the demand was advertised. A copy of the advertisement must be exhibited to the affidavit.

The court may decline to file the petition if not satisfied that the creditor has taken all required steps (see Practice Direction 4/86, page 51) to bring the statutory demand to the attention of the debtor.

(f) Domicile

A bankruptcy petition may not be presented to the court unless by s 265 the debtor is domiciled in England and Wales, is personally present in England and Wales on the day on which the petition is presented; or at any time in the period of three years ending with that day, has been ordinarily resident, or has had a place of residence or has carried on business in England and Wales (see page 36 as to carrying on business).

(g) Following the failure of a voluntary arrangement

The procedure for presentation by a creditor otherwise bound by a voluntary arrangement will be subject to s 276; see below.

(h) Withdrawal of petition

A bankruptcy petition may not be withdrawn without leave of the court. This provision is an important safeguard against misuse of the legal machinery of bankruptcy.

6. Supervisor's petition

The rules relating to the presentation of the supervisor's petition are the same as for the presentation of a creditor's petition with a court fee of £45 plus VAT and a deposit of £200. The court must be satisfied under s 276 as to any one of the following matters:

- (a) that the debtor has failed to comply with his obligations under the voluntary arrangement under Part VIII; or
- (b) that information which was false or misleading in any material particular or contained material omissions was contained in any statement of affairs or other document, or was otherwise supplied in connection with the proposed arrangement or made available to his creditors; or
- (c) that the debtor has failed to do all such things as may for the purposes of the voluntary arrangement have been reasonably required of him by the supervisor of the arrangement.

This requirement also applies to a *creditor* bound by the arrangement who wishes to petition in bankruptcy. "Creditor" means in relation to an individual to whom a bankruptcy petition relates, a person who would be a creditor in the bankruptcy provided that a bankruptcy order were to be made on that petition (s 383(1)(b)).

It may be assumed that a supervisor is not allowed to retain assets in his hands as against the trustee of the subsequent bankruptcy, even for his costs (*Smith* v *Dresser* (1866) 14 WR 469); and that he is only entitled to payment for his services provided that they were beneficial to the estate; see, for example, *Re George ex parte Greener* (1880) 41 LT 739 and *Re Foster ex parte Official Receiver* (1895) 43 WR 428 as to compositions under the old law where bankruptcy supervened.

Where a bankruptcy order is made any expenses properly incurred as expenses of the administration of the voluntary arrangement are a first charge on the bankrupt's estate in priority to the distribution (see page 231).

7. Service of the petition

The petition is to be served personally, by delivery of a sealed copy, by an officer of the court, by the creditor or his solicitor, or by a person instructed by the creditor or his solicitor.

Service is proved by affidavit, to which must be exhibited a sealed copy of the petition, and, where substituted service has been ordered, a sealed copy of the order. The affidavit must be filed in court immediately after service (Form 6.17).

Rule 12.12 provides that a petition may be served outside England and Wales, with the leave of the court and in such manner as the court may direct. Where any process, order of the court or other document needs to be served on a person who is outside England and Wales the court may order service to be effected within such time, on such person, at such place and in such manner as it thinks fit, and may require such proof of service as it thinks fit. Application for leave to serve outside the jurisdiction must be supported by affidavit stating the grounds of the application and the place or country in which the person to be served is or probably is.

If the debtor dies before service, the court may order service on his personal representatives or such other person(s) as the court thinks fit (by Form 6.15 or by notice in the Gazette - Form 6.16).

The court may, if satisfied that the debtor is avoiding service, or for any other reason, order substituted service of the petition in such manner as it thinks fit. Practice Direction Bankruptcy 4/86 [1987] All ER 605 contains the following provision:

> " ...... 4. *Order for substituted service of a bankruptcy petition* In most cases, the following evidence will suffice to justify an order for substituted service:
>
> (a) one personal call at the residence and place of business of the debtor where both are known or at either of such places as is known. Where it is known that the debtor has more than one residential or business address, personal calls should be made at all addresses;
>
> (b) should the creditor fail to effect service, a first class prepaid letter should be written to the debtor referring to the call(s), the purpose of the same and the failure to meet with the debtor, adding that a further call will be made for the same purpose on the day of 19 at hours at [*place*]. At least two business days' notice should be given of the appointment and copies of the letter sent to all known addresses of the debtor. The appointment letter should also state that (i) in the event of the time and place not being convenient, the debtor is to name some other time and place reasonably convenient for the purpose; (ii) (statutory demands) if the debtor fails to keep the appointment the creditor purposes to serve the debtor by advertisement (see para 2) *or* post *or* insertion through a letter box *or* as the case may be, and that, in the event of a bankruptcy petition being presented, the court will be asked to treat such service as service of the demand on the debtor, (iii) (petitions) if the debtor fails to keep the appointment, application will be made to the court for an order for substituted service either by advertisement or in such other manner

as the court may think fit;
(c) in attending any appointment made by letter, inquiry should be made whether the debtor has received all letters left for him. If the debtor is away, inquiry should also be made whether or not letters are being forwarded to an address within the jurisdiction (England and Wales) or elsewhere;
(d) if the debtor is represented by a solicitor, an attempt should be made to arrange an appointment for personal service through such solicitor. Practitioners are reminded that the rules provide for a solicitor accepting service of a statutory demand on behalf of his client but there is no similar provision in respect of service of a bankruptcy petition;
(e) the supporting affidavit [Form 6.18] should deal with all the above matters including all relevant facts as to the debtor's whereabouts and whether the appointment letter(s) has/have been returned.
5. Where the court makes an order for substituted service by first class ordinary post, the order will normally provide that service be deemed to be effected on the seventh day after posting. Practitioners serving a statutory demand by post may consider using the same method of calculating service."

8. Hearing of petition

A petition is not usually heard until at least fourteen days have elapsed after service. However, the court may hear the petition earlier, on such terms as it thinks fit, if:

(i) it appears the debtor has absconded; or
(ii) the court is satisfied that it is a proper case for an expedited hearing; or
(iii) the debtor agrees.

The petitioning creditor, the debtor and any other creditor who has given notice may be heard on the petition. A creditor wishing to be heard must give notice (Form 6.20) of his intention to the petitioning creditor. The notice must state:

"(a) the name and address of the person giving it, and any telephone number and reference which may be required for communication with him or with any other person (to be also specified in the notice) authorised to speak or act on his behalf;
(b) whether his intention is to support or oppose the petition; and
(c) the amount and nature of his debt."
(Rule 6.23(2))

The notice must reach the addressee not later than 4 pm on the business day before the day fixed for the hearing or adjourned hearing. If the notice requirements are not met, a creditor may only be heard with the leave of the court.

The petitioning creditor must prepare for the court, a list (Form 6.21) of any persons who have given notice (Form 6.20) that they wish to be heard, giving their names and addresses and, if known, their respective solicitors. Any person who has not complied with the notice requirements but has been given leave to appear by the court should be added to the list. The list must show whether each creditor appearing intends to support or oppose the petition, and a copy of the list must be handed to the court before the commencement of hearing.

Practice Direction No 1 of 1986 [1987] 1 WLR 120 provides that:

> "On the hearing of a petition for a bankruptcy order, to satisfy the court that the debt on which the petition is founded has not been paid or secured or compounded for the court will normally accept as sufficient a certificate signed by the person representing the petitioning creditor in the following form:
>
> > 'I certify that I have/my firm has made inquiries of the petitioning creditor(s) within the last business day prior to the hearing/adjourned hearing and to the best of my knowledge and belief the debt on which the petition is founded is still due and owing and has not been paid or secured or compounded for (save as to .....).
> > Signed .... Dated ....
>
> For the convenience of practitioners this certificate will be printed on the attendance slips. It will be filed after the hearing. A fresh certificate will be required on each adjourned hearing."

A petition based on a moneylending transaction made before 27 January 1980, where the creditor was a licensed moneylender at the time of the transaction, must be supported at the hearing by an affidavit setting out the particulars required by s 9(2) Moneylenders Act 1927.

If the debtor wishes to oppose the petition, he must, not later than seven days before the date fixed for the hearing:

(i) file in court a notice (Form 6.19) specifying the grounds on which he will object to the making of a bankruptcy order; and

(ii) send a copy of the notice to the petitioning creditor or his solicitor.

(a) Decision on the hearing

Rule 6.25 provides:

> "(1) On the hearing of the petition, the court may make a bankruptcy order if satisfied that the statements in the petition are true, and that the debt on which it is founded has not been paid, or secured or compounded for.
>
> (2) If the petition is brought in respect of a judgment debt, or a sum ordered by any court to be paid, the court may stay or dismiss the petition on the ground that an appeal is pending from the judgment or order, or that execution of the judgment has been stayed [Form 6.22].
>
> (3) A petition preceded by a statutory demand shall not be dismissed on the ground only that the amount of the debt was over-stated in the demand, unless the debtor, within the time allowed for complying with the demand, gave notice to the creditor disputing the validity of the demand on that ground; but, in the absence of such notice, the debtor is deemed to have complied with the demand if he has, within the time allowed, paid the correct amount."

If the petitioning creditor fails to appear at the hearing, he may not petition again in respect of the same debt, either alone or jointly with another, except with leave of the court to which the first petition was presented.

(b) Adjournment of hearing

If service has not been effected, the petitioning creditor may apply for an extension of time for the hearing. The application must state the reasons why the petition has not been served, and no costs may be allowed other than by order of the court. If another day is appointed for the hearing, the petitioning creditor must give notice to any other creditor who has notified him that he wishes to be heard.

If the hearing is adjourned, the petitioning creditor must, unless the court otherwise orders (Form 6.23), send to the debtor and any creditor who has given notice that he wishes to be heard, notice of the adjournment (Form 6.24), stating the venue for the adjourned hearing. The grant of repeated adjournments coupled with payments into court under some form of trust is a wholly irregular substitute for the normal process of a bankruptcy or schemes of arrangement: *per* Sir Robert Megarry VC in *Re A Debtor (No 72 of 1982 and No 26 of 1983)* [1984] 2 All ER 266.

(c) Substitution of petitioner

The court may order that another creditor be substituted as petitioning creditor, where it is found that the petitioning creditor is not entitled to present the petition, or where he:

- (i) consents to withdraw his petition or to allow it to be dismissed, or
- (ii) consents to an adjournment; or
- (iii) fails to appear in support of his petition; or
- (iv) appears but does not apply for an order in the terms of the prayer in the petition.

The person substituted will be a creditor who has given notice of his intention to appear, who wishes to prosecute the petition, and who was, when the petition was presented, in a position to have presented a bankruptcy petition.

(d) Change of carriage of petition

At the hearing, a person claiming to be a creditor, who has given notice of his intention to appear, may apply to the court for the carriage of the petition in place of the petitioning creditor, without amending the petition. The court may make an order accordingly if satisfied that:

"(a) the applicant is an unpaid and unsecured creditor of the debtor, and

(b) the petitioning creditor either -

  (i) intends by any means to secure the postponement, adjournment or withdrawal of the petition, or

  (ii) does not intend to prosecute the petition, either diligently or at all."

(Rule 6.31(2))

The court may not, however, make the order if satisfied that the petitioning creditor's debt has been paid, secured or compounded for by means of a disposition of property made by some person other than the debtor; or by a disposition of the debtor's own property made with the approval of, or ratified by, the court.

A change of carriage order may be made whether or not the petitioning creditor appears at the hearing, and if the order is made, the person given carriage of the petition may rely on all evidence previously adduced in the proceedings (whether or not by affidavit).

(e) Dismissal or withdrawal of petition

The court has a general power, if it appears to it appropriate to do so on the grounds that there has been a contravention of the rules or for any other reason, to dismiss a bankruptcy petition or to stay proceedings on such a petition; and where it stays proceedings on a petition, it may do so on such terms and conditions as it thinks fit.

If the petitioner applies to the court for the petition to be dismissed, or for leave to withdraw, he must file an affidavit stating the grounds and circumstances of the application, unless the court otherwise orders.

If, since the petition was filed, any payment has been made to the petitioner by way of settlement (in whole or in part) of the debt(s) on which the petition was brought, or any arrangement has been entered into for securing or compounding for it, the affidavit must state:

"(a) what dispositions of property have been made for the purposes of the settlement or arrangement, and

(b) whether, in the case of any disposition, it was property of the debtor himself, or of some other person, and

(c) whether, if it was property of the debtor, the disposition was made wth the approval of, or has been ratified by, the court (if so, specifying the relevant court order)."

(Rule 6.32(2))

No order giving leave to withdraw may be made before the petition is heard; see *Re a Debtor (No 44 of 1978)* [1980] 1 WLR 665.

If the petition is dismissed or withdrawn by leave of the court, an order is made permitting vacation of the registration of the petition as a pending action. The court sends to the debtor two sealed copies of the order. A bankruptcy petition may not be withdrawn without leave of the court. This provision (s 266(2)) is an important safeguard against misuse of the legal machinery of bankruptcy. If it appears to the court appropriate to dismiss a bankruptcy petition or to stay proceedings on such a petition on the grounds that there has been a contravention of the rules or for any other reason, it may do so on such terms and conditions as it thinks fit. It may authorise a creditor's petition to be amended by s 271(5) by the omission of any creditor or debt, and to be proceeded with as if things done for the purposes of it has been done only by or in relation to the remaining creditors or debts.

The deposit paid by the debtor is to be repaid in full where a bankruptcy petition is dismissed, withdrawn or annulled unless a fee has become payable to the nominee. However, where the assets of the estate are sufficient to pay the whole or part of his fee, then the deposit is repaid to the petitioning creditor(s).

(f) Security for costs

Where the petition is based on a debt for a fixed amount payable at some future time, and it is claimed that the debtor appears to have no reasonable prospect of being able to pay, the debtor may apply for an order that the petitioning creditor give security for the debtor's costs. The nature and amount of the security is in the discretion of the court, and if an order is made, the petition is not heard until the amount of the security has been given in full, to which the Rules of the Supreme Court and the County Court Rules apply. It is not stated whether the costs of arranging the security are allowable in priority or at all. In the proceedings before the court the court may order costs to be taxed.

9. Consolidation; insolvent partnerships

Where two or more petitions have been presented against the same individual the court may give directions for consolidating the proceedings on such terms as it thinks fit. If more than one debtor is named in the petition and the petition has not been served on both or all of them, it may be heard separately or collectively in respect of those who have been served, and may then be heard separately or collectively as regards the remainder, as and when they are served.

Where, after a bankruptcy petition has been presented to the court, the attention of the court is drawn to the fact that the person in question is a member of an insolvent partnership, the court may make an order as to the future conduct of the insolvency proceedings, for example as an insolvent partnership under the Insolvent Partnerships Order 1986.

Application may be made by the official receiver, any responsible insolvency practitioner or any other interested person. An order made may include provisions as to the administration of the partnership, in particular as to the joint estate of the partnership and any separate estate of any member (see Chapter 20, page 293).

One fee only is payable where more than one petition is presented in relation to a partnership.

Chapter 6

The bankruptcy order and receivership

1. The interim receiver

(a) Appointment

After the presentation of a bankruptcy petition and before the making of a bankruptcy order, where it is shown to be necessary for the protection of the debtor's property, the court may under s 286 appoint the official receiver, or an insolvency practitioner, to be interim receiver of the debtor's property, and will direct him to take immediate possession (Form 6.32). Application to the court may be made by a creditor or debtor, or by the insolvency practitioner who has been appointed under s 273 to report to the court following a debtor's petition (see page 38).

References to the debtor's property are to all his property, whether or not it would be comprised in his estate if he were adjudged bankrupt.

(b) Application to the court

The application, supported by affidavit states:

> "(a) the grounds on which it is proposed that the interim receiver should be appointed,
> (b) whether or not the official receiver has been informed of the application and, if so, has been furnished with a copy of it,
> (c) whether to the applicant's knowledge there has been proposed or is in force a voluntary arrangement under Part VIII of the Act, and
> (d) the applicant's estimate of the value of the property or business in respect of which the interim receiver is to be appointed."
> (Rule 6.51(2)).

If an insolvency practitioner has been appointed under s 273 and it is proposed that he, rather than the official receiver, should be appointed interim receiver, and someone other than the insolvency practitioner has made the application for the appointment of interim receiver, the affidavit must state that he has consented to act (Rule 6.51(3)).

Copies of the application and affidavit must be sent to the person proposed as interim receiver, and if the person proposed is the official receiver and an insolvency practitioner has been appointed who is not the applicant, to the insolvency practitioner also. If it is not practicable to send copies, the person proposed, and if appropriate, the insolvency practitioner, must be informed of the application in time for him/them to attend the hearing. Those persons may then attend the hearing and make representations (Rule 6.51(4) and (5)).

On the hearing of the application, the court may order the appointment on such terms as it thinks fit, for example by directing that his powers should be limited or restricted in any respect.

(c) Security

Rule 6.53 provides for a deposit from the person applying for the order:

"(1) Before an order appointing the official receiver as interim receiver is issued, the applicant for it shall deposit with him, or otherwise secure to his satisfaction, such sum as the court directs to cover his remuneration and expenses.

(2) If the sum deposited or secured subsequently proves to be insufficient, the court may, on application by the official receiver, order that an additional sum be deposited or secured. If the order is not complied with within 2 days after service on the person to whom the order is directed, the court may discharge the order appointing the interim receiver.

(3) If a bankruptcy order is made after an interim receiver has been appointed, any money deposited under this Rule shall (unless it is required by reason of insufficiency of assets for payment of remuneration and expenses of the interim receiver, or the deposit was made by the debtor out of his own property), be repaid to the person depositing it (or as that person may direct) out of the bankrupt's estate, in the prescribed order of priority."

Where the insolvency practitioner was appointed under s 273 to report on a proposal for a Part VIII arrangement, then the cost of providing the security is paid in the first instance by the interim receiver, but if a bankruptcy order is not made, the person so appointed is entitled to be reimbursed out of the property of the debtor, and the court may make an order against the debtor accordingly. If a bankruptcy order is subsequently made, he is entitled to be reimbursed out of the estate in the prescribed order of priority (see page 231).

As to his failure to give or keep up security, by Rule 6.55:

"(1) If the interim receiver fails to give or keep up his security, the court may remove him, and make such order as it thinks fit as to costs.

(2) If an order is made under this Rule removing the interim receiver, or discharging the order appointing him, the court shall give directions as to whether any, and if so what steps should be taken for the appointment of another person in his place".

(d) Order of appointment

"6.52 - (1) The order appointing the interim receiver shall state the nature and a short description of the property of which the person appointed is to take possession, and the duties to be performed by him in relation to the debtor's affairs.

(2) The court shall, forthwith after the order is made, send 2 sealed copies of it to the person appointed interim receiver (one of which shall be sent by him forthwith to the debtor). "

The court also requires that person to take immediate possession of the debtor's property or that part of it to which his powers as interim receiver are limited or restricted in any respect. Otherwise he has all the rights, powers, duties and immunities of a receiver and manager under a receivership (see page 74), other than for trust property (see page 108).

(e) Effect on proceedings

After an interim receiver is appointed, and in the interregnum before the making of the bankruptcy order or dismissal of the petition, no creditor may have any remedy against the property or person of the bankrupt in respect of the debt, as if the appointment were the making of such an order.

(f) Property of the debtor

The debtor is required to provide the interim receiver with an inventory of his property (whether or not it would be comprised in his estate if he were adjudged bankrupt) with other information and to attend on him at such times as he may reasonably require, for the purpose of carrying out his functions.

The interim receiver has the same power, by s 368, as the official receiver or the trustee (following the making of a bankruptcy order; see page 77) to apply to the court to inquire into the debtor's dealings and property or to use their powers of enforcement under s 367.

The court also has the discretion in these circumstances, on application by the official receiver, to appoint any person to be the special manager of the property or business of the debtor with such powers as they may entrust to him (see page 89).

(g) Remuneration

The remuneration of an interim receiver (other than the official receiver) is fixed by the court from time to time on his application, taking into account:

"(a) the time properly given by him (as interim receiver) and his staff in attending to the debtor's affairs,

(b) the complexity (or otherwise) of the case,

(c) any respects in which, in connection with the debtor's affairs, there falls on the interim receiver any responsibility of an exceptional kind or degree,

(d) the effectiveness with which the interim receiver appears to be carrying out, or to have carried out, his duties as such, and

(e) the value and nature of the property with which he has to deal."

The interim receiver's remuneration (whether the official receiver or another) is paid to him and expenses reimbursed:

(a) if a bankruptcy order is not made, out of the property of the debtor (and the court may make an order on the debtor accordingly), and

(b) if a bankruptcy order is made, out of the estate in the prescribed order of priority,

or, in either case (the relevant funds being insufficient), out of the deposit under Rule 6.53. (Rule 6.56).

Where an insolvency practitioner has not been appointed then the official receiver's fee is calculated on the total hourly rate specified in the table to Regulation 20 (see Appendix 5(3)) plus a percentage of one half per cent of the sale price of the property, or £110, whichever is the greater (Regulation 21).

(h) Termination of appointment

By s 286(7)(a), a person ceases to be interim receiver if:

(i) the bankruptcy petition is dismissed;

(ii) a bankruptcy order is made on the petition; or

(iii) the court otherwise terminates the appointment.

The appointment may be terminated by the court on the application of the interim receiver himself, or on that of the official receiver, the debtor or any creditor. On termination of the appointment, the court may give such directions as it thinks fit with respect to the accounts of his administration and any other matters which it thinks appropriate. In particular it may:

(a) direct that any expenses properly incurred by the interim receiver during the period of his appointment, and any remuneration to which he is entitled, be paid out of property of the debtor, and

(b) authorise him to retain out of that property such sums as are required for meeting his expenses and remuneration,

or make such order as it thinks fit with respect to those matters. (Rule 6.57)

2. The bankruptcy order

A bankruptcy order means an order adjudging an individual bankrupt. By s 278 an individual is officially bankrupt commencing with the day on which the bankruptcy order is made and continues until he is discharged. The order may be made following a petition by a creditor (Form 6.25), debtor (Form 6.30) or supervisor of a voluntary arrangement (Form 6.30), or on a petition based on a criminal bankruptcy order, by the bankruptcy judge or registrar in bankruptcy of the High Court, or the judge, the registrar or deputy registrar of a county court.

(a) Following a creditor's petition

The court will make a bankruptcy order (Form 6.25) on a creditor's petition if it is satisfied that the debt, or one of the debts, in respect of which the petition was presented is either a debt which, having been payable at the date of the petition or having since become payable, has been neither paid nor secured or compounded for, or is a debt which the debtor has no reasonable prospect of being able to pay when it falls due.

The bankruptcy order is settled by the court and states the date of presentation of the petition and the date and time of making the order; it contains a notice requiring the bankrupt, forthwith after service of the order on him, to attend the official receiver at the place stated in the order. Subject to s 346 (effect of bankruptcy on enforcement procedures), the order may include provision staying any action or proceeding against the bankrupt. (Rule 6.33)

At least two sealed copies of the bankruptcy order are sent forthwith by the court to the official receiver, who then sends one of them to the bankrupt. Unless the court has, on the application of the bankrupt or a creditor (supported by affidavit stating the grounds), ordered the official receiver to suspend such action pending further order, the official receiver must:

(i) send notice (Form 6.26) of the making of the order to the Chief Land Registrar, for registration in the register of writs and orders affecting land;

(ii) cause the order to be advertised in such local paper as the official receiver thinks fit; and

(iii) cause the order to be gazetted.

(Rule 6.34)

The bankrupt is required to submit a statement of his affairs to the official receiver within 21 days beginning with the date of the order, unless that period has been extended (see Chapters 8 and 9).

(b) Following a debtor's petition

The court is bound to make a bankruptcy order in the circumstances where the aggregate amount of indebtedness is more than the small bankruptcies level of £20,000; where the value of the assets is less than the minimum amount of £2,000; and in any event in those cases where the debtor has been adjudged bankrupt within the preceding five years; or where it appears to the court that it would be inappropriate to make an interim order (debts above small bankruptcies level) and appoint an insolvency practitioner to prepare a report under s 274 with a view to the debtor entering into a voluntary arrangement.

If the court has no option but to make an order, then it may include provisions staying any further proceedings against the bankrupt. It requires him to attend on the official receiver, except that, on the application of either the bankrupt or a creditor, the court may order the official receiver to suspend advertising the order and causing registration with the Land Registry pending a further order (see page 143).

If the amount of the debts is less than £5,000 then the debtor should consider filing a request for an administration order as an alternative to bankruptcy (see page 335). Careful reference therefore needs to be made to the description of debts that are provable in bankruptcy and the variety of possibilities thereunder. Note that a creditor by Rule 6.114 may prove for a debt where payment was not due as at the date of the bankruptcy order but was due later, even after discharge. If either the debtor or creditor is dissatisfied then he may appeal under s 303.

The debt is usually for all practical purposes based on the amount of the estimated sum that is provable in the bankruptcy. Otherwise it is based on the estimated amount that is accepted by the court under s 322(4) at that time, and, by s 382 includes any debt or liability to which the bankrupt is subject at the commencement of the bankruptcy together with any debt or liability to which he may become subject by reason of any obligation incurred before the commencement of the bankruptcy.

The procedure for the making of the order on Form 6.30 is otherwise the same as in the case of a creditor's petition (see above).

(c) Following a supervisor's petition

The court should not make a bankruptcy order on a petition by the supervisor, or any person (other than the individual) who is for the time being bound by a voluntary arrangement approved under Part VIII, unless it is satisfied as to the following matters:

- (i) that the debtor has failed to comply with his obligations under the voluntary arrangement; or
- (ii) that false or misleading information was contained in the statement of affairs supplied by the debtor or made available by him at a meeting of his creditors; or
- (iii) that he has failed to do all things as may have been reasonably required of him by his supervisor.

Following a supervisor's petition, the rules for issue of a bankruptcy order on a debtor's petition are effectively the same as following a creditor's petition and any expenses properly incurred as expenses of the administration of the voluntary arrangement in question are a first charge on the bankrupt's estate.

(d) Petition based on a criminal bankruptcy order

The court makes a bankruptcy order on production of a copy of the criminal bankruptcy order on which the petition (Form 6.79) is based, and made against the individual by the Official Petitioner (s 402) or by any person specified in the order in pursuance of s 39(3)(b) of the Powers of Criminal Courts Act 1973, unless it appears to the court that this has been rescinded on appeal.

(e) Restrictions after presentation of petition

When an individual has been adjudged bankrupt, the court may stay an action, execution or other legal process against the property or person of the debtor or bankrupt, or allow them to continue on such terms as it thinks fit. No person who is a creditor in respect of a debt provable in the bankruptcy has any remedy against the property or person of the bankrupt in respect of that debt; nor may he, before the discharge, commence any action or other legal process except with the leave of the court and on such terms as it may impose. This is, however, subject to s 346 (enforcement procedures) and s 347 (limited right to distress) discussed at page 174 *et seq.*

On adjudication in bankruptcy, any disposition of property made in the period beginning with the day of the presentation of the petition and ending with the vesting of the bankrupt's estate in a trustee, is void unless made with the consent of, or is subsequently ratified by, the court. As to registration with the Chief Land Registrar, see page 143, and for mistake in the bankruptcy order, see page 145.

These provisions do not give a remedy against any person who received in good faith, property or payment before the commencement of the bankruptcy, for value and without notice that the petition had been presented, or which derives from an interest in respect of which there is no remedy.

(f) Member of Parliament

It is the duty of the court to advise the Speaker of the House of Commons following the adjudication in bankruptcy of a member of parliament, which takes effect after six months, when his seat is vacated (see page 270).

Where the seat of a member becomes vacant during a parliamentary recess, it is the duty of the Speaker upon receipt of a certificate of vacancy to issue his warrant during a recess of the House (whether by prorogation or by adjournment) to the Clerk of the Crown in Chancery to make out a new writ for electing another member because of his bankruptcy. However, by the House of Commons Disqualification Act 1975 as amended to 1 January 1987, the Speaker may, if it appears to him that an opportunity should be given to that House to consider the making of an order, defer the issue of his warrant pending the determination of that House.

A "certificate of vacancy" is a certificate issued under section 427(6)(a) of the Act, where the seat has become vacant because of a Member's bankruptcy.

(g) Amendment of title of proceedings

At any time after the making of a bankruptcy order, the official receiver or trustee may apply to the court for an order amending the full title of the proceedings. Where such an order is made, the official receiver must send notice of it to the Chief Land Registrar, for corresponding amendment of the register, and, if the court so directs, he must have notice of the order gazetted, and advertised in such local newspaper as the official receiver thinks fit. (Rule 6.35).

(h) In summary administration

Where the court issues a certificate for summary administration the certificate may be included in the bankruptcy order (see page 44).

Where under a contract of insurance a debtor was insured against liabilities to third parties, his rights against the insurer are, on his bankruptcy, transferred to and vest in the third party to whom the liability was incurred (s 1 Third Parties (Rights Against Insurers) Act 1930).

3. Official receivership

(a) *Role as "official trustee"*

Following the bankruptcy order the official receiver takes over the bankrupt estate on a "protective trust", without putting the estate into formal receivership, pending the subsequent appointment of a trustee by the creditors. The title "official receiver" is however an historical anachronism left over from the old law.

His authority under the old law was established by the making of a receiving order by virtue of which, as an official of the court, he was constituted receiver of the debtor's estate, with no estate, interest or powers to bring or defend actions. He stood in a different position from the trustee: see for example *Re Berry, Duffield* v *Williams* [1896] 1 Ch 939.

That has all changed; the nearest a receivership *per se* could now be realistically allied to insolvency law, is in connection with a mortgage deed or appointment under an instrument such as a debenture secured by a floating charge in company insolvency. It is submitted that that is a long way from his role of protection in individual insolvency under s 287, which is more akin to his minor role as trustee under a certificate for summary administration (under s 275); or where he is not replaced by the Secretary of State (s 296(1)); or in a criminal bankruptcy (s.297(3)).

Surprisingly the opportunity was not taken by parliament to reflect the true nature of his role by naming him: "official trustee", to mean in plain English the official custodian of the bankrupt's estate pending the appointment of the creditor's trustee. Moreover, both the trustee (pursuant to s 311(2)) and the official receiver (s 287(2)), have like powers as if they were respectively receiver or manager appointed by the High Court.

If the Insolvency Service was properly designated as the "official trustee" there would not be a misunderstanding by the uninitiated of his role and responsibilities in the administration, particularly in those serious cases of bankruptcy for which the new legislation opens a more particular role for him; they are unlikely to be about receivership. That, however, is for future correction or as may be; at the moment his title, if not his role, remains officially "receiver" (s 399).

(b) *Function as receiver and manager*

His function whilst acting under s 287 is essentially to protect the estate, and for this purpose he has the same powers as if he were a receiver or manager appointed by the High Court; he is entitled to sell or otherwise dispose of any perishable and other goods the value of which is likely to diminish if they are not disposed of. The property may subsequently be claimed for the estate by the trustee, but if it is not then he is not required to do anything that involves his incurring expenditure unless he is so directed by the Secretary of State. He may summon a general meeting of creditors, and must do so if directed by the court.

By s 400 other functions may be conferred on him by the Secretary of State.

(c) Remuneration

The remuneration of the official receiver while acting as trustee is calculated in accordance with the table to Regulation 19 (see Appendix 5).

In *Evans* v *Clayhope Properties Ltd* [1987] 2All ER 40 there were insufficient assets to meet the receiver's remuneration: per Vinelott J "a receiver should not take office unless he is satisfied that the assets of which he is appointed receiver will be adequate to meet his remuneration". However in bankruptcy the official receiver, by s 287(1), has no choice once the bankruptcy order is made (although the *dictum* might come to the aid of the reluctant nominee under a proposed voluntary arrangement).

(d) Duty to investigate

By s 289(1) it is the duty of the official receiver to investigate the conduct and affairs of every bankrupt, and to report to the court as he thinks fit (see below). His report is *prima facie* evidence of the facts stated in it in any proceedings. Following a creditor's petition, he gives the bankrupt instructions for the preparation of his statement of affairs and the forms required for that purpose. "Conduct and affairs" include the conduct and affairs of the debtor before the making of the order. In *Khan* v *Khan* [1982] 1 WLR 513 there was an unsuccessful objection to the swearing of an affidavit disclosing where certain moneys were, on the grounds of self-incrimination. See also *Rank Film Distributors* v *Video Information Centre* [1982] AC 380.

The bankrupt is required to attend on the offical receiver or his deputy and staff (s 401) for the "preliminary examination" at such time as the official receiver may reasonably require for questioning by him or his examiners, and to make a background statement dealing with his history and the likely causes of his failure. He is also required to give an inventory of his estate: see *Re Poh* (1983) 1 WLR 2 and *Lane* v *Esdaile* [1891] AC 210, failing which he is guilty of contempt of the court and liable to be punished.

As to the bankrupt's duty to the official receiver, see page 272.

(e) Information to creditors

At least once after the making of the bankruptcy order the official receiver is bound to send a report on the state of the bankrupt's affairs to the creditors, ie those known to him or identified in the bankrupt's statement of affairs (see Chapter 8) (Rule 6.74). His report contains a summary of the statement where there is one, together with such observations as he thinks fit with respect to it or to the bankrupt's affairs generally. The court may relieve him of this duty or authorise him to carry out the duty in a different manner having regard to the amount of funds available in the estate and to the extent of the interest of creditors or any particular class of them. Likewise the court may allow limited disclosure only of the statement where it would otherwise prejudice the conduct of bankruptcy.

Where the bankrupt has been released from the obligation to submit a statement of affairs, the official receiver sends a report to creditors with respect to his affairs (so far as within his knowledge) and his observations, unless he has previously reported to the creditors and there is nothing new to be brought to their attention (Rule 6.76).

(f) Inspection of secured goods

Where any goods of an undischarged bankrupt (whether or not comprised in the estate) are held by any person by way of pledge, pawn or other security, the official receiver may inspect the goods after giving notice in writing under s 285(5) of his intention to do so. (For proofs by secured creditors, see page 196.)

(g) Liability in negligence

Where he seizes or disposes of any property not comprised in the estate, but has reasonable grounds for believing that he is so entitled, then the official receiver is not liable to any person in respect of any loss or damage resulting other than that which is caused by his negligence.

(h) Expenses

However, he retains a lien on the property or the proceeds of its sale for such of the expenses (including damages) of the bankruptcy as were incurred in connection with the seizure or disposal. Any expenses incurred by him in connection with proceedings taken against him are to be treated as expenses of the insolvency proceedings.

(i) General rule as to reporting

On application the court may relieve him of any duty to report to the creditors or authorise him to carry out the duty differently having regard to the cost, to the amount of funds available in the estate, and to the extent of the interest of creditors or any particular class of them (Rule 6.77). The reporting requirements cease should the bankruptcy order be annulled (Rule 6.78).

4. Appeals against the order

Every bankruptcy court may review, rescind or vary any order made by it in the exercise of that jurisdiction; the Secretary of State may appeal from an order of the court rescinding, annulling or discharging a bankruptcy order (Rule 7.48(1)). A rehearing is, however, a "matter of indulgence" and will only be allowed in special circumstances: see *Re May, ex parte May* (1884) 12 QBD 497. A rehearing may take place even though an appeal is pending: *Re Wike, ex parte Keighley* (1874) 30 LT 407.

In the case of an order made by a county court or by a registrar of the High Court, the appeal lies to a single bankruptcy judge of the High Court under s 375 (see Appendix 2); and an appeal from a decision of that judge on such appeal lies, with the leave of the bankruptcy judge or the Court of Appeal to the Court of Appeal. The procedure under RSC O 59 is by application and not by summons: no appeal lies to the House of Lords against the Court of Appeal's refusal of leave to appeal.

The court has the discretion to annul a bankruptcy order if at any time it appears to the court that the order ought not to have been made, or that to the extent required by the rules, the bankruptcy debts and expenses have all either been paid or secured to the satisfaction of the court (see page 288).

In bankruptcy proceedings an appeal lies at the instance of the Secretary of State from any order of the court made on an application for the rescission or annulment of a bankruptcy order.

No insolvency proceedings are invalidated by any formal defect or by any irregularity, unless the court before which objection is made considers that substantial injustice has been caused by the defect or irregularity, and that the injustice cannot be remedied by any order of the court.

By s 376 where the time for doing anything is limited, the court has a discretion to extend the time either before or after it has expired.

5. Inquiry by the court following the bankruptcy order

(a) Generally

For the purposes of inquiry into the bankrupt's affairs, the court may, at any time after a bankruptcy order has been made and on the application of the official receiver or the trustee under s 366, summon to appear before it:

- the bankrupt;
- the bankrupt's spouse or former spouse;
- any person known or believed to have any property comprised in the estate in his possession or to be indebted to the bankrupt;
- any person able to give information concerning the bankrupt's dealings, affairs or property; this includes British subjects resident abroad; see *Re*

Tucker (a Bankrupt) [1987] 2 All ER 23 (who was resident in Belgium).

Until the bankrupt is discharged, no creditor has any remedy against the property or person in respect of a debt provable in the bankruptcy, other than the right to prove, nor may he commence any action or other legal proceeding except with the leave of the court and on such terms as the court may impose.

The court may stay any action, execution or other legal process against the property or person of the debtor or bankrupt. Any court in which proceedings are pending may, on proof that a bankruptcy petition has been presented or that the debtor is an undischarged bankrupt, either stay the proceedings or allow them to continue on such terms as it thinks fit.

(b) Application for examination (Form 9.1)

The application for examination must be in writing, accompanied by a brief statement of the grounds, and must sufficiently identify the respondent. It must state whether the application is for the respondent to:

(i) be ordered to appear before the court and/or;
(ii) answer interrogatories (and if so, particulars of the matters in respect of which answers are required must be given); and/or
(iii) submit affidavits (and if so, details of the matters to be sworn to must be included); and/or
(iv) produce books, papers or other records (and, if so, the items).

The application may be made *ex parte* (Rule 9.2).

(c) Order of the court

The court may make any order for which it has appropriate power, whatever the purpose of the application (Form 9.1). If it orders the respondent to appear before it, the court must specify a date not less than fourteen days from the date of the order. If he is ordered to submit affidavits, the order must specify the matters to be dealt with and the time within which they are to be submitted to the court. If the order is to produce books, papers or other records, the order must state the time and manner of compliance. The order must be served immediately on the respondent, and must be served personally unless the court otherwise directs. (Rule 9.3).

The court may cause a warrant to be issued for the purpose of bringing that person and anything in his possession including books, papers, records, money or goods before the court.

(d) Procedure for examination

Any person who appears or is brought before the court may be examined on oath either orally or by interrogatories, concerning the bankrupt or the bankrupt's dealings, affairs and property (Rule 9.4).

If it appears to the court, on consideration of any evidence obtained under s 366 or 367, that any person has in his possession any property comprised in the bankrupt's estate, the court may order that person to deliver the whole or any part of the property to the official receiver or the trustee at such time, in such manner and on such terms as the court thinks fit. It may order any debtor of the bankrupt to pay the whole or part of the money due, whether in full discharge of the debt or otherwise.

(e) Record of examination

Under Rule 9.5, the written record of the examination, answers to interrogatories and any affidavits submitted, are not filed in court unless the court so orders. In so far as the court file shows the grounds of the application or consists of copies of proposed interrogatories, the written record, answers and affidavits are not open to inspection without a court order, except to the applicant for the order or any person who could have applied for such an order. The court may give directions as to the custody and inspection of any documents, and the furnishing of copies or extracts.

(f) False claims

Where the rules provide for a creditor or any other person to inspect documents, whether in the possession of the court, the trustee or the official receiver, it is an offence for any person, with the intention of inspecting documents he is not entitled to see, falsely to claim a status which would entitle him to see them (Rule 12.18).

(g) Costs

Where the court has ordered an examination (s 366; Rule 9.6) and it appears the examination was necessitated by the unjustifiable refusal of information by the respondent, it may order him to pay the costs. Where an order is made under s 367(1) (to deliver up property which belongs to the bankrupt); or under s 367(2) (to pay any amount in discharge of debt due to the bankrupt), the court may order the respondent to pay the costs of the application. The applicant's costs are paid out of the insolvent estate, unless the court directs otherwise.

A person summoned to attend for examination must be tendered a reasonable sum for travelling expenses; other costs falling on him are at the court's discretion. Where the examination is on the application of the official receiver otherwise than in the capacity of trustee, no order may be made for the payment of costs by him.

6. Public examination of the bankrupt

(a) Application to the court by the official receiver

The official receiver may apply to the court for the public examination of the bankrupt under s 290(1) at any time before discharge, provided that a bankruptcy order has been made. The court must then direct that a public examination of the bankrupt be held on a day appointed by the court, requiring him to attend on the appointed day to be publicly examined in open court as to his affairs, dealings and property. If without reasonable cause he fails to attend his examination, he is guilty of contempt of court and liable to be punished accordingly.

(b) Order on request by creditors

If one of the bankrupt's creditors gives notice (Form 6.56) to the official receiver under s 290(2), and has the concurrence of not less than one half in value (including the creditor giving notice) of the other creditors, then unless the court otherwise orders, the official receiver must make an application for a public examination.

Where the creditor making the request has a claim of at least one half of the total debt then he has no more to do than give to the official receiver a statement of his reasons for requesting the examination. Where his own claim is insufficient then his request must be in writing and accompanied by a list of those creditors who concur with the request (to make up at least the one half in value), stating the amount of their respective claims, together with his statement of reasons.

Before the application is made, the person requesting it must deposit with the official receiver a sum determined by the official receiver as a deposit for the expenses of the public examination. The court may later order that a proportion of the expenses of the public examination be paid out of this sum of money rather than from the estate. The costs of a public examination never fall to the official receiver personally.

The official receiver then makes the application to the court within 28 days of receiving the request. If, however, he thinks the request unreasonable, he may apply to the court for an order that he need not make the application. If the court makes such an order on an *ex parte* application, notice of it is given to the person requesting the examination; otherwise the official receiver must make the application for a public examination forthwith.

(c) Order for public examination

Rule 6.172 provides that if the official receiver applies under s 290 for a public examination of the bankrupt, a copy of the court's order [Form 6.55] shall, forthwith after its making, be sent by the official receiver to the bankrupt. The order appoints a venue for the hearing, and directs the bankrupt to attend. The official receiver must give at least fourteen days notice of the hearing:

(i) if a trustee has been nominated or appointed, to him;
(ii) if a special manager has been appointed, to him; and
(iii) subject to any contrary direction of the court, to every creditor of the bankrupt who is known to the official receiver or is identified in the bankrupt's statement of affairs.

The official receiver may, if he thinks fit, cause notice of the order to be given, by public advertisement in one or more newspapers, at least fourteen days before the date fixed for the hearing.

(d) Who may take part

The following persons may take part in the public examination and may question the bankrupt concerning his affairs, dealings and property and the causes of his failure:

- the official receiver;
- the official petitioner (in criminal proceedings);
- the trustee of the bankrupt's estate (where appointed);
- the special manager;
- creditors who have proved.

(e) Procedure at the hearing

Rule 6.175 governs the procedural matters:

"(1) The bankrupt shall at the hearing be examined on oath; and he shall answer all such questions as the court may put, or allow to be put to him.

(2) Any of the persons allowed ...... to question the bankrupt may, with the approval of the court (made known either at the hearing or in advance of it), appear by solicitor or counsel; or he may in writing authorise another person to question the bankrupt on his behalf.

(3) The bankrupt may at his own expense employ a solicitor with or without counsel, who may put to him such questions as the court may allow for the purpose of enabling him to explain or qualify any answers given by him, and may make representations on his behalf.

(4) There shall be made in writing such record of the examination as the court thinks proper. The record shall be read over either to or by the bankrupt, signed by him, and verified by affidavit at a venue fixed by the court {Form 6.58}.

(5) The written record may, in any proceedings (whether under the Act or otherwise) be used as evidence against the bankrupt of any statement made by him in the course of his public examination.

(6) If criminal proceedings have been instituted against the bankrupt, and the court is of opinion that the continuance of the hearing would be calculated to prejudice a fair trial of those proceedings, the hearing may be adjourned."

The court may adjourn the hearing to a fixed date or generally (Form 6.59). In the latter case, on the application of the official receiver or the bankrupt, the court may arrange a resumption of the examination and give directions in connection with it, by order appointing a new time (Form 6.60).

(f) Bankrupt unfit for examination

Rule 6.174 covers situations where the bankrupt is unable to proceed with the public examination:

"(1) Where the bankrupt is suffering from any mental disorder or physical affliction or disability rendering him unfit to undergo or attend for public examination, the court may, on application in that behalf, either stay the order for his public examination or direct that it shall be conducted in such manner and at such place as it thinks fit." (Form 6.57)

The application may be made by:

(i) a person who has been appointed by a court in the United Kingdom or elsewhere to manage the affairs of, or represent, the bankrupt;
(ii) a relative or friend of the bankrupt whom the court considers a proper person to make the application; or
(iii) the official receiver, when it may be made *ex parte* and may be supported by evidence in the form of a report by the official receiver.

In cases (i) and (ii), then:

(i) unless the bankrupt is a patient within the meaning of the Mental Health Act 1983, the application must be supported by an affidavit from a registered medical practitioner as to the bankrupt's medical and physical condition;
(ii) at least seven days' notice of the application must be given to the official receiver and to any trustee; and
(iii) before any order is made, the applicant must deposit with the official receiver such sum as the official receiver certifies to be necessary for the additional expenses of any examination that may be ordered. Any order subsequently made may include an order that the expenses of the examination be met, as to a specified proportion, out of this deposit rather than out of the estate.

7. Production of documents by Inland Revenue

For the purposes either of enquiry by the court or for the public examination of the bankrupt, the court may by s 369 order an Inland Revenue official to produce any return or account(s) submitted, whether before or after the commencement of the bankruptcy, by the bankrupt to any Inland Revenue official; or any assessment or determination made; or any correspondence between the bankrupt and any Inland Revenue official. The court must address the order to an Inland Revenue official whom the court is satisfied is dealing, or has dealt, with the affairs of the bankrupt. Where any document to which an order relates is not in the possession of the official, it is his duty to take all reasonable steps to secure possession of it and, if he fails to do so, to report the reasons for his failure to the court.

Rules 6.194 - 6.196 set out the procedure for applying for an order. The application must specify the documents the production of which is required, "with such particularity as will enable the order, if made, to be most easily complied with". It must also name the official to whom the order is to be addressed. The court fixes a venue for hearing and gives notice, with a copy of the application, to the Commissioners of Inland Revenue at least 28 days before the hearing. The notice requires the Commissioners, not later than seven days before the date fixed for the hearing, to inform the court whether they consent or object to the making of the proposed order.

If they consent, they inform the court of the name of the official to whom the order should be addressed, if it is someone other than the official named in the application. If they object, they must ensure an officer attends the hearing and, not less than seven days before it, they must deliver to the court a statement of the grounds of their objection. A copy of the statement must be sent to the applicant.

On hearing the application the court may make the order applied for, with any modification that may appear appropriate in the light of any representations made by the Commissioners. The order may be addressed to an Inland Revenue official other than the one named in the application. It specifies a time, not less than 28 days after service of the order, within which it must be complied with; and may include requirements as to the manner in which the documents are to be produced.

A sealed copy of the order must be served by the applicant on the official to whom it is addressed. If the official cannot comply because he does not have the relevant documents in his possession, and has been unable to obtain them, he must deliver to the court a written statement of his reasons for non-compliance. A copy of any such statement must be sent by the official to the applicant.

When, under such an order, original, rather than copy, documents are produced, any person who has them in his possession or custody is responsible to the court for their safe keeping and return as and when directed by the court.

Where the court has made an order under s 369(1) for the purposes of any examination or proceedings, the court may, at any time after the document to which the order relates is produced to it, authorise its disclosure (or of any part of its contents) to the official receiver, trustee or creditors by order (Form 6.70).

8. Reference to the Ombudsman

The Parliamentary Commissioner for Administration is engaged to investigate complaints referred to him by MPs from members of the public who claim to have sustained injustice in consequence of maladministration in connection with administrative action or inaction. Official receivers are therefore legitimately included in their administrative capacity rather than as a result of decisions flowing from their duty as a trustee. Enquiries may be made to the Office of the PCA, Church House, Great Smith Street, London SW1P 3BW.

Chapter 7

Appointment of the trustee and special manager

1. The trustee in bankruptcy

A trustee in relation to a bankruptcy and the bankrupt means the trustee of the bankrupt's estate (s 385). Nobody may be appointed as trustee of a bankrupt's estate unless he is, at the time of the appointment, qualified to act as an insolvency practitioner in relation to the bankrupt (see page 19 *et seq*). A person who is not an individual is not qualified to so act and a person who acts when he is not qualified to do so is liable to imprisonment or a fine, or both. References to trustees are without prejudice to provisions under which the official receiver is in certain circumstances to be trustee of the estate. The trustee must not tout for the work and must retain professional independence at all time (see "ethical statement", page 25).

(a) Power to make appointment

The trustee is appointed by the creditors, the court or the Secretary of State for Trade and Industry, and is a licensed insolvency practitioner. He normally reports to a committee of creditors and is personally responsible for any misapplication of the funds of the estate or any loss resulting from misfeasance or breach of fiduciary or other duty as trustee.

The appointment of any person as trustee takes effect only if that person accepts the appointment in accordance with the rules. Subject to this, the appointment of any person as trustee takes effect at the time specified in his certificate of appointment (Form 6.40).

(b) Joint trustees

Any power to appoint a person as trustee includes power to appoint two or more persons as joint trustees, but such an appointment must make provision in the certificate of appointment (Form 6.41) as to the circumstances in which the trustees must act together and the circumstances in which one or more of them may act on behalf of the others. The ethical guidance notes (page 25) apply to joint appointments.

2. Appointment of trustee by the creditors

A general meeting of creditors has the power under s 292(1)(a) to appoint a person as trustee, except where a certificate for the summary administration of the bankrupt's estate is in force.

(a) First meeting of creditors

Where a bankruptcy order has been made it is the duty of the official receiver under s 293 as soon as practicable within twelve weeks (four months according to Rule 6.79) beginning with the day on which the order was made, to decide whether to summon a general meeting of the creditors to appoint a trustee (see page 205).

If the official receiver decides to summon a meeting he advertises it and gives notice to the court, and to every creditor known to him or identified in the statement of affairs.

(b) Advertisement of appointment

Under Rule 6.124, where the trustee is appointed by a creditors' meeting, he must, forthwith after receiving his certificate of appointment, give notice of his appointment in such newspaper as he thinks most appropriate for ensuring that it comes to the notice of the bankrupt's creditors. The advertisement is an expense of the bankruptcy and the trustee is entitled to be reimbursed.

(c) Failure of meeting to appoint

Where a creditors' meeting is held but fails to appoint a trustee it is then the duty of the official receiver to decide whether or not to refer the need for an appointment to the Secretary of State. Should he decide not to refer the matter then he gives notice of his decision to the court and becomes the trustee under s 295(4).

(d) Decision not to hold a creditors' meeting

If the official receiver has decided not to summon a meeting, then, before the end of twelve weeks, he gives notice of his decision to the court and to every creditor of the bankrupt who is known to the official receiver or is identified in the bankrupt's statement of affairs under s 293(2). On giving this notice to the court he becomes trustee of the bankrupt's estate. This avoids useless expenditure and a waste of the creditors' time, presumably where it is known that they do not want to appoint a trustee.

(e) Power of creditors to call a meeting

Where the official receiver has not yet summoned, or has decided not to summon, a general meeting of the creditors and a certificate for the summary administration of the estate is not in force, any creditor may request the official receiver to summon such a meeting under s 294 for that purpose. If the request appears to the official receiver to be made with the concurrence of not less than one quarter in value of the bankrupt's creditors including the creditor making the request, it is his duty to summon the requested meeting. Accordingly he is required neither to reach a decision to hold a creditors' meeting, (s 293(1), *(a)* above) nor if he has reached a decision (*(d)* above), to serve any notice under s 293(2).

3. Appointment of trustee by the court

The court will be concerned to appoint a trustee:

(a) when the creditors fail to agree among themselves;

(b) where the court issues a certificate for the summary administration of a bankrupt's estate, the official receiver is from the date of issue of that certificate the trustee; the court may, however, appoint a person other than the official receiver to be trustee;

(c) under a debtor's petition where an insolvency practitioner's report has been submitted to the court (and no certificate for summary administration has been issued), the court may appoint the person who made the report under s 274. No meeting of creditors is necesary;

(d) at the time where there is a supervisor of a voluntary arrangement in which case it may on making the order appoint the supervisor of the arrangement the trustee under s 297(5); again no meeting of creditors is necesary.

The order of the court will not issue unless and until the person appointed has filed in court a statement that he is a duly qualified insolvency practitioner and that he consents to act. The court sends two copies of its order to the official receiver, one of which is sealed and is sent by the official receiver to the person appointed as trustee. The trustee's appointment is effective from the date of the order. (Rule 6.121)

An appeal from a decision of the High Court on the validity of an objection to the appointment of a trustee lies to the Court of Appeal; see *Re Lamb, ex parte Board of Trade* [1894] 2 QB 805. If on making the appointment there would be serious conflict between the trustee's interest as a creditor and his duty as trustee then the objection of the (then) Board of Trade, now the Department of Trade and Industry, was valid.

Where the trustee has been appointed by order of the court (Form 6.42, or 6.43 for two or more trustees), he must give notice to the bankrupt's creditors of his appointment, or, if the court so allows, advertise his appointment in accordance with the directions of the court. In the notice or advertisement he should state the following:

(a) whether he proposes to summon a general meeting of the bankrupt's creditors for the purpose of establishing a creditors' committee under s 301 (see page 218); and

(b) if he does not propose to summon such a meeting, set out the power of the creditors to require him to summon one (see page 210).

4. Appointment of trustee by the Secretary of State

A request to the Secretary of State to make an appointment of a trustee arises:

(a) by reference from the official receiver following a meeting of creditors which fails to agree under s 295; or

(b) following application by the official receiver when he is acting as trustee under s 296; or

(c) 28 days after a vacancy (including the need for a revival of trusteeship) first came to the official receiver's attention and he has not summoned and does not propose to summon a general meeting of creditors (s 300).

If he duly makes an appointment he sends two copies of the certificate to the official receiver who then transmits one copy to the person appointed and files the other copy in court. The certificate specifies the date from which the trustee's appointment is to be effective (Rule 6.122) and may be advertised (as above) if the court allows and in accordance with their directions.

The Secretary of State either makes an appointment or declines to make one. Where he declines to make an appointment, the official receiver continues to be trustee of the bankrupt's estate but without prejudice to his power to make a further reference.

5. Authentication of appointment

Where a trustee is appointed in any of the ways described in this chapter, a sealed copy of the order of appointment or, as the case may be, of the certificate of his appointment, may be adduced as proof in any proceedings that he is duly authorised to exercise the powers and perform the duties of the trustee.

He is entitled to receive remuneration for his services as fixed by the creditors' committee (see page 221). So far as costs and taxation are concerned, O 62 of the Rules of the Supreme Court applies to insolvency proceedings in the High Court and O 38 County Court Rules applies to such proceedings in the county court, with any necessary modifications in either case. Unless otherwise directed or authorised costs are allowed on the standard basis (see page 257).

6. Vacancy in the office of trustee

Where the appointment fails to take effect the official receiver is trustee until the vacancy is filled on giving notice to the court under s 293(2). He may summon a general meeting of the creditors for the purpose of filling the vacancy and shall do so if required by s 294 (creditors' requisition; see page 210).

If at the end of 28 days beginning with the day on which the vacancy first came to the official receiver's attention, he has not summoned, and is not proposing to summon, a general meeting of creditors for the purpose of filling the vacancy, he refers the need for an appointment to the Secretary of State who may either make an appointment or decline to make one (see page 87). If he does not, then the official receiver continues as trustee, but without prejudice to his power to make a further reference.

Reference to a vacancy includes the case where it is necessary to revive the trusteeship (ie after holding a final meeting under s 331 or the giving of a notice by the official receiver under s 299(2)) in relation to any property which is or may be comprised in a bankrupt's estate.

7. Replacement of official receiver as trustee

(a) Hand over of estate to trustee

Under Rule 6.125, where the bankrupt's estate vests in the trustee following a period in which the official receiver is the receiver and manager of the estate according to s 287, or the trustee is appointed in succession to the official receiver acting as trustee, the official receiver must forthwith do all that is required for putting the trustee into possession of the estate, as soon as his appointment takes effect (s 312(2)). On taking possession of the estate, the trustee discharges any balance due to the official receiver on account of:

(i) expenses properly incurred by him and payable under the Act or the Rules, and

(ii) any advances made by him in respect of the estate, together with interest on such advances at the rate specified in s 17 of the Judgments Act 1838 on the date of the bankruptcy order.

Alternatively, the trustee may, before taking office, give to the official receiver a written undertaking to discharge any such balance out of the first realisation of assets. The official receiver has a charge on the estate in respect of any such sums due to him. But, where the trustee has realised assets with a view to making those payments, the official receiver's charge does not extend to sums deductible by the trustee from the proceeds of realisation, as being expenses properly incurred therein.

The trustee from time to time must, out of the realisation of assets, discharge all guarantees properly given by the official receiver for the benefit of the estate, and pay all the official receiver's expenses.

The official receiver must give to the trustee all such information, relating to the affairs of the bankrupt and the course of the bankruptcy, as he (the official receiver) considers to be reasonably required for the effective discharge by the trustee of his duties in relation to the estate. The trustee must also be provided with any report of the official receiver to the creditors.

(b) Transitional arrangements

Where a person is adjudged bankrupt before the appointed day, or after that day but on a petition presented before, the official receiver may apply to the Secretary of

State for the appointment of a trustee in bankruptcy. On such application the Secretary of State may either make an appointment or decline to make one.

(c) Land registration

When the official receiver is replaced as trustee the insolvency pracititoner is registered as proprietor in his place on production of the evidence required by Rule 176(1) Land Registration Rules 1925.

8. The special manager

Immediately on the making of a bankruptcy order and pending the appointment of a trustee, the official receiver acts as a receiver and manager of the bankrupt's estate (see page 74), including his business, unless and until a special manager is appointed. He will therefore consider an appointment where pressed by the creditors and where it appears to the official receiver (or trustee if appointed) that the nature of the estate, property or business, or the interests of the creditors generally, require the appointment of another person to manage it.

The introduction of the special manager procedure depends upon the need to keep the business going, the level of business activity and the swiftness with which a general meeting of the creditors can be called to appoint a trustee in the bankruptcy and to obtain their views. For if the business has, for example, failed through overtrading rather than fraudulent pursuits this appointment gives an outside expert the opportunity of putting in hand a major reorganisation of it, getting in the book debts, and converting any partly finished product with a view to ultimately selling the business as a going concern.

(a) Application to the court

A special manager may be appointed by the court, following application by the official receiver or trustee under s 370, to a bankrupt's estate, or the business of an undischarged bankrupt, or to the property or business of a debtor in whose case the official receiver was appointed interim receiver (Form 6.54).

An application is supported by a report setting out the reasons for the application and includes the applicant's estimate of the value of the estate, property or business in respect of which the special manager is to be appointed (Rule 6.167). The grounds would, basically, be that unless the business receives the constant personal attention of an expert until such time as it can profitably be sold, there will be a considerable loss of assets to the estate.

(b) Appointment

The special manager is appointed by the court on application by the official receiver or trustee, to manage the business of an undischarged bankrupt, or the property or business of a debtor where the official recevier has been appointed interim receiver.

Any person may be appointed to be special manager, not necessarily or only an insolvency practitioner, and may be appointed either before or after the court makes a bankruptcy order. Where an interim receiver has been appointed then that person (ie the official receiver or insolvency practitioner) has the powers and duties of a manager; the power is purely discretionary and the court will not interfere with the official receiver's exercise of it: see *Re Frederick Whitaker* (1884) 50 LT 510.

Where an interim receiver has been appointed, the court may appoint any person to be the special manager of the property or business of a debtor with such powers as may be entrusted to him by the court; the court therefore retains a continuing role in the control of his functions so that effectively it has the same power as it would have in relation to any of the functions of either the official receiver, the interim receiver or trustee; security is required and accounts are to be prepared and appointment may be renewed by order of the court.

(c) The order making the appointment of special manager (Form 6.54)

The set form leaves open the particular needs of the appointment as to the special manager's responsibility over the debtor's property or bankrupt estate, the powers to be entrusted to him under s 370(4), the period of his appointment and his remuneration:

(i) Powers - the special manager has such powers as may be entrusted to him by the court, which by s 370(4) must include power to direct that any relevant provision of the Act that has effect in relation to the official receiver, interim receiver (see page 67) or trustee, shall have the like effect in relation to the special manager for the purposes of carrying out those functions. The powers should expressly enable him to carry on the business of ...... at ...... with authority to retain those employees he may deem necessary and to engage others with their terms of employment defined as necessary.

(ii) Remuneration - the amount of remuneration will be governed largely by the nature and extent of the business and to the level of duties required. It may take the form of a percentage or a fixed salary agreed at £*x*; if on a *quantum meruit* basis it would not be given according to a fixed scale, regard being had to the degree of facility or difficulty in carrying out the duties in each case. The percentage may be given on net profits if that appears to be a fairer scale of remuneration than on gross receipts. It may vary in amount according to the nature of the moneys to be collected: see *Buckmaster* v *Buckmaster* (1859) 28 LJ Ch 564. However, his remuneration may be fixed from time to time by the court, and is allowed in the order of ranking of the distribution as an expense under Rule 6.224(1)(j) (see page 233), for the rules are otherwise silent as to his reimbursement; it would seem that he is bound to submit the gross proceeds of the business to the Department of Trade and Industry before being paid whatever he is entitled: see *AB & Co No 2* [1900] 2 QB 429.

(iii) Responsibilities - the special manager's responsibilities include to pay over all moneys to the official receiver; to produce receipts and payments accounts; to pay

disbursements and salaries; to give receipts; and to account for all expenditure with supporting vouchers. Where a trustee is appointed, the special manager must produce accounts. The special manager must produce accounts, containing details of his receipts and payments, for approval by the trustee. The accounts must relate to three months, or lesser periods if there is less than three months between the last and the penultimate sets of accounts. When the accounts have been approved, the special manager's receipts and payments are added to those of the trustee.

(iv) Period - the appointment may be until the first meeting of creditors; for a period of *x* weeks until the giving of security or until such further time as the court may direct; until the appointment of an interim receiver or until a resolution of the creditors is passed requesting that the appointment be terminated.

(v) Security - The special manager is required to give such security under s 370(5)(a) as may be prescribed. Rule 6.168 requires that the appointment does not take effect until the person appointed has given (or, being allowed by the court to do so, undertaken to give) security to the person who applies for him to be appointed. Security need not be given for each separate bankruptcy, but it may be given specially for a particular bankruptcy, or generally for any bankruptcy in relation to which the special manager may be employed as such. The amount of the security must not be less than the value of the estate, property or business in respect of which he is appointed, as estimated by the applicant in his report under Rule 6.167(1).

When the special manager has given security to the person applying for his appointment, that person's certificate as to the adequacy of the security should be filed in court.

The cost of providing the security is paid in the first instance by the special manager; but -

(i) where a bankruptcy order is not made, he is entitled to be reimbursed out of the property of the debtor, and the court may make an order on the debtor accordingly, and
(ii) where a bankruptcy order is made, he is entitled to be reimbursed out of the estate in the prescribed order of priority. (Rule 6.168(5))

(vi) Indemnity - The appointment continues to be valid unless and until it is set aside by the court, and therefore gives validity to everything done - even though it may turn out to have been erroneous.

The fact that the special manager has been in possession of, and carrying on the business, does not entitle the alleged debtor, on the petition being dismissed, to treat him as a wrongdoer nor to deprive him of his right to protection as an officer of the court: see *Re A B & Co* [1900] 2 QB 429. Consequently he is entitled to be reimbursed out of the receipts of the business (see Rule 6.168(5)(a), above). Following a bankruptcy order the special manager is paid in priority (see Rule 6.224(1)(j), page 233).

(d) Termination of appointment as special manager

A special manager's appointment terminates if the bankruptcy petition is dismissed or if an interim receiver is discharged without a bankruptcy order having been made. If the official receiver or the trustee is of the opinion that the employment of a special manager is no longer necessary or profitable for the estate, he may apply to the court, which may terminate the appointment. The like application is to be made to the court if the creditors resolve to request that the appointment be terminated (Rule 6.171).

(e) Failure to give or to keep up security

If the special manager fails to give the required security within the time required in the order appointing him, or within any extension of time allowed, the official receiver or trustee, as the case may be, must report the failure to the court and the court may discharge the order appointing the special manager. Similarly, if the special manager fails to keep up his security, the court may remove him and make such order as it thinks fit as to costs. In either case, the court gives directions as to what steps should be taken to appoint a replacement special manager. (Rule 6.169).

(f) Liability of the official receiver when acting as special manager

Where the special manager happens to seize or dispose of any property which is not in fact comprised in the estate but has reasonable grounds for believing that he is entitled to seize or dispose of that property, whether in pursuance of an order of the court or otherwise, then he, under s 287(4), is not liable to any person in respect of any loss or damage resulting from the seizure or disposal except in so far as that loss or damage is caused by his negligence. He has a lien on the property or the proceeds of its sale for such of the expenses of the bankruptcy as were incurred in connection with the seizure or disposal.

(g) Formal defects

The acts of a person whilst acting as a special manager are valid notwithstanding any defect in the appointment, election or qualifications of the manager (s 377).

9. Acting without qualification

By s 389 a person who acts as an insolvency practitioner in bankruptcy at a time when he is not qualified to do so is liable to imprisonment, a fine or both. However, this does not apply to the official receiver or a special manager.

Chapter 8

The statement of affairs - creditors

1. Introduction

The bankrupt's statement of affairs contains particulars of his creditors, debtors and other liabilities and assets, together with such other information as may be prescribed, and is considered in this and the next chapter.

By s 283(1)(a) of the Act a bankrupt's estate comprises all property belonging to *or vested in* the bankrupt at the commencement of the bankruptcy. By virtue of s 283(4), property in the bankrupt's estate includes any power exercisable by the bankrupt over or in respect of property unless it cannot be so exercised for the benefit of the bankrupt and is excluded from the vesting order (see page 150), or excluded from "after-acquired" property (see page 161).

It is also important to understand at the outset that all claims by creditors are provable as debts against the bankrupt whether they are present or future, certain or contingent, ascertained or sounding only in damages, except for any fine imposed for an offence, and any obligation arising under an order made in family or domestic proceedings.

In any proceedings, whether or not under the Act, a statement of affairs may be used in evidence against any person making or concurring in making the statement (s 433).

2. Submission of the statement of affairs following a creditor's petition

Where a bankruptcy order has been made otherwise than on a debtor's petition, the official receiver gives the bankrupt Form 6.33 on which he is to prepare the statement of his affairs, together with Guidance Notes (Form B44.01, available from the Department of Trade and Industry). He is required to return the statement, completed and verified by affidavit, together with one copy, to the official receiver within 21 days of the commencement of bankruptcy. It is then filed in the court by the official receiver. If the bankrupt finds that he himself cannot prepare the statement then the official receiver has the authority to employ someone to assist him, at the expense of the estate.

(a) Affidavit

The statement of affairs is verified by affidavit and delivered to the official receiver, together with one copy. It may be sworn before an official receiver or a deputy official receiver, by an officer of the Department of Trade and Industry or by an officer of the court duly authorised in that behalf. The official receiver files one copy in court (Rule 6.60).

(b) Release or extension of time

The official receiver may release the bankrupt from his duty or extend the period of 21 days. If he refuses then the bankrupt has the right to apply to the court for a release or extension, which the court may grant if it thinks fit. If the court thinks no sufficient cause is shown for the application, it may dismiss it, but not unless the bankrupt has had an opportunity to attend court for an *ex parte* hearing of which he had at least seven days notice. If the application is not so dismissed, the court fixes a venue for it to be heard and gives notice to the bankrupt accordingly.

At least fourteen days before the hearing, the bankrupt must send to the official receiver a notice stating the venue, a copy of the application and any evidence which the bankrupt intends to adduce in support of it. The official receiver may appear and be heard on the application and whether or not he does so he may file a written report of any matter he considers should be brought to the court's attention. A copy of any such report must be sent to the bankrupt not later than five days before the hearing.

Sealed copies of any order made on the application are sent by the court to the bankrupt and to the official receiver.

On an application for a release from the duty to submit a statement of affairs or to extend the time therefor, the bankrupt's costs must be paid by him, and unless the court orders otherwise, no allowance towards them may be made out of the estate (Rule 6.62).

(c) Failure to submit statement

A bankrupt who without reasonable excuse fails to comply with the obligation imposed or submits a statement that does not comply with the requirements is guilty of a contempt of court and liable to be punished accordingly.

(d) Assistance in preparation

Rule 6.63 provides help for the bankrupt in the preparation of his statement and pursuant to Rule 6.64, to assistance in preparation of accounts:

"(2) At the request of the bankrupt, made on the grounds that he cannot himself prepare a proper statement, the official receiver may authorise an allowance payable out of the estate (in accordance with the prescribed order of priority [see Rule 6.224(1)(k), page 233]) towards expenses to be incurred by the bankrupt in employing some person or persons to assist him in preparing it.

(3) Any such request by the bankrupt shall be accompanied by an estimate of the expenses involved: and the official receiver shall only authorise the employment of a named person or a named firm, being in either case approved by him.

(4) An authorisation given by the official receiver under this Rule shall be subject to such conditions (if any) as he thinks fit to impose with respect to the manner in which any person or a named firm, being in either case approved by him.

(5) Nothing in this Rule relieves the bankrupt from any obligation with respect to the preparation, verification and submission of his statement of affairs, or to the provision of information to the official receiver or the trustee."

(e) Accounts

Accounts are governed by rules 6.64 and 6.65. Rule 6.64 requires the bankrupt, at the request of the official receiver, to furnish him with accounts relating to his affairs of such nature, as at such date and for such period as he may specify. The period specified may begin from a date up to three years preceding the date of the presentation of the bankruptcy petition, although the court may, on the official receiver's application, require accounts in respect of any earlier period. Assistance in preparing the statement of affairs (see above) is available.

Rule 6.65 provides that the accounts shall, if the official receiver so requires, be verified by affidavit, and (whether or not so verified) delivered to him within 21 days of the request under Rule 6.64(1), or such longer period as he may allow. Two copies of the accounts and (where required) the affidavit must be delivered by the bankrupt to the official receiver, who files one copy in court (with the affidavit, if any).

3. Submission of the statement of affairs with a debtor's petition

Where the debtor wishes to present his own petition to the court, it has to be accompanied by a statement of the debtor's affairs on Form 6.28, the majority of which is set out as straightforward questions. The form, with guidance notes (Form B44.24) is available from the court.

The rules contain provisions identical with those for creditors' petitions (although with differing rule numbers), except that the debtor has no choice as to the submission of a statement of his affairs and can get no help in preparing it, at least officially.

Two copies of the statement are filed in court verified by affidavit (Rule 6.42); if required he must submit accounts (Rule 6.69) and may have assistance for preparation of them (Rule 6.71). The rule as to further disclosure also applies (Rule

6.72), but not that, of course, related to limited disclosure, for the matter will already have had an initial airing before the court.

4. The forms considered

The statement is made out in either of two ways - on Form 6.33 following a bankruptcy order made on a creditor's petition, or on Form 6.28 to accompany the debtor's petition to the court. Each comprises a series of lists (or pages) for completion by the creditor or debtor respectively. Lists A and B (creditors) are the same for both forms, but there are differences between the two for list C (assets - see Chapter 9, page 107) with further disclosures being required from debtors for the immediate assistance of the court. Further, lists D to G relate to the debtor's petition only and are designed to elicit details of his personal affairs, while further aspects of his debts and means are dealt with at the end of this chapter. Following a creditor's petition these aspects of his affairs would, of course, be picked up on general inquiry and investigation by the official receiver after the bankruptcy order had been made (see page 75).

(a) Secured and unsecured debts

In the case of a creditor who has both secured (List A) and unsecured (List B) debts, the debts should be treated separately and listed accordingly, and likewise the secured part of a debt may be divorced.

(b) Discounts

All trade and other discounts receivable are deducted from the creditor's claim provided that they would have been available to the bankrupt, except for his bankruptcy, other than those discounts in respect of immediate, early or cash settlement.

(c) Interest

The creditor's claim may include interest on the debt for periods before the bankruptcy order, although not previously reserved or agreed. This need not concern the debtor's statement of affairs at this stage for the rate of interest will be determined at the date of the bankruptcy order by the trustee and as specified in s 7 of the Judgments Act 1838.

(d) Damages

Any damages payable by the bankrupt by virtue of an order of the court in respect of a contract to which he is a party are provable as a bankruptcy debt. The court may make an order discharging obligations under the contract on the application of any other party to it, on such terms as to payment by the applicant or the bankrupt of damages for non-performance or otherwise as appear to the court to be equitable.

(e) VAT default surcharges

A concession by HM Customs & Excise means that a default surcharge will not be levied in respect of pre- or post- bankruptcy default in the submission of VAT returns.

(f) Debt in foreign currency

The amount of a debt in foreign currency is converted into sterling at the official exchange rate prevailing on the date of the bankruptcy order. The official exchange rate is the middle market rate at the Bank of England as published for the date in question. The debtor serving his own petition is advised to use the rate prevailing on the date of service.

5. List A: secured creditors

The debtor here needs to consider both what the security is worth, the amount owed on that security and whether or not there is a lien on his property. The debtor is asked to list the names and addresses of all secured creditors and to provide an answer to two questions:

- what is the "amount owed to [each] creditor?"
- what of yours is claimed and what is it worth?

Note however, that the petitioning creditor may have given up his security under s 269.

(a) "Secured"

The original meaning of the word "secured" comes down through the mists of time and refers to a situation where a person holds a mortgage, charge or lien on the property of the debtor, or any part thereof, as a security for a debt due to him from the debtor.

The grantee or holder of the security holds, as against the grantor of the security, a right to some property or fund of the grantor for the satisfaction of some demand - after satisfaction of which the balance of the property or fund belongs to the grantor. For example the debentures of a company are securities, as are goods held by any person by way of pledge, pawn or other security (s 285(5)).

This does not affect the right of the secured creditor to split his security between the secured and the unsecured element and to treat them as separate debts, or to prove in the bankruptcy for the full amount of value before allowing for the value of his security. He has the right not to enforce the security or to give it up for the benefit generally of the creditors (see page 196) for the purposes of the bankruptcy petition .

To put it another way, the deduction of a security is never made in bankruptcy except when it is on the property of the bankrupt; see *Re Leigh & Armstrong ex parte Parr* (1811) 34 ER 242 LC. It must also be a security for the debt of the debtor, and for this purpose the property of a partnership is distinct from the property of an individual partner.

The effective date for all such transactions is the date of the bankruptcy order and not the date of the petition.

(b) Lien

A lien is the right to hold the property of another as security for the performance of an obligation. A possessory lien gives the creditor the right to retain possession of the debtor's property until the debt has been satisfied. A particular lien exists only as a security for the particular debt incurred, while a general lien is available as a security for all debts arising out of similar transactions between the parties.

However, a lien is unenforceable to the extent that its enforcement would deny possession of any books, papers or other records to the official receiver or the trustee of the bankrupt's estate; this does not extend to a lien on documents which give a title to property and are held as such. For example, a solicitor has a lien on his client's documents in order to secure his costs provided that title deeds are not included.

(c) Right of redemption

Where goods are held by any person by way of pledge, pawn or other security, the official receiver may give notice in writing that he wishes to inspect the goods held. That person is not entitled, without leave of the court, to realise his security unless he has given the trustee a reasonable opportunity of inspecting the goods and of exercising the bankrupt's right of redemption.

(d) The amount owed to [each] creditor

The amount owed should be clearly available and for the purposes of the list it will be sufficient to state the amount owing that day, for example, as per a building society pass book or latest statement from a finance house. There is seemingly no requirement to include in the amount owed any additional costs or extra interest payments which may have been agreed in the event of early redemption or failure to keep to the terms of a contract. In the event of any disagreement as to the amount owed, the debtor is reminded that he is required to swear (or affirm) the Statement of Affairs. Strangely, List B allows for alternative amounts.

(e) What of yours is claimed

The absence of gobbledegook in the new forms is obviously admirable, although the removal of the singular all-embracing word "consideration" and its replacement by this question is perhaps to be regretted, for it poses the problem of the clash of a "use" with occupation and that of "possession" with or without occupation. It is therefore submitted that to make the question logical "use" needs to be coupled with title in this instance. However a *Romalpa* type reservation of title would not be a bar to a full valuation for this class of property or goods (*Aluminium Industries Vaasen BV* v *Romalpa Aluminium Ltd* [1976] 1 WLR 676). This was discussed at some length in the Cork Report (Report of the Review Committee 1982 Cmnd 8558) and summarised at para 1618 in the following terms:

> "As the law now stands therefore it is possible to obtain protection against the insolvency of a purchaser of goods by means of a reservation of title clause where the goods or chattels sold remain in the possession of the purchaser intact in the form sold, or where proceeds of sale in respect of an onward sale of the goods in that form are separately identifiable in his possession. The protection may well extend beyond the price of the goods themselves to other sums due from the purchaser to the supplier, possibly to sums due on any account whatsoever. On the other hand, the preservation of a property interest in the goods supplied after they become mixed with other goods or consumed in some process of manufacture, is far more difficult and may be impossible. In such a case the appropriate course for the creditor to adopt is to obtain a charge in his favour, either fixed or floating, both requiring registration under [s 396 of the Companies Act 1985]."

However the Department of Trade and Industry requires that contracts where the creditor is claiming full title to goods in the possession of the bankrupt be shown on list B (below).

The Act states that the matter of priority of debts is without prejudice to any provision of this or any other Act under which the payment of any debt is to have a particular priority in the event of bankruptcy.

Therefore the creditor's proof may not necessarily agree at this stage with the debtor's statement of affairs. Likewise, where there is a surety guaranteeing the payment of money owed, a bank is nevertheless entitled to prove for the payment of all sums of money which were then due or owing to the bank from a customer and without any deduction for the amount received from the surety; see *Re Sass, ex parte National Provincial Bank* [1896] 2 QB 12.

It is worth noting that should the secured creditor, in proving for his debt, not mention his security, then that will not concern the debtor because it must then be surrendered for the benefit of the general body of creditors, so that it would consequently emerge as an additional asset and the *quid pro quo* would be complete.

(f) " .... and what is it worth?"

The worth or value of the security can only be subjective at this stage unless the official receiver is persuaded that a formal valuation is appropriate. This would normally only be so for a commercial operation. A residential valuation on a "with a view to sale" basis should easily be obtainable at no cost from an estate agent. However, in either case, if the property is mortgaged, the court may order a valuation to be prepared with a view to fixing a reserve or minimum price prior to a sale by auction or by private treaty.

However, normally for the smaller estate, the debtor will have to do the best he can. He will soon realise that he is in what is known as a forced sale situation and that he may not be given the benefit of time for normal market forces to operate to his advantage. If, as a mortgagor he defaults on the payment of interest, then the mortgagee may (subject to the rights of occupation set out in s 336 of the Act with regard to the matrimonial home) sell the property or seek to foreclose, which would have the effect of extinguishing the mortgagor's equity of redemption and with it any potential profit for the benefit of the creditors. Whether or not the mortgage repayments continue after the commencement of bankruptcy, they cannot affect the bankrupt's interest and should not therefore be taken into the consideration of the property's worth.

Valuations: The most usual valuations to be met in practice relate to homes, businesses and goods and chattels, which it now seems appropriate to consider briefly.

It should be borne in mind that from the resultant valuation should be deducted values in respect of any mortgage, the right of a spouse to occupy under the Act, any property adjustment order made in matrimonial proceedings (see page 173), and any beneficial interest accruing in equity (see page 138).

The role of the professional valuer: Where a qualified valuer is formally instructed to prepare asset valuations then in order to discharge the duty of care of an ordinary competent valuer he must have regard to many matters of principle and fact; for example, see *Corisand Invesment Ltd* v *Druce & Co* [1978] EGD 769 and *Singer & Friedlander Ltd* v *John D Wood & Co* (1977) 243 EG 213. The bankrupt, however, is not thereby relieved of his duty to provide the information.

Valuation of a residential property: The market value or market price of a house or flat may be considered to be the amount of money which can be obtained for that interest in the property as vacant for sale or to let, at the particular time, from persons able and willing to purchase it.

Thus any value applied is not intrinsic but results from carefully considered estimates of the worth to purchasers, ie those who are both able and willing. A professional valuer would therefore be able to assess the probable value to potential purchasers of the benefit of owning the property, and sale prices of similar property will be but one yardstick in the process of deciding.

Council tenants and others who have taken advanatage of the "right to buy" provisions of the Housing Acts may have a saleable interest capable of inclusion as an asset. For valuation purposes it will be necessary to take account of the mandatory discount repayment in respect of early realisation of their interest, thus leading to a reduced asset value, whether or not the trustee in his administration decides that the property should be sold (see page 136).

Valuation of a business: An estimate of the value of a commercial or industrial business will be needed on a going concern basis. This may be considered to be the aggregate value of the land, buildings and plant in the hands of a purchaser who acquired them as part of a business for which they are designed and used; it would not normally be valued on the footing of a forced sale; see *In Re Gomersall* (1875) LR 20 EG 291.

Such a purchaser will have regard to the amount of profit which he will make out of the business and if the property, the subject of the valuation, is not being put to its most profitable use, the going concern value will in all probability be lower than the market value. The essential difference is that as a going concern it is the business which is valued, not the property as it would be if it was stripped away from the business. At this stage it is presumably too late to start thinking of the potential for asset stripping and the indulgence of creditors will extend no further along such paths to any allegorical rainbow's end.

The method of valuation depends on the business; whether barrels of beer sold, room occupancy or trading profits; but in essence a ceiling figure needs first to be fixed for the cost of the buildings or value of the profit rent of the lease. This is judged on comparison or by applying a cost of rebuilding, because no owner of a business should pay more for his premises than either the amount he would have to pay for similar premises or the amount they would cost to construct after allowing for repairs and modernisation necessary to bring them up to current standards.

The resultant ceiling figure will have to be scaled down where the buildings are, say, of bad layout and design, and may also have to be further reduced where regard is to be had to a valuation of the concern on a profits basis (if any).

The amount of "profits" as shown will probably have no regard to reality and must be adjusted by reference to a rate of return enjoyed by such a business in normal market circumstances. The amount of profit will be expressed as a percentage of the working capital plus the ceiling figure. Where the resultant percentage is less than the fair percentage of profit normally associated with the type of business then the ceiling figure needs to be reduced to such as would give a more normal rate of profit.

If a leasehold value is required then the rental value of the business should first be ascertained and capitalised by the use of a year's purchase, ie discounting a reasonable investment yield for the property.

For example:

X owns a factory of 25,000 square feet on a site of 2 acres. The buildings are 10 years old and all the usual services are connected. It is suitable for a number of alternative uses.

Rental value:	£
25,000 sq. ft. @ £3.00 per sq. ft. per annum	75,000
Year's purchase to assume a yield of 10%	10
	750,000
Add value of plant and machinery	25,000
Total "ceiling figure"	£775,000

If a reasonable amount of profit from trading were to be £100,000 p a and the working capital was £50,000, then £100,000 must be expressed as a percentage of the ceiling figure of £775,000 together with the amount of working capital:

$$\frac{100{,}000 \times 100}{50{,}000 + 775{,}000} = 12\%$$

If 12% is equal to or greater than a fair annual rate of profit then the valuation can remain at its ceiling figure of £180,000; if it is less than the real rate, which is 20%, then the values must total:

$$\frac{100{,}000 \times 100}{20} = £500{,}000$$

and after deducting working capital of £50,000, leaves the value of the land and buildings, together with its plant and machinery, at £450,000 (£500,000 - £50,000). A forced sale may, depending on the circumstances, require this capital sum to be further reduced by between 20% and 40%:

	£
Value of land, buildings, plant, machinery and working capital	500,000
Deduct working capital	50,000
Value as going concern	450,000
Forced sale, say 20% of £450,000	90,000
Value in individual insolvency	£360,000

Other considerations that may be of assistance in the circumstances are the amount of real capital employed and the turnover of the failed business.

Valuation of goods and chattels: In considering the value of moveable items or white goods it is very easy to be lulled into a false sense of value which may only become apparent when the goods are sold by auction. It is of no real benefit to anyone to produce an inflated impression of value out of proportion to that which they are actually capable of realising.

(g) The secured creditor of a partnership

If a creditor of a partnership has a security on the separate property of one of the partners, he may retain his security and yet prove for his whole debt in the bankruptcy of the firm, because the security is not on property belonging to the firm; see *Re Turner, ex parte West Riding Bank* (1881) 30 WR 239. If one partner has deposited securities with a bank to secure the firm's overdraft, and has given his personal guarantee for the overdraft, the bank can prove on the guarantee in his bankruptcy without giving credit for the securities, for the securities were not deposited in respect of his debt; see *Re Dutton, Massey & Co, ex parte Manchester & District Banking Co Ltd* [1924] 2 Ch 199.

6. List B: unsecured creditors

The debtor is required to write in under List B, the names and addresses of all those persons and companies to whom a debt is owing.

(a) Amount the creditor says you owe him/her

It is a matter of convenience that, as the form states, the names of the unsecured creditors should be listed with the full details of their addresses and the amounts they say are due to them. Unusually for the law the female joins the male on this singular occasion - as a creditor; the debtor continues to remain a mere male.

The effect of any entry in List B is not an acknowledgement which takes a simple contract out of the Statute of Limitations, because no promise to pay the debt can be inferred from the insertion of the debt on the form; see *Everett* v *Roberton* (1858) 28 LJQB 23.

(b) Amount you think you owe

It sometimes happens that, included among the creditors' claims, are some that are disputed by the debtor, so the alternative columns to allow for areas of actual and potential dispute are useful, for the debtor is asked only to swear on the affidavit "to the best of my knowledge and belief". For the moment it will be sufficient to have the debtor put down the nearest estimate he can give and to mark it "estimated".

It will be up to the insolvency practitioner later to enquire further into the matter in detail with the proof of the debt (Form 6.37), verified as the case may be by a sworn affidavit (Form 6.39), from the creditor before him.

Where there is a *contra* account held against the creditor which is less than the amount of the claim against the estate, the amount of the creditor's claim, and the amount of the *contra* account, should be shown with the balance only inserted.

(c) Creditors for rents, rates etc recoverable by distress

The full amount of the debt outstanding will be declared after allowing for the distraint, if any, which has taken place.

Regardless of his right to distrain, the landlord has a right to prove for any bankruptcy debt in respect of rent. Where he has distrained upon the goods and effects then he may, basically, retain not more than six months rent, and must prove for the remainder. The right to distrain is lost if the landlord neglects to exercise the right whilst the goods remain on the demised premises; see *ex parte Descharmes* (1742) 1 Atk 103.

(d) Hire purchase or conditional sale agreements

Such agreements form part of the property of the bankrupt's estate. To take an old (1883) case by way of example, in *Re Davis & Co ex parte Rawlings* v *Dewars* (1888) 37 WR 141 the debtors deposited a hire purchase agreement in respect of furniture with a creditor by way of security. Before the second instalment became due the debtors were adjudicated bankrupt. It was held that the amount payable under the agreement was a debt growing due to the bankrupts in the course of their trade and the trustee was entitled to the benefit of it.

Goods bailed under a hire purchase or a consumer hire agreement, and goods agreed to be sold under a conditional sale agreement or subject to a regulated agreement, now remain the property of the bankrupt notwithstanding the service of a default notice under the Consumer Credit Act 1974, unless the trustee gives notice that he intends to avoid the agreement and disclaim it by virtue of s 315 (see page 180), or to seek an order under s 343 (extortionate credit transactions; see page 170).

The trustee is therefore entitled to the bankrupt's rights under a hire purchase agreement at the commencement of bankruptcy and may claim the interest in such goods notwithstanding any term in the agreement providing that it should terminate upon the hirer becoming insolvent. Thus the trustee can continue with it and obtain the property by completing the instalments.

(e) Preferential creditors

The creditors paid in priority over others are listed here; they include the Inland Revenue, HM Customs and Excise, social security, and employees, who are subject to payment limits; see page 234 *et seq.*

(f) Bankers and finance houses

Included in List B must be those amounts owed where no security is held; otherwise, see List A (above).

(g) Checklist of general items to be listed in List B

General items include electricity, gas, oil, general and water rates, telephone, insurances, leasing agreements, guarantees or indemnities given, goods or services supplied, creditors claiming that they own goods in the debtor's possession, and customers who have paid money for goods and services which have not been supplied by the debtor.

7. List C (assets)

See Chapter 9, page 107 *et seq.*

8. List D (debtor's petition)

Further questions here are designed to elicit details of the personal affairs of the debtor:

Dependants: this certainly includes those members of the family who rely on the bankrupt for support. "Family" is defined in the Act as the persons (if any) who are living with the bankrupt and who are *dependent* on him. It is submitted that this is not exhaustive and others not living with him or those not in the immediate family, and whether or not they are living with him, may be dependent on him, or may have a beneficial interest in occupation.

Thus by s 336 (security of occupation of the matrimonial home - see page 126) the interests of the spouse, former spouse and children are taken into account, and by s 310 (income payment orders - see page 272 *et seq*), the court is bound to consider the "reasonable domestic needs" of the bankrupt and his family.

The meaning of a relative is widened by s 435 (defining "associate") to include the individual's brother, sister, uncle, aunt, nephew, niece, lineal ancestor or lineal descendant, treating any relationship of the half blood as a relationship of the whole blood, and the step child or adopted child of any person as his child, and an illegitimate child as the legitimate child of his mother and reputed father. References to a husband or wife include a former husband or wife and a reputed husband or wife. The significance of this section is, of course, in respect of mutual dealings and transactions prior to adjudication etc, in which dependants could have played a part in the events leading up to the bankruptcy.

Distress: The right of a landlord to distrain on the goods and effects for rent due to him is only available for six months' rent accrued due before the commencement of the bankruptcy (he may prove for the remainder as a non-preferential creditor; see page 174). This means that the details, including the date of the distress, are important.

Where a bankruptcy order is subsequently made, any amount recovered by way of distress which is in excess of the amount which would have been recoverable after the commencement of the bankruptcy, or is in respect of rent for a period or part of a period after the distress was levied, is held for the bankrupt as part of his estate.

9. List E (debtor's petition)

Court judgments: detailed here are any processes in hand and value of any property involved. At any time when the petition is presented, the court may stay any action, execution or other legal process against the property or person of the debtor. The accuracy of the answers is important since they are admissible as evidence against any person making or concurring in making the statement.

Attachment of earnings: this refers to any order(s) under the Attachment of Earnings Act 1971, whereby the employer deducts specified sums from the debtor's earnings and pays them to the collecting officer of the county court to secure payment of a sum due under a judgment or order.

10. List F (debtor's petition)

Tried to come to an agreement: The significance of anything entered here may be judged from the fact that a voluntary arrangement cannot be entered into while a bankruptcy petition presented by the creditor is pending, whereas an arrangement can lead from a debtor's petition. If agreement has been sought by the debtor, it is submitted that the court is unlikely to make a bankruptcy order but to give the voluntary arrangement a second chance by making an interim order and appointing an insolvency practitioner to report on whether a meeting of the creditors should be summoned to consider the proposal for a voluntary arrangement with a view to his acting on it. If successful this would avoid the need for a bankruptcy order.

Voluntary arrangement under Part VIII: This is the Part dealing with any moratorium for insolvents so that effectively no bankruptcy petition may be presented or proceeded with and no other proceedings, execution or legal process, may be commenced or continued against the debtor or his property except with leave of the court on hearing the supervisor of the arrangement (see Chapter 1).

11. List G (debtor's petition)

Statement of means: Listed here are the items of regular monthly income, including salary or wages, maintenance receivable, interest under a settlement etc, offset against household and other expenditure (rent, rates, light, heat, insurances, maintenance, fees, travelling, laundry, clothing etc). This determines the surplus or deficit on revenue which could, if in surplus, give rise to "the minimum amount" for a voluntary arrangement (see page 40).

Chapter 9

The statement of affairs - assets

In the sense used in the statement of affairs for either the creditor's or the debtor's petitions, "assets" means that property, whether real or personal, which is available for the payment of the debts in the bankruptcy. It has little relationship to a balance sheet even if there is an up to date one to hand. This chapter deals with the assets list "C" in cases of both creditors' and debtors' petitions, together with the statement of affairs in individual voluntary arrangements, partnerships, and for deceased debtors.

1. Property available for inclusion in the statement

Subject to important exceptions and protective provisions the main assets available to the trustee which he may recover on behalf of the creditors are as follows:

(a) all that which belongs to or is vested in the bankrupt at the commencement of the bankruptcy (s 283(1));
(b) after-acquired property, ie property acquired by the bankrupt since the commencement of the bankruptcy and before his discharge (s 307);
(c) certain items of excess value where it appears to the trustee that the realisable value exceeds the cost of a reasonable replacement (s 308);
(d) goods held by way of pledge, pawn or other security (s 311);
(e) transactions at an undervalue within five years of the bankruptcy petition (s 341(1)(a));
(f) property transferred to an associate within two years of the bankruptcy petition (s 314(1)(b));
(g) property transferred to a creditor within six months of the bankruptcy petition which transfer has the effect of giving a preference (s 341(1)(c));
(h) property surrendered to the trustee under a credit transaction within three years of the commencement of the bankruptcy (s 343);
(i) certain proceeds resulting from the general assignment of existing or future book debts (s 344);
(j) proceeds of certain executions, eg in respect of rent (s 347(2));
(k) property (or its value) disposed of by the bankrupt with intent to defraud creditors (s 357).

2. List C (creditors' petition): assets

Listed are six items of personal property together with a space for "other property". It is under this latter item that real property discussed in Chapter 8 should be included if it has not already appeared as an item of secured property on List A.

(a) Cash at bank or building society

This includes the final balances of both current and deposit accounts after allowing for the accumulation of interest and deduction for charges. Cheques "in the pipeline" at the date of the bankruptcy order and on notice to the bank would not be cleared, but note that certain transactions have been deemed to be retrospective (see page 167). Likewise any moneys received by it would be paid direct to the official receiver or trustee.

Where the bankrupt has incurred a debt to a banker or other person by making a payment which is void after the commencement of bankruptcy, that debt is deemed to have been incurred before the commencement of bankruptcy unless the banker or person has notice of the bankruptcy before the debt was incurred, or it is not reasonably practicable for the amount of the payment to be recovered from the person to whom it was made.

A disposition of property in the period after the presentation of the petition and ending with the vesting of the bankrupt's estate in a trustee is void notwithstanding that it is not, or would not be, comprised in the bankrupt's estate, unless the property is held by the vendor on trust for another person.

It is to be noted that cash in hand and petty cash moneys are excluded from this item.

Trust property: Funds held by the bankrupt in a trust account for another do not form part of his estate in bankruptcy and are therefore not included in this item.

The trust beneficiary has the right to claim the trust property if it is still in the hands of the bankrupt, but he can also follow it if it has been converted, so long as it is in any way traceable. Thus if a trustee sells the trust property and pays the proceeds into his own account at the bank, the trust beneficiary has a first claim on the money standing to the trustee's credit not exceeding the lowest balance on the account since the payment in; see *Roscoe* v *Winder* [1915] 1 Ch 62. If, however, the trust property or its proceeds cannot be traced into any specific property in the hands of the trustee the trust beneficiary has no remedy except to prove in the bankruptcy.

Therefore, a professional who is handling clients' money in the course of his work prior to the commencement of his (the professional's) bankruptcy, and who is required to pay it into a separate clients' account, for example under the Estate Agents Act 1979, the Insurance Brokers (Registration) Act 1977 or the Solicitors Act 1974, continues to administer that money as a "bankrupt trustee" unless a replacement trustee has been appointed by the court under s 41 of the Trustee Act

1925; see *Re A Solicitor* [1951] 1 All ER 133.

Where the clients' money cannot be separately identified and has been merged in the general pool, then the money forms part of the bankruptcy estate and should be listed as such.

Finally, as a rule, solicitors and accountants who receive money from a debtor after the commencement of the bankruptcy must refund it to the trustee.

(b) Household furniture and belongings

Listing of these personal assets is clearly one of the most evocative parts of the whole bankruptcy process, putting great emotional strain on trustees and family alike. It emphasises the point that bankruptcy is not just about business but that the statement of affairs is designed to cover each and every part of the bankrupt's assets and liabilities including his private assets and liabilities which would have been ignored in the audited accounts of his business.

The trustee may greet with relief the news that some pieces of household furniture are claimed by a wife or third party. Nevetheless the trustee has his duty to perform and must satisfy himself as to the claim; for household goods bought by the wife but with the husband's money, even though the receipts are made out in the wife's name, belong to the husband. Where, however, it can be established that the goods were purchased by the wife out of savings from housekeeping money then the Matrimonial Proceedings and Property Act 1970, as amended by the Matrimonial and Family Proceedings Act 1984, will apply.

When there is no claim by a third party to the household furniture other than necessities, then the trustee has the alternative of selling it, usually at auction, but possibly by tender, or, more satisfactorily, by offering it to relatives or friends of the debtor at the valuation of a competent valuer with the approval of the creditors' committee.

As between the sexes there appears to be no distinction; s 329 of the Act does not differentiate between spouses or between the treatment of a husband's property on the bankruptcy of his wife and the treatment of a wife's property on the bankruptcy of her husband. Likewise, where a man and woman were living together unmarried in a case involving a business loan it was decided that it made no difference whether or not they were formally married; see *Re Meade* [1954] Ch 774, and this principle seems to carry through here.

Necessities: A bankrupt's estate does not include such clothing, bedding, furniture, household equipment and provisions as are necessary for satisfying the basic domestic needs of the bankrupt and his family. This is, interestingly, subject to a new test of reasonableness: where it appears to the trustee that the realisable value of the whole or any part of that property comprising the necessities, exceeds the cost of reasonable replacement(s), the trustee may claim that property for the bankrupt's estate. The trustee's warning shot comes in the form of a notice in writing to claim the property or part of it. On service it vests in the trustee as part of the bankrupt's estate. His title relates back to the commencement of the bankruptcy, except against a purchaser in good faith for value and without notice of the bankruptcy.

(c) Life policies

In return for the payment of premiums at regular intervals, life assurance policies provide payment of a fixed sum on the death of the insured, or, with endowment policies, on completion of a set term of years, and a value which can be realised by early surrender. A policy "with profits" entitles the holder to a share in the profits of the company during the term of the policy, which can amount to a considerable sum. Such policies have to be realised for the benefit of the estate and there are three basic ways of dealing with them:

- surrender;
- legal assignment;
- equitable assignment.

Surrender: This produces the amount payable on the yielding up of the policy, usually at a nominal value, unless it has the benefit of a with-profits policy which has been running a number of years.

For the immediate purpose of the statement of affairs, the surrender value as obtained from the life assurance company should be inserted until such time as the trustee agrees the method of disposal, otherwise it might be void against him, with the policy passing to him on the making of the bankruptcy order. It will be an unusual trustee taking a pique against the bankrupt who insists on surrendering on a cash basis without first making clear to the debtor and his immediate family the alternatives available.

Legal assignment: Assignment can be effected by private sale, for example by offering the policy to the debtor's family at surrender value plus a percentage addition, or by auction at one of the recognised specialist sales held at the London Auction Mart, 25 Little Trinity Lane, EC4.

A policy may have been issued on the debtor's life for the benefit of his wife under the Married Women's Property Act 1964. The trustee has no title to such and will be able to confirm this by reference to the policy itself or to the insurance comapny.

Equitable assignment: these are assignments permitted in equity and are not legal assignments of the policy whereby the trustee takes the rights of the bankrupt subject to equities. For example, where the bankrupt contracted to pay premiums without telling his trustee, the official receiver is entitled to the policy money: see *Tapster* v *Ward* (1909) 101 LT 503. The persons who have been paying the premiums have no legal right to reimbursement for there is no weight of contract with the trustee. If the trustee wishes he may claim the whole of the proceeds of the policy; except that as an officer of the court he is bound to act equitably, ie he must not do *violent* justice in operating the law. He should therefore realise the proceeds, refund those who have paid the premiums and treat the residue as part of the debtor's estate. Such a situation may only be resolved years after the event for in practice the life company will probably have noted the bankruptcy from the *London Gazette* and even if the debtor or his friends continue to pay the premiums, the company is bound to need the authority of the original trustee for the disposal of the proceeds when the policy eventually falls due for payment because it still forms part of his estate, and may then be worth a considerably larger sum.

(d) Money owed to you

Listed here are all those persons indebted to the estate in respect of accounts outstanding, whether or not bills have been submitted. This list constitutes an important part of the trustee's early collection.

Where any debtors are also creditors but for a lesser amount than their indebtedness, the gross amount due to the estate, as well as the amount of the *contra* account should both be shown in the list, the balance only being inserted in the £ column.

Bad and doubtful debts: It is not sufficient for the debtor merely to satisfy himself as to the correctness of the balances on his sales or fee ledgers; it is also his duty to ascertain from all the evidence at his fingertips whether any of the balances represent debts which are not recoverable or are of a doubtful nature. The trustee will, of course, enquire most closely into those debts which are not soon paid and doubtless will require full disclosure of the reasons for the debtor's billing and will ultimately consider employing an outside agency or a solicitor to collect the debts.

Mutual dealings: It is a very old established rule in bankruptcy that where there have been mutual dealings between the bankrupt and a creditor, only the balance is to be paid to the bankrupt estate by s 323(4). In other words, where there is mutual credit between the bankrupt and the person who sues him, which has ended in a debt, then the trustee is entitled to recover only the balance due from the bankrupt: see *MacFarlane* v *Norris* (1862) 6 LT 492 and further consideration at page 192.

Bills of exchange: A bill of exchange is defined as an unconditional order in writing, addressed by one person to another, signed by the person giving it, requiring the person to whom it is addressed to pay on demand, or at a fixed or determinable future time, a sum certain in money to, or to the order of, a specified person or to a bearer.

The essential feature is payment at a fixed future time. If bills are sent to a banker for collection at maturity, ie entered as "short", such of the bills as are still in the bank's possession at the commencement of the bankruptcy do not pass to the trustee unless there is an express or implied contract between the banker and the customer that they should be treated as immediate cash. If so they would be the banker's property and he would be merely a debtor to the customer for the amount of the bills, and not in any sense a trustee.

The debtor should estimate the amount the bill is expected to produce. If their acceptors do not meet the bills at maturity the trustee will have a right of recourse against the drawer or any prior indorser. As it will not be known at the date of the statement of affairs whether all those bills will be met, a note of the net estimate should be given to to allow for the contingent liability. The instrument or security itself, or a certified copy, will in any event be required to be produced.

Promissory notes: A promissory note is an unconditional promise in writing made by one person to another, signed by the maker of it engaging to pay, on demand or at a fixed or determinable future time, a sum certain in money, to, or to the order of, a specified person or to bearer. It may also contain a pledge of collateral security. Negotiable instruments are clearly of value to the estate provided that they are capable of being enforced by the holder in due time: see *Clayson* v *Bradley* [1987] 1 All ER 522. For a promissory note given by way of compromise of an action (for seduction) see *Ex parte Mumford* (1808) 15 Ves 289.

Cheques: Dishonoured, post-dated or unrepresented cheques may be thought of as securities by some, but they confer no rights whatsoever on third parties and therefore form no part of these assets.

(e) Stock in trade

This means goods in the bankrupt's trade or business. Furniture in a private home is not stock in trade, even though it belongs to a trader, but furniture in the hands of a landlord who takes in lodgers is within the meaning, notwithstanding that he might not provide them with board.

Most people are familiar with the publicity for "bankrupt stock" sales: But how is it to be valued and what price is to be put on partly finished goods? The answer in most cases is to amply mark down the stock to a figure acceptable in a finicky buyers' market and thereafter the trustee takes over responsibility for selling.

The position as to farming stock, whether livestock or growing crops, is more complex as it is bound up with statute law coupled with the requirements of good husbandry.

Farming stock: The basis of valuation of livestock should be cost or market value, whichever is the lower. A special treatment - the "herd basis" - is in certain circumstances accorded to dairy herds and ewe flocks which have been maintained for the purpose of producing a saleable article, namely milk, wool or lambs.

Milk quota: Schedule 1 to the Agricultural Holdings Act 1986 concerns the payment to certain agricultural tenants, on the determination of their tenancies, of compensation in respect of milk quota. Where, on the termination of the tenancy of any land, the tenant has a milk quota registered as his in relation to a holding consisting of or including the land, the tenant is entitled, on quitting the land, to obtain from his landlord a payment, and this will be for the benefit of his estate in the following circumstances:

(i) where the tenant had milk quota allocated to him in relation to land comprised in the holding (allocated quota), in respect of so much of the relevant quota as consists of allocated quota;

(ii) where the tenant had milk quota allocated to him or was in occupation of the land as a tenant on 2 April 1984 (whether or not under the tenancy which is terminating), in respect of so much of the relevant quota as consists of quota transferred to him by virtue of a transaction the cost of which was borne wholly or partly by him.

A tenant is not entitled to more than one payment under this provision in respect of the same land.

Relevant quota: this means the milk quota registered in relation to the holding where the holding consists only of the land subject to the tenancy, otherwise such part of that milk quota as falls to be apportioned to that land on the termination of the tenancy.

Transferred quota is milk quota transferred to the tenant by virtue of the transfer to him of the whole or part of a holding.

Growing crops: Growing crops are valued according to the "reasonable costs of seeds sown and cultivations, fallows and acts of husbandry performed". Guidance on cost is published by the Country Landowners Association.

(f) Motor vehicles

Detailed here will be the present value of motor bicycles and cars owned, together with model and registration numbers. For motor bicycles, the value will be written down to a value based on the year of manufacture; for cars the value will be based on the age and condition of the vehicle and whether or not the average mileage is higher or lower than 10,000 miles per annum. An allowance must be made for any exceptional wear and tear over day-to-day use and a sum added to take account of any important additions over the standard specification.

The forced sale value of such items as motor vehicles can best be judged by reference to the auction sale rooms and *Glass's Guide* to trade values. The original cost price of the vehicle will not therefore assist the trustee in arriving at a proper asset value.

3. List C (creditor's petition): other property

This form is blank so that the bankrupt can list as applicable to his case:

Agricultural land : When the tenancy of an an agricultural holding comes to an end, the outgoing tenant or his estate, is entitled to compensation under the Agricultural Holdings Act 1986 for many kinds of improvement and for other matters which the outgoing tenant has to leave behind, either by law or necessity, to benefit the next occupier. So far as insolvency is concerned the position as to compensation for the estate appears not to be materially different.

If at the date of the notice to quit it is stated that the tenant had become insolvent, then the notice will have immediate effect (rather than after twelve months) under Case F of that Act, and neither the trustee nor bankrupt can serve a counter-notice. A farm tenant is insolvent if he has been adjudged bankrupt or has made a composition or arrangement with his creditors.

Schedules 7 to 9 of that Act comprise a catalogue of items that an outgoer may claim for, and ss 64 - 69 establish the tenant's rights to claim compensation for improvements and tenant-right matters, while s 70 covers compensation in respect of the adoption of a special system of farming.

Building contractors - upon the contractor's bankruptcy the benefit and burden of the contract passes to the trustee subject to the effect of any valid forfeiture clause, unless the contract is personal. If it is, then it is up to the contractor to complete, and the moneys are payable to, or recoverable by, the contractor's trustee and listed as such.

The trustee has a right, by giving notice under s 315, to disclaim any unprofitable contract but if he decides to complete then he is liable; otherwise disclaimer brings the contract to an end and the employer can thereupon prove in the bankruptcy for his prospective loss.

In *Re Keen & Keen, ex parte Collins* [1902] 1 KB 555 materials brought on to site were considered to be the property of the employer and were not to be removed without the consent of the architect. The contractor became bankrupt and the employer gave the builders and the trustee notice to proceed with the work; upon non-compliance the employer claimed that the plant and material were forfeited. The trustee claimed the materials but it was held that the contractor was the true owner of the materials at the time of his bankruptcy, so that the title of the trustee was determined by the forfeiture and accordingly the employer was entitled to seize and retain the materials.

If, however, it is the employer who is made bankrupt then the position is governed by the ordinary law of bankruptcy and the contractor, being an unsecured creditor, would be entered on List B (see page 102).

Cash in hand includes moneys held in petty cash which will be available for the official receiver on the commencement of bankruptcy and for which a receipt will have been given by him. Loose change collected for or on behalf of charities or as an agent for, eg a lottery, will be specifically excluded as being in the nature of trust funds.

Chose in action: Property which consists of things in action, such as debentures, annuities, shares, a partner's share of interest in a partnership, is deemed to have been assigned to the trustee unless the petitioning creditor has agreed to give up his security for the benefit of all the creditors.

Where the deemed assignment is from the bankrupt himself, the trustee must perfect his title by giving notice in order to avoid the risk of being postponed to an assignee who takes without notice of the bankruptcy and protects his title by giving notice; see s 137(10) Law of Property Act 1925. The chance of receiving a legacy from a relative is not an interest that can pass as such; see *Johnson* v *Smiley* (1853) 1 WR 440.

Copyright: Here the asset comprises only the benefit of transactions entered into after 29 December 1986, and not before, unless before that date the debtor was not required to pay royalties and/or a share of the profits to the author of the work. Thus the bankrupt will, it appears, now receive the full benefit of the royalties or a share of the profits in respect of any copyright or interest in copyright comprised in the bankrupt's estate whether or not he previously paid over royalties and/or a share of the profits.

Where, however, the transaction was entered into before 29 December 1986, s 60 of the Act of 1914 will still apply by virtue of Sch 11(15) to the Act in relation to the trustee of that estate as it applies in relation to a trustee under the Act of 1914.

The position would then be that copyright vested in the bankrupt passes to his trustee, but if the bankrupt is liable to pay the author of the work royalties or a share of the profits, the trustee is then not entitled to sell or authorise the sale of any copies of the work except on the terms of paying to the author his royalties or share of the profits. Nor can he without the consent of the author or of the court, assign the copyright or grant a licence except on terms which secure to the author payments by way of royalty or share of profits at a rate not less than that which the bankrupt was liable to pay.

Extortionate credit transactions: Where the debtor has entered into a credit transaction not more than three years before the commencement of the bankruptcy the court may, on the application of the trustee, order that the transaction was extortionate, ie the terms of it were such as to require grossly exorbitant payments or otherwise grossly contravened ordinary principals of fair dealing. Any sums paid under it are surrendered to the trustee and comprised in the estate. The debtor will therefore need to include it on his statement; it will be up to the trustee to argue the merits of the case (see page 169).

Factoring - credit factoring is the continuing legal relationship between a financial institution, the factor, and a business concern, the client. The client sells goods or provides services to trade customers, and the factor purchases the client's book debts, either with or without recourse to the client, and in return controls the credit extended to customers and administers the sales ledger. The question of asset value depends on the facts.

The basic rule is that an assignment of debts to a factor prior to the commencement of bankruptcy, which is valid against the client, is generally void as against the client's trustee in bankruptcy unless the assignment has been registered under the Bills of Sale Act 1878. For the purpose of registration under that Act, an assignment of book debts is to be treated as if it were a bill of sale given otherwise than by way of security for the payment of a sum of money.

Thus an agreement for the sale of all future debts, coupled with the legal assignment as they arise is registrable, but a factoring "agreement to agree" which contemplates subsequent agreements for the sale of existing specified debts as they arise in the future is not covered by this section and could probably be avoided by the trustee.

Farms: In respect of owner-occupied farms sold, the Inland Revenue publishes average prices of farms sold with vacant possession, which may be used by way of comparison.

Improvements to business premises: Where notice has been served under Part I of the Landlord and Tenant Act 1927 by the tenant, to entitle him on quitting the premises to be paid compensation by his landlord for any improvements made by him as a tenant and which at the termination of the tenancy adds to the letting value of the holding, this is a recoverable asset. However, compensation is not available in respect of trade or other fixtures which the tenant is by law entitled to remove, and is subject to conditions and the landlord's right to object.

Compensation for any improvement cannot exceed the net additional value of the premises as a whole as a direct result of the improvement, or the reasonable cost of carrying out the improvement at the end of the tenancy, subject to a deduction of an amount equal to the cost (if any) of putting the works constituting the improvement into a reasonable state of repair, except so far as such cost is covered by the liability of the tenant under any covenant or agreement as to the repair of the premises.

Leasehold property and tenancies: A leasehold interest in property is one where the leaseholder holds under a lease for a term of years subject to the payment of an annual rent and to the observance of covenants in the lease.

If the rent which the leaseholder has agreed to pay is less than the true rental value of the premises then the difference represents the value on which his interest depends. However, in order to counteract the effect of inflation and increased costs, normally a rent review clause is incorporated in business leases which will restore the position as to full rental value; in that event the interest, or profit rental, would be for a limited term only. It may further be reduced by the cost of putting right any covenants, for example as to decoration and repair, which have not been observed by the tenant.

Tenancies, including regulated and shorthold tenancies with security of tenure in which the landlord is only able to regain possession on clearly defined grounds, will not normally give rise to an asset value in the property capable of inclusion in the statement as an asset, but see page 129.

Matrimonial home: If the matrimonial home is free from mortgage and is comprised in the estate, then if the trustee cannot sell it he may apply to the court for a charging order (see page 146). If the court imposes a charging order the amount of the charge is enforceable up to the value from time to time of the property secured save for the amount owing to unsecured creditors under s 313. Subject thereto the property ceases to be comprised in the estate. Inevitably, therefore, an indication of value is needed at this stage.

Not in actual possession: Property which is not actually in the possession of the bankrupt, eg goods at sea, may still be included in the bankrupt's estate if the bankrupt is in possession of the bill of lading or other document of title. He can determine his constructive possession by endorsement and delivery of the bill to a purchaser: see *C Simeons & Co* v *Durand's Trustee* [1928] 2 KB 66.

Plant and machinery: The right of a trustee to remove trade fixtures and machinery is somewhat more extensive than the right to remove domestic fixtures. For example, a market gardener or nurseryman may remove the greenhouses he has erected together with his shrubs and trees, but a tenant of domestic premises has no right to do so. On trade premises some engines, machinery and the like necessitate a degree of attachment which, in the case of domestic fixtures, might be sufficient of itself to preclude the right of removal. If the property is mortgaged then one can expect that the mortgage deed conveys to the mortgagee not only the fabric of the building but everything attached thereto.

Before any sale of plant and machinery can take place it is necessary to have a clear understanding with the mortgagee as to what items he claims to be his. A possible answer is to have an auctioneer who is acceptable to both parties to decide which items are "fixed" and those which are "loose". The question of fixed plant concerns the mortgagee, who may appear as a partly secured creditor, in which case his security would include it. If the mortgagee is able to realise sufficient from a sale of the building to clear his mortgage then the proceeds of the sale of the fixed plant would be available for the estate. In the meanwhile it is wise to have some agreement at this stage, so that a realistic estimate can be inserted in the statement of affairs.

Rebates for rates and taxes: Tax losses resulting in an overpayment of tax may give rise to a claim for relief to be officially sworn by the trustee, thus constituting an asset.

Likewise both general and water rates, which are non-preferential items, will be refundable upon the termination of rateable occupation of the premises. In the event of alteration of the use and occupation of premises following the bankruptcy, then, provided a proposal is made to the local valuation office of the Inland Revenue, before 31 March in the year of the alteration, a change in the basis of assessment may result in a rebate which may be backdated for up to twelve months.

Reversionary or other interests under Wills etc: A bankrupt's reversionary interest in an estate passes to his trustee. If he received a legacy prior to the bankruptcy this also passes, and therefore should be listed at its face value; likewise any future interest, provided that he has not been totally discharged from the bankruptcy.

In *Carr* v *Living* (1860) 54 ER 514, a case involving a life interest to be applied for maintenance etc of the bankrupt and her children, the trust was only for the benefit of those children requiring support. The widow having become insolvent, her estate was entitled to receive merely the surplus over and above what was necessary for the maintenance and support of her children.

By a marriage settlement, a wife's property was settled on her husband for life with a share if he survived the wife, with remainder to the wife. The husband became bankrupt and the wife was entitled to have her interest protected and to prove by a trustee, the interest on the amount recovered to accumulate for her benefit; see *Re Saunders, ex parte Saunders* (1834) S Deac & Ch 568; see also page 167 - transactions at an undervalue and page 173 - provisions against debt avoidance.

Secret formulae: the bankrupt is bound to disclose secret formulae used by him in his business, as an asset capable of being valued. In *Re Keene* [1922] 2 Ch 475 the bankrupt had refused to disclose them on the general ground that they existed only in his brain as the result of his skill and capacity, but it was held that they were part of the goodwill and assets of his business; he was bound to communicate them to his trustee.

Stocks and shares: where any part of the estate consists of stock or shares in a company, shares in a ship or any other property transferable in the books of a company, office or person, the trustee may exercise the right to transfer the property to the same extent as the bankrupt might have exercised it if he had not become bankrupt. The trustee is therefore entitled to be registered as owner, even though the bankrupt may be indebted to the company in which he holds shares. The value will be based on the estimated selling price published daily in the City pages of the press, or that which is available from the company's managers. This appears to apply to any form of shareholding including shares quoted on the Stock Exchange, the Unlisted Securities Market and shares held in private companies.

Tools of trade etc: the significance here is that although tools of the trade are excluded from the bankrupt's estate, the trustee may nevertheless claim part or all of them for the estate where it appears to him that the realisable value of the whole or any part of that property exceeds the cost of a reasonable replacement. In that event, the trustee is required to purchase a reasonable replacement, a duty in priority over his obligation to distribute the estate. Thus there is a need to assess the value as a basis for negotiation (see page 150).

Trade fixtures and fittings: If it appears that these were annexed for the purpose of the tenant's trade, it may be presumed that the tenant intended to remove his fixtures on quitting and that he had no intention of making his fixtures a permanent part of the premises; see *Fisher* v *Dixon* (1845) 12 Cl&F 312. If so there is a positive asset value, except that loss on forced sale can be upwards of 50% on equivalent retail price. On the other hand, the tenant may so annex a fixture in connection with his trade as to show a contrary intention, ie where its removal would necessitate its destruction and thereby preclude any value being applied to that asset.

By way of a footnote it may be found that landlords will seek to lay claim to fixtures and fittings. The landlord who claims that such fixtures and fittings are his property should be asked to establish his title by proving their purchase and fitting. If they have been erected by the tenant then, of course, the answer is clear; to counter a threatened claim for damage caused in removal it may be pointed out that any such damage has already been caused by erection and will constitute a claim against the bankrupt's estate to rank only for dividend.

Trade marks: A trade mark will usually have value and is therefore capable of being classed as an asset and subsequently sold by the trustee. The assignment of the business and the trade mark need not be contemporaneous; see *Hammond & Co* v *Malcolm, Brunker & Co & Collyns* (1892) 8 TLR 324.

4. List C (debtor's petition): assets

The questions here are set out in easy yes/no answer form with an explanation, and generally cover all matters referred to above so that the court can have a reasonable overview of the situation before granting the petition requested.

5. The statement of affairs in individual voluntary arrangements

Where a debtor makes a proposal to his creditors for a voluntary arrangement, ie a composition in satisfaction of his debts or a scheme of arrangement of his affairs, with a view to an application for an interim order, a statement of affairs is required to accompany his proposal.

This statement is not on a set form but comprises particulars made up to a date not earlier than two weeks before the date of the notice to the nominee (unless the nominee allows an extension of that period), and for which guidance may be obtained under the various headings above.

(a) Particulars required

The particulars required are set out in Rule 5.8(3):

> "(a) a list of his assets, divided into such categories as are appropriate for easy identification, with estimated values assigned to each category;
> (b) in the case of any property on which a claim against the debtor is wholly or partly secured, particulars of the claim and its amount, and of how and when the security was created;
> (c) the names and addresses of the debtor's preferential creditors ..... with the amounts of their respective claims;
> (d) the names and addresses of the debtor's unsecured creditors, with the amounts of their respective claims;
> (e) particulars of any debts owed by or to the debtor to or by persons who are associates of his;
> (f) such other particulars (if any) as the nominee may in writing require to be furnished for the purposes of making his report to the court on the debtor's proposal."

The statement is then certified by the debtor as correct, to the best of his knowledge and belief.

(b) Following a debtor's or creditor's petition

Where the debtor has already delivered a statement of affairs on either Form 6.28 or 6.33 following a petition, then he need not deliver a further statement unless he is required to do so by the nominee with a view to supplementing or amplifying the former statement.

6. Statement of affairs for insolvent partnerships

Where a bankruptcy order has been made the bankrupt submits a statement of his affairs which contains particulars of the bankrupt's creditors, debts, other liabilities and assets to the official receiver within 21 days of the bankruptcy, specifying:

(a) the individual member's interest in the assets of the insolvent partnership; and

(b) those debts and liabilities which are attributable to the separate and joint estates respectively.

No different forms for bankrupt partners are prescribed; for those partnership wound up as unregistered companies by the court, Form 4.17 (not reproduced in this volume) should be used.

7. Statement of affairs in the administration of insolvent estates of deceased persons

In this case the personal representative submits a statement of the deceased debtor's affairs, together with an affidavit containing particulars of the assets and liabilities of the estate as at the date of the order, together with other particulars of his affairs as required by Form 7 in the administration order (see Appendix 6). Guidance notes (Form B44.25) are also available from the Department of Trade and Industry.

It is similar to a statement following a debtor's petition and details further items, in particular the assets discussed in this chapter, and may be compared as shown in the table on page 121. For an explanation of the terms used in List B, see the relevant parts of the text. There are no equivalent lists for D to G of the debtor's statement.

Table of comparison between debtor's (Form 6.28) and creditor's (Form 6.33) statements of affairs

Form 7	*Form 6.28*	*Form 6.33*	*Detail*
A	A	A	Creditors claiming property of the deceased
B			Hire-purchase/conditional sale/leasing agreements and claiming title to goods
C	B	B	Unsecured creditors
D	C(1-3)	C	Assets, viz bank, building society, savings, life policies etc
E	C(1-3)		Debts due to the estate
F	C(1-3)	C	Cash, stock-in-trade, growing crops, household furniture, stocks and shares, motor vehicles etc
G			Funeral, testamentary and administrative expenses
H			Receipts and payments account since death.

Chapter 10

The matrimonial home

1. Introduction

One of the more distressing aspects of bankruptcy is that there may be insufficient realisable assets to pay the creditors other than by the sale of the family home. The Act therefore contains special provisions to ameliorate the effect of bankruptcy on the rights of occupation of the married woman in this all too frequent situation, and by overriding s 2(7) Matrimonial Homes Act 1983 ("MHA"), it enshrines the protection she is given by law as a beneficiary of equitable ownership in the matrimonial home.

It also gives effect to the moratorium (which the courts have tended to hand down on actions for possession of the property by the trustee) by introducing a twelve month stay of possession for the bankrupt owner-occupier. This is designed to give the family time either to move out of the home, or to arrange finance for a buy-out with the help of family or friends. Likewise it gives the courts time to assess the needs and conduct of the family together with any other circumstances, before the sins of the parent have to be visited on the children; for the duty of the court is to be just before it is generous.

The rights of the spouse in s 336 of the new Act sit comfortably with Lord Wilberforce's *dictum* in *Williams & Glyn's Bank Ltd* v *Boland and Another* [1981] AC 487 (HL) that where there is a sole trustee for sale, actual occupation acquires the status of an overriding interest. This view was approved in *City of London Building Society* v *Flegg* [1987] 2 WLR 1266 (HL). Neither the Act, nor the courts before it, have cast aside as irrelevant the undoubted fact that, if the two wives in the (joint) appeal in *Boland* had not succeeded against the bank, the protection afforded to them could be considerably weakened and even destroyed by an unscrupulous husband. In the *Boland* case, which was not specifically on insolvency, the reverse is true; the law was strengthened and now provides a launching pad for consideration of all rights flowing from the bankruptcy of the owner or co-owner of the matrimonial home and the normally innocent family.

As Lord Denning has pointed out in *Bull* v *Bull* [1955] 1 QB 234 (referred to by Lord Wilberforce), to describe the interest of spouses in a house jointly bought to be lived in as a matrimonial home, as merely an interest in proceeds of sale, or rents and profits until sale, was just a little unreal. For similar reasons one might concede that it was unreal for it to be vested in the trustee at all and that the matrimonial home should stay with the family at least in summary cases and/or in those cases where fraud is absent, and so not become part of the bankrupt's estate.

This chapter concentrates on co-ownership and occupation, considering initially the rights of ownership and occupation of the family (defined in s 385 as the persons (if any) who are living with the bankrupt and are dependent on him) and the bankrupt. This is followed by rights of other interested parties, for example the co-habitee who is other than spouse by marriage; and the safety of the divorced spouse's investment in the matrimonial home. And while the spouse's interest in the home could, by *Boland*, overrule a bank's claim (but that is unlikely in cases of new lending now that lenders are aware), in what circumstances can a spouse now step into the trustee's shoes. The home which is tenanted is also briefly considered, as is the tenant who has exercised his right to buy.

The general answers to such questions are in ss 336 and 337. It is first necessary for the trustee to decide by what legal rights of occupation the bankrupt and/or his spouse occupy the home, or what security of tenure they enjoy, and whether or not the right of the trustee supervenes. In considering these rights, it is necessary to look at family and property law outside insolvency, and for the trustee to establish whether or not a conveyance or settlement by the debtor in favour of his spouse or family prior to the bankruptcy is a voidable settlement (as to which, see Chapter 12).

2. Rights of co-ownership

The trustee can take no better title than that which is held by the bankrupt; otherwise the interests of the parties, which are unaffected by the Act, may be briefly stated as follows:

(a) Trust for sale

A trust for sale of land means an immediate binding trust for sale, whether or not exercisable at the request or with the consent of any person, and with or without power to postpone the sale enabling the land to be permanently retained. By s 34 Law of Property Act 1925 ("LPA"), whenever land is owned, whether freehold or leasehold, by more than one legal owner it is subject to a trust for sale, and is held subject to statutory trusts. Therefore, if the trustees refuse to sell, then the trustee in the bankruptcy may apply to the court, either for a vesting order or for an order directing the trustees for sale to give effect to the trust for sale.

A trust for sale may arise as follows:

(i) As joint tenants in a trust for sale: Here the respective shares in the property are given full effect by s 36(1) LPA: "Where a legal estate ...... is beneficially limited to or held in trust for any persons as joint tenants, the same shall be held on

trust for sale *in like manner* as if the persons beneficially entitled were tenants in common, but not so as to sever their joint tenancy in equity". "In like manner" simply refers back to ss 34(2) and 35 LPA which provide in effect that where the legal estate in land is expressed to be conveyed to *sui juris* persons as tenants in common, the conveyance operates as if the legal estate had been conveyed to them as joint tenants on trust for sale and to hold the net proceeds of sale on such trusts as may be requisite for giving effect to the rights of the person interested in the land: *Goodman* v *Gallant* [1986] 1 All ER 311. In *City of London Building Society* v *Flegg* [1987] 2 WLR 1266, it was confirmed that a sale by two trustees for sale puts to an end the interests of beneficiaries under the trust for sale who were in occupation of the property.

(ii) Express declaration of trust: By s 53(1)(b) LPA an express trust must be manifested and proved by some writing and signed, or created by an agreement of which equity will grant specific performance, although formal words are not required. Where the relevant conveyance contains an express declaration of trust which comprehensively declares the beneficial interests in the property or its proceeds of sale, there is no room for the application of the doctrine of resulting, implied or constructive trusts (s 53(2) LPA) unless and until the conveyance is set aside or rectified. Until that event the declaration contained in the document speaks for itself: *Goodman* v *Gallant* (above) and with it any possible discretionary jurisdiction relating to the assessment or valuation of the parties' beneficial shares which might otherwise exist; see *Turton* v *Turton* [1987] 2 All ER @ 649.

(iii) Resulting trust: Where property is conveyed on a purchase into the name of someone other than the purchaser, there is a resulting trust in favour of the person who advances the purchase money except where it would defeat the policy of the law or where there is a presumption of advancement. The trustee may be able to defeat a resulting trust as a preference by way of voidable settlement (see page 171) and where there is no occupation the property vests in him; where the spouse is in occupation then the rights of occupation under the MHA apply.

(iv) Postponed trust for sale: By s 25 LPA the trustees for sale have unlimited power to postpone the sale enabling the property to be permanently retained but subject to the effect of bankruptcy; there are three elements to this:

(i) where a person and his spouse or former spouse are trustees for sale of a dwelling-house and that person is adjudged bankrupt, and the trustees refuse to sell, any application by the trustee in bankruptcy for an order under s 30 LPA (see page 125) is made to the court having jurisdiction in relation to the bankruptcy by virtue of s 336(3). The court must then consider all the circumstances;

(ii) where the spouse has rights of occupation, they are a charge on the estate or interest of the other spouse under s 2 MHA by virtue of s 336(2) and the trustee and those deriving title from him are bound by the charge;

(iii) by virtue of s 337(1), the bankrupt has rights of occupation against the trustee of his estate:

- where he is entitled to occupy by virtue of a beneficial estate or interest; and

- where any person under the age of eighteen with whom the bankrupt had at some time occupied the dwelling-house, had their home with the bankrupt at the time when the bankruptcy petition was presented and at the commencement of the bankruptcy.

(b) The beneficiaries under the trust

Where a legal estate is held in trust, the trustees for sale will generally be the beneficiaries, except where part of the purchase price has been contributed by someone who is not otherwise a party to the purchase and does not therefore have a legal interest in land (*Irani Finance Ltd* v *Singh* [1971] Ch 59), but obtains an equitable interest in the property. This was confirmed in *City of London Building Society* v *Flegg* (above). This may, of course, initially prove to be as unobvious to the trustee in a bankruptcy as was Mrs Boland's interest to the bank, and may transpire to be a joint tenancy or tenancy in common:

(i) Joint tenants: Here each joint tenant has the same estate or interest in the land and is entitled to possession of the whole of the land. By s 36 LPA, where a legal estate (not being settled land) is beneficially limited to or held in trust for any persons as joint tenants, it is held on trust for sale in favour of a purchaser of the legal estate.

(ii) Tenants in common: Where two or more persons are entitled to land in such a manner that they have an undivided possession without exclusivity, each is entitled to occupy the whole in common with the others. They have divided shares which may be of different size. By s 1(6) and s 34 LPA no undivided share in land is capable of being created other than as an equitable interest under a settlement or a joint tenancy. For the purpose of insolvency there is no practical difference other than in calculating the value of the respective shares of the proceeds following a sale of the property (see page 138).

(c) Orders under s 30 LPA

Section 30 applies to an express or implied trust for sale, with or without power to postpone the sale. If the trustees for sale refuse to sell, any person interested, including the trustee in bankruptcy, may apply to the court for an order under s 30 directing the trustees for sale to give effect to the proposed transaction. The court will have regard to the following:

(i) the interests of the bankrupt's creditors;
(ii) the conduct of the spouse or former spouse so far as contributing to the bankruptcy;
(iii) the needs and financial resources of the spouse or former spouse;
(iv) the needs of any children;
(v) all the circumstances of the case (other than the needs of the bankrupt).

The court makes such order as it thinks just and reasonable. It may grant a vesting or other order for giving effect to the proposed transaction, or an order directing the trustees for sale to give effect thereto.

In *Re Soloman* [1967] 1 Ch 573 the issue was between the wife and trustee in bankruptcy when the court ordered a sale under s 30; the principle (on the limited grounds then available to the court), laid down in *Re Buchanan-Wolleston's Conveyance* [1939] 2 All ER 301, was that the court has a complete discretion to do what is right and proper.

(d) Co-habitee

While status establishes the spouse's equitable interest, no such rights attach to the unmarried co-habitee. Therefore where there is no express declaration of trust to decide the matter the home has to be sold under s 30 LPA 1925. The co-habitee may wish to establish a claim to a beneficial interest in the property. Where one of the partners has earlier left the property then the beneficial interest does not cease, but endures until the property is eventually sold; see *Turton* v *Turton* (1987) (see page 139).

Of the "common law wife" Lord Denning has said: "No such woman was known to the common law, but it means a woman who is living with a man in the same household as if she were his wife. She is to be distinguished from a "mistress" where the relationship may be casual, impermanent and secret": *Davis* v *Johnson* [1978] 2 WLR @ 187.

3. Security of occupation in the matrimonial home

(a) Generally

The matrimonial home is defined as the place where a husband and wife have lived together and have rights of occupation under s 1 MHA 1983; thus the dwelling-house which has never been the matrimonial home does not give rise to rights of occupation; the co-habitee who is unmarried has no such status and cannot claim any occupational rights to the home as such. The "dwelling-house" includes any building or yard or part of a building which is occupied as a dwelling and any yard, garden, garage or outhouse belonging to the dwelling-house and occupied with it (s 385). The spouse is given protection from eviction or exclusion by the Act of 1983, but the divorcee may have rights through a property adjustment order under ss 24 and 24A Matrimonial Causes Act 1973 (ie without rights of occupation but with rights ensuing on the sale of the property by s 7 Matrimonial Homes and Property Act 1981).

(b) Statutory security

Under s 1(1) MHA 1983, if in occupation, the spouse has a right not to be evicted or excluded; if not in occupation the spouse has a right to enter and occupy. So long as one spouse has rights of occupation either may apply to the court for an order:

(i) declaring, enforcing, restricting, or terminating those rights; or
(ii) prohibiting or suspending the exercise of the rights to occupy.

Occupation by one spouse is deemed to be that of the other spouse for, *inter alia*, security of occupation following bankruptcy by the first spouse, or for preserving a statutory tenancy (see page 129).

For a unique summary of the development of the "beneficial interest" given by Lord Denning during the committee stage of the Insolvency Bill in the House of Lords, see *Hansard* 7 February 1985, Cols 1264/5.

(c) Security as a charge on the estate

Where one spouse is entitled to occupy by virtue of a beneficial estate or interest, then the other spouse's rights of occupation are a charge on that estate or interest having the like priority as if they were an equitable interest created at whichever is the later of the dates when the spouse acquired the estate or interest, or marriage. The right is capable of registration under s 2 Land Charges Act 1972.

By s 336(2) of the Act and Sch 10 of the 1985 Act repealing s 2(7) MHA, the charge now continues to subsist notwithstanding the bankruptcy of the other spouse, and subject to the provisions of that Act binds the trustee and persons deriving title under the trustee.

An application under s 336(2) of the Act of 1986 may be made to the bankruptcy court for an order under s 1 of the Act of 1983. The court will make such order as it thinks just and reasonable having regard to the five factors listed (i) to (v) on page 125 above.

Where such an application by the bankrupt's spouse is delayed until after the end of one year beginning with the first vesting of the estate in a trustee, the court is required to assume, unless the circumstances of the case are exceptional, that the interests of the bankrupt's creditors outweigh all other considerations. Here, therefore, the situation will be very much as it was before the new Act.

The trustee may consider alternative action against the spouse under the MHA which, by s 1(3), enables the court to make any order it thinks just and reasonable as a contribution for the spouse's right of occupation in the home. This may take the form of periodic payments together with obligations as to repairs, maintenance and other liabilities.

(d) Implied licence to occupy

A spouse who has an equitable interest in a dwelling-house or in the proceeds of sale (not being a spouse in whom is vested a legal estate in fee simple or a term of years absolute), is to be treated for the purpose only of determining rights of occupation, as not being entitled to occupy the dwelling-house by virtue of that interest (s 1(11) MHA).

An "implied licence" has been described as "the irreducible minimum right which the court would enforce by virtue of its inherent jurisdiction and where the interests of children were concerned"; see *S* v *S* (1980) 124 SJ 219.

However there would be no such licence of occupation where the house has never been the matrimonial home of the spouse in question; the MHA would not then apply (s 1(10)); see *Hall* v *King* [1987] TLR 24 June 1987 where a husband took a tenancy of a house for his wife (with whom he was no longer living) and the house had never been their joint home. She acquired no security of tenure under the Rent Act 1977 because the house had never been a matrimonial home and she had not occupied it on behalf of her husband.

(e) Security for the bankrupt

Whether or not the bankrupt's spouse (if any) has rights of occupation under the Act of 1983, the bankrupt has security under s 337(2) as against the trustee:

if in occupation - a right not to be evicted or excluded from the dwelling-house or any part of it except with the leave of the court;

if not in occupation - a right, with the leave of the court, to enter into and occupy the dwelling-house.

The bankrupt's rights are a charge, having the like priority as an equitable interest created immediately before the commencement of the bankruptcy, on so much of his estate or interest in the dwelling-house as vests in the trustee. Any charge on the estate or interest of the trustee is to be taken as a charge under the MHA on the estate or interest of a spouse.

Application may be made under s 337(2)(a) or otherwise to the bankruptcy court for leave, for an order under s 1 MHA. The court makes such order under s l of the Act of 1983 as it thinks just and reasonable having regard to:

(i) the interests of the creditors;
(ii) the bankrupt's financial resources;
(iii) the needs of the children; and
(iv) all the circumstances of the case other than the needs of the bankrupt.

Where such application by the bankrupt is not made until after the end of one year beginning with the first vesting of the estate in a trustee, the court is required to assume, unless the circumstances of the case are exceptional, that the interests of the bankrupt's creditors outweigh all other considerations.

If the bankrupt has the whole beneficial interest then the trust has ended and all legal and equitable interests will indubitably vest in his trustee.

(f) The home of the mistress

It has been held that so far as matrimonial rights are concerned, a man may have just as much right to continue living in the home of his mistress, even when his wife is still living and they are not divorced, where he has not necessarily set himself up as married to his mistress, but they live together each continuing to use their separate names.

In *Watson* v *Lucas* (1980) TLR 7 July 1980 the question before the court was whether the bankrupt was a member of his mistress's family and the answer "could no longer be decided by any moral preference for the family to which his wife belonged". Also see *Re Lowrie* [1981] 3 All ER 353 and *Re Holliday* [1981] Ch 405.

(g) In the initial period

Nothing occurring in the period beginning with the day of the presentation of the petition and ending with the vesting of the bankrupt's estate in the trustee is to be taken as giving rise to any rights of occupation under the MHA in relation to a dwelling-house comprised in the bankrupt's estate. Thus the spouse's rights are determined by the date on which the petition giving rise to the bankruptcy order is presented.

4. Security of tenure under the Act

(a) For the bankrupt tenant

What then of the secured tenant with rights of occupation, for example the council tenant or one holding under an assured, restricted or shorthold tenancy. The matter of the vesting in the trustee of this type of home is more a question of what is its worth as an asset (see page 99); should the official receiver or trustee disclaim the tenancy as onerous property and indeed does he have that right? (see page 180)

A contractual tenant does not have security of occupation against the trustee, because leaseholds forming part of a bankrupt's own property vest absolutely in the trustee who is personally liable for the observance and performance of the tenant's covenants while he is in possession (s 283) subject to his power to disclaim them under s 317.

On the other hand, where the bankrupt is a statutory tenant under the Rent Acts, the spouse's rights do not vest in the trustee; they are regarded as purely personal, and the statutory tenancy is preserved by s 1 MHA.

Where the trustee disclaims the tenancy the statutory tenant may continue in possession: see *Sutton* v *Dorf* [1932] 2 KB 304. As to *who* is the tenant depends on whether the tenancy was in the bankrupt's name alone or joint names.

Following a divorce the landlord is entitled to possession when the premises are occupied only by the ex-wife who was not the tenant; see *Metropolitan Properties Co Ltd* v *Cronan* (1982) 44 P&CR 1, unless she seeks a transfer before a decree absolute: see *Lewis* v *Lewis* [1985] AC 828.

(b) Bankrupt landlord

The reversionary estate of a bankrupt landlord will vest in the trustee, who may then act as any other assignee of a lease, eg by disposing of it (subject to any covenant against assignment and whether or not it extends to involuntary assignments). A tenancy at will is determined from the time the tenant learns of the bankruptcy of the landlord.

(c) *Forfeiture*

While a lease entitles the landlord to re-enter if, *inter alia,* the tenant becomes bankrupt, the tenant is nevertheless under an obligation not to become bankrupt. A right of re-entry or forfeiture against the tenant is enforceable without service of a notice under s 146 LPA. Relief from forfeiture may be granted where the tenant's interest is sold within one year from the bankruptcy or, if it is not sold within the year, then application needs to be made before the expiration of that year in order to obtain the relief.

The fact that the tenancy can be brought to an end before the expiry of the term because of a breach of the obligation not to become bankrupt, does not prevent the tenancy being a shorthold tenancy under s 52(1)(a) Housing Act 1980; see *Paterson* v *Aggio* (1987) 137 NLJ 809. Although on a strict construction of the relevant provision it might be said that the requirement not to become bankrupt was not an "obligation" on the tenant, that would defeat the plain intent of the legislation.

5. Assessment by the court

(a) *Generally*

By s 336(4) of the Act, the conduct, needs and financial resources of the spouse or former spouse, together with the needs of the children, are considered by the court together with all the circumstances of the case before making an order under s 1 MHA or s 30 of the Act of 1925.

(b) *The needs of the family and other creditors compared*

In considering the needs of the family and other creditors, the question before the court is: on what ground if any should the trust for sale be postponed? In a case involving the trustee and a former or existing spouse, Walton J in *Re Bailey (a Bankrupt) ex parte the Trustee* v *Bailey* [1972] 2 All ER 26 summed up the problem thus:

> "The situation must vary enormously from family to family ...... where, for example, a house had been specially adapted to suit the needs of a handicapped child, where there are obviously special circumstances; so special that, undoubtedly the court would hesitate long before making an immediate order for sale. Further than that one cannot go, because one does not know what the counteracting hardship on the other side might be at the same time when the matter comes for decision. One does not know whether there would be a likelihood of creditors being paid in full, what they would have to pay by way of interest for any borrowing they may, themselves, have to make to fill the gap until they get their money, and so forth."

As to the meaning of "needs", in *Burke* v *Burke* [1974] 1 All ER @ 1068 Lawton LJ said:

> "If the circumstances are such that the parents buy a house in which to accommodate themselves and any children of the marriage, for my part, I cannot see why the children should not be beneficiaries under any implied trust which may come into existence on the purchase of the house."

This has been extended to cases where the courts could find good reason for saying that the trust for sale should not be enforced immediately, for example where the former wife was left on her own and burdened with the obligation to provide a home for the three children of the marriage.

In *Re Holliday (a Bankrupt)* [1981] Ch 405, an order was made that the family home should not be sold until the time when the elder daughter would have passed her seventeenth birthday; the creditors had an unassailable right to be paid out of the assets of the bankrupt, but when one of those assets was an undivided share in land in respect of which the debtor's right to an immediate sale was not absolute, that was an asset in the bankruptcy which was liable to be affected by the interest of any other party interested in the land. However, in a case involving children *under* school age, the court decided that there were no such special circumstances to justify any substantial postponement of a possession order and sale; see *Re Lowrie (a Bankrupt)* (page 129).

Whether an order for sale should be made is a matter for the discretion of the court and the question was "whose voice ought in equity in all the circumstances of the case, to prevail". The trustee has a statutory duty (now subject to s 336) that normally gives him the stronger claim; see *Re Turner, a Bankrupt* [1975] 1 All ER 255. Where the bankrupt and his wife were ready to co-operate with the trustee if a sale were ordered, the court might therefore refrain from making an order for delivery up of possession to the trustee (in addition to an order of sale) because of the bankrupt's domestic circumstances (one of the four children suffering from a disablement); see *In re McCarthy, a Bankrupt* [1975] 1 WLR 807.

In the event of an order being deferred until a child attains a given age, consideration needs to be given to whether the intention is to terminate the order precisely on the relevant birthday or on cessation of full time education; if the latter, the words "or ceases full time education (whichever is the later) or further order" should be added to the order.

(c) Conduct

By s 336(4) the conduct of the spouse or former spouse so far as contributing to the bankruptcy, is considered by the court before making an order under s 1 MHA or s 30 LPA. "Conduct" is taken to mean whether or not the spouse contributed in any way to the bankrupt's downfall, for example, by living off the creditors.

There is, however, no specific guidance in the new Act, and one must therefore look further afield. Section 13 Debtors Act 1869, which is of general application, may be applied to any person in the bankruptcy: see *R* v *W Jones* [1898] 1 QB 119, in respect of the loss of any substantial part of the estate within a period of one year before the date of the petition, or between that date and the date of the adjudication. If, at the request of the official receiver, the spouse or bankrupt fails to give a satisfactory explanation of the manner in which loss to the estate occurred, they will be liable provided that their financial position is taken into consideration in determining whether any speculations were rash and hazardous. However, no prosecutions can be instituted under s 13 except by an order of the court.

(d) "All the circumstances"

The court is bound to look into all the circumstances of the case and consider whether or not, at the particular moment and in the particular circumstances when the application is made to it that it would be right and proper that an order should be made and to ask itself whether or not the person applying for an order for execution of the trust for sale is a person whose voice should be allowed to prevail; see *Re Buchanan-Wolleston's Conveyance* [1939] 2 All ER 301, and *Re Holliday (a Bankrupt)* [1981] Ch 405.

The prospects for an annulment of the bankruptcy, or a pending application for a voluntary arrangement, will clearly weigh upon the court, as will the availability of security over and above that available in the equity of the matrimonial home. Whilst the views of the creditors may be considered, the decision nevertheless rests upon a view of all the circumstances: see for example *Re Ezekiel's Settled Trust* [1942] Ch 230, a case considering the needs of beneficiaries.

6. Possession claims by mortgagees

(a) Claims by mortgagee

A statutory or express power of sale made exercisable by reason of the bankruptcy of the mortgagor, cannot be exercised without leave of the court; see *Re Huddersfield Building Society* (1940) WN 247.

Any person claiming to be a legal or equitable mortgagee of land belonging to the bankrupt may apply to the court for an order that the land be sold. The court may, if satisfied as to the applicant's title, require accounts to be taken and enquiries made to establish the principal, interest and costs due under the mortgage and, where the mortgagee has been in possession, the rents and profits, dividends, interest or other proceeds received by him or on his behalf. The court may require such accounts and enquiries in respect of any mortgage of the same property other than that of the applicant. Any of those concerned may be examined by the court for these purposes, including by interrogatories, and must produce to the court, on oath, such documents in their custody or under their control relating to the bankrupt's estate as the court may require. In any proceedings between a mortgagor and mortgagee, or the trustee of either of them, the court may order accounts to be taken and enquiries made in the same manner as in the Chancery Division (Rule 6.197)

The court may order that the land, or any part of it, be sold. Any party in possession, or in receipt of rents and profits, may be ordered to deliver up possession or receipt to the purchaser or to such other person as the court may direct. The court may permit the person having the conduct of the sale to sell the land in such manner as he thinks fit, or direct the manner in which it is to be sold. The order may also contain directions:

(i) appointing the person who is to have the conduct of the sale;
(ii) as to the manner of sale - eg by private treaty, by auction;
(iii) as to the particulars and conditions of sale;
(iv) as to obtaining evidence of the value of the property and fixing a reserve or minimum price;
(v) requiring particular persons to join in the sale and conveyance;
(vi) requiring the payment of the purchase money into court, to trustees or to others;
(vii) if the sale is to be by auction, fixing any security to be given by the auctioneer, and his remuneration, and directing that the mortgagee may appear and bid on his own behalf.

See Rule 6.198 and *Quennell* v *Maltby* [1979] 1 All ER 568 (CA).

A building society should not, in practice, immediately seek to enforce its security, or at all, where the mortgage repayments are secured by family or friends.

(b) Action for foreclosure

Under the terms of the mortgage deed, where the building society brings an action for foreclosure in which a claim for possession of the mortgaged property is also made, the court has a discretion; in accordance with s 36(2) Administration of Justice Act 1970, it may either adjourn the proceedings, or on giving judgment or making an order for delivery of possession of the mortgaged property, may either:

(i) stay or suspend the execution of the judgment or order; or
(ii) postpone the date for delivery of possession for such period or periods as the court thinks reasonable,

at any time before the execution of such judgment or order.

In exercising its power under s 36 the court may also, by s 8 Administration of Justice Act 1973, adjourn the case where repayment of arrears is expected within a reasonable period.

The court may ignore any provision for early repayment of the mortgage on default, provided arrangements are made to pay off the arrears, even over the length of the mortgage term: see *Western Bank* v *Shindler* [1976] 2 All ER 393. Section 8 extends to cases of endowment mortgages: see *Bank of Scotland* v *Grimes* [1985] 2 All ER 254.

(c) Proceeds of sale

The proceeds of sale are to be applied:

(i) in paying the expenses of the trustee in the application to the court, the sale, and any costs arising out of taking accounts and making inquiries (Rule 6.197); and

(ii) in payment of the amount due to any mortgagee for principal, interest and costs.

Any balance is retained by or paid to the trustee. Where the proceeds of sale are insufficient to pay in full the amount due to any mortgagee, the mortgagee may prove as a creditor for the deficiency and may receive dividends rateably with other creditors, but not so as to disturb any dividend already declared.

(d) Housing Act advances

In respect of advances originally made under the Small Dwelling Acquisition Acts 1899-1923 (before the Housing (Consequential Provisions) Act 1985), when the proprietor of any such house becomes bankrupt or makes an arrangement under Sch 18 para 3(4) to the Housing Act 1985, the local authority may suspend the condition as to residence during the continuance of the arrangement to allow the bankrupt to remain in occupation. The local authority may either take possession of the house or order its sale without taking possession, and should do so except in pursuance of some arrangement to the contrary with the trustee (para 5(3)).

(e) In the initial period

If a bankrupt has purported to mortgage his property or give other security or a charge after the presentation of the petition, the transaction would be restricted under s 284 and wholly ineffective against the trustee, unless it is made with the consent of the court.

(f) Mortgage repayments after adjudication

Under s 1(5) MHA 1983 the spouse has the right to continue paying or to pay off the outstanding mortgage. Where the bankrupt continues in occupation on condition that he makes repayment or pays towards other outgoings, the bankrupt cannot *prima facie* thereby purchase an interest in the estate property (s 338).

7. Realisation of the property

(a) Generally

By s 314(1)(b) and Sch 5 Part 2 of the Act the trustee has a general power of sale of any part of the property in the bankrupt's estate. Expenses of sale have priority under Rule 6.224(1)(a) (see page 232). The trustee or creditors' committee may agree with the person entitled to payment, or may request taxation by the county court (Rule 7.34). The trustee is a "trust corporation" and as such can make a contract by his official name and can give a receipt for the proceeds of the sale (s 3 Law of Property Act 1926). Where there are beneficial or other interests in the property they will be paid out of the proceeds of sale before funds are passed to the estate for distribution.

(b) Postponed trust for sale

Under s 30 LPA any beneficiary or other person interested may apply for an order directing the trustees to sell to recoup their share of the purchase price. As an alternative to outright sale the trustee in the bankruptcy may invite the other to buy out the bankrupt's share. Under s 25 LPA the trustees for sale have unlimited power to postpone the sale enabling the property to be permanently retained. By s 336(3), however, the power to order the sale to be postponed is subject to the court having regard to the needs of the creditors and family (see above).

(c) "Right to buy" homes

Under the Housing Act 1985: Trustees of bankrupt ex-tenants of housing association and council houses who have purchased the freehold or long lease of their own homes under the "right to buy" provisions of the Housing Acts 1980-85 will have a liability to repay part or all of the discount received by the bankrupt following an early disposal before the end of the discount period. No provision is made under the Act of 1986 to modify those repayment provisions on an insolvency, and likewise there is no power to recoup the original discount from the bankrupt. Indeed it is hard to see under what legal or moral grounds such an action could be perpetrated. Section 2 Housing and Planning Act 1986 reduces from five to three years the period during which disposal obligates all or some of the discount repayment, provided that the property was purchased before the operative date for that Act of 7 January 1987. Repayment of the discount is, by s 156 Housing Act 1985, a charge on the dwelling-house taking effect as if it had been created by deed expressed to be by way of legal mortgage.

Whenever the disposal takes place by virtue of a property adjustment order under s 24 Matrimonial Causes Act 1973 in connection with divorce, the disposal is exempt from repayment of the discount. It is not, however, exempt where the disposal is by way of a sale pursuant to s 24A of that Act whereby "the court may make a further order for the sale of such property ...... being property in which, or in the proceeds of sale of which, either or both of the parties to the marriage has or have a beneficial interest, either in possession or reversion".

In *Re Rushmoor Borough Council ex parte Barrett & Another* [1987] 1 All ER 353 on the true construction of s 160(1)(c) of the Housing Act 1985, a "disposal ...... in pursuance of an order made under s 24 of the Matrimonial Causes Act 1973" contemplated a transfer or settlement of property under s 24 which involved continued occupation of the property by a spouse and/or children of the family whereby no liquid cash advantage was gained. Accordingly, such a disposal did not include the sale of a matrimonial home by order of the court in proceedings for financial relief after divorce, since in making such an order, the court was exercising the power conferred on it by s 24A of the 1973 Act to order the sale of property and it followed therefore that the applicants were obliged to repay £10,120 (being 80% of the original discount) in accordance with the covenant in the conveyance, to the local authority.

Under the Landlord and Tenant Act 1987: A tenant of a flat that falls within the scope of s 1 Landlord and Tenant Act 1987, will have a right of first refusal to buy his flat upon a "relevant disposal" by the landlord, provided that he is what is known as a "qualifying tenant". In the event of the landlord's bankruptcy the question will arise as to whether there is a "relevant disposal" within the terms of the 1987 Act. The answer appears to be that there will not; for by s 4(2)(b) the vesting of the landlord's interest in the trustee in bankruptcy is not a relevant disposal to which the Act would apply.

(d) Disposal to the spouse or to the bankrupt

The general power of the trustee to sell property is not restricted by the new Act and confirms the practical effect of s 55 of the old Act (following *Kitson* v *Hardwick* (1872) 26 LT 846 and a similar provision in the 1869 Act), that property may be transferred to the bankrupt himself. This reasoning was strongly supported over one hundred years later in *Ramsey* v *Hartley* [1977] 2 All ER 680. Now the same result may be achieved by use of the trustee's general powers under Sch 5 Part II to dispose of the property (and if necessary for a nominal sum) to the bankrupt.

Where the property (for whatever reason) otherwise satisfies s 315 as an "onerous property" (see page 180) it would be transferable to "any person" under s 320(6); imputing *Kitson* v *Hardwick*, a bankrupt could not be excluded.

In any event, and so as to prevent him being exposed to a subsequent charge of maladminstration before (or even after) his release, the trustee will be advised to take professional advice from a surveyor and valuer, and/or apply for directions from the court.

Whichever method is used to administer the affairs of the estate will largely depend on the facts as the trustee finds in the particular case. There is, of course, no question of re-vesting the property in the trustee in bankruptcy following a transfer to the bankrupt howsoever obtained, for equity will not permit a statute to be a cloak for fraud. Obviously in many cases a higher price might be obtained by selling direct to the spouse or family who, for both sentimental and practical reasons, might give a higher price than a stranger, even on a fair market basis.

(e) Proceeds of sale

A purchaser of a legal estate from trustees for sale is not to be concerned with the trusts affecting the proceeds of sale (s 27 LPA). The proceeds are distributed in accordance with the respective shares or other interests as set out on page 138.

8. Capital gains tax

Under the Capital Gains Tax Act 1979, liability to tax on realisation of the property depends not on whether the property is the matrimonial home but on whether or not it is the principal residence. The disposal of an individual's principal residence is exempt from tax. On the appointment of the trustee, the residence vests in him and, by s 61, he is responsible for tax due, if any; see *Re Mesco Properties Ltd* [1980] 1 WLR 96. Whilst remaining occupied by the bankrupt and his family until disposal, there is no liability to tax.

If part of the residence has been wholly and exclusively used for business or professional purposes, that part is not exempt, and the gain is apportioned, but the distinction between part use of a residence for business purposes and exclusive use is a fine one with each case decided on its merits. Likewise special rules relate to gains on a main residence which has been partly let.

However, where the debtor owns more than one property the question which is to be treated as the main one is usually a question of fact, and may be determined by notice given by the trustee jointly with the occupier unless notice has previously been served on the Inspector of Taxes by the debtor.

CGT applies only to gains accruing since 5 April 1965. Reliefs take the form of exemption from liability or deferment, plus indexation relief in the form of a further deduction after the unindexed gain has been arrived at.

By way of illustration: B owned a second home for a period of three years from May 1984 until he sold in May 1987. He purchased for £25,000, spent £4,000 on improvements, and the trustee in bankruptcy sold it for £40,000 net (after allowing for the costs - probably special terms - of the disposal). The assessable gain is computed as follows:

Proceeds of sale £40,000 - £29,000	11,000	
Deduct allowable costs		
Unindexed gain; annual examption 1987/88	6,600	
Gain	4,400	
*Indexation allowance		
$\frac{101.9 \text{ x } 89.0}{89.0}$ = 0.145 x 40,000		5,800
Chargeable gain		£ Nil

(May '84 =RI=89.0, May '87=RD=101.9

$$\frac{RD - RI}{RI}$$

Where RD = retail price index figure for the month in which the disposal is received; RI = the index for the month in which expenditure incurred.

In a case where tax is payable then it would be paid by the trustee out of the estate as per the order of payment of expenses shown in Rule 6.224(1)(p) in priority to the distribution to any preferential creditor (see page 233). When spouses are living together only one exemption relief is given, allocated between them *pro rata* to their net gains.

9. Valuation of trusts and other interests

(a) Co-ownership

The parties hold on a statutory trust for sale; each is entitled to an undisputed share in the home, the share of either being declared in the conveyance that they were to hold the proceeds of sale of the property upon trust for themselves as joint tenants. Such a declaration of trust exhaustively states the respective beneficial interests: *Goodman* v *Gallant* (above, page 124).

Lord Diplock in *Gissing* v *Gissing* [1970] 2 All ER @ 789: "Where the trust is expressly declared in the instrument by which the legal estate is transferred to the trustee or by a written declaration of trust by the trustee, the court must give effect to it"; and see *Turton* v *Turton* [1987] 2 All ER 641; *Goodman* v *Gallant* (above) where the conveyance into joint names contained an express declaration it was also held that on severance of the tenancy a tenancy in common in equal shares was created.

Failing an express declaration, the owners are jointly beneficially entitled to the proceeds of sale so that the share of each will be in proportion to his or her respective contribution to the purchase price: see *Jones* v *Challenger* [1968] 1 QB 176; *Walker* v *Hall* (1984) 5 FLR 126 about unequal contributions; *Re Pittortou (a Bankrupt)* [1985] 1 All ER 285 where the husband's business and personal debts were deductible only from his share of the property. "In matrimonial disputes Parliament has given a very wide discretion to adjust and determine the property rights of the parties according to what was just and reasonably conferred by the Matrimonial Causes Act 1973." (*Walker* v *Hall*)

(b) The beneficial interest

This relates to the interest of a beneficiary (as contrasted with the interest of the legal owner) where for example the wife has contributed part of the purchase price or paid for improvements to the matrimonial home even though it was bought in the husband's name alone: see *Rimmer* v *Rimmer* [1953] 1 QB 63. In that event she would have a quantifiable beneficial interest in the property: *Bull* v *Bull* [1954] 2 WLR 80 where there was a resulting trust in favour of the parents who provided a loan for the purchase price as against the trustee in bankruptcy.

Therefore, a spouse who makes the purchase possible by means of a loan or pays for an extension acquires an equitable interest, ie a beneficial share proportionate to the total value of the house, and the trustee takes subject to that beneficial share. This happily brings the law down to the simple question of establishing the facts in a particular case and thereafter assessing the appropriate proportions on the making of a bankruptcy order.

But how does one measure beneficial interest? "It has been thought better not to prescribe any rule that the share must be commensurate with or proportionate to the cost or value of the improvements, but to allow the court in the event of a dispute, to make such order as it thinks just in all the circumstances". (*Report on Financial Provision in Matrimonial Proceedings (Law Commission No 25)* following the confusion left by the House of Lords in *Pettit* v *Pettit* [1969] 2 All ER 385).

In *Heseltine* v *Heseltine* [1971] 1 All ER 952: "in the usual way, the court imputes a trust under which the husband is to hold it for them both jointly in equal shares; but half and half is not an invariable decision. If some other decision is more fair the court will adopt it". See, for example, *Gissing* v *Gissing* [1970] 2 All ER 780.

Nourse LJ in a long and important judgment in *Turton* v *Turton* (above):

> "It must always be remembered that the basis on which the court proceeds is a common intention, usually to be inferred from the conduct of the parties, that the claimant is to have a beneficial interest in the house. In the common case where the intention can be inferred only from the respective contributions, either initial or under a mortgage, to the cost of its acquisition it is held that the house belongs to the parties beneficially in proportions corresponding to those contributions."

Note also the position of the divorcee under a beneficial interest; see *Re Holliday (a Bankrupt)* (above).

(c) Constructive trust

The "constructive trust" is an equitable lien distinguished from the beneficial interest by virtue of 53 LPA; by it the court can enable an aggrieved party to obtain restitution where the legal owner cannot conscientiously keep the property for himself alone; it does not *ipso facto* provide any right to occupation. It therefore allows another to have the property, or the benefit of it, or a share in it; see *Husey* v *Palmer* [1972] 1 WLR 1290, *per* Lord Denning:

> "it is a trust imposed by law whenever justice and good conscience require it ...... thus we have repeatedly held that where one person contributes towards the purchase price of a house, the owner holds it on a constructive trust for him, proportionate to his contribution, even though there is no agreement between them and no declaration of trust to be found."

The doctrine cannot be invoked where there is an express declaration which comprehensively declares the beneficial interest or its proceeds of sale because such a declaration is exhaustive and conclusive of the position unless and until the conveyance is set aside or rectified; see *Goodman* v *Gallant* (above). It may be imputed at the outset when the property is acquired, or later on, as the circumstances may require.

Common intention: If a common intention is found that the plaintiff should have a beneficial interest in the property, then equity will construct a trust to give effect to it; see *Grant* v *Edwards and Edwards* [1987] 1 FLR 87 at page 93, Nourse LJ:

> "In a case such as the present where there has been no written declaration or agreement, nor any direct provision by the plaintiff of part of the purchase price, so as to give rise to a resulting trust in her favour, she must establish a common intention between her and the defendant, acted upon by her, that she should have a beneficial interest in the property. If she can do that, equity will not allow the defendant to deny that interest and will construct a trust to give effect to it."

Oral intention: Where, although there has no been no writing, the parties have orally declared themselves in such a way as to make their common intention plain the court does not have to look for conduct from which the intention can be inferred, but only for conduct which amounts to acting upon it by the claimant. Although that conduct can undoubtedly include the incurring of expenditure on buying the house it need not necessarily be so; see *Grant* v *Edwards and Edwards* (above).

Imputation in favour of the donor: A constructive trust applies in favour of the donor in the following situations: where a wife has helped pay mortgage instalments (*Leake (formerly Bruzzi)* v *Bruzzi* [1974] 2 All ER 1196); helped in a business (*Heseltine* v *Heseltine*, above); where a mistress has contributed money or money's worth to building the house (*Cooke* v *Head* [1972] 1 WLR 518); where a son built a bungalow on his father's land (*Inwards* v *Baker* [1965] 2 QB 29); and where another pays for an extension (*Unity Joint Stock Bank* v *King* (1858) 25 Beav 72, *Husey* v *Palmer*, above). Likewise a relative or in-laws may be involved through assistance with the original price; see *Re Sharpe, Trustee* v *Sharpe* [1980] 1 All ER 198 as to moneys advanced by loan without occupation.

(d) Relinquishing the ex-wife's claim to a property adjustment order

Among the orders that may be made under the Matrimonial Causes Act 1973 following on, or after, the granting of a decree of divorce, nullity or judicial separation, are property adjustment orders.

The fact that a settlement or transfer of the property had to be made to comply with a property adjustment order will by s 39 of the 1973 Act, not prevent that settlement or transfer from being a transaction in respect of which an order may be made under s 339 or 340 of the 1986 Act (so as to avoid transactions at an undervalue and at a preference - see page 173). For example, in *Re Abbott (a Bankrupt)* [1983] 1 Ch 45, at the time of the order the husband was insolvent and subsequently made bankrupt. The trustee mounted a challenge against the settlement (under s 42(1) of the old Act) under the property adjustment order. However, as the ex-wife was a purchaser of that right for valuable consideration within the terms of that section the settlement was not void against the trustee.

Before the 1985 Insolvency Act, such rights could be challenged; now in order that the property can be realised and the balance made available for the creditors, it would seem that the ex-wife need only relinquish her claim to such an order by consent in return for the right to part of her husband's share of the proceeds of sale.

(e) The doctrine of the beneficial interest applied to co-habitees

In the case of unmarried couples, to establish a claim to a beneficial interest in the property by a non-owning party, it is firstly necessary to establish that such a beneficial interest was the common intention of the parties, eg by virtue of conduct; and secondly to ascertain what each contributed to creating the trust property, ie to the purchase price.

Having established the common intention of the parties, the unmarried claimant must then show that she had acted upon it to her detriment. There is a distinction to be made between the sort of conduct from which a common intention could be inferred, and conduct amounting to an acting upon a common intention already established.

In *Grant* v *Edwards and Edwards* (1987) 1 FLR 87 in a dispute between an unmarried couple as to the beneficial ownership of a house in which they formerly lived together, the court took into account the defendant's payment of the insurance moneys into a joint account, their common intention, and indirect contributions by the plaintiff towards the mortgage payments, and concluded that the plaintiff woman was entitled to a half interest in the property. This followed the reasoning in *Burns* v *Burns* [1984] Ch 317 that the court has to look for expenditure relating to the acquisition of the home. If it is found to have been incurred, it will perform the two-fold function of establishing the common intention and of showing that the claimant has acted upon it.

When the co-habitees are unmarried, no jurisdiction exists to make a formal division of property between them under statute law; cf Matrimonal Causes Act 1973. Their rights have to be decided otherwise; see *Pettit* v *Pettit* (above) and *Gissing* v *Gissing* [1970] 2 All ER 780. If there is a resulting trust the beneficiaries acquire interests in the trust property by operation of law. In *Hall* v *Hall* (1982) 3 FLR 379, a case where a family home was bought in the joint names of a man and a woman, the general conditions were identified as follows:

- (i) as a consequence of a legal process the intention must be identifiable;
- (ii) there must be more than expectations which at some later date require valuation by the court;
- (iii) the interest must not be capable of being brought to an end by the happening of an unrelated event, eg by the separation of the co-habitees;
- (iv) the interest must be capable of being turned into another form of property, eg proceeds of sale.

Supposing, however, one of the partners has left the property before it beomes necessary (eg by bankruptcy) to determine the respective interests. Then the valuation date is paramount; whether the original co-habitees hold their home on an express or an implied trust for sale, the beneficial interest would appear to endure until the property is sold.

There is no discretion to apply an earlier "cut-off" point simply because the purpose of the trust had come to an end, namely that the property was no longer used as a family home, for the trust for sale imposed by statute as a result of the transfer of property in joint names did not come to an end but continued until either the property is sold in execution of the trust for sale, or one party - by buying out the other - became solely and absolutely entitled to the property in equity. Therefore the beneficial interests of both parties established by their contributions to the original purchase would not automatically cease or be quantified as fixed sums until it was later sold; see *Walker* v *Hall* (1984) 4 FLR 126.

This principle was applied in *Turton* v *Turton* [1987] 2 All ER 641 so that Carol, who left her co-habitee Edward in the house they occupied, took a half share in the net proceeds (ie £15,000), rather than a half share in a valuation of the property at the time she had left it (£2,750), and was thereby considerably better off.

Kerr LJ (in *Turton* at page 649) also confirmed that an express declaration of trust covering the respective beneficial interests of the parties is conclusive and excludes any possible resulting or implied trust, and with it any possible discretionary jurisdiction relating to the assessment or valuation of the parties' beneficial shares which might otherwise exist.

(f) Equity of exoneration

Where the wife stands in the position of surety for her husband she may then prove in her husband's bankruptcy in the same order of priority as the creditor would have had. *Re Cronmire ex parte Cronmire* [1901] 1 KB 480 established the entitlement of a wife, who deposited her own securities to secure her husband's debts, to prove in his bankruptcy in respect of the indemnity which he owed her. Indeed she may also be able to claim for an enhanced proprietary interest; see *Re a Debtor (No 24 of 1971) ex parte Marley* v *Trustee of the Property of the Debtor* [1976] 2 All ER 1010.

> "The equity of exoneration is a principle of equity which depends on the presumed intention of the parties. If the circumstances of a particular case do not justify the inference, or indeed the circumstances negate the inference, that it was the joint intention of the joint mortgagors that the burden of the secured indebtedness should fall primarily on the share of that of them who was the debtor, then that consequence will not follow."; see *Pittortou (a Bankrupt) ex parte Trustee* v *The Bankrupt and Another* [1985] 1 All ER @ 288.

Therefore, if the beneficial interests of husband and wife have been kept quite distinct in the transaction and each spouse has kept moneys separately for this purpose, the husband's share is debited with the whole of the outstanding mortgage and unpaid interest charged on the house, together with premiums on the endowment policy, if any, related thereto ; see *Coucher* v *Coucher* [1972] 1 All ER 959.

Thus building societies and other institutional lenders will seek to establish the purpose of the borrowing and that the charge is executed by the wife as well as the husband to satisfy*Williams and Glyn's Bank* v *Boland* and *Flegg* (above). To the extent that bank drawings in *Pittortou* charged on the wife's interest represented payments for the joint benefit of the household, the doctrine of exoneration should not apply; however, payments made by the bankrupt purely for business purposes and, therefore, any payments made by him for the purposes of a second home he was supporting, should as between the bankrupt and his spouse be treated as charged primarily on the bankrupt's half share in the mortgaged property.

(g) Fraud or mistake

The trustee will be on his guard against possible claims against the bankruptcy estate arising out of mistake or fraud. Where the bankrupt has conveyed his property before the commencement of bankruptcy, it is fraudulent only if the grantor becomes bankrupt within five years of its execution (s 357). It cannot be set aside if no bankruptcy proceedings are taken within that time; see *Re Hirth* [1899] 1 QB 612; if they are then the court may take action under s 423 for restoring the position (see page 170).

Once a trust has been effectively declared, it can only be extinguished by rescinding the document containing the declaration of trust on the ground of fraud or mistake, or rectifying it in the appropriate manner to vary or delete the declaration of trust (Lord Upjohn in *Pettit* v *Pettit* [1969] 2 All ER 385).

Conveyancers should guard against claims for professional negligence in respect of mistakes in conveying on behalf of co-habitees; they are advised to ascertain and record the intention of the parties when clients give or jointly contribute to the purchase price in unequal amounts; see *Conveyancers Beware the Co-habitee*, Law Society's Gazette 6 May 1987 at page 1309. Also, Griffiths LJ:

> "I would wish to underline the point as strongly as I can and to suggest that the courts may soon have to consider whether a solicitor acting for joint purchasers is not guilty of negligence if he fails to find out and record what the joint purchasers' beneficial interests in the relevant property are to be" (*Bernard* v *Josephs* (1983) 4 FLR 178).

The parties cannot go behind a conveyance which declares in whom the beneficial title between them is to vest in the absence of fraud or mistake at the time of the transaction; see *Leake (formerly Bruzzi)* v *Bruzzi* [1974] 2 All ER 1196.

As to the trustee's duty not to take advantage of a mistake see *Re Byfield (a Bankrupt) ex parte Hill Samuel & Co Ltd* [1982] 1 All ER 249.

10. Land registration

Upon the bankruptcy of the proprietor of any registered land or charge his trustee (where appointed) is entitled to be registered as proprietor in his place, under the Land Registration Rules 1986. The official receiver or the trustee furnishes the prescribed evidence that the land or charge is comprised in the bankrupt's estate.

(a) Protection of spouse

The right of occupation of the spouse under the MHA exists as a charge on the estate or interest of the other spouse, or the trustee for the other spouse; notwithstanding the bankruptcy of the other spouse, the charge continues to subsist and binds the trustee in bankruptcy (s 336(2)).

(b) Protection of creditors

As soon as practicable after registration of a petition in bankruptcy as a pending action under the Land Charges Act 1925 the Chief Land Registrar registers a "creditors' notice" against the title of any proprietor of any registered land or charge which appears to be affected. This notice protects the rights of all creditors and, unless cancelled by the registrar, remains in force until a bankruptcy inhibition is registered or the trustee is registered as proprietor.

Where, under a disposition to a purchaser in good faith for money or money's worth, such purchaser is registered as proprietor of an estate or a charge, then notwithstanding that the person making the disposition is adjudged bankrupt, the title of his trustee as from the date of such disposition, is void as against such purchaser unless at that date either a creditors' notice or a bankruptcy inhibition has been registered. A purchaser who, at the date of the execution of the registered disposition has notice of the bankruptcy petition or the adjudication will not be deemed to take in good faith.

Where the estate or assets of a bankrupt proprietor suffer loss by reason of the omission of the registrar to register a creditors' notice or bankruptcy inhibition; or because of the execution or registration of a disposition after a petition is registered as a pending action; or after a bankruptcy order is registered and before the registration of a creditors' petition or bankruptcy inhibition, the trustee is entitled to indemnity as a person suffering loss by reason of the omission from the register.

(c) Inspection of the register

The official receiver or trustee may inspect the register so far as it relates to any proprietor against whom a bankruptcy order has been made. Any creditor, on behalf of himself and all other creditors, or the official receiver or trustee, may lodge a caution against any such proprietor in respect of any minor interest affecting the registered land.

(d) Action of the registrar

Where:

- (i) any doubt arises as to the identity of the debtor or bankrupt; or
- (ii) the registration of a pending action in respect of a bankruptcy petition is vacated; or
- (iii) the bankruptcy order is annulled; or
- (iv) the bankruptcy proceedings do not affect or have ceased to affect the

statutory powers of the bankrupt under the Act,
the registrar must take such action as he thinks advisable as soon as practicable after receiving notice thereof, and after making such enquiry and giving such notice (if any) as he deems necessary.

(e) Mistake in bankruptcy order

Where a mistake has occurred in a bankruptcy order or where any amendment in the land register appears to be required, it is the duty of the official receiver, or the trustee if appointed, as soon as it comes to his knowledge, to notify such mistake or to suggest such amendment to the registrar, who shall, thereupon, after making such inquiries and giving notice, if any, as he deems necessary, make such amendment in the register as may be necessary.

The official receiver or trustee may apply to the court for an order amending the full title of the proceedings which the official receiver immediately sends to the registrar for corresponding amendment of the registration. The notice may also be advertised and Gazetted (Rule 6.35).

(f) Dismissal of petition

If the petition is dismissed or withdrawn by leave of the court, then an order is made at the same time permitting vacation of the registration of the petition as a pending action (Rule 6.27).

11. Non-realisation of interests

(a) Disclaimer of onerous property

In the unfortunate circumstances that the debt to the building society matches or exceeds the equity in the property, then to avoid incurring further expense on sale, the trustee may serve notice to disclaim the property under s 318 of the Act and s 52 LPA on the grounds that it may otherwise give rise to a liability on the estate to pay money or perform any other onerous act.

For a disclaimer to be effective a copy of the disclaimer must be served on every person in occupation of or claiming a right to occupy the dwelling-house and either no application is made to vest the property within fourteen days, or where such an application has been made, the court directs that the disclaimer is to take effect. See page 180 for disclaimer generally.

(b) Trust property

It is expressly provided by s 283(3)(a) of the Act that property held by the bankrupt on trust for any other person is not vested in the trustee and the legal estate remains vested in the bankrupt. Under s 41 Trustee Act 1925 the court has a wide power to appoint a new trustee in substitution for or in addition to the bankrupt. However if there is no danger to the trust property, bankruptcy by itself will not necessarily induce the court to remove him; see *Re Barker's Trusts* [1875] 1 Ch 43 (see also page 266).

(c) Settled land

By s 103 Settled Land Act 1925 the legal estate in settled land (as defined by s1 of that Act) that is comprised in or claimed for the bankrupt's estate does not vest in his trustee unless and until the bankrupt becomes absolutely and beneficially entitled to the land free from all limitations, powers and charges taking effect under the settlement, by virtue of Sch 8 to the Act of 1985.

If, however, it is shown to the satisfaction of the court that by reason of, *inter alia*, his bankruptcy he has ceased to have a substantial interest in the settled land, and has unreasonably refused to exercise the statutory powers, an order may be made authorising the trustee of the settlement to exercise the powers in his name (s 24(1) of that Act).

(d) Charging order

Where any property consists of an interest in a dwelling-house which is included in the estate and is occupied by the bankrupt or by his spouse or former spouse, and the trustee is, for any reason, unable for the time being to realise that property, the trustee may apply to the court under s 313 for an order imposing a charge on the property for the benefit of the bankrupt's estate. That charge is enforceable, up to the value from time to time of the property secured, for the payment of any amount which is due otherwise than to the bankrupt out of the estate, together with interest on that amount at the prescribed rate. This has the effect of taking the house out of the estate and (subs (3)) subject to the charge (and any prior charge), vesting it in the bankrupt, thereby saving the home for the family.

Thus if the spouse is served with a possession order, she can now plead that power to impose such a charge enables the trustee's application for possession to be rebutted. Where the trustee applies to the court for an order, the spouse or former spouse is respondent to the application and the court may, if it thinks fit, direct other persons to be made respondent also, in respect of any interest which they may have in the property. The trustee must report to the court on the extent of the bankrupt's interest in the property and the amount which, at the date of the application, remains owing to unsecured creditors. The terms of the charge to be imposed may be agreed between the trustee and the bankrupt, or, failing agreement, settled by the court. As to the final general meeting of creditors in those circumstances, see page 214.

Section 3 of the Charging Orders Act 1979 applies and provides that a charging order may be made either absolutely, or subject to conditions as to notifying the debtor of the time when the charge is to become enforceable. The possibility of the debtor's subsequent insolvency alone will not be sufficient to convince the county court that an order absolute should be made, and certainly not in a case where instalments as ordered were being regularly paid by the judgment debtor; see *Mercantile Credit Co*

Ltd v *Ellis* [1987] ILR 17 March 1987. A creditor in whose favour a charging order *nisi* has been made under that Act is not a secured creditor in the bankruptcy; see *Roberts Petroleum Ltd* v *Bernard Kenney Ltd* [1983] 1 All ER 564.

The Land Charges Act 1972 and the Land Registration Act 1925 also apply in relation to charging orders. A charge imposed by a charging order has the same effect as an equitable charge created by the debtor in writing. When a charging order has been protected by an entry under those Acts an order under s 3(5) of the Act of 1979 discharges the charging order and directs that the entry be cancelled.

Chapter 11

Administration by the trustee

1. Introduction

The function of the trustee is to get in, realise and distribute the bankrupt's estate. In carrying out that function, and in the management of the bankrupt's estate, he is entitled to use his own discretion, both with and without the permission of the creditors, the Secretary of State, or the court; but his duties may not relate to property held by the bankrupt in trust. He may act on his own in a case of emergency provided he seeks ratification of his actions without undue delay.

The following matters arising in the trustee's administration of the bankrupt are covered by the Regulations and are discussed in the Chapters indicated:

- (a) the preparation and keeping of books, accounts and other records, and their production to such persons as may be authorised or required to inspect them (Chapter 15);
- (b) the auditing of accounts (Chapter 17);
- (c) the manner in which trustees (including the official receiver when acting as receiver and manager under s 287) are to act in relation to the bankrupt's books, papers and other records, the manner of their disposal by the responsible insolvency practitioner, or others (Chapters 15 and 17);
- (d) the supply by the trustee to creditors and the creditors' committee of copies of documents relating to the insolvency and the affairs of the individual on payment of the specified fee (Chapter 15);
- (e) the manner in which insolvent estates are to be distributed by trustees, including provision with respect to unclaimed funds and dividends (Chapters 16 and 21);
- (f) the manner in which moneys coming into the hands of a trustee in the course of his administration are to be handled (Chapter 17);
- (g) the amount (or the manner of determining the amount) to be paid to the official receiver by way of remuneration when acting as interim receiver (Chapter 6) or trustee (Chapter 15).

2. Official name

The full title of the trustee is "the trustee of the estate of ...., a bankrupt", referred to as the trustee in bankruptcy of the particular bankrupt. All proceedings are headed "IN BANKRUPTCY".

3. Vesting and transfer of property

The bankrupt's estate vests in the trustee immediately on his appointment taking effect, and property vests in him without any other conveyance, assignment or transfer. The exception is income, for which an income payments order is required.

"Property", by s 436, includes money, goods, things in action, land and every description of property wherever situated, together with obligations and every description of interest, whether present or future, vested or contingent, arising out of or incidental to property. It does not include income.

Except as against a purchaser in good faith, for value and without notice of the bankruptcy, the trustee's title to property dates back to the commencement of bankruptcy.

As to the general rules for vesting and transferring property to the trustee, see below. For an analysis of individual personal and other property of the bankrupt which will normally be declared on his statement of affairs as "assets", see Chapter 9.

(a) Duty to deliver up

Where a bankruptcy order has been made the bankrupt is under a duty (by s 312(1)) to deliver possession of his estate to the official receiver, or the trustee if appointed, and to deliver up to him all books, papers and other records of which he has possession or control and which relate to his estate and affairs (including any which would be privileged from disclosure in any proceedings). He cannot lawfully resist his trustee's application for possession of premises comprised in that property; see *Fryer* v *Brook* (1984) TLR 2 August 1984, but note the position now as to the matrimonial home (Chapter 10, page 122).

The property to be delivered up comprises all the property that belonged to or vested in the bankrupt at the commencement, other than certain excluded property reclaimable by the trustee, and exempt property (see page 150).

While the official receiver is acting as receiver and manager of the estate he takes all such steps as he thinks fit for protecting any property which may be claimed for the estate by the trustee, except that he is not required to do anything that involves his incurring expenditure. He must deliver up possession of the property, books, papers or records to the trustee. So too must a person who has ceased to be supervisor of a voluntary arrangement or a person who has ceased to be trustee (s 312(2)).

Any banker or agent of the bankrupt who holds any property to the account of, or for, the bankrupt, must pay or deliver up all property in his possession or under his control which forms part of the bankrupt's estate and which he is not by law entitled to retain as against the bankrupt or trustee, failing which he is guilty of contempt of court (s 312(3)).

(b) Property excluded from the vesting order

The general power of vesting under s 306 is, however, controlled by other sections of the Act:

(i) Trust property By s 283(3)(a) property held on trust by the bankrupt for any other person is excluded. It should not have been subsumed with the assets and he must retain control of the trust property. For example, in *Re Kayford Ltd* [1975] 1 All ER 604 a mail order firm set up a separate trust fund for moneys received from customers in respect of goods not yet delivered. The existence of a separate bank account, which a useful indicator but not conclusive, may also be required by statute; see s 13 Estate Agents Act 1979.

(ii) Income Income does not vest in the trustee without an income payments order (see page 272). "Income" means every payment in the nature of income which is from time to time made to the bankrupt or to which he becomes entitled. The word "income" is defined by Jessel MR as "as large a word as can be used" to denote personal receipts, including a retirement pension; see *Re Huggins* (1882) 21 Ch 85. It includes maintenance payable to the bankrupt under an order of the divorce court; see *Re Landau* [1934] Ch 549, and any payment made in respect of the carrying on of any business or of any office or employment (s 310(7)). A person may receive income though he cannot legally sue for payment, as is the case with a barrister. However, income from capital that has vested in the trustee belongs to the trustee and is therefore not income in respect of which an income payments order may be made, unless, of course, the trustee has for some reason authorised the disclaimer.

(iii) Exempt property Exempt property comprises such tools, books, vehicles and other items of equipment as are necessary to the bankrupt for use personally by him in his employment, business or vocation, and such clothing, bedding, furniture, household equipment and provisions as are necessary for satisfying the basic domestic needs of the bankrupt and his family. However, even this property (or part of it) may now be claimed by the trustee if it appears to him to have a realisable value greater than the cost of a "reasonable replacement". In such a case the trustee may serve notice on the bankrupt under s 308, whereupon the property vests in him (see below).

(c) Replacement of exempt property

Property is a reasonable replacement for other property if it is reasonably adequate for meeting the needs met by the other property. The onus is on the trustee to provide funds for the bankrupt rather than go out and do the shopping himself. A notice by the trustee or his successor must be served within 42 days of the property first coming to his knowledge or on his appointment, whichever is the later.

The purchase may be made either before or after realisation of the value of the property. However, the trustee is under no obligation to apply funds to the purchase of a replacement for property vested in him, unless and until he has sufficient funds in the estate for that purpose.

Where a third party proposes that he should provide the estate with a sum of money in lieu of property which would otherwise vest in the trustee, then the trustee may accept the money, provided it is a reasonable amount, and provided that the estate will benefit to the extent of the value of the property in question, less the cost of a reasonable replacement.

However, it was the view of the Blagden Committee (Minutes 1957; HMSO Cmnd 59944) that a bankrupt should be allowed to keep the tools of his trade, apparel, bedding and other excluded property without replacement provided they had been used and worn, and whatever value they were; after property of that kind has been used it is a very clever man who is able to say "this or that is outside the limit, and we are going to take it away." (See also page 265 for the bankrupt's point of view.)

(d) Secured property

Where any goods of the bankrupt, whether or not comprised in the estate, are held by any person by way of pledge, pawn or other security, the official receiver may, after giving notice in writing of his intention to do so under s 285(5) inspect the goods. Thereafter that person is not entitled to realise his security without leave of the court, unless he has given the trustee a reasonable opportunity of inspecting the goods and of exercising the bankrupt's right of redemption. Security does not include a lien on books, paper or other records, except to the extent that they consist of documents which give a title to property and are held as such.

(e) Choses in action

These are deemed to have been asssigned to the trustee on adjudication (see also page 114). Notice need not be given except in so far as it is necessary for protecting the priority of the trustee, in a case where the deemed assignment is from the bankrupt himself.

(f) Goods pledged

The trustee may exercise his right of redemption in respect of any goods held by any person by way of pledge, pawn or other security. A notice served by the trustee has the same effect as a notice served by the official receiver under s 285(5) to inspect the goods and restrict their disposal (see above).

(g) Stocks and shares in a company

This includes shares in a ship or any other property transferable in the books of a company, office or person; the trustee may exercise the right to transfer the property to the same extent as the bankrupt might have exercised if he had not become bankrupt.

(h) Options to purchase

An option in personal or real property passes to the trustee who is entitled to intervene to exercise the option, as if he were the debtor; see *Mason* v *Schuppisser* (1899) 8 ITLT 147.

(i) Seizure

Any time after the making of a bankruptcy order, the court may, on the application of the official receiver or the trustee under s 365, issue a warrant authorising a person to seize any property in the estate comprising books, papers or records which are in the possession of or under the control of the bankrupt or any other person. They may break open any premises or receptacle which contains or is believed to contain anything that may be so seized.

(j) Concealment

If, after a bankruptcy order has been made, the court is satisfied that any property comprised in the estate is, or any books, papers or records relating to the bankrupt's estate or affairs are, concealed in any premises not belonging to him, it may issue a warrant authorising any constable or officer to search the premises and to seize any property of the bankrupt found. The search warrant (Form 7.13, not reproduced in this volume) must be executed in the prescribed manner and in accordance with its terms.

(k) Disposal of books, papers and other records

Provided he has authority from the official receiver, the trustee may sell, destroy or otherwise dispose of the bankrupt's books, papers and other records at any time during his tenure of office, or on vacating office. Administration records are, however, to be retained for not less than six years following his release.

(l) Mistake or fraud

The trustee has no better right to property delivered to a bankrupt under a mistake as to identity, or which has been obtained by him by fraud, than had the bankrupt. The true owner can recover it from the trustee just as he could have recovered it from the bankrupt. When the goods have been purchased on credit by the debtor with the fraudulent intention of not paying for them, the vendor, on discovering this fact is entitled to disaffirm the sale within a reasonable time, and retake possession of the goods although he has knowledge of the bankruptcy.

(m) Lien

The principle is the that trustee should have full access to all records. Therefore no person can enforce a lien on books, papers or records so as to prevent the trustee taking them into his possession (s 349). This provision does not, however, extend to documents which give title to property and are held as such.

4. Powers of the trustee in the administration

(a) General powers

The trustee has general powers of control, among which he may himself:

- (i) sell any part of the estate including goodwill and book debts of any business;
- (ii) give receipts which effectually discharge the person paying from all responsibility;
- (iii) prove, rank, claim and draw a dividend in respect of debts due to the bankrupt;
- (iv) exercise his powers under the Act;
- (v) deal with any property to which the bankrupt is beneficially entitled as tenant in tail;
- (vi) issue an invoice showing VAT,

which matters are covered in the text below (s 314(1), Sch 5 Part II).

(b) Sanction of the committee

With the permission of the committee (see page 221 *et seq*) , or failing that the court, he may:

- (vii) carry on any business so as to wind it up beneficially;
- (viii) bring or defend any action;
- (ix) accept a future consideration;
- (x) mortgage or pledge;
- (xi) exercise any right, option or other power;
- (xii) refer to arbitration;
- (xiii) make a compromise with debtors and creditors;
- (xiv) appoint the bankrupt:
    - to superintend the management of the estate;
    - to carry on his business (if any) for the benefit of his creditors;
    - to assist in administering the estate.

(s 314(1), Sch 5 Part I, set out in full at page 224).

Permission to exercise functions (vii) to (xiv) may not be given on a general basis but must be specific to each proposed exercise of the power in question. A person dealing with the trustee in good faith and for value is not to be concerned to enquire whether any permission required in either case has been given. Where the trustee has done anything without permission, the court or the creditors' committee may ratify what he has done to enable him to meet his expenses out of the bankrupt's estate.

(c) Ancillary powers

In connection with the exercise of any of his powers the trustee may, in his official name:

- (i) hold property of every description;
- (ii) make contracts;
- (iii) sue and be sued;

(iv) enter into any engagements binding on himself and, in respect of the bankrupt's estate, on his successors in office;
(v) employ an agent;
(vi) execute any power of attorney, deed or other instrument;
(vii) do anything else necessary or expedient for the purposes of or in connection with the exercise of those powers

(s 314(5), Sch 5 Part III).

(d) Bankruptcy of a plaintiff

The bankruptcy of the plaintiff in any action in a county court which the trustee might maintain for the benefit of the creditors does not cause the action to abate if, within such reasonable time as the court orders, the trustee elects to continue the action and to give security for the costs of the action. The hearing may be adjourned until such time as an election is made, and where the trustee does not elect to continue the action and to give security as required by the order, the defendant may avail himself of the bankruptcy as a defence to the action.

(e) The Crown

By s 434 the Act binds the Crown so far as affecting or relating to remedies against, or against the property of, individuals, priority of debts, transactions at an undervalue or preferences; voluntary arrangements approved under Part VIII; and discharge from bankruptcy.

(f) Application for directions

The trustee may apply to the court for directions in relation to any particular matter arising under the bankruptcy. See also pages 217 and 229.

(g) Employing agents

There are no published fee scales under the new legislation, for example for solicitors or estate agents acting at the instruction of the trustee. The fees are therefore a matter for separate negotiation between the parties, bearing in mind that taxation by the court is now discretionary. Thus if a creditors' committee so resolves, the trustee must require taxation (see page 257).

However, where the costs of anyone employed by the insolvency practitioner are required to be taxed, this does not preclude the practitioner making payments on account to such a person on the basis that the recipient will repay immediately, with interest, any money which may, on taxation, prove to have been overpaid.

If the trustee intends to appoint the bankrupt to superintend the management of his estate, to carry on his business or otherwise to assist with the administration he should obtain the permission of the creditors' committee or the court.

If there is a creditors' committee, the trustee must give notice to them if he disposes of any property comprised in the estate to an associate of the bankrupt, or if he employs a solicitor (s 314(6)(b)).

(h) Justices' licence

In the case of the bankruptcy of, or arrangement by, the holder of a justices' licence, the justices' licence is transferred to the insolvency practitioner. He is in the same position as regards carrying on the business under the licence as a person to whom a protection order had been validly granted on the date on which he became trustee or supervisor.

(i) Public utilities

The effect on supplies of gas, water, electricity and telephone when a bankruptcy order is made is that payment of any charges for supplies may be guaranteed by the office-holder. Public utilities cannot withhold supplies or make it a condition of supply that any charges outstanding before the relevant day are paid (s 372).

(j) As receiver

The trustee is in the same position as if he were a receiver of property appointed by the High Court for the purpose of acquiring or retaining possession of the bankrupt's estate.

(k) Right of redemption

Where any goods of an undischarged bankrupt (whether or not comprised in his estate) are held by any person by way of pledge, pawn or other security, the trustee must be given a reasonable opportunity of inspecting the goods and of exercising the bankrupt's right of redemption. This requirement does not affect the right of a secured creditor to enforce his security. As for the right of the official receiver to inspect the goods, see page 151.

(l) Saving

The acts of a person as trustee are valid notwithstanding any defect in the appointment, election or qualifications of the trustee. Where he has done anything without permission, the court or the creditors' committee may ratify what he has done to enable him to meet his expenses out of the bankrupt's estate.

(m) Tenant in tail

If the bankrupt is entitled to an entailed interest, the trustee may bar the entail and dispose of the land for the benefit of the creditors in accordance with his general powers (above). If property is settled upon a tenant for life, and then upon such of his children as may be living at his death, the future interest of a child who becomes bankrupt before his life tenant's death likewise passes to the trustee.

5. Duties of the trustee

(a) Administrative records

The trustee must keep administrative records containing:

(i) the minutes of any meeting of creditors and their committee, including a record of every resolution passed;

(ii) copies of every resolution by post (see page 227) and a note that the relevant concurrence was obtained; and

(iii) any other matter that may be necessary to give an accurate record of the administration.

For the records to be kept by an insolvency practitioner, see page 25.

(b) Capital gains tax

Section 61 Capital Gains Tax Act 1979 applies to the trustee as if the assets were vested in him, so that tax in respect of any chargeable gains which accrue to him are assessable on and recoverable from him. Acquisitions from, or disposals to him by, the bankrupt are disregarded. For CGT on the principal residence, see *Re Mesco Properties Ltd* [1980] 1 WLR 96 and page 137. The position of the trustee on the death of the bankrupt is different (see page 312).

(c) Confidentiality of documents

The trustee may refuse a person otherwise entitled, inspection of a document forming part of the records, where he considers that it should be treated as confidential or is of such a nature that its disclosure would be calculated to be injurious to the interests of the creditors.

(d) Copy accounts

If the trustee is asked by the bankrupt or any creditor for a copy of an account of his receipts and payments for any period (including future periods) he must send them a copy free of charge. The copy of the account should be sent within fourteen days either of his sending it for audit to the Secretary of State, or fourteen days of the request, whichever is the later.

(e) Copyright

By virtue of the Copyright Act 1956 (Amendment) Act 1982, amending s 21 of the 1956 Act, the trustee may need to be personally aware that any person who, at the time when copyright subsists in a sound recording or in a cinematograph film by way of trade, has in his possession any article which he knows to be an infringing copy of the sound recording or film, is guilty of an offence.

(f) Creditors

The trustee's general duty to hold creditors' meetings is considered at page 212 and his duty to report to the creditors' committee is discussed at page 222.

(g) Financial records

The trustee should prepare and keep separate financial records for each insolvent for whom he is trustee, and enter all receipts and payments. The financial records must be submitted to the creditors' committee when required. If the committee is dissatisfied with the accounts, they may inform the Secretary of State, with their reasons, and request the Secretary of State to require an audit.

Where the trustee carries on the business of the bankrupt, he must:

(i) keep separate trading accounts, including, if appropriate, particulars of all local bank account transactions; and

(ii) incorporate into the financial records the total weekly amounts of the receipts and payments made in relation to the trading account.

He is required to submit his accounts of the administration for annual audit by the Secretary of State (see page 253).

(h) Land registration

Where any amendment in the land register appears to be required, it is the duty of the official receiver, or the trustee if by then appointed, to suggest such amendment to the registrar as soon as it comes to his knowledge. The registrar must then, after making such inquiries and giving such notice, if any, as he thinks necessary, make such amendment in the register as appropriate (see also page 145).

(i) Notices

All notices required or authorised must be in writing unless it is otherwise provided in the Act or Rules or the court allows the notice to be given in some other way. The sending or giving of it may be proved by means of a certificate that the notice was duly posted, which may be endorsed on a copy or specimen of the notice to which it relates.

(j) Duty of trustee to official receiver

It is the duty of the trustee to furnish the official receiver with such information as he may reasonably require for the purpose of enabling him to carry out his functions in relation to the bankruptcy. The trustee is also required to produce such books, papers and other records as the official receiver may reasonably require and to assist him generally.

(k) Stamp duty

Stamp duty is not charged on any document in bankruptcy, namely a deed, conveyance, assignment, surrender, admission or other assurance.

6. Redundancy fund

Following the termination of his employment by the trustee (or official receiver when so acting), an employee is given the right to claim unpaid wages or salary through the Secretary of State from a redundancy fund established under the Redundancy Payments Act 1965 (now the Employment Protection (Consolidation) Act 1978), provided that at the relevant date the employee was entitled to be paid the whole or any part of any debt following the termination of his employment.

This gives recognition to an employee's rights in his job and, by giving some financial protection on the insolvency of his employer, is designed to mitigate the hardship caused.

In addition the Secretary of State is given the power to pay out of the redundancy fund, and into an occupational pension scheme, certain unpaid contributions to that scheme which are due from an insolvent employer. Before such a payment from the redundancy fund may be made, the following conditions must have been fulfilled:

- (i) a written application for payment into the funds of the scheme must be made to the Secretary of State by the trustee or official receiver;
- (ii) the Secretary of State must be satisfied as to the employer's insolvency and that at the date of insolvency any relevant contributions had been unpaid and were still owing to the scheme;
- (iii) the Secretary of State must have received, in a case where a trustee or receiver or manager has been or is required to be appointed, a statement from such officer of the apparent amount of the unpaid contributions on the date on which the employer became insolvent and remain unpaid.
- (iv) the amounts calculated under (i) - (iii) and the sum payable in respect of the employer's unpaid contributions must have been certified by the relevant officer, eg the trustee.

In certain circumstances, however, the Secretary of State may, on the request of the persons making the application, or of his own motion, make a payment into the funds of the scheme even though no statement or certificate has been received.

Any persons who are competent to act in respect of an occupational pension scheme or a personal pension scheme and who have applied for a payment to be made into the resources of the scheme may, within a period of three months beginning with the date on which the decision of the Secretary of State on that application was communicated to them, or if that is not reasonably practicable, within such further period as is reasonable, present a complaint to an industrial tribunal that the Secretary of State has failed to make such payment, or that any such payment made by him is less than the amount which should have been paid. Where the tribunal finds that the Secretary of State ought to make the payment it must make a declaration to that effect and must also declare the amount of any such payment which it finds he ought to make.

Under the Employment Act 1978 the employee may make an application in writing to the Secretary of State and claim for the following:

(i) any arrears of pay, up to £158 per week, in respect of the whole or any part of the period or periods not exceeding sixteen weeks before the relevant date; and

(ii) any amount which the employer is liable to pay the employee, up to £158 per week, for the minimum period of notice required under the Employment Act or for any failure of the employer to give the required period of notice; and

(iii) any holiday remuneration, up to £158 per week, in respect of any period of employment before the relevant date; and

(iv) any basic award of compensation for unfair dismissal; and

(v) any reasonable sum by way of reimbursement of the whole or part of any fee or premium paid by an apprentice or articled clerk.

By virtue of s 218(4) of the 1985 Act and s 122(4) of the Employment Act "arrears of pay" includes a guarantee payment, remuneration on suspension on medical grounds, any payment for time off, remuneration under a protective award made under s 101 of the Employment Protection Act 1975, and statutory sick pay payable under Part I of the Social Security and Housing Benefits Act 1982.

Any remuneration payable by the debtor to a person in respect of a period of holiday or of absence from work through sickness or other good cause is deemed to be wages or salary in respect of services rendered to the debtor in that period. References to remuneration in respect of a period of holiday include any sums which, if they had been paid, would have been treated for the purposes of the enactments relating to social security as earnings in respect of that period.

The minimum statutory periods of notice are one week where employment has continued for four weeks or more but less than two years; one week for each year of employment if it has continued for two years or more but for less than twelve years; and twelve weeks where the employment exceeds twelve years.

"Holiday remuneration" means pay in respect of a holiday actually taken, or any accrued holiday pay which under the employee's contract of employment would in the ordinary course have become payable to him in respect of the period of a holiday if his employment had continued until he became entitled to be allowed the holiday. It is payable in respect of any period of employment before the relevant date, to a person whose employment by the debtor has been terminated, whether before, on or after that date.

"Reasonable sum", for the purposes of (v) above, has the same meaning as in s 348, ie as the trustee thinks fit in the light of the amount of the fee, the proportion of the period in respect of which the fee was paid that has been served by the apprentice or clerk before the commencement of the bankruptcy, and the other circumstances of the case.

The "relevant date" for determining debts payable out of the fund means, in relation to arrears of pay (not being remuneration under a protective award made under s 101 of the Employment Protection Act 1975) and to holiday pay, the date on which the employer became insolvent; in relation to such an award and to a basic award of compensation for unfair dismissal, it means whichever is the latest of:

(i) the date on which the employer becamc insolvent;
(ii) the date of the termination of the employee's employment; and
(iii) the date on which the award was made.

In relation to any other debt, it means whichever is the later of the dates in (i) and (ii) above (s 218(3) 1985 Act amending s 122(2) Employment Act).

The sums referred to are subject to review and may be varied by the Secretary of State. Although arrears of pay, holiday pay and payments in lieu of notice over £800 are not given preferential status and are therefore not covered by the scheme, the debts in respect of a basic award and reimbursement of apprentice's or articled clerk's fees may be settled in full unless it is possible to transfer the indenture or articles to another employer (and see page 232 as to priority payment).

In respect of a period shorter than one week, the amount payable is an amount bearing the same proportion to £158 as that shorter period bears to a week.

An employee must give credit for any sums which he has earned in other employment during the period of notice. Where these sums equal or exceed the amount of compensation to which the employee is entitled, because he has suffered no loss he is *not* entitled to make a claim: see *Secretary of State for Employment* v *Wilson* (1978) ICR 200.

The Department of Employment makes clear that the employee is under a duty to reduce his or her loss to a minimum, for example by claiming all social security benefits to which he is entitled, by making every effort to find a new job and by drawing his contractual salary in new employment during the notice period. If the employee could have reduced the loss but did not, compensation will be reduced by the value of the unclaimed benefits or the amount that could have been earned from the new job.

Although insolvency practitioners do not appear to owe a duty to employees of the insolvent firm, they are discouraged from seeking to take advantage of employees under an existing contract. In *Nicholl* v *Cutts* TLR 20 May 1985 where a receiver appointed under the winding-up provisions of the 1985 Act, only terminated a contract of employment some weeks after his appointment and did not pay the employee's wages for this period, the employee tried to make the receiver personally responsible but failed because the contract of employment was a contract entered into prior to the appointment of the insolvency practitioner. So far as insolvent limited companies are concerned, the matter has probably been corrected by a new s 37; the position of the special manager in bankruptcy, however, appears to remain as stated above.

Any debt owed in excess of the statutory limits may of course be proved as a non-preferential debt.

7. After-acquired property

(a) By the bankrupt

Section 307 applies to property acquired by the bankrupt before he obtains his discharge which, with the exception of income, passes to the trustee. Upon service of a notice by the trustee on the bankrupt the property vests in the trustee as part of the estate, with the trustee's title having relation back to the time at which it was acquired by, or devolved upon, the bankrupt. It is immaterial that the person dealing with the bankrupt has notice of the bankruptcy provided that the transaction is *bona fide* and for value; see *Hunt* v *Fripp* [1898] 1 Ch 675.

By s 309 the notice must be served by the trustee or his successor within 42 days of the acquisition or devolution of the property first coming to his knowledge, or on his appointment, whichever is the later.

(b) From the bankrupt

However, the trustee is not entitled to property which a person acquired from the bankrupt *in good faith, for value and without notice* of the bankruptcy. This also applies where a banker enters into a transaction without such notice. Provided that he can show good faith he is protected from action by the trustee to recover the property or its value where the transaction was completed before intervention on the part of the trustee.

If the bankrupt disposes of property before giving notice to the trustee, or otherwise in contravention of Rule 6.200, the trustee may serve notice on the person to whom it has been transferred, claiming the property as part of the estate under s 307(3). This notice must be served within 28 days of the trustee's becoming aware of the disponee's identity and an address at which he can be served. Any expenses incurred are paid out of the estate in the prescribed order of priority.

If the bankrupt without reasonable excuse fails to comply with any obligation imposed he is guilty of contempt of court and liable to be punished accordingly. Income, which may be the subject of an income payments order under s 310, is not included in after-acquired property.

(c) Bankrupt carrying on business

Where the bankrupt is continuing to trade with permission, problems could arise if the trustee were to use s 307 to intervene in the course of business to claim, for example, stock-in-trade, for the creditors of the estate. However, by the rule in *Troughton* v *Gitley* (1766) 27 ER 408, the trustee is estopped from claiming any after-acquired property from a creditor where he knows that the creditor was relying on the bankrupt's apparent ownership. For the rule to be effective it appears that the trustee should know that the bankrupt is so trading and has received the permission of the creditors' committee or the court under s 314(2)(b). Likewise, if he afterwards gets the consent of the creditors to sell the business to the bankrupt before he has obtained his discharge, then the creditors would not be allowed to claim the profits of the bankrupt thereby acquired ; see *Re Caughey ex parte Ford* [1876] 1 Ch 521. As to the bankrupt's duty to the trustee, see page 271.

8. Second bankruptcy

Where the existing trustee has been given notice of the presentation of the petition for the later bankruptcy (by Form 6.78) any distribution or other disposition by him of any property or money is void except to the extent that it was made with the consent of the court, or is or was subsequently ratified by the court.

Under s 335, with effect from the commencement of a later bankruptcy, anything which is comprised in the estate of an undischarged bankrupt is to be treated as comprised in the estate under the second bankruptcy. Pending the appointment of a trustee of that estate, it is administered by the first trustee.

Any sums which are payable under an income payments order (see page 272) are payable after the commencement of the later bankruptcy to the existing trustee, but form part of the second bankruptcy. The court may give consequential directions modifying the income payments order. There is a first charge in favour of the existing trustee, for any bankruptcy expenses incurred by him in relation to anything comprised in the first bankruptcy, whether in the hands of the first or later trustee. Personal property of the bankrupt exceeding a reasonable replacement value is not included in the second bankruptcy.

The creditors of the bankrupt in an earlier bankruptcy cannot be creditors in a later bankruptcy for the same debts. By s 335(5) the existing trustee may prove in the later bankruptcy for:

- (a) the unsatisfied balance of the debts (including the same debts in both bankruptcies) provable against the bankrupt's estate in the earlier bankruptcy;
- (b) any interest payable on that balance; and
- (c) any unpaid expenses of the earlier bankruptcy.

However, any of these amounts provable rank in priority after all the other debts provable in the later bankruptcy, and after interest on those debts. Accordingly, amounts outstanding under the earlier bankruptcy are not paid unless the debts and interest of the second bankruptcy are paid out in full (see Chapter 16).

Rules 6.226 and 6.227 provide for the handover from the trustee in the earlier bankruptcy to the trustee in the later bankruptcy:

"6.226 - (1) Subject as follows, the existing trustee shall take into his custody or under his control all such property and money, in so far as he has not already done so as part of his duties as trustee in the earlier bankruptcy.

(2) Where any of that property consists of perishable goods, or goods the value of which is likely to diminish if they are not disposed of, the existing trustee has power to sell or otherwise dispose of those goods.

(3) The proceeds of any such sale or disposal shall be held, under the existing trustee's control, with the other property and money comprised in the bankrupt's estate.

6.227 The existing trustee shall, as and when requested by the trustee for the purposes of the later bankruptcy, deliver up to the latter all such property and money as is in his custody or under his control in pursuance of Rule 6.226."

The existing trustee (not the individual creditors) will be treated as a creditor with a right to prove in the later bankruptcy for the unsatisfied balance of the debts in the first bankruptcy, any interest payable on that balance, as well as for any unpaid expenses. This right cannot be barred by lapse of time: see *Re Cullwick* [1918] 1 KB 646.

9. Reciprocal jurisdiction inside and outside England and Wales

Where a trustee claims property situated in any part of the UK, then, under s 426, he has the same rights in respect of it in all other parts of the UK, and the courts in those other parts must assist.

Likewise, nothing in the Act is to be construed as restricting the capacity of the trustee to exercise any of his powers outside England and Wales (s 314(8)), particularly in the relevant countries and territories (SI 1986 No 2123), including parts of the Commonwealth as well as the Republic of Ireland; the courts have a reciprocal duty to assist those courts having corresponding jurisdiction in any relevant country or territory overseas. For example, the Federal and Supreme Courts of Australia have a duty to act in aid of prescribed countries including the UK, and the appropriate order is for the official receiver of the relevant district to be appointed receiver in Australia; see *Re Ayres* (1981) 51 FLR 395.

In the Channel Islands, the Jersey en d'ésastre proceedings were held to be proceedings in bankruptcy, whereby the Viscount of the Royal Court of Jersey could be appointed to give effect to an order in aid, as receiver (without security) of all the movable property of the debtor (an English solicitor); see *In Re a Debtor, Viscount of the Royal Court of Jersey* v *the Debtor* TLR 20 May 1980.

Chapter 12

Administration - prior transactions

1. Introduction

This chapter is concerned with what used to be known as "antecedent transactions", now called "prior transactions", and their particular effect on trustees' title and property available to the creditors.

The aim of the law, both then and now, is to benefit the creditors by avoiding any unsatisfactory dealings by the debtor within a period before the bankruptcy, and, basically, to restore the position to what it would have been if the transaction had not been entered into. The law is concerned with relating back transactions entered into prior to the commencement of the bankruptcy and catching those deemed unacceptable to the general body of creditors in the subsequent bankruptcy.

The vesting of property in the trustee is effective on the making of the bankruptcy order, and may relate back further by reference to "relevant time" so as basically to restore the position to what it would been if subsequent transactions had not been entered into. Conversely the trustee might not like what he now finds vested in his possession and he may disclaim any unprofitable contracts as unsaleable property even though he has taken possession of them. Certain settlements by a debtor are cancelled by the bankruptcy or are at the least voidable by the trustee; further a landlord who has distrained for rent is only entitled to rent for six months; and unless he has completed the execution or attachment before the commencement of the bankruptcy, the execution creditor may not retain the proceeds unless the judgment debt is for less than £500.

There are, on the other hand, important exceptions to this traumatic interference with past dealings, for protection is given by the Act to certain *bona fide* transactions.

2. Relevant time

Preferences (s 340) and transactions at an undervalue (s 339) assume significance if made at a "relevant time" (s 341). The relevant time varies according to the type of transaction and whether or not the debtor is insolvent at the time.

The old law provided for the avoidance of transactions which took place prior to the commencement of the bankruptcy and which could be considered unacceptable to the body of creditors in the subsequent bankruptcy. The new legislation redefines the time limit by reference to the "relevant time" for transactions at an undervalue or preferences; for extortionate credit transactions the time limit is, more simply, three years before the commencement of the bankruptcy.

The time a transaction was entered into by a debtor prior to the bankruptcy, which determines whether or not it can be swept up by the trustee into his vesting bowl, varies:

(a) Three to six months

A landlord has the right, subject to conditions, to distrain for six months rent; however he may not be able to keep it all, for if it turns out that he has distrained within three months of the adjudication, the debts to which priority is given are a first charge on the goods or proceeds. In the case of a preference which is not a transaction at an undervalue (or to an associate) the relevant time is six months and ends with the day on which the petition is presented, and not afterwards.

(b) Two years

In the case of a preference which is not a transaction at an undervalue and is given to a person who is an associate of the individual (provided he is not an employee), the time is two years ending with the day on which the petition is presented.

(c) Three years

This term is relevant where the bankrupt has received credit in respect of a transaction which is extortionate or exorbitant, so that the terms may, for example, be varied or set aside for a period three years back.

(d) Five years

In the case of a transaction at an undervalue, then the relevant time is the period of five years ending with the day on which the bankruptcy petition is presented.

A fraudulent disposal can be clawed back for up to five years before the bankruptcy.

It is to be observed that s 341 does not apply where a preference or transaction at an undervalue is given *after* the presentation of the petition in bankruptcy, so that by *Re Seymour* [1937] Ch 668 such a transaction is protected under s 342 (see page 167).

3. Contracts to which the debtor was a party

(a) Contracts not protected

On the application of any other party to the contract, the court may make an order under s 345 discharging obligations under a contract made with a person who is subsequently adjudged bankrupt, on terms as to payment by the applicant or the bankrupt of damages for non-performance or otherwise as appear to the court to be equitable. Where an undischarged bankrupt is a contractor in respect of any contract jointly with any person, that person may sue or be sued in respect of the contract without the joinder of the bankrupt. Any damages payable by the bankrupt under the order are provable as a bankruptcy debt.

(b) Contracts protected

All contracts with persons providing income to the bankrupt are protected whether or not they take place after the commencement of the bankruptcy; they are therefore not void as against the trustee. This protection is afforded by s 310 and comprises "every payment in the nature of income which is from time to time made to him or to which he from time to time becomes entitled and includes the carrying on of any business or in respect of any office or employment" (s 310(7)).

(c) Transactions deemed to be retrospective

Certain transactions by and with the bankrupt are protected in certain circumstances, either during the initial period or after the making of the bankruptcy order, and are deemed to be retrospective to the day prior to the making of the bankruptcy order:

- *(i)* *De minimus debts*: In the matter of a small debt, unless a person had notice of the bankruptcy, and it is not reasonably practicable for the amount of the payment to be recovered from the person to whom it was made, the debt is deemed to have been incurred before the commencement of the bankruptcy.
- *(ii)* *Debt to a banker:* In the case where the bankrupt incurred a debt to his banker, or other person, after the commencement of his bankruptcy (and which would thereby be void under s 284(1) - see below) that debt is nevertheless deemed to have been incurred before the commencement of the bankruptcy unless either the banker or other person had notice of the bankruptcy before the debt was incurred, or it is not reasonably practicable for the amount of the payment to be recovered (s 284(5)). This prevents the trustee from claiming any amounts paid into the credit of the debtor's account without allowing the bank a *contra* credit for any amounts withdrawn during the period that they are unaware of the bankruptcy.

As to the date when a payment by cheque is received, see *Re Hone* [1951] 1 Ch 85 discussed in *Parkside Leasing Ltd* v *Smith* [1985] 1 WLR 310.

For reference to the meaning of "insolvency" under the Banking Act 1987, see s 59 of that Act with reference to the deposit protection fund established by s 21 Banking Act 1979.

(d) Assignment of book debts

Before 1913 an assignment made by a trader of book debts due or to become due to him in his business was valid against his trustee in bankruptcy unless the debts were still in his order and disposition at the commencement of bankruptcy (or unless the assignment was fraudulent). There was no need to register the assignment under the Bills of Sale Act 1878 because choses in action were excluded from the definition of "personal chattels" given in s 4 of that Act.

Since then, however, and re-enacted in the 1986 Act (see s 344), a general assignment to another person of his existing or future book debts, or any class thereof (including an assignment by way of security or charge on book debts), will be void against the trustee in his subsequent bankruptcy to the extent of any debts which have not been paid before the presentation of the bankruptcy petition, unless the assignment has been registered as if it were a bill of sale.

A general assignment does not, however, include an assignment of book debts due at the date of the assignment from specified debtors or of debts becoming due under specified contracts, or an assignment of book debts included either in a transfer of a business made in good faith and for value, or in an assignment of assets for the benefit of creditors generally.

For the purposes of registration under the Act of 1878 an assignment of book debts is to be treated as if it were a bill of sale given otherwise than by way of security for the payment of a sum of money. The provisions of that Act with respect to the registration of bills of sale apply accordingly, with such necessary modifications as may be made by rules under that Act.

4. Effect on bankruptcy of a transaction at an undervalue or preference

Following bankruptcy, the court may under s 342 make an order affecting the property or imposing an obligation either on the person with whom the bankrupt entered into the transaction at undervalue, or on the person to whom a preference was given. Such an order may:

(a) require any property transferred or proceeds received to be vested in or returned to the trustee as part of the estate;

(b) require any property to be vested if it represents the proceeds of sale of property or money so transferred;

(c) release or discharge any security given by the individual in whole or in part;

(d) require any person to pay, in respect of benefits received by him from the individual, such sums to the trustee as the court may direct;

(e) provide for any surety or guarantor whose obligations to any person were released or discharged, in whole or in part, under the transaction or by the giving of the preference to be under such new or revived obligations to that person as the court thinks appropriate;

(f) require security to be provided for the discharge of any obligation imposed by or arising under the order, to be charged to the property, and for the security or charge to have the same priority as a security or charge released or discharged (in whole or in part) under the transaction or by the giving of the preference; and

(g) provide for the extent to which any person whose property is vested by the order, or on whom obligations are imposed, to be able to prove in the bankruptcy for debts or other liabilities which arose from, or were released or discharged in whole or in part under or by the transaction or the giving of the preference.

The order may affect the property of, or impose an obligation on, any person whether or not he was the individual who benefited from the transaction or preference. However, it should not prejudice any interest in property which was acquired from a person, other than that individual, in good faith, for value and without notice of the relevant circumstances, or prejudice any interest deriving from such an interest. Where a person received a benefit from the transaction or preference in good faith, for value and without notice of the relevant circumstances, then the order should not require him to repay it, unless he was a party to the transaction, or the payment required by the order is to be in respect of a preference given to him when he was a creditor of the person benefiting from the transaction or preference.

5. Void settlements by the debtor

Certain settlements are void as against the trustee. This means that the settlement is avoided from the time when the trustee takes title to the property; consequently until then it is "voidable": see *Re Brall* (1893) 2 QB 381. Anyone who claims under the settlement for valuable consideration without notice of the bankruptcy therefore has a good title.

(a) Disposition of property after presentation of petition

Any disposition of property by the bankrupt, including payment in cash or otherwise, in the period beginning with the day of the presentation of the petition and ending with the vesting of the bankrupt's estate in a trustee, is void (s 284(1)). The exception is where it is or was made with the consent of the court or is or was subsequently ratified by the court. Such a disposition of property is void notwithstanding that the property is not, or would not be, comprised in the bankrupt's estate. However, any disposition made in respect of trust property is *not* affected.

"Protected dealings" include those concerning property or payments received before the commencement of the bankruptcy, in good faith, for value and without notice that the petition had been presented, and remain enforceable despite the bankruptcy. Any interest in property deriving out of such a dealing is also protected.

(a) Extortionate credit transactions

Section 343 is new to the world of bankruptcy and derives in part from s 138 of the Consumer Credit Act 1974, to apply to a bankrupt who has received credit within the three years preceding the commencement of the bankruptcy. The 1974 Act is thereby extended to give the trustee (in place of the debtor), as well as the surety (if any), the right to apply to the court for an order with respect to the transaction, if the transaction is or was extortionate and was not entered into more than three years before the commencement of the bankruptcy.

A transaction is extortionate if, having regard to the risk accepted by the person providing the credit, the terms of it are or were such as to require grossly exorbitant payments to be made (whether unconditionally or in certain contingencies) in respect of the provision of credit, or it otherwise grossly contravened ordinary principles of fair dealing. The "persuasive" burden of proof rests throughout on the creditor, for it is an express presumption that a transaction to which the application relates is extortionate unless the contrary is proved. If the trustee has sufficient evidence to raise the issue in the first place, it is therefore for the creditor to satisfy the court that the credit bargain was in fact not extortionate. It is, however, necessary for the office holder initially to prove the "evidential burden", ie sufficient evidence to raise the issue that the transaction was extortionate in the first instance.

Relevant factors so far as the debtor is concerned include his age, experience, business capacity and state of health, and the degree to which, at the time of making the credit bargain, he was under financial pressure, including the nature of the pressure.

For a consideration of the factors that should be taken into account in determining whether payments are grossly exorbitant, it is submitted that reference needs to be made directly to the 1974 Act, in particular as to whether or not the interest charged is excessive having regard to the interest rates prevailing at the time it was made. Other factors that come into play include whether or not the advance was secured; the degree of risk having regard to any security provided; the relationship of the creditor to the debtor; (ie whether the transaction was a linked transaction - see below) and whether or not a cash price was quoted for any goods or services included in the credit bargain. An excessive rate of interest may not of itself render the repayments grossly exorbitant.

"Otherwise grossly contravened ordinary principles of fair dealing" might apply where the repayments are excessive but not so excessive as to be grossly exorbitant, or other circumstances might be present which enable the court to say that they grossly contravene the ordinary principles of fair dealing. The court, however, is by subs (3) to have regard to the risk accepted by the person providing the credit. As to the degree of risk, it is not what the real risk transpired to be, as ascertained after the event, which has to be looked at, but how the matter presented itself to the lender at the time of the loan, with the experience he certainly would have had of borrowers; see *Carringtons Ltd* v *Smith* [1906] 1 KB 179.

In considering a "linked transaction" under the Consumer Credit Act, the question is how far the transaction was reasonably required for the protection of the debtor or creditor, or was in the interest of the debtor or was entered into in compliance with a term of the principal agreement. A transaction is "linked" where it is entered into by the debtor or hirer or a relative of his with any other person (s 19 of that Act).

(c) Order of the court in respect of extortionate credit transactions

Under s 343(4) an order of the court in respect of an extortionate credit transaction may provide for one or more of the following:

(i) setting aside the whole or part of any obligation created by the transaction;

(ii) varying the terms of the transaction or the terms on which any security is held;

(iii) requiring any person who is or was party to the transaction to pay the trustee any sums paid to that person by virtue of the transaction, by the bankrupt;

(iv) requiring any person to surrender to the trustee any property held by him as security for the purposes of the transaction;

(v) directing accounts to be taken between any persons.

Any sum or property required to be paid or surrendered to the trustee in accordance with an order of the court is comprised in the bankrupt's estate.

A credit agreement may generally be reopened under the Consumer Credit Act on an application by the debtor or surety on the ground that it is extortionate, but in the case of a bankrupt's estate, neither the trustee nor the undischarged bankrupt is entitled to make such an application in respect of any agreement by which credit is or has been provided to the bankrupt. Nonetheless, by s 343(6) of the 1986 Act, the powers under s 343 described above are exercisable concurrently with any other powers under the Act in relation to that transaction as one at an undervalue.

(d) Fraudulent dispositions

The bankrupt is guilty of an offence under s 357 if he makes any gift, transfer of or charge on his property within a period of five years of the commencement of the bankruptcy, unless he proves that at the time of the conduct constituting the offence, he had no intent to defraud. If a debtor acts innocently but on the advice of an agent who acts fraudulently, the payment will still be fraudulent; see *Re Drabble Bros* [1930] 2 Ch 211.

The reference to the making of a "transfer of" or a "charge on" any property includes causing or conniving at the levying of any execution against that property. To prove the intention to prefer, evidence of other acts of fraudulent preference committed by the debtor about the same time, may be presented; see *Re Ramsay ex parte Deacon* [1913] 2 KB 80.

When a transaction is impeached as a fraudulent preference then it must be proved that the debtor was insolvent at the time and that he made the payment or transfer with the intention of preferring the creditor or surety; see *Re Laurie ex parte Green* (1898) 46 WR 491, except that it is not necessary to show this as the debtor's sole motive; see *Re Bird, ex parte Hill* (1883) 459 LT 278. The court must be satisfied under s 423(3) that the transaction was entered into by the debtor for the purposes of:

(i) putting assets beyond the reach of a person who is making, or may at some time make, a claim against him; or
(ii) otherwise prejudicing the interests of such a person in relation to the claims which he is making or may make.

If so the order made by the court under s 423(2) will:
(i) restore the position to what it would have been if the transaction had not been entered into; and
(ii) protect the interests of persons who are victims of the transaction.

6. Voidable settlements of the debtor

Certain settlements made prior to the bankruptcy may be avoided by the bankruptcy of the settlor. The court may restore the position to what it would have been if the transaction had not been entered into, to protect the interests of persons who are victims of the transaction. The court must be satisfied that the purpose was to put assets beyond the reach of a creditor who is making, or may at some time make, a claim against him, or otherwise to prejudice the interests of such a person in relation to the claim which he is making or may make. "Transactions" include a gift, agreement or arrangement and references to entering into a transaction are construed accordingly (s 436).

The application is made to the court by the official receiver, the trustee, a victim of the transaction (with the leave of the court where the debtor has been adjudged bankrupt), or by the supervisor of a voluntary arrangement. However, any application made is to be treated as made on behalf of every victim of the transaction.

The section only applies to dealings between debtor and creditor; "creditor" is, nevertheless, given a wide meaning to include any person, including a surety, who at the date of the payment or charge is entitled to prove in the bankruptcy; see *Re Blackpool Motor Car Co Ltd* [1901] 1 Ch 77.

An individual enters into a transaction with a person at an undervalue (s 339) or with a view to defrauding creditors (s 423; see page 173) by putting assets beyond their reach or otherwise prejudicing their interests in relation to a claim they are making or may make, in the following circumstances:

(a) Consideration missing

Where the debtor makes a gift to the other person or he otherwise enters into a transaction with the other on terms that provide for him to receive no consideration, that transaction is voidable on application to the court under s 339.

(b) Preference

Where the debtor gives a preference which has been *influenced* by what is termed "a desire to produce in relation to that person", ie in the event of the individual's bankruptcy, a better position than he would have been in if that thing had not been done, then that settlement is voidable. It is to be noted that the presumption of fraudulence enshrined in the earlier legislation has been done away with in favour of *proof of influence*.

Thus an individual gives a preference to a person where:

(i) that person is one of the individual's creditors or a surety or guarantor for any of his debts and liabilities; and

(ii) the individual does anything or suffers anything to be done which (in either case) has the effect of putting that person into a position which, in the event of the individual's bankruptcy, will be better than the position he would have been in if that thing had not been done (s 340(3)).

The trustee may apply to the court for an order to restore the position to what it would have been if the individual adjudged bankrupt had not given that preference. In *Re FP and GH Mathews Ltd* [1982] Ch 257 the bank was sued to set aside a preference and so enjoined the guarantor, who had been the beneficiary of the preferential payment, in the action.

Where a preference has been given to an associate (other than an employee) he is presumed to have been influenced by the desire referred to unless the contrary intention is shown. It is up to the creditor to satisfy the court that he was not a preferred creditor at the time:

> "For example, there would be nothing wrong in paying a brother-in-law, but if it could be proved that the brother-in-law was a preferred creditor because of evidence that the debtor was insolvent at the time, he would be debarred by the [section - 340(5)]. We have said that it is up to the creditor to satisfy the court that he was not a preferred creditor at the time." (*Hansard*: Standing Committee E 18 June 1985 Col 410).

The fact that something has been done following the order of the court does not, without more, prevent that thing from constituting the giving of a preference.

(c) On marriage

If a person enters into a transaction at an undervalue with another person in consideration of marriage, the court may make an order to claim back the assets under s 339.

(d) Undervalue

Where an individual entered into a transaction at an undervalue or gave a preference at a time mentioned above (but, in the case of a transaction at an undervalue, within two years of the end of the period), then that time is only relevant if he is insolvent or becomes insolvent in consequence of the transaction or preference. For these purposes, an individual is insolvent if he is unable to pay his debts as they fall due, or the value of his assets is less than the amount of his liabilities, taking into account his contingent and prospective liabilities.

The debtor enters into a transaction with another person where the value of the consideration in money or money's worth, is significantly less than the value of the consideration provided by himself, the court may make an order to restore the position under s 339.

In so far as he has entered into any such transaction with an "associate", other than an employee of his, these requirements are presumed to be satisfied, unless the contrary is shown.

(e) Property adjustment orders

A property adjustment order may be made under s 24 Matrimonial Causes Act 1973 following on, or after, the granting of a decree of divorce, nullity or judicial separation, to settle property on the children, spouse or family. The fact that a settlement or transfer had to be made in order to comply with such an order does not by s 39 of the 1973 Act prevent the settlement or transfer from being a settlement of property to which the Insolvency Act applies with the consequence that flows therefrom. The trustee may accordingly challenge it as being either a transaction at an undervalue or at a preference, and apply to the court for an order under s 339 or 340 respectively of that Act. As to relinquishing the ex-wife's claim to a property adjustment order, see page 140.

7. Provisions against debt avoidance which may be made by order under s 423

An application may be made to the court under s 424 by the trustee, supervisor or the debtor, to correct a (voidable) settlement. Section 425(1) provides:

"(1) Without prejudice to the generality of section 423, an order made under that section with respect to a transaction may (subject as follows)-

(a) require any property transferred as part of the transaction to be vested in any person, either absolutely or for the benefit of all the persons on whose behalf the application for the order is treated as made;

(b) require any property to be so vested if it represents, in any person's hands, the application either of the proceeds of sale of property so transferred or of money so transferred;

(c) release or discharge (in whole or in part) any security given by the debtor;

(d) require any person to pay to any other person in respect of benefits received from the debtor such sums as the court may direct;

(e) provide for any surety or guarantor whose obligations to any person were released or discharged (in whole or in part) under the transaction to be under such new or revived obligations as the court thinks appropriate;

(f) provide for security to be provided for the discharge of any obligation imposed by or arising under the order, for such an obligation to be

> charged on any property and for such security or charge to have the same priority as a security or charge released or discharged (in whole or in part) under the transaction."

"Security" means any mortgage, charge, lien or other security.

An order under s 425(2) may affect the property of, or impose any obligation on, any person whether or not he is the person with whom the debtor entered into the transaction.

However, such an order may not:

- (i) prejudice any interest in property which was acquired from a person (other than the debtor in good faith, for value and without notice of the relevant circumstances;
- (ii) prejudice any interest deriving from such an interest;
- (iii) require a person who received a benefit from the transaction in good faith, for value and without notice of the relevant circumstances to pay any sum unless he was a party to the transaction.

The "relevant circumstances" in relation to a transaction are the circumstances by virtue of which an order under s 423 may be made in respect of the transaction. For the transitional arrangements, see page 185.

8. Distress for rent

A landlord or other person to whom rent is payable has the right, either before or after the commencement of the bankruptcy, to distrain for rent upon the goods and effects of an undischarged bankrupt comprised in the bankrupt's estate. However, this remedy is available in respect of six months' rent only accrued due before the commencement of the bankruptcy (s 347), except that, unlike under the old law, this is not limited by a date and can now suit the landlord's pleasure. Thereafter the landlord has the right to prove in the bankruptcy in respect of remaining rent (if any).

Where a distraint has been made before a bankruptcy order, any amount recovered by way of that distress which is in excess of six months' rent or is in respect of rent for a period or part of a period after the distress was levied is held for the bankrupt as part of his estate. For a case under the old s 41(1) where the notice of a receiving order was served on the sheriff after the goods were taken in execution but before the execution was completed, see *Re Cooper (A Bankrupt) ex parte Trustee* v *Registrar and High Bailiff of the Peterborough and Huntingdon County Courts* [1958] Ch 922.

Where any person has distrained upon the goods or effects of an individual who is adjudged bankrupt before the end of three months beginning with the distraint, so much of those goods or effects, or of the proceeds of their sale as is not held for the bankrupt is charged for the benefit of the bankrupt's estate with the preferential debts of the bankrupt to the extent that the bankrupt's estate is for the time being insufficient for meeting those debts (see page 240 as to the landlord's proprietorial rights). In *Re Memco Engineering Ltd* [1985] 3 All ER 267 it was held that on yielding up the proceeds Customs and Excise became a preferential creditor *pari passu* with other preferential creditors.

Thus the right to distrain is not denied even if the property has vested in the trustee, but it will be lost if the landlord neglects to exercise it during the time that the goods remain on the premises: see *ex parte Descharmes* (1742) 1 Atk.103. If the trustee takes possession and does not disclaim the lease, distress continues to be available to the landlord for rent actually due (s 347(9)). It is difficult for other creditors to understand why a landlord should still be in a position at that stage to obtain a preference over them.

Where execution has been levied on the tenant's goods, the landlord has no power of distress because the goods are in the custody of the law. However, it is provided by s 1 Landlord & Tenant Act 1709 and s 102 County Courts Act 1984 that the goods should not be removed until the landlord had been paid all rent claimed by him, not exceeding one year's arrears which gives an advantage to the process of execution over distress. It was held in *Re Neil Mackenzie ex parte Sheriff of Herts* [1899] 2 QB 566, on the equivalent earlier legislation, that this entitled the landlord to be paid a year's rent even though notice (of the then receiving order) was served on the sheriff before he had parted with the proceeds of the execution; therefore the landlord sometimes receives a year's rent after the commencement of the bankruptcy because of the circumstance of levying of execution (which is, of course, made without regard for the bankruptcy). Clearly where there has been no execution but the landlord had distrained, he could not have kept more than six months arrears.

But, by s 347(6) of the Act, if the debtor is adjudged bankrupt *before* the notice of claim is served, the landlord is restricted to six months rent, which does not extend to any rent payable for a period after the notice of claim is served on the sheriff or other officer charged with the execution. This is, of course, without prejudice to his right to prove for the remainder.

Where an execution creditor has satisfied the landlord's claim out of his own pocket and where the execution is subsequently avoided by the bankruptcy, the sheriff must deduct from the proceeds of sale not only his costs of the levy, but the amount so paid by the execution creditor; this sum must be repaid to him and consequently only the balance of the proceeds of sale are handed to the trustee in the bankruptcy.

9. Other distraint

Nothing in the Act affects any right to distrain otherwise than for rent (s 347(8)) and by any person (s 347(3)), except that it is not available after the discharge of the bankrupt. Any such right is at any time exercisable without restriction against property comprised in the bankrupt's estate. This is not restricted by the fact that in any other enactment, the right is expressed to be exercisable like a distraint for rent. Particular among such cases are distress for the collection of rates (under the General

Rate Act 1967 s 96), for the collection of taxes under the Taxes Management Act 1970 s 60, and rentcharge under the Law of Property Act 1925 s 121(3).

10. Recovery from execution and attachment creditors

(a) Relationship of insolvency to the County Court Act 1984 (CCA)

At any time when proceedings on a bankruptcy petition are pending or an individual has been adjudged bankrupt, the court may, by s 285 of the Insolvency Act, *inter alia* stay any execution aganst the property of the debtor.

Generally, enforcement under the CCA is subject to the provisions of s 346 of the Insolvency Act. Otherwise, purchasers acquire a good title where any goods in the possession of an execution debtor are sold. This refers to the time of the seizure by a registrar or other officer charged with the enforcement of a warrant or other process of execution issued from a county court under s 98 CCA and sold by them without any claim having been made on them by the trustee. However, by s 346 the creditor is not entitled to retain the benefit against the official receiver or trustee, unless the execution or attachment was completed or the sum paid before adjudication.

(b) Property liable to execution or attachment

Reference to the bankrupt's "property" is to any of his property, whether or not comprised in his estate, except that by s 346(7) of the Act nothing entitles the trustee to claim goods from a person who has acquired them in good faith under a sale by a sheriff or other officer charged with an execution. Money paid to avoid seizure would not appear to come within the section, so that the execution creditor would be entitled to it even if the sum was in excess of the minimum amount and notice of a bankruptcy petition had been given under s 346(3) within the fourteen days referred to (see below): see *Bower* v *Hett* [1895] 2 QB 51.

(c) As to the petitioning creditor

If the sheriff appropriates the proceeds of sale towards the petitioning creditor's debt so as to reduce the amount of his debt below the statutory minimum (presently £750) that would be fatal to the petition if such appropriation constituted payment of the debt: see *Re a Debtor (No. 2 of 1977) ex parte the Debtor* v *Goacher* [1979] 1 All ER 870. However the question whether the execution is or is not for this sum may depend on the cost of the realisation viz a viz the costs and poundage after the sheriff has been in possession.

(d) Where execution not void against the trustee

Execution completed before bankruptcy: An execution creditor is entitled to retain the benefit of an execution against the goods or land of a debtor or of an attachment of a debt or any sums paid to avoid it where he has completed the execution or attachment before commencement of the bankruptcy (s 346(1)). It is therefore necessary to establish precisely when an execution or an attachment is "completed" and what is its "benefit":

(i) Completion - an execution against goods is either completed by seizure and sale, or by the making of a charging order under s 1 Charging Orders Act 1979; an execution against land is completed by seizure, by the appointment of a receiver, or by the making of a charging order under s 1 of that Act; an attachment of a debt is completed by the receipt of the debt.

(ii) Benefit - In *Re Andrew* [1937] 1 Ch 122 it was held that this meant only the prior charge obtained at common law by the writ of execution over the debtor's goods. Consequently s 346 (1) may deprive a judgment creditor of the benefit of such a charge where an execution is still subsisting.

After-acquired property unclaimed by the trustee: The execution or attachment of property acquired by or devolving upon the bankrupt following the commencement of his bankruptcy is likewise not void against the trustee unless at the time the execution is issued and before it is completed, he has claimed it for the estate under s 307 (see page 161); also a copy of the notice given under that section should have been or is being served on the sheriff or other officer charged with the execution.

Judgment less than the minimum amount: Where the judgment debt is less than £500 the execution creditor is entitled to retain the benefit as against the trustee in the bankruptcy whether or not the execution or attachment was complete or the money was paid before the commencement of the bankruptcy.

(e) Where execution void against the trustee in respect of goods unsold

Where any goods have been taken in execution, if, before the completion of the execution, notice is given under s 346(2) to the sheriff or other officer charged with the execution that the debtor has been adjudged bankrupt, then he must deliver the goods to the official receiver or trustee when requested, together with any money seized or recovered in part satisfaction of the execution unless set aside by the court in favour of the creditor.

The notice must be in writing and delivered by hand or sent by recorded delivery; it is to the effect that the judgment debtor has been adjudged bankrupt or that a bankruptcy petition has been presented in respect of him. Where the execution is in the county court and the officer in charge of it is the registrar of that court, then if there is filed in that court in respect of the judgment debtor a bankruptcy petition, or the court has made a bankruptcy order or an order appointing an interim receiver, then notice is deemed to have been served or given.

The costs of the execution are a first charge on the goods or money so delivered, and the official receiver or trustee may sell the goods (or a sufficient part of them) for the purpose of satisfying that charge and may require in writing that the sheriff's bill of costs is taxed under Rule 7.36 in accordance with r Rule 7.35(4) (and see page 257).

(f) *Where execution void against the trustee in respect of goods sold (or debtor paid up)*

Goods sold: Where any goods of a person have been taken in execution for a judgment debt exceeding £500 (the minimum amount) in respect of which there is a moratorium period of fourteen days from the day of the sale (or of the payment by the debtor), the sheriff may not during that time at once hand over the proceeds of sale (or debt paid up to avoid a sale) but must deduct the costs of the execution and retain the balance for fourteen days. If within that time he is given notice of a bankruptcy petition and that a bankruptcy order is being or has been made on that petition, then by s 346(3) the amount recovered on the sale (or money paid) goes to the bankrupt's estate for the benefit of the creditors generally and not exclusively to the execution creditor.

These enforcement procedures only apply where the debtor is the "person" to whom the seized goods belong and if, for example, a creditor levies on the property of a firm so that within fourteen days after a sale one of the partners becomes bankrupt, then his trustee cannot claim the proceeds against the execution creditor: see *Dibb* v *Brook* [1894] 2 QB 338.

The effect of a judgment in excess of the minimum amount of £500 is to transfer the right to the proceeds from the execution creditor to the trustee, and therefore where there are several executions - some over and some under £500 - the writs will be paid in order of priority, with the trustee standing in the place of those over £500, unless set aside by the court.

The fourteen day moratorium period commences to run from the date of the sale and not from the date when the proceeds of the sale are received by the sheriff: see *Re Cripps, ex parte Ross* (1888) 21 QBD 472. If the sale extends over several days, then the time is calculated from the last day: see *Jones* v *Parsell* (1883) 11 QB 430.

The general point seems to be that a creditor does not have the benefit of his execution if, before sale, notice is given to the sheriff, or if, the amount being over £500, notice is given to the sheriff within fourteen days after the date of sale. That seems to give fair notice to the creditors of the time within which a petition in bankruptcy must be presented, otherwise the execution creditor should "reap the benefit of his diligence": see *Re Cripps* (above). Accordingly, the sheriff must not dispose of the balance either within the fourteen days or while the bankruptcy petition is pending, and must then pay the balance to the official receiver or to the trustee as the case may be.

Payment by the debtor: Payment to the sheriff would only amount to payment to the creditor when the creditor was in a position to maintain an action against the sheriff for money had and received. Such an action could be maintained only if he could prove that he was entitled to the money, ie if the sheriff had retained the money for at least fourteen days without notice either of the bankruptcy or the bankruptcy order.

For example, in a case under the 1883 Act (where the relevant judgment debt exceeded the then minimum amount of £20); - on 3 February the sheriff seized the goods of the debtor under an execution for more than (£20); on 4 February before sale, the debtor paid the amount of the debt plus costs, and notice to this effect was given to the judgment creditors who on 11 February assented to the payment and asked the sheriff for the money. On 13 February a petition in bankruptcy was presented against the debtor who was adjudicated bankrupt thereon and the trustee laid claim to the money so paid. It was held that the money was received by the sheriff for the judgment creditors who were entitled to it as against the trustee: *Re Pearson ex parte West Cannock Colliery Co* (1886) 3 Morr 187.

Several judgment creditors both above and below the minimum amount: In a case where there was a succession of writs, some for more and some for less than the then minimum amount, and the sheriff sold the goods, the writs were payable in order of priority so long as there were funds and if he received notice of a bankruptcy petition within fourteen days of the sale, only those writs were entitled to be paid which were for less than the minimum amount and which would have been paid had not bankruptcy supervened: *Re Pearce, ex parte Crossthwaite* (1865) 14 QBD 966.

Costs of the execution: The costs of the execution are paid in priority to the claim of the execution creditor and the trustee, and are first deducted from the proceeds of sale which the trustee may require to be taxed (as above). If by Rule 7.36(3) any amount is disallowed on taxation, the sheriff must make up the costs by paying a sum equal to that amount to the trustee for the benefit of the estate.

(g) Method of sale

Under s 89 CCA where any goods are seized in execution and the registrar has notice of another execution or other executions, the court must not consider an application to sell privately where the value exceeds £50 until notice has been given to the other execution creditor or creditors, who may appear before the court and be heard upon the application.

Where the sheriff sells goods under an execution for more than £20 the sale must, by virtue of s 97 of the CCA, be by public auction unless the court from which the process issued otherwise orders, and must be publicly advertised by the registrar on and during the three days preceding the day of sale.

(h) Setting aside by the court

The rights conferred on the official receiver and the trustee may be set aside by the court in favour of the execution creditor under s 346(6) of the Act or in favour of the creditor who has attached the debt.

(i) Execution, attachment and relation back

There is in fact no need for a trustee to rely on s 346 if the debtor's property was seized by the sheriff after the commencement of bankruptcy and even though the trustee has served notice of same, since he can rely on his right to relate back to the "relevant time" under s 341. The execution creditor can probably rely on s 346(1), that is other than for his costs pursuant to s 346(3)(c).

11. Trustee's right to disclaim onerous property

(a) Power of disclaimer

The trustee has the general power to disclaim certain kinds of onerous property of the bankrupt under s 315 in order to free himself and the estate from the burdens attaching to them.

In giving leave to the trustee to disclaim a leasehold, the court has power to impose a condition, such as payment to the lessor of the rent in full up to the date of the disclaimer even though no third party has acquired an interest in the lease from the bankrupt. But the lessor will not be compensated for its use unless it has been used by the trustee for the benefit of the estate. A person interested in preventing a disclaimer should apply at once to stay proceedings under the order pending his appeal. The restriction on the trustee effecting such a disclaimer after twelve months under the old law has been removed so that he is now placed on the same footing as the official receiver when acting as trustee, and may disclaim at any time with the exception of replacement (see page 150) and after-acquired property (see page 161).

(b) "Onerous property"

For the purpose of disclaiming, the following are classed as onerous property:
- (i) any unprofitable contract: and
- (ii) any other property comprised in the bankrupt's estate which is unsaleable or not readily saleable, or is such that it may give rise to a liability to pay money or perform any other onerous act (s 315(2)).

(c) Trustee's notice

The trustee's notice disclaiming must contain such particulars of the property as enable it to be easily identified (Form 6.61). It must be signed by the trustee and filed in court with a copy. The court seals and endorses one copy with the date of filing and that copy is returned to the trustee. The original notice is marked by the court with the manner in which the copy notice was returned to the trustee (Rule 6.178).

(d) Effect of giving notice

The effect of the notice is to discharge the trustee from all personal liability in respect of the property disclaimed as from the date when the property vested in him. However, he is not freed from any personal liability that he may have incurred by having injured the property before disclaimer, nor from liability to pay rates for a period during which he was himself in occupation of the property. This applies whether or not he has taken possession of it, endeavoured to sell it, or otherwise exercised rights of ownership in relation to it.

A disclaimer determines the rights, interests and liabilities of the bankrupt as from the date of the disclaimer and discharges the trustee from all personal liability in respect of that property from the commencement of his trusteeship. It does not, however, affect the rights or liabilities of any other person. Any person sustaining loss or damage becomes a creditor to that extent and accordingly may prove for the loss or damage as a bankruptcy debt.

(e) Communication to persons interested

The trustee must send or give copies of the notice of disclaimer, showing the date endorsed on it by the court, within seven days of its being returned to him by the court, to the following persons:

- (i) where the property disclaimed is of a leasehold nature, every person who (to his knowledge) claims under the bankrupt as underlessee or mortgagee;
- (ii) where the property disclaimed is a dwelling-house, every person who, to his knowledge, is in occupation of, or claims a right to occupy, the house;
- (iii) in any case, to every person who, to his knowledge, claims an interest in the disclaimed property or is under any liability in respect of it, not being a liability discharged by the disclaimer;
- (iv) if the disclaimer is of an unprofitable contract, to all such persons as, to his knowledge, are parties to the contract or have interests under it;
- (v) any person who subsequently comes to the trustee's notice as being entitled to notice under (i) - (iv) above.

However, notice is not required if the trustee is satisfied that the person in question has already been made aware of the disclaimer and its date; or where the court, on the trustee's application, orders that notice is not required in the particular case (Rule 6.179).

Under Rule 6.180, the trustee may also, at any time, give notice of disclaimer to any person who, in his opinion, in the public interest or otherwise, should be informed of it. The trustee must keep the court informed of those to whom notice has been given, with their names, addresses and the nature of their respective interests.

If it appears to the trustee that there is some person who claims, or may claim, to have an interest in the property, he may give him notice by Form 6.63, calling on him to declare within fourteen days whether or not he claims such interest, and if so the nature and extent of it. Failing compliance with the notice, the trustee is entitled to assume that the person concerned has no such interest in the property as will prevent or impede its disclaimer (Rule 6.184).

(f) Notice to elect

In the case of property which cannot be disclaimed without leave of the court, any application to the trustee under s 316 by any interested party for a decision as to whether property is to be disclaimed or not must be delivered to the trustee personally or sent by registered post. It must be in Form 6.62 or a substantially similar form. If, within the requisite 28 days, the trustee applies to the court for leave to disclaim, the court extends the time allowed for giving notice of disclaimer to a date not earlier than the date fixed for the hearing of the application. The trustee is deemed to have adopted any contract which by virtue of s 316 he is not entitled to disclaim.

(g) Bankrupt's personal and after-acquired property

The power to disclaim is not available under s 315 in respect of any "after-acquired property" or personal property of the bankrupt exceeding reasonable replacement value (see page 150), except with the leave of the court. The trustee may apply for such leave *ex parte*. The application must be accompanied by a report:

- (i) giving such particulars of the property proposed to be disclaimed as enable it to be easily identified;
- (ii) setting out the reasons why, the property having been claimed for the estate, the court's leave to disclaim is now applied for; and
- (iii) specifying the persons (if any) who have been informed of the trustee's intention to make the application.

If the report recites that any consent(s) has been obtained to the disclaimer, a copy of such consent(s) must be annexed.

The court may, before granting leave, order that notice of the application be given to all such persons who, if the property is disclaimed, will be entitled to apply for a vesting or other order under s 320 (see below), and fix a venue for the hearing of the application.

(h) Vesting of property following disclaimer

Where the trustee has disclaimed property under s 315 the court may make an order vesting or delivering up the disclaimed property to the person interested. The effect of any such order is taken into account in assessing the extent of any loss or damage sustained by any person in consequence of the disclaimer.

An application for such an order under s 320 may be made by any person who claims an interest, including anyone who is under any liability in respect of the disclaimed property, not being a liability discharged by the disclaimer. Where the property is a dwelling-house, any person who, at the time when the bankruptcy petition was presented, was in occupation of or entitled to occupy the dwelling-house, may make an application.

An order vesting property in any person including the bankrupt by s 320(6) need not be completed by a conveyance, assignment or transfer.

The application must be made within three months of the applicant becoming aware of the disclaimer, or of his receiving a copy of the trustee's notice of disclaimer, whichever is the earlier.

The application must be accompanied by an affidavit under Rule 6.186:

(i) stating whether the application is under s 320(2)(a) - claim of interest in the property; s 320(2)(b) - liability not discharged; or s 320(2)(c) - occupation of dwelling-house;

(ii) specifying the date on which the applicant received a copy of the trustee's notice of disclaimer or otherwise became aware of it; and

(iii) specifying the grounds of the application and the order requested.

The court fixes a venue for the hearing and the applicant must, not later than seven days before the date fixed, give the trustee notice of the venue, and copies of the application and affidavit. On hearing the application, the court may give directions as to any other persons who should be given notice of the application and the grounds thereof. Sealed copies of any order made are sent by the court to the applicant and to the trustee.

(i) Order of the court

The court may on application under s 320 make an order for vesting the disclaimed property in, or for its delivery to:

(i) a person entitled to it or a trustee for such person;

(ii) a person who is under any liability in respect of the disclaimed property, not being a liability discharged by the disclaimer; or

(iii) where the disclaimed property is property in a dwelling-house, any person who at the time when the bankruptcy petition was presented was in occupation of or entitled to occupy the dwelling-house.

The court will not make an order by (ii) except where it appears to the court that it would be just to do so for the purpose of compensating the person subject to the liability in respect of the disclaimer.

The effect of any order is taken into account in assessing the extent of any loss or damage sustained by any creditor under s 315(5) in consequence of the disclaimer.

(j) Leasehold property

By s 317 the disclaimer of any property of a leasehold nature does not take effect unless a copy of the disclaimer has been served on every person claiming under the bankrupt as underlessee or mortgagee, and either:

(i) no application under s 320 (see below) is made with respect to the property before the end of fourteen days beginning with the day on which the last notice was served; or

(ii) where such an application has been made, the court directs that the disclaimer is to take effect.

Where the court gives a direction under (ii) it may, instead of or in addition to any order it makes under s 320, make orders with respect to fixtures, tenant's improvements, and other matters arising out of the lease.

Where the trustee has disclaimed a leasehold property, the court has no power to make an order vesting all or part of it in any person except (s 321(1)):

- (i) by making that person subject to the same liabilities and obligations as the bankrupt was subject to under the lease on the day the bankruptcy petition was presented;
- (ii) subject to the same liabilities and obligations as that person would be subject to if the lease had been assigned to him on that day.

These requirements also apply to part only of a leasehold property. Where nobody is willing to accept the order the court may vest the estate or interest in any person who is liable to perform the lessee's covenants in the lease (whether personally or in a representative capacity and whether alone or jointly with the bankrupt).

Where (i) applies, if a person interested declines to accept the order then he is excluded from all interest in the property.

The court's order should include a direction giving effect to the disclaimer except where, at the time when the order is issued, other applications under s 320 are pending in respect of the same property.

(k) Person interested

A person interested in a disclaimed property may be:

- (i) a person, or his trustee, entitled to it;
- (ii) any person, or his trustee, who is under any liability in respect of it;
- (iii) a person either in occupation or entitled to be in occupation of the dwelling-house.

The court should not make an order under (ii) above except where it appears that it would be just to compensate the person subject to the liability.

(l) Disclaimer presumed valid and effective

Any disclaimer of property by the trustee is presumed valid and effective unless it is proved that he is in breach of his duty as to giving notice.

(m) Rentcharge

Where any land that is subject to a rentcharge vests in the Crown or any other person "the proprietor", as a consequence of the disclaimer, the proprietor and successors in title are not subject to any personal liability in respect of any sums becoming due under the rentcharge, except those becoming due because he has taken possession or control of the land or has entered into occupation of it (s 319).

(n) Statutory tenancy

Where the debtor is a statutory tenant under the Rent Acts and is subsequently adjudicated bankrupt, the spouse's rights do not vest in the trustee; they are regarded as purely personal; see *Sutton* v *Dorf* [1932] 2 KB 304. Thus on a disclaimer by the trustee a statutory tenant may continue in possession. Note that on the other hand a contractual tenant may not continue in possession because leaseholds forming part of a tenant debtor's property, vest absolutely in the trustee who is personally liable for the observance and performance of the tenant's covenants while he is in possession (see *(j)* above, and page 129 as to the matrimonial home).

12. Transitional arrangements

A preference given, assignment made or other transaction entered into before the appointed day may not be set aside except to the extent that it could have been set aside under the law in force immediately before that day. This also applies to the making of any order which varies or reverses the effect of a preference, assignment or other transaction.

Chapter 13

Proof of debts

1. Introduction

All unsecured claims by creditors are provable as debts against the bankrupt. It is immaterial whether the debt or liability is present or future, certain or contingent, or whether its amount is fixed or liquidated or is capable of being ascertained by fixed rules or sounding only in damages. "Liability" means a liability to pay money or money's worth, including any liability under any enactment, any liability for breach of trust, any liability in contract, tort or bailment and any liability arising out of an obligation to make restitution.

Any fine imposed for an offence is not provable; neither is any obligation arising under an order made in family or domestic proceedings. An obligation arising under a confiscation order made under s 1 of the Drug Trafficking Offences Act 1986 is likewise not provable.

The creditor is said to "prove" for his debt, and the document by which he seeks to establish his claim is his "proof". The proof of any bankruptcy debt by a secured or unsecured creditor of the bankrupt and the admission or rejection of any proof by s 322(1) takes place in accordance with the rules, and may be withdrawn or varied as to the amount claimed at any time by agreement between the creditor and trustee.

Debts should be proved as soon as possible after the bankruptcy order on Form 6.37, (or Form 6.38 where an existing trustee proves in a later bankruptcy) which is then lodged with the official receiver or trustee, if there is one. It is these claims that are called "proof of debt" and in certain circumstances must be in the form of an affidavit (Form 6.39).

More controversially, however, s 281 of the Act also determines that discharge does not affect "the right of any creditor of the bankrupt to prove in the bankruptcy for any debt from which the bankrupt is released". What, it has to be asked, is this intended to mean? At common law, bankruptcy only frees the debtor from debts and liabilities that are provable, which highlights the need for the statement of affairs to be as complete and open as possible.

A liability existing at the relevant date but which cannot be quantified until after the relevant date is nevertheless a sum due: see *In re Daintrey* [1900] 1 QB 546.

When a trustee is appointed, the official receiver must send him all the proofs which he has so far received, together with an itemised list of them which the trustee signs and returns. From then on all proofs of debt are sent to the trustee and retained by him. He deals with every creditor's proof within seven days from the last date for proving, by admitting or rejecting it in whole or in part, or by making such provision for it as he thinks fit. He is not obliged to deal with proofs lodged after the last date for proving but may do so if he thinks fit. As to the declaration and payment of dividends see page 243 *et seq.*

Where a debt is due to the Crown or a government department, the proof need not be in the prescribed form, as long as it shows all the particulars which appear in a normal proof and are relevant in the circumstances (Rule 6.96(4)).

2. Provable debt

(a) Contingencies

The debt is usually for all practical purposes based on the amount of the estimated sum that is provable in the bankruptcy. Otherwise it is based on the estimated amount that is accepted by the court under s 322(4) at that time.

Such an obligation to pay is not a debt due even though the contingency subsequently occurs and the obligation to pay arises under the contract entered into before the due date; see *In Re a Debtor (No 66 of 1955) ex parte the Debtor* v *Trustee of Waite (A Bankrupt)* [1956] 3 All ER 225.

The trustee estimates the value of any debt that does not bear a certain value. By s 382 it includes any debt or liability to which the bankrupt is subject at the commencement of the bankruptcy, together with any debt or liability to which he may become subject by reason of any obligation incurred before the commencement of the bankruptcy.

If the debtor or creditor is dissatisfied then either may appeal under s 303.

(b) Damages

Damages are provable where payable by the bankrupt in respect of non-performance or otherwise on such terms as appear to the court to be equitable (s 345).

(c) Disclaimed property

Where the trustee has disclaimed onerous property under s 315 (see page 180) the resulting claims against the estate for loss or damage are provable.

(d) Discounts

Trade and other discounts that would have been available to the bankrupt are deducted from the amount of the claim. Discounts that are allowed would be for immediate, early or cash settlement.

(e) Estimated debts

Where the value of a debt is estimated either by the trustee (subject to contingencies) or the court (general control under s 303) the amount payable in the bankruptcy is the amount of the estimate (s 322(4)).

(f) Foreign currency debts

When proving a debt incurred in a foreign currency, the amount is converted to sterling at the official exchange rate prevailing on the day of the bankruptcy order. The "official exchange rate" is the middle market rate at the Bank of England as published for the date in question. In the absence of such published rate, the court determines the rate. (Rule 6.111)

(g) Future debts

A creditor may prove for a debt, payment of which has not fallen due at the date of the bankruptcy order, but subject to adjustment for the purposes of a dividend, by an amount calculated as follows: $\frac{I \times M}{12}$

where I is 5% and M is the number of months (expressed if need be as including fractions of months) between the declaration of dividend and the date when payment of the creditor's debt would otherwise be due.

(h) Interest

Where a bankruptcy debt bears interest, that interest is provable as part of the debt except for interest accruing during any period after the commencement of the bankruptcy. If the debt arises out of a written instrument and is payable at a certain time, interest may be claimed for the period from that time to the date of the bankruptcy order. Otherwise, it may be claimed only if, before the presentation of the petition, a demand for payment was made in writing by or behalf of the creditor, and notice given that interest would be payable from the date of the demand to the date of payment; here interest may be claimed for the period from the date of that demand to the date of the bankruptcy order (Rule 6.113).

The rate of interest is that specified in s 17 of the Judgments Act 1838 on the date of the bankruptcy order, except in the case of a notice mentioned above, where the rate is that specified in the notice, but not exceeding the rate under the Judgments Act.

(i) Licensed moneylender

A proof in respect of a moneylending transaction made before 27 January 1980, where the creditor was at the time of the transaction a licensed moneylender, must have endorsed on or annexed to it a statement setting out in detail the particulars mentioned in s 9(2) of the Moneylenders Act 1927, since repealed (Rule 6.102).

(j) Negotiable instruments

Unless the trustee allows, a proof in respect of money owed on a bill of exchange, promissory note, cheque or other negotiable instrument or security cannot be admitted unless the instrument or security itself, or a copy certified true by the creditor or his authorised representative, is produced. (Rule 6.108)

(k) Partnerships

For the purpose of proving a debt a partnership is treated as a person distinct from its members. The general rule is that a partnership may not prove upon the insolvent estates of its members. The exceptions are as follows:

- where the debt has been incurred by fraud;
- where goods were supplied to the partner in a separate trade;
- when the parties may be said to have acquiesced by their conduct.

For example, where the bankrupt has taken property from the partnership fund and applied it to his own use without the knowledge of the other partners, the partnership can prove in the bankrupt's estate (see page 297).

(l) Payments of a periodical nature

In the case of rent and other periodical payments, the creditor may prove for amounts due and unpaid up to the date of the bankruptcy order. Where at that date any payment was accruing due, the creditor may prove for as much of it as would have fallen due at that date if accruing from day to day. (Rule 6.112)

(m) Rent

A landlord has the right to lodge a proof in bankruptcy for rent. He has the right to distrain for six months rent accrued due before the commencement of bankruptcy (see page 174); otherwise he ranks as an ordinary creditor.

(n) Tax penalties

Tax penalties arise out of the failure to make returns for income or capital or to notify chargeability to tax under ss 93 and 94 Taxes Management Act 1970, incorrect returns being penalised under s 95 or mitigated under s 102 of that Act.

The Revenue stated (Press Release 1 August 1977) in connection with s 115 Income and Corporation Taxes Act 1970 that it does not seek to get more by way of tax penalties overall, and is prepared to accept somewhat less than the statutory maximum where the debtor taxpayer gives his full and complete co-operation to the Inspector. It is therefore incumbent upon the trustee and his debtor bankrupt to proceed diligently, with a view to expunging and reducing the proofs of HM Inspector of Taxes.

Tax penalties have been debts provable in bankruptcy since *Re Pascoe Trustee* v *The Lords Commissioners of HM Treasury* [1944] 1 All ER 593. The only way the Inland Revenue may be able to enforce the payment of tax penalties is by instituting bankruptcy proceedings; see *Re Hurren (a Bankrupt) ex parte the Trustee* v *Inland Revenue Commissioners* [1982] 3 All ER 982. However, it was then necessary to bring the trustee into the matter and the view was taken in that case that this was an unnecessary complication of the issue.

The amount of the penalty varies but can be as much as twice the evaded tax; furthermore interest is chargeable on the amount by which the tax is underpaid. Under s 102 there is the discretion to mitigate or entirely remit the penalty. In *IRC* v *Elcock* (1953) 35 TC 27 it was decided that where the penalty is expressed to be a sum not exceeding a named figure, then it is open to the court to consider the appropriate amount to impose in the circumstances of the case. In *Re Hurren* (above) the trustee asked the court to determine whether the Commissioners might prove for the amount of penalties claimed by the Revenue. The penalties were held to be *contingent* liabilities and as such were provable debts.

Discharge does not necessarily release the bankrupt from a penalty for an offence under an enactment relating to the public revenue, or a recognisance.

Since *Re Hurren*, "it is also to be observed that an order of discharge does not have the effect of releasing the bankrupt from any debt etc ...... relating to any branch of public revenue; it is a matter of fact that the Treasury is therefore required to certify their consent to the eventual discharge of such a debtor" (133 New Law Journal 732); but this is now restricted to second or subsequent bankruptcies.

The fact that a fine is also a punishment does not make it any less a debt. The Commissioners may accept a composition for penalties without *ipso facto* commencing bankruptcy proceedings, but they may alternatively enforce an agreement for compensation which would appear to be at their discretion.

(o) Liability in tort

In determining whether liability in tort is a bankruptcy debt, the bankrupt is deemed to become subject to that liability under s 382(2) by reason of an obligation incurred at the time when the cause of action accrued. Damages arising will be considered liquidated and provable if their amount is settled by final judgment, award or compromise before adjudication; see *Re Newman, ex parte Brooke* (1876) 25 WR 261. At present unliquidated damages in tort are not provable in bankruptcy; see *Re Berkeley Securities (Property) Ltd* [1980] 1 WLR 1589 (see also page 242).

3. Claims not provable

(a) Drugs

An obligation arising under a confiscation order made under s 1 of the Drug

Trafficking Offences Act 1986 is not provable (Rule 12.3(2)).

(b) Fines

Any fine imposed for an offence is not provable.

(c) Guarantees

Before payment of the debt, the guarantor cannot prove in the bankruptcy of the principal debtor unless the creditor has renounced his right to prove; otherwise the bankrupt's estate might be subject to a proof for each of two claims for the same liability; see *Re Fenton ex parte Fenton Textile Association* [1931] Ch 85.

Where the guarantee is for the full amount of the debt and the creditor has only recovered a part of the debt, it is doubtful that the guarantor can prove for the amount he has paid. Nor is he entitled to any dividends except any that may be received by the creditor after he has received the full amount of the debt from the guarantor and the estate. However, where it is given for a part only of an ascertained debt which the guarantor has paid in full, then he would be entitled, in the absence of agreement to the contrary, to a proportionate part of the dividend; see *Ex parte Rushforth* (1805) 10 Ves 414.

(d) Maintenance

Any obligation arising under an order in family or domestic proceedings as defined by the Matrimonial and Family Proceedings Act 1984 is not provable (Rule 12.3(2)).

(e) Previous proceedings under Part VIII

Where a bankruptcy order has been made following the discharge of an interim order, or where a voluntary arrangement has been revoked or suspended, it is unclear whether or not liabilities and expenses incurred by creditors in good faith under the arrangement are provable in the subsequent bankruptcy. There is no express provision, only the general rule as to priority for official costs etc (see page 231), and as to general applications to the court.

It may also be assumed that a supervisor is not allowed to retain assets in his hands as against the trustee of the subsequent bankruptcy (see page 60).

(f) Statute barred debts

Debts barred by the Limitation Act 1980 cannot be proved. For the purposes of proof, time does not run against a debt after adjudication; see *Re Tynte* (1880) 15 Ch 125.

(g) Unliquidated damages

Demands in the nature of unliquidated damages are, by s 267(2), not provable as they are incapable of valuation. They may become liquidated and therefore provable by agreement made or judgment signed before adjudication.

4. Mutual credit and set-off

In some cases, if the creditor is indebted to the bankrupt, the debts are set off against each other and the balance only is proved for or paid. This is a statutory right which the parties do not have power to waive. It would be contrary to the policy of insolvency laws that any particular claim should be excluded; see *Victoria Products Ltd* v *Tosh & Co Ltd* (1940) 165 LT 178. For a discussion on set-off, see *BICC plc* v *Burndy Corporation* [1985] 1 Ch 247. Where the same creditor is owed both a preferential and non-preferential debt, the set-off should be apportioned rateably between the two debts; see *Re Unit 2 Windows Ltd* [1985] 1 WLR 1389.

(a) Between the same parties

Section 323 provides that where (before the commencement of the bankruptcy) there have been mutual credits, mutual debts or other mutual dealings between the bankrupt and any creditor proving or claiming to prove for a bankruptcy debt, an account must be taken of what is due from each party to the other in respect of the mutual dealings; and the sums due from the one party shall be set off against the sums due from the other party, and only the balance of the account is provable as a bankruptcy debt or payable to the trustee as part of the estate. A person is not entitled to claim the benefit of any set-off where he had notice, at the time of giving credit, that a bankruptcy petition relating to the bankrupt was pending.

(b) Set-off in an action

There can be no set-off where the debt, though legally due to the creditor from the bankrupt, is really due to him as trustee for another, and although recoverable in a cross action, would not have been recovered by the debtor for his own benefit; see *Forster* v *Wilson* (1843) 12 M&W 19 and applied in *Re Unit 2 Windows Ltd* [1985] 1 WLR 1389.

(c) Mutual credits and debts

The expression "mutual credits" is wider than the term "mutual debts" and will include a case where there are simple contract debts presently due on the one side, and a speciality debt not due on the other; mutual credits must terminate in debts, as where a debt is due from one party, and credit given by him on the other hand for a sum of money which is payable at a future date, and which will then become a debt; see *Rose* v *Hart* (1818) 2 Smith's LC 298.

(d) Mutual dealings

The term "mutual dealings" is wider still and includes the case of transactions which will most likely end in debts provided that they both end in a pecuniary payment. See for example *Re Taylor, ex parte Norvell* [1910] 1 KB 103. The result is that all claims provable in the bankruptcy may be set-off against a pecuniary claim by the bankrupt provided that they arise out of a contract. Unliquidated damages for breach of contract may be set-off against a claim in an action on the contract by the trustee; see *Peat* v *Jones* (1881) 30 WR 433, and an equitable debt may be set-off against a legal debt: see *Mathieson's Trustee* v *Burrup, Mathieson & Co* [1927] 1 Ch 562.

In *Rolls-Razor* v *Cox* [1967] 1 QB 552, the company had engaged a salesman to sell washing machines and other appliances on a commission basis, and supplied him with both types for demonstration purposes and for sale to customers. Each week he was required to pay over all the cash he had received without deducting his commission; the company then paid him his commission less a small percentage which they paid into a retention fund against default by the salesman, but repayable in the event of the termination of these arrangements by the company. Rolls-Razor went into liquidation and the liquidator sought to recover both machines and cash from the salesman and in turn he sought to set-off his own claims to commission as well as repayment of the amount in the retention fund. On appeal the court found mutual dealings entitling the salesman to a set-off both for the cash and for the articles he held for sale, but not for the demonstration machines. There could be no set-off in respect of the value of goods entrusted to the salesman for use and not for sale and those goods or their value were to be returned to the company.

(e) Set-off against the Crown

See County Court Rules O 42 r 9 and the Crown Proceedings Act 1947, which makes provision, by s 35, for a creditor to seek the leave of the court during any proceedings by the Crown in order to avail himself of any right of set-off which relates to a different government department. An opinion preferred by law officers was that all ministries or departments of the Crown were one and indivisible for the purpose of mutual credit and set-off (*Blagden Report*; HMSO Cmnd 221, para 83).

5. The proof

The trustee should examine every proof (Form 6.37) and, in writing, either admit or reject it in whole or in part, or require further evidence in support of it or require it to be verified by affidavit (Form 6.39) if in doubt; see Bigham J in *Re Van Laun* [1907] 1 KB 162: "The trustee's right and duty when examining a proof for the purpose of admitting or rejecting it is to require some satisfactory evidence that the debt on which the proof is founded is a real debt."

A creditor has 21 days to appeal against the trustee's decision, and the bankrupt, or any other creditor, has 21 days of becoming aware of his decision to express dissatisfaction.

(a) Double proofs

Only one proof may be lodged, for the same debt cannot be proved twice against the same estate. Thus where the bankrupt owes money to joint creditors, they must lodge a joint proof and not individual proofs. For example, a guarantor cannot prove if the creditor has lodged a proof. For illustrations of this important principle see *Re Kent County Gas Light & Coke Co* [1913] 1 Ch 92 and *Day & Dent Constructions Pty Ltd* v *N Australian Properties Pty Ltd* (1982) 40 ALR 399. As to partnerships, see page 246.

(b) Supply of forms

Forms for use to prove debts are sent by the official receiver or trustee to all known creditors. The forms must accompany the earliest of:

(i) the notice to creditors under s 293(2) (official receiver's decision not to call meeting of creditors);
(ii) the first notice calling a meeting of creditors;
(iii) where a certificate of summary administration has been issued, the notice sent by the official receiver under Rule 6.49(2); or
(iv) where a trustee is appointed by the court, the notice of his appointment sent by him to creditors.

Where, with the leave of the court (s 297(7)), the trustee advertises his appointment, he must send proofs to the creditor within four months after the date of the bankruptcy order. The court may, however, dispense with the requirement to send out forms of proof, or may alter the time limits for sending them. (Rule 6.97)

(c) Contents of the proof

The proof must contain the following information:

"(a) the creditor's name and address;
(b) the total amount of his claim as at the date of the bankruptcy order;
(c) whether or not that amount includes outstanding uncapitalised interest;
(d) whether or not the claim includes value added tax;
(e) whether the whole or any part of the debt falls within any (and if so which) of the categories of preferential debts [see page 234];
(f) particulars of how and when the debt was incurred by the debtor;
(g) particulars of any security held, the date when it was given and the value which the creditor puts on it; and
(h) the name, address and authority of the person signing the proof (if other than the creditor himself)."

(Rule 6.98)

The proof must also specify any documents substantiating the debt, but they do not need to be attached to, or submitted with, the proof. The trustee may, however, require any such document to be produced if he thinks it necessary.

A proof may at any time, by agreement between the creditor and the trustee, be withdrawn or the amount claimed may be varied (Rule 6.106).

(d) Cost of proving

Unless the court orders otherwise, every creditor bears the cost of proving his own debt, including the cost of providing documents and evidence, eg for substantiating his claim (Rule 6.100(1)). Costs incurred by the trustee in estimating the value of a bankruptcy debt, which by reason of its being subject to any contingency or contingencies does not bear a certain value, fall on the estate as an expense of the bankruptcy unless the court otherwise orders (Rule 6.100(2)).

(e) Trustee to allow inspection of proofs

As long as proofs lodged with him remain in his possession, the trustee must allow them to be inspected, at all reasonable times on a business day, by:

(i) any creditor who has submitted his proof of debt, unless that proof has been wholly rejected;
(ii) the bankrupt; and
(iii) any person acting on behalf of either of the above.

(Rule 6.101)

(f) Admission and rejection of proofs

A proof may be admitted for dividend either for the whole amount claimed by the creditor, or for part of that amount. If the trustee rejects a proof in whole or in part, he must prepare a written statement of his reasons for doing so and send it to the creditor straight away under Rule 6.104. Rule 6.94 provides for the procedure at creditors' meetings (see page 208).

The trustee has seven days from the last date for proving to deal with every creditor's proof by admitting or rejecting it in whole or in part, or by making such provision as he thinks fit. After the last date for proving he is not *obliged* to deal with proofs, but *may* do so (Rule 11.3).

(g) Appeal against decision

A creditor may apply to the court for the trustee's decision on his proof to be varied or reversed. The application must be made within 21 days of his receiving the trustee's statement of reasons for rejecting the proof in whole or in part. The bankrupt himself or any other creditor may likewise apply to the court if aggrieved by the admission or rejection, in whole or in part, of a proof.

When the application is received, the court fixes a venue for the hearing of the application; notice of it is sent by the applicant to the creditor whose proof is in question, and to the trustee. The trustee must then file in court the relevant proof, together with, where relevant, a copy of his statement of reasons for rejection in whole or in part. After the hearing the proof is returned to the trustee, unless it has been wholly disallowed. The official receiver is not personally liable for costs incurred by any person in making an application of this kind unless the court so orders (Rule 6.105). As to payment of the dividend in those circumstances, see page 244.

(h) Expunging the proof by the court

Under Rule 6.107 the court may expunge a proof or reduce the amount claimed:

(i) on the trustee's application, where he thinks that the proof has been improperly admitted or ought to be reduced; or

(ii) on the application of a creditor if the trustee declines to interfere in the matter.

Where an application is made to the court to exercise these powers, the court must fix a venue for the hearing. The applicant then sends notice of it to the creditor who made the proof (if not himself) and, if appropriate, to the trustee. If the proof is expunged or reduced after it has been admitted, the creditor is liable to repay any amount overpaid by way of dividend under Rule 11.8(3). As to omission by a secured creditor to declare his security, see page 199.

(i) Information about proofs lodged

A creditor who has lodged a proof has the right to apply in writing to the trustee to furnish him with a list of all the creditors who have lodged proofs of debt, and the amounts of the respective debts admitted by the trustee. He must supply the list but is entitled to charge the appropriate fee (see Appendix 5) for so doing.

6. Proofs by secured creditors

A debt is secured under s 383(2) to the extent that the person to whom the debt is owed holds any security for it over any property of the debtor. Security does not, however, include a lien on books, papers or other records except to the extent that they consist of documents which give title to property and are held as such (s 383(4)).

A secured creditor is in a different position from an unsecured creditor for he has a direct claim on an asset of the debtor whereas the unsecured creditor has his personal remedies only. It is unacceptable to both business practice and consumer law to make them both equal in the event of bankruptcy for that would strike at the root of soundly secured enterprise, consequently, the secured creditor has the following options open to him:

(i) to rely entirely on the security (eg to sell it) and not prove in the bankruptcy (Case A); or

(ii) to give up the security to the trustee for the benefit of all the creditors, and prove for the whole of his debt as an unsecured creditor (Case B); or

(iii) to realise his security independently of the bankruptcy and prove for the balance, if any, still due to him (Case C); or

(iv) to re-value his security and prove for the difference between the total debt due to him and the estimated value of the security (Case D), except that the trustee may require the property to be sold where:

(v) he disagrees with the re-valuation under (iv) (Case E), or

(vi) he requires to redeem the security in any event (Case F).

These options are discussed below.

Case A: Selling the security

Such a sale takes place outside bankruptcy. The effect of this action is that any proceeds in excess of the creditor' debt (plus interest) are paid to the trustee.

Case B: Surrender

This is an unusual option in which either the petitioning creditor states that he is willing to abandon his security voluntarily for the benefit of all creditors, or the petition is expressed not to be made in respect of the secured part of the debt; the creditor is then deemed to have given up the security specified in the statement. If he voluntarily gives it up for the general benefit of creditors, he may prove for his whole debt as if it were unsecured (Rule 6.109(2)).

Case C: Realisation of security by the creditor

If a creditor who has valued his security later realises it, the amount realised must be substituted for the value previously put on the security by the creditor. That amount is treated in all respects as an amended valuation by Rule 6.119, and he may prove for the balance still owing (Rule 6.109(1)).

Case D: Re-valuation

Secured creditors may alter the value which they have put upon their security in their proof of debt only with the agreement of the trustee or the leave of the court, and that amount is treated in all respects as an amended valuation by Rule 6.119. However, where the secured creditor is the petitioning creditor and has placed a value on his security, or voted in respect of the unsecured balance of his debt, he may only re-value his security with the leave of the court (Rule 6.115) as a re-valuation may, of course, affect the value placed on the estate by the court before being satisfied as to the correctness of the issue of a bankruptcy order etc.

Where the creditor is relying on security which is initially incapable of valuation and the debt turns out to be more than anticipated, it has been held that whilst the creditor was to be allowed to readjust his claim (a situation reinforced by the present rules), he was not thereby to create any injustice to the other parties in a bankruptcy and/or to interfere with anything that had been done prior to the change of his proof; see *Re McMurdo, Penfield* v *McMurdo* [1902] 2 Ch 684.

Assistance may also be had from a Canadian case where the debt turned out to be less than expected; in *Bank of Ottawa* v *Newton* [1906] 4 WLR 508 the creditor, having ranked for the balance of his debt after deducting the amount of his valuation, subsequently realised his security for more than that amount. It was held that he could not then be required to re-value his security, but note the subsequent position by Rule 11.9 (see page 199).

It is therefore submitted that a subsequent lower or higher valuation by creditors will not affect the basis of the aggregate amount of the debt at the commencement, even if it turns out to have been excessive. In the meanwhile, any further resolution of the matter will await consideration by the courts.

As for re-valuation after a dividend has been declared, see 8 below, and for potential disqualification from dividend see page 245.

Case E: Disposal by the trustee

If the trustee is dissatisfied with the value which the creditor puts on his security he may require any property comprised in the security to be offered for sale. The terms of sale are such as may be agreed or as the court may direct. If the sale is by auction, the trustee on behalf of the estate, and the creditor on his own behalf, may appear and bid. The rule does not apply where the security has been re-valued and the re-valuation has been approved by the court (Rule 6.118).

Case F: Redemption by the trustee

In any event it would appear that the trustee is enabled to redeem the security under Rule 6.117, which provides that he may at any time give notice to a secured creditor that he proposes to redeem the security 28 days from the date of the notice, at the value placed on it in the creditor's proof. The creditor then has 21 days, or such longer period as the trustee may allow, to exercise his right to re-value his security, but with the leave of the court if, for example, he is the petitioner. If the creditor re-values his security, it may only be redeemed at the new value. The cost of transferring the security on redemption is borne by the estate. A secured creditor may, at any time, by notice in writing, call on the trustee to elect whether or not to exercise his power of redemption at the value then placed on the security. The trustee then has six months in which to exercise the power or decide not to exercise it. A creditor in whose favour a charging order has been made under the Charging Orders Act 1979 is not a secured creditor; see *Roberts Petroleum Ltd* v *Bernard Kenney Ltd* [1983] 1 All ER 564.

7. Affidavit of debt

The proof may consist of an affidavit [Form 6.39] if the trustee thinks it necessary, notwithstanding that a proof of debt has already been lodged and sworn. The affidavit may be sworn before an official receiver or duly authorised officer of either the Department of Trade & Industry or of the court.

The usual High Court rules of procedure governing affidavits apply in insolvency proceedings unlcss inconsistent with Rule 7.57(3) and (4). These provide that where, in insolvency proceedings, an affidavit is made by the official receiver or responsible insolvency practitioner, the deponent must state the capacity in which he makes it, the position he holds and the address at which he works; and that, notwithstanding O 41 r 8 of the Rules of the Supreme Court (affidavit not to be sworn before party's own solicitor), a creditor's affidavit of debt may be sworn before his own solicitor.

8. Alteration of proof or valuation after dividend paid

(a) Re-valuing of security

Where a creditor re-values his security at a time when a dividend has been declared, Rule 11.9 provides that:

"(2) If the re-valuation results in a reduction of his unsecured claim ranking for dividend, the creditor shall forthwith repay to the responsible insolvency practitioner, for the credit of the insolvent estate, any amount received by him as dividend in excess of that to which he would be entitled having regard to the re-valuation of the security.

(3) If the re-valuation results in an increase in his unsecured claim, the creditor is entitled to receive from the insolvency practitioner, out of any money for the time being available for the payment of a further dividend, before any such further dividend is paid, any dividend or dividends which he has failed to receive, having regard to the re-valuation of the security.

However, the creditor is not entitled to disturb any dividend declared (whether or not distributed) before the date of the re-valuation."

(b) Omission to declare

If a secured creditor omits to disclose his security in his proof of debt, he surrenders it for the general benefit of creditors unless the court relieves him on the ground that the omission was inadvertent (see *Re Piers ex parte Piers* [1898] 1 QB 627 and *Re Rowe* [1904] 2 KB 489); or the result of an honest mistake. If the court grants that relief, it may require or allow the creditor's proof of debt to be amended, on such terms as may be just. (Rule 6.116). As to entitlement to vote at a creditors' meeting, see page 207.

(c) Effect of overpayment

If, after being admitted, a proof is withdrawn, expunged, or the amount of it is reduced, the creditor must refund the overpayment to the trustee for the credit of the estate.

9. Second and subsequent bankruptcies

The creditors of the bankrupt in the earlier bankruptcy and the creditors in any bankruptcy prior to the earlier one, are not to be creditors in the later bankruptcy for the same debts. Therefore the existing trustee may prove in the later bankruptcy (Form 6.38) for:

(i) the unsatisfied balance of the debts in the earlier bankruptcy;
(ii) any interest payable on that balance; and
(iii) any unpaid expenses of the earlier bankruptcy.

Chapter 14

Creditors' meetings - general business

1. Voluntary arrangement

(a) Summoning of creditors' meeting following interim order

Where the nominee has reported to the court under s 256, following the making of an interim order (see page 6), that a meeting of the debtor's creditors should be summoned, the nominee or his replacement must then summon that meeting for the time, date and place proposed in the report. If the court is satisfied that a meeting should be summoned to consider the debtor's proposal, the court then directs that the interim order be extended to enable the debtor's proposal to be considered by his creditors.

The persons to be summoned to the meeting are every creditor of the debtor of whose *name* and address the person summoning the meeting is aware. Note the Act says "claim" rather than "name" but in the author's submission the latter would have been more logical for not all those named may yet have claimed. This is especially so because for this purpose, the creditors of a debtor who is an undischarged bankrupt include every person who is a creditor of the bankrupt in respect of a bankruptcy debt, and every person who would be such a creditor if the bankruptcy had commenced on the day on which notice of the meeting is given.

The meeting must be held at least fourteen days and not more than 28 days from the day the nominee's report is filed in the court. Notice of the meeting must be sent out at least fourteen days before the date fixed. The notice must:

- (i) specify the court to which the nominee's report on the debtor's proposal has been delivered;
- (ii) explain the effect of Rules 5.18 (1), (3) and (4) concerning requisite majorities;
- (iii) be accompanied by a copy of the proposal; a copy of the statement of affairs, or, if the nominee thinks fit, a summary of it; and the nominee's comments on the proposal.

(Rule 5.13(3))

The nominee is bound to have regard to the convenience of creditors, to summon the meeting to start between 10 am and 4 pm on a business day, and to send out forms of proxy (Form 8.1). Apart from the forms of proxy, there are no set forms to be used.

(b) The meeting of creditors following interim order

The meeting is summoned to decide whether to approve the arrangement and may, with the debtor's approval, modify it. The result is to bind everyone who had notice of the meeting; and the supervisor(s), who may be the original nominee, then implements the scheme, applying to the court for directions as necessary.

The meeting may not approve any proposal or modification which affects the right of a secured creditor of the debtor to enforce his security except with the concurrence of the creditor concerned. By s 258(5) the meeting may not approve any proposal or modification under which the priority attaching to a preferential debt is lost or modified, except with the concurrence of the preferential creditor concerned.

After the conclusion of the meeting, the chairman reports the results of it to the court within four days, by filing a copy of his report in court. The court endorses the copy with the date of filing. Immediately after so reporting he gives notice of the result of the meeting to all those who were sent notice of the meeting. The chairman's report must:

"(a) state whether the proposal for a voluntary arrangement was approved or rejected and, if approved, with what (if any) modifications;
(b) set out the resolutions which were taken at the meeting, and the decision on each one;
(c) list the creditors (with their respective values) who were present or represented at the meeting, and how they voted on each resolution; and
(d) include such further information (if any) as the chairman thinks it appropriate to make known to the court."

(Rule 5.22(2))

(c) Chairman of meeting

The nominee takes the chair at the meeting. Where he is unable to attend, he may nominate in his place either a person qualified to act as an insolvency practitioner in relation to the debtor, or an employee of the nominee or his firm who is experienced in insolvency matters (Rule 5.15).

The chairman may not use any proxy he holds to vote to increase or reduce the remuneration or expenses of the nominee or supervisor, unless the proxy specifically directs him so to vote (Rule 5.16). If he does so, that vote will not count towards a majority (see below for the requirements as to majorities).

(d) Voting rights

By Rule 5.17 all creditors who had notice of the meeting may vote at it. Votes are calculated according to the amount of the creditor's debt at a certain date - in Case 1 as at the date of the bankruptcy order, and in Case 2 as at the date of the meeting. A creditor may not vote in respect of a debt whose value is unliquidated or otherwise not ascertained, unless the chairman agrees an estimated minimum value for the debt for the purpose of entitlement to vote.

The chairman may admit or reject a creditor's claim in whole or in part for the purpose of his entitlement to vote. The chairman's decision on entitlement to vote is subject to appeal to the court by any creditor, or by the debtor. If the chairman is in doubt whether a claim should be admitted or rejected, he should mark it as objected to and allow the creditor to vote, subject to his vote being subsequently declared invalid if the objection to the claim is sustained. If on an appeal the chairman's decision is reversed or varied, or a creditor's vote is declared invalid, the court may order another meeting to be summoned, or make such other order as it thinks just, but the court may only exercise this power if it considers that the matter is such as to give rise to unfair prejudice or a material irregularity. An application to the court by way of appeal against the chairman's decision may not be made after the end of the 28 days from the day on which the chairman's report to the court is made under s 259. The chairman is not personally liable for any costs incurred by any person in respect of an appeal resulting therefrom.

(e) Requisite majorities

A resolution approving any proposal or modification must be by a majority of at least three quarters in value of the creditors *present in person or by proxy* and voting on the resolution (Rule 5.18). Any other type of resolution requires a majority of at least half. As to majorities in value, see page 208.

Where:

- (i) written notice of the claim was not given either at or before the meeting to the chairman or nominee; or
- (ii) the claim is wholly or partly secured; or
- (iii) the claim is in respect of a debt wholly or partly on or secured by a current bill of exchange or promissory note, unless the creditor is willing (1) to treat the liability to him on the bill or note of every person who is liable on it antecedently to the debtor, and against whom a bankruptcy order has not been made (or, in the case of a company, which has not gone into liquidation), as a security in his hands, and (2) to estimate the value of the security and (for the purpose of entitlement to vote, but not of any distribution under the arrangement) to deduct it from his claim,

then a creditor's vote in respect of that claim or part of a claim is left out of account. It is for the chairman to decide whether a vote is to be left out under this provision.

A resolution is not valid if those voting against it include more than half in value of the creditors; the only creditors, however, who will be counted for this purpose are those who had notice of the meeting, whose votes were not left out of account under the provisions explained above, and who are not, to the best of the chairman's belief, associates of the debtor. It is for the chairman to decide whether or not a person is an associate of the debtor (see s 435), and in so doing he may rely on information provided by the debtor in his statement of affairs or otherwise.

An appeal is available against the decision of the chairman as to the leaving out of a vote and as to whether a person is an associate of the debtor. The procedure is the same as for an appeal against a decision of the chairman on voting rights (see page 202).

(f) Adjournment of meeting

On the day on which the creditors' meeting is to be held, it may be adjourned from time to time. If on that day the requisite majority to approve the voluntary arrangement (with or without modification) is not obtained, the chairman may adjourn the meeting for not more than fourteen days, and must do so if the meeting so resolves. If there are then further adjournments, the final adjournment shall be to a day no later than fourteen days after the date on which the meeting was first held. Notice of an adjournment must be given by the chairman to the court. If, following the final adjournment of the meeting, the proposal, whether or not modified, is not agreed to, it is deemed rejected. (Rule 5.19)

(g) Business at the creditors' meeting following interim order

The meeting of the creditors is summoned under s 257(1) and Rule 5.13, for the time date and place proposed in the nominee's report under s 256. The meeting stands adjourned for up to 21 days if a quorum is not present within 30 minutes of the appointed time. The chairman and three proxies constitute a quorum; if fewer than three creditors (or proxies) attend, then the meeting may only elect the chairman, admit creditors' claims and adjourn the meeting (Rule 6.92).

The proceedings at the meeting are as follows:

AGENDA FOR THE MEETING OF CREDITORS FOLLOWING THE INTERIM ORDER

(i) *The Chairman* This is the nominee, an insolvency practitioner appointed by the court. He may nominate another qualified member to take the meeting (Rule 5.15).

(ii) *Notice of meeting* Notice should be verified as having taken place in accordance with Rule 5.13(3) (above).

(iii) *Creditors in attendance* The chairman draws up a list of creditors attending, showing those whose claims have been admitted, and those whose claims he has rejected (Rule 5.17). If he is in doubt he should mark the claim "objected to" and allow the creditor to vote pending appeal (Rule 5.17(6)).

(iv) *Proxies* The chairman declares the proxies he has received prior to the meeting on Form 8.1 and allowed for voting (Rule 6.93). He confirms that they are available for inspection by any person attending the meeting (Rule 8.5(4)), and explains that proxy holders with a financial interest in a resolution must not vote in favour unless the proxy specifically directs his vote (Rule 8.6).

(v) *Report on the scheme of arrangements* The nominee, having circulated a copy or summary of the proposals together with his comments, invites discussion on the advantages to the creditors, and circumstances which would give rise to a suspension of the arrangement, for example that the debtor might be unable to comply with his obligations thereunder.

(vi) *Bankrupt's statement* The chairman may invite the bankrupt to address the meeting if he considers that an explanation of his proposals and undertakings would be helpful. He may also answer questions at the discretion of the chairman (Rule 6.84) and must give his consent (or refusal) to any modifications proposed by the meeting under s 258(2). However, any such amendments may not be such as to cease to make it a s 253 proposal (on which the interim order was based) (s 258(3)); neither may they affect the right of a secured debtor to enforce his security (s 258(4)), nor become a proposal that prejudices a preferential creditor without his concurrence (s 258(5)).

(vii) *Resolutions to be taken* (Rule 6.80)

- Amendments to the proposals
- The proposed arrangement (including the modifications if approved)
- Adjourning the meeting for not more than fourteen days (if requisite majority not obtained) (Rule 5.19)
- Appointment of the supervisor of the arrangement (if approved) (Rule 5.20)
- Any other resolution which the nominee thinks it right to allow.

Voting on resolutions: The proposal is passed when a majority in excess of three quarters in value, voting in person or by proxy, votes in favour of it (Rule 5.18(1)). For any other resolution the majority is one half (Rule 5.18(2)).

(viii) *Report of the meeting* The chairman prepares a report of the proceedings under s 259, and files a copy in the bankruptcy court within four days, with a copy to all creditors who were sent notice of the meeting (Rule 5.22).

2. Rules for creditors' meetings following a bankruptcy order

(a) *Resolution for appointment and removal of trustee*

For the appointment of a trustee at a first general meeting, see page 212 below. If a meeting is held but no appointment of a person as trustee is made, it is the duty of the official receiver to decide whether to refer the need for an appointment to the Secretary of State (see page 87).

The chairman may at any time put to the meeting a resolution for the joint appointment of two or more nominees. In respect of a vote given by a person as creditor or as proxy for a creditor, where a resolution affects a person's remuneration or conduct as trustee, or as proposed or former trustee, the vote of that person and of any partner or employee of his, shall not be count towards a majority. (Rule 6.88(3) and (4)).

By s 298 the trustee may be removed from office only by an order of the court or by a general meeting of creditors summoned specially for that purpose. If he was appointed by the Secretary of State he may be removed by the direction of the Secretary of State (see page 318). A general meeting of the creditors may be summoned for the purpose of replacing the trustee only if the trustee thinks fit, the court so directs, or the meeting is so requested by one of the bankrupt's creditors with the concurrence of not less than one quarter in value of the creditors (including the creditor making the request).

Where the appointment fails to take effect the official receiver is trustee until the vacancy is filled. He may summon a general meeting of the creditors for the purpose of filling the vacancy and shall do so if required by s 314(7) (creditors' requisition; see page 212).

Reference to a vacancy includes the case where it is necessary to revive the trusteeship (ie after holding a final meeting under s 331 or after the giving of a notice by the official receiver under s 299(2)) in relation to any property which is or may be comprised in a bankrupt's estate.

As to the need for trustees to be licensed as insolvency practitioners, see page 19; for the fixing of their remuneration see page 221 and as to their release, see page 314.

(b) Deposit for expenses of summoning meetings

The expenses of summoning and holding a meeting at the instance of someone other than the official receiver or trustee fall to that person, who must deposit security for the payment of those expenses with the trustee, or, if no trustee has been appointed, with the official receiver. The trustee or official receiver determines the amount of the security and it must be deposited before the matter may proceed. The meeting may subsequently decide that the expenses should be paid out of the estate. If it transpires that any deposit or part of a deposit so paid is not needed for paying the expenses of summoning and holding the meeting, it is to be refunded. (Rule 6.87)

(c) Creditors' committee

The creditors' committee is established by resolution at the first meeting (see page 211).

(d) Chairman

Where a meeting is convened by the official receiver, he or his nominee is chairman of the meeting. In the latter case, the nomination must be in writing unless it is of another official receiver or a deputy official receiver. Where the meeting is convened by someone other than the official receiver, then he, the convener, or a person nominated by him in writing, is chairman. A chairman nominated other than by the official receiver must be qualified to act as an insolvency practitioner in relation to the bankrupt, or he must be an employee of the trustee or of his firm and experienced in insolvency matters.

(e) Quorum

A quorum comprises three creditors entitled to vote, or all the creditors if their total is less than three, present in person or by proxy. A quorum is not needed to elect a chairman; for the admission by the chairman of proofs for the purpose of their entitlement to vote; or to adjourn a meeting. One person alone is a quorum where he is himself a creditor entitled to vote and, with his own vote, holds sufficient proxies to meet the above requirements; or is the chairman or any other person and where he holds sufficient proxies to ensure the quorum requirement is met. (Rule 6.92) In calculating a quorum under Rule 6.92, only those entitled to vote under Rule 6.93 may be reckoned; see *Re Thomas ex parte Warner* (1911) 55 SJ 482.

(f) Entitlement to vote

A person may only vote at a creditors' meeting as a creditor if he has lodged his proof as required in the notice convening the meeting, and the claim has been admitted for the purpose of entitlement to vote (Rule 6.93). He must also have properly lodged any requisite proxy (see page 215). In exceptional circumstances the court may permit a creditor to vote without proving his debt and in such a case, the court may, on the application of the trustee, make such consequential order as it thinks fit.

A creditor may not vote in respect of a debt which is unliquidated or whose value is not ascertained, unless the chairman agrees to an estimated minimum value for the purpose of entitlement to vote and admits the proof for that purpose. A secured creditor may vote only in respect of the balance of the debt after deducting the value of the security as estimated by him.

If a secured creditor votes in respect of his whole debt and omits to disclose his security, then he will be deemed to have surrendered his security unless the omission was inadvertent or the result of an honest mistake (see page 199), or that the security covers other debts not proved; see *Re Pawson* [1917] 2 KB 527.

A creditor may not vote in respect of a debt on, or secured by, a bill of exchange or promissory note unless he is willing:

(i) to treat the liability to him on the bill or note of every person who is liable on it antecedently to the bankrupt, and against whom a bankruptcy order has not been made, as a security in his hands, and

(ii) to estimate the value of the security and (for the purpose of entitlement to vote but not for dividend) to deduct it from his proof.

(g) Admission and rejection of proofs

For the purpose of ascertaining a creditor's entitlement to vote at a meeting, the chairman has power to admit or reject his proof. This power is exercisable with respect to the whole or any part of his proof (Rule 6.94).

Rule 6.94 also provides that the chairman's decision under this Rule, or in respect of any matter arising under Rule 6.93 is subject to appeal to the court by any creditor or by the bankrupt. If the chairman is in doubt whether or not to admit a proof, he should mark it "objected to" and allow the creditor to vote, subject to his vote being declared invalid later if the objection to the proof is sustained. If on appeal the chairman's decision on a proof is varied or reversed, or a creditor's vote declared invalid, the court may order another meeting, or make such other order as appears just. Neither the official receiver nor any person nominated by him to be chairman is personally liable for costs incurred by any person in respect of an application to the court under Rule 6.94. The chairman (if other than the official receiver or a person so nominated) is not so liable unless the court makes an order to that effect.

The chairman's decision is not binding on a chairman at a subsequent meeting; see *Re Potts* [1934] Ch 356. On an appeal from the chairman's rejection of a proof the bankrupt has no *locus standi* to appear and to oppose the appeal even if he is served with notice of an appeal; see *Re Knight ex parte Smith* (1884) 1 Mor 74.

(h) Majority in value

Where voting rights are based on a majority in value of creditors, this means a majority in value of all debts (after deducting the value of security held by creditors, if any), in respect of those creditors entitled to vote and be present at the meeting, either in person or through their proxies (see page 215). A Companies Act case on the subject is *Clay* v *Grand Junction Waterworks Co* 21 TLR 31. For a case on valuation by the court of a proof of debt, see *Re Burghart ex parte Varnish* (1841) 10 LJ Bcy 50.

(i) Attendance of bankrupt

Whenever any meeting is summoned, the person convening the meeting must give 21 days notice of it to the bankrupt on Form 6.36. If the meeting is adjourned, the chairman must notify the bankrupt if he was not present, unless it appears to the chairman unnecessary or impracticable to do so. The convener may, if he thinks fit, notify the bankrupt that he is *required* to be present or in attendance at a particular meeting, and the creditors do not appear to be able to waive this requirement; see *Re Best, ex parte Best* (1881) 45 TLT 95. At the discretion of the chairman, the bankrupt may be admitted to any meeting, as may any other person who has given reasonable notice that he wishes to be present. The chairman's decision is final as to what, if any, intervention may be made by the bankrupt or any person admitted to the meeting. (Rule 6.84)

If the bankrupt is absent from a meeting and it is desired to question him, the chairman may adjourn the meeting so as to secure the bankrupt's attendance. Where the bankrupt is present at a creditors' meeting, the questions which may be put to him are at the chairman's discretion.

The chairman has the power to prevent improper and immaterial questions being put to him, but such power has to be exercised honestly and its exercise is open to review by the creditors; see *Re Hope ex parte Hope* (1878) 9 Ch 398.

(j) Record of proceedings

The chairman must arrange for minutes to be taken of all creditors' meetings. The minutes must include a record of all resolutions passed. He must sign and retain the minutes. He must also arrange for a list of creditors attending the meeting to be compiled and kept. The chairman must ensure that particulars of all resolutions passed are certified by him and filed in court not more than 21 days after the date of the meeting. (Rule 6.95)

A minute of proceedings at a meeting signed by a person describing himself as, or appearing to be, the chairman of that meeting is admissible in insolvency proceedings without further proof (Rule 12.5).

(k) Suspension and adjournment of meetings

Once only in the course of a meeting, the chairman may at his discretion and without adjournment, declare the meeting suspended for a period of up to one hour (Rule 6.90).

At his discretion he may, and must if the meeting so resolves, adjourn the meeting to such time and place as seems appropriate; however, the consent of at least one half in value of the creditors present and entitled to vote is needed to adjourn a meeting chaired by the trustee or his nominee where a resolution removing the trustee has been proposed.

If, within 30 minutes from the time appointed for the commencement of a meeting, a quorum is not present, the meeting is automatically adjourned to such time and place as may be appointed by the chairman. An adjournment under these powers shall be for not more than 21 days and the usual rules about venue (see *(l)* below) apply to the adjourned meeting.

If at a meeting there is no person to act as chairman, some other person present and entitled to vote may, with the agreement of the others present, appoint the time and place to which the meeting will be adjourned. If agreement is not reached, the adjournment shall be to the same time and place a week following, or, if that is not a business day, to the business day immediately following. Where a meeting is adjourned in this way, proofs and proxies may be used if lodged at any time up to noon on the business day immediately before the adjourned meeting. (Rule 6.91)

(l) Venue

When fixing a venue for a meeting, the convener must have regard to the convenience of creditors. Meetings must be summoned to commence between 10 am and 4 pm on a business day unless the court otherwise directs, and forms of proxy (Form 8.2) must be sent with every notice summoning a creditors' meeting. (Rule 6.86)

(m) Notice of meetings by advertisement only

The court may order that notice of any meeting be given by public advertisement rather than by individual notice to those concerned. In considering whether or not to make such an order, the court must have regard to the cost of advertising, the amount of funds in the estate, and the extent of the interest of creditors or any particular class of them, ie whether or not in priority. The proceedings are intituled "In Bankruptcy". (Rule 6.85)

3. First meeting of creditors following bankruptcy order

Where a bankruptcy order has been made (see page 70) and no certificate for the summary administration of the bankrupt's estate has been issued, it is the duty of the official receiver to decide whether or not to summon a general meeting of creditors to appoint a trustee of the bankrupt's estate.

(a) Summoning the meeting

The official receiver has twelve weeks beginning with the day on which the bankruptcy order was made, to decide whether or not to summon the meeting. If he does decide to summon a meeting of creditors under s 293(1) and Rule 6.79(2), he fixes a venue not more than four months from the date of the bankruptcy order. Notice is given to the court forthwith, and, at least 21 days before the date fixed, to every creditor known to the official receiver or identified in the statement of affairs. The notice to the creditors must give a time and date, not more than four days before the date fixed for the meeting, by which they must lodge their proofs and (if applicable) proxies, in order to be entitled to vote at the meeting. Notice must also be given by advertisement.

If he decides not to, then he must give notice of his decision before the end of the twelve weeks to every creditor known to him or identified in the statement of affairs, and he becomes trustee of the bankrupt's estate.

(b) Power of creditors to requisition a meeting

Where the official receiver has not yet summoned, or has decided not to summon, a first meeting of the bankrupt's creditors to appoint a trustee under s 293, and a certificate for the summary administration is not in force, any creditor of the bankrupt may request the official receiver to summon such a meeting for that purpose (on Form 6.34). It is his duty to summon the meeting provided it is requested by not less than one quarter in value of the bankrupt's creditors, which includes the creditor making the request (s 294).

Following such a request he is then also bound to withdraw any notice under s 293(2) (that he has decided not to summon a meeting), and must fix the venue for not more than three months from his receipt of the creditor's request; he then proceeds on the basis of *(a)* above under Rule 6.79(6).

(c) Business at the first meeting

Where a first meeting of the creditors is summoned under s 293(1) and Rule 6.79(2) by the official receiver, or requisitioned by the creditors under s 294 and Rule 6.79(6), and provided there is a quorum, the normal proceedings are as set out below. The meeting stands adjourned for up to 21 days if a quorum is not present within 30 minutes of the appointed time. The chairman and three proxies constitute a quorum; if fewer than three creditors (or proxies) attend then the meeting may only elect a chairman, admit creditors' proofs and adjourn the meeting.

AGENDA FOR THE FIRST MEETING OF CREDITORS

(i) *The Chairman* This is the official receiver or a person nominated by him under Rule 6.82.

(ii) *Notice of meeting* It should be verified as taking place in accordance with Rule 6.79, or requisitioned in accordance with Rule 6.83.

(iii) *Creditors in attendance* The chairman draws up a list of creditors attending, showing by class those whose claims have been admitted, and by class those whose proofs he has rejected (Rule 6.94).

(iv) *Proxies* The chairman declares the proxies he has received prior to the meeting on Form 8.2 and allowed for voting (Rule 6.93). He confirms that they are available for inspection by any person attending the meeting (Rule 8.5(4)), and explains that proxy holders with a financial interest in a resolution must not vote in favour unless the proxy specifically directs his vote (Rule 8.6).

(v) *Report on the bankruptcy* The official receiver gives a summary of the bankrupt's affairs as known to him (Rules 6.75 and 6.76) and may distribute a copy of the statement of affairs (if available). He details steps so far taken, including the public examination (if any) held to recover property for the estate, and gives any views he may have as to the administration, for example, whether or not to ask the court to appoint a special manager under s 370.

(vi) *Bankrupt's statement* The chairman may invite the bankrupt to address the meeting when he considers that an explanation would be helpful. He may also answer questions at the discretion of the chairman (Rule 6.84)

(vii) *Resolutions to be taken* (Rule 6.80)

- to appoint a named insolvency practitioner as trustee in bankruptcy, or two or more named insolvency practitioners as joint trustees (Rule 6.120; see *(d)* below);
- to establish a creditors' committee (Rule 6.151);
- unless it has been resolved to establish a creditors' committee, to specify the terms on which the trustee is to be remunerated or defer the same (Rule 6.138);
- if, and only if, joint trustees are appointed, to specify whether acts are to be done by both or all of them or by one only (Rule 6.88(2));
- where the meeting has been requisitioned, to authorise payment of the cost of summoning and holding the meeting from the estate as an expense of the bankruptcy (Rule 6.87);
- to adjourn the meeting for not more than three weeks (Rule 6.91);

- any other special resolution which the chairman thinks it right to allow for special reasons (Rule 6.88(1)).

Voting on resolutions: A resolution is passed when a majority in value, voting in person or by proxy, vote in favour (Rule 6.88(1)). Specifically, the first meeting may not resolve to appoint the official receiver as trustee. Where the resolution is for the appointment of a trustee:

- if on any vote there are two nominees for appointment, the person who obtains the most support is appointed;
- if there are three or more nominees, and one has a clear majority over both or all the others, that one is appointed; and
- in any other case, the chairman shall continue to take votes (disregarding at each vote any nominee who has withdrawn or, if no nominee has withdrawn, the nominee who obtained least support last time) until a clear majority emerges (Rule 6.88(2))

(viii) *Minutes of the meeting* The chairman signs the minutes of the proceedings and files a copy in the bankruptcy court within 21 days (Rule 6.95).

(d) Resolution for appointment of a trustee

Where a meeting is held which resolves to appoint a trustee under s 292(1)(a), then the following procedural points should be noted:

(i) the chairman of the meeting must certify the appointment (Form 6.40), but not unless and until the person to be appointed has provided him with a written statement to the effect that he is an insolvency practitioner, duly qualified under the Act to act as trustee in relation to the bankrupt, and that he consents so to act;

(ii) the chairman (if not himself the official receiver) shall send the certificate to the official receiver;

(iii) the official receiver shall in any case file a copy of the certificate in court; the trustee's appointment is effective as from the date on which the official receiver files the copy certificate in court, that date to be endorsed on the copy certificate. The certificate, so endorsed, is sent by the official receiver to the trustee. (Rule 6.120)

4. General meetings of creditors

(a) General power to call meetings

The trustee *may* summon a general meeting of the bankrupt's creditors at any time, under s 314(7); and *must* do so where requested by a creditor of the bankrupt if the request is made with the concurrence in value of not less than one tenth of the creditors (including the creditor making the request). The official receiver or trustee may at any time call subsequent general meetings to ascertain the wishes of the creditors on any matter arising in the bankruptcy (Rule 6.81). The person summoning a meeting is referred to as "the convener", and he must give 21 days notice of any meeting to all creditors known to him or identified in the bankrupt's statement of affairs. The notice (Form 6.35) must state the purpose of the meeting and give a date (not more than four days before the meeting) by which proxies, and proofs in the case of those who have not already filed them, must be filed to establish entitlement to vote at the meeting. Notice may also be given by advertisement if the convener thinks fit or if the court so orders.

(b) General power of creditors to requisition a meeting under s 314(7)

By Rule 6.83, in the case of a requisitioned meeting, where the creditors request the official receiver or trustee to summon a meeting of creditors, the meeting shall be summoned and the notice shall be accompanied by:

(i) a list of creditors concurring with the request and the amount of their claims;
(ii) the written confirmation of his concurrence from each concurring creditor;
(iii) a statement of the purpose of the meeting.

However, (i) and (ii) need not be complied with if the requisitioning creditor's debt is alone sufficient to request the meeting, ie it is at least one tenth the value of the creditors. The official receiver or trustee then fixes a date for the meeting, which must be not more than 35 days from the date of receiving the request, and gives 21 days notice to the creditors of the venue for it (Form 6.35).

Any creditor appears to have the right to request the official receiver or the trustee to summon a general meeting for the purpose of replacing the trustee provided he makes his request with the concurrence of not less than one quarter in value of the creditors, including the creditor making the request. However, this is without prejudice to the right of the creditors to replace the trustee if they think fit or if the court so requires; see page 316 *et seq*. As to control by general meeting of the creditors, see page 248.

(c) Business at a general meeting

When a meeting of creditors is summoned under s 314(7) and Rule 6.81 by the official receiver or by the trustee, or requisitioned by a creditor under s 314(7) and Rule 6.83, and provided there is a quorum (the quorum requirement is as for the first meeting, page 207), the normal proceedings are as follows:

AGENDA FOR A GENERAL MEETING

(i) *The chairman* This will be the official receiver or the trustee (Rule 6.81(1)).
(ii) *Notice of meeting* Notice should be verified as having been in accordance with Rule 6.81 or requisitioned in accordance with Rule 6.83.
(iii) *Creditors in attendance* (Rule 6.94 - as for first meeting; see page 211).
(iv) *Proxies* (Form 8.2) Rules 6.93, 8.5(4) and 8.6 - as for first meeting.
(v) *Report on the bankruptcy* Rules 6.75 and 6.76 - as for first meeting.
(vi) *Bankrupt's statement* Rule 6.84 - as for first meeting.
(vii) *Resolutions to be taken* The following resolutions may be taken:
- where the meeting has been requisitioned, authorising the payment of

the cost of summoning and holding the meeting from the estate as an expense of the bankruptcy (Rule 6.87);

- adjourning the meeting for not more than three weeks (Rule 6.91);
- any other resolution (Rule 6.88)

A resolution is passed when a majority in value, voting in person or by proxy, vote in favour (Rule 6.88(1)). Where the resolution is for the appointment of a trustee:

- if on any vote there are two nominees for appointment, the person who obtains the most support is appointed;
- if there are three or more nominees, and one has a clear majority over both or all the others, that one is appointed; and
- in any other case, the chairman shall continue to take votes (disregarding at each vote any nominee who has withdrawn or, if no nominee has withdrawn, the nominee who obtained least support last time) until a clear majority emerges (Rule 6.88(2))

(viii) *Minutes of the meeting* Rule 6.95 - as for first meeting (see page 212).

5. Final general meeting of creditors

(a) Summoning the meeting under s 331

The trustee summons a final meeting, at least 28 days before the date fixed, to receive his report and determine whether or not he should have his release under s 299. The notice may be given at the same time as giving notice of the final dividend under s 330(1) in accordance with Rule 11.2. But if summoned for an earlier date, that meeting should be adjourned, and if necessary further adjourned, until a date on which the trustee is able to report to the meeting that the administration of the bankrupt's estate is for all practical purposes complete. The notice is sent to all creditors who have proved their debts and to the bankrupt.

(b) Where trustee unable to dispose of the matrimonial home

Where the trustee has for any reason been unable to realise the dwelling-house which is occupied by the bankrupt or by his spouse or former spouse, he only summons a final general meeting under s 332 if:

(i) the court has made an order under s 313 imposing a charge on that property for the benefit of the bankrupt's estate; or

(ii) the court has declined, on an application under that section, to make such an order; or

(iii) the Secretary of State has issued a certificate to the trustee stating that it would be inappropriate or inexpedient for such an application to be made in the case in question.

See also Chapter 10 on the matrimonial home, and page 146 for charging orders applying to it.

(c) Business at the final meeting

A meeting of creditors is summoned under Rule 6.137(1) by the trustee, and a quorum is required (as for the first meeting, page 207). If there is no quorum, he reports to the court that a final meeting was summoned in accordance with the rules but there was no quorum. The meeting is deemed to have been held, and the creditors not to have resolved against his release (Rule 6.137(5)). Otherwise proceedings are as follows:

AGENDA FOR A FINAL MEETING

(i) *The chairman* This will be the trustee (s 331(2)).

(ii) *Notice of meeting* Notice should be verified as having been in accordance with Rule 6.137(1) and s 330 if applicable.

(iii) *Creditors in attendance* (Rule 6.94 - as for first meeting).

(iv) *Proxies* Form 8.2 (Rules 6.93, 8.5(4)) and Form 8.6 as for final meeting; see page 211

(v) *Trustee's report* He reports to the meeting on his administration of the bankrupt's estate and that it is for practical purposes complete. He circulates a summary of the receipts and payments, together with a statement that he has reconciled his account with that held by the Secretary of State in respect of the bankruptcy. The meeting may question him with respect to any matter contained in his report (Rule 6.137(2) and (3)).

(vi) *Bankrupt's statement* Rule 6.84 - as for first meeting; see page 211.

(vii) *Resolutions to be taken* The following resolutions may be taken:

- adjourning the meeting for not more than three weeks (Rule 6.91);
- any other resolution (Rule 6.88);
- release of the trustee (s 299(3)(d), Rules 6.135(1) and 6.137(6); see page 315.

(viii) *Minutes of the meeting* Rule 6.95 - as for first meeting (see page 212) with notice to the court under Rule 6.137(4).

6. Voting by proxy

Votes at meetings may be cast personally or by proxy. Proxies should be given in the prescribed form (Form 8.1 for individual voluntary arrangements, and Form 8.4 for bankruptcy) and personally signed by the creditor or some person authorised by him. Rules 8.1 to 8.6 contain the detailed rules governing the use of proxies:

(a) Meaning of "proxy"

A proxy is "an authority given by a person ("the principal") to another person ("the proxy holder") to attend a meeting and speak and vote as his representative". A person may give only one proxy for any one meeting, and may give it to one person only, who must be aged eighteen or over. The principal may, however, specify one or more others to be proxy holder in the alternative, in the order in which they are named in the proxy. A proxy may be given to the chairman of the meeting or the official receiver. (Rule 8.1)

(b) Forms

There is only one form for the proxy, but it provides for a general or special direction. The proxy requires the proxy holder to cast the principal's vote on matters arising at the meeting, or to abstain, either as directed or in accordance with the holder's own discretion. It may also require the holder to propose a resolution in the principal's name.

When notice of a meeting is issued with a proxy form (Form 8.1 in voluntary arrangements; Form 8.4 in bankruptcy), the forms must not have inserted on them the name or description of any person. Forms of proxy used at a meeting must be those sent out with the notice of meeting, or forms substantially similar. The proxy must be signed by the principal or someone authorised by him; if the latter, the nature of the authority must be stated (Rule 8.2). The signature must be witnessed and the person appointed to act as proxy cannot himself be the attesting witness; see *Re Parrott ex parte Cullen* [1891] 2 QB 151.

(c) Use of proxies

A proxy given for a particular meeting may be used at an adjournment of that meeting. Where the official receiver has been appointed proxy, his deputy or any other official receiver may act as proxy holder in his place, or the official receiver may give written authorisation to an officer of the Department of Trade and Industry to act for him at the meeting and as proxy holder. Where an insolvency practitioner holds proxies to be used by him as chairman of a meeting, and some other person acts as chairman, the other person may use the insolvency practitioner's proxies as if he were himself proxy holder. (Rule 8.3). Proxies which have been used for voting are retained by the chairman of the meeting, who, after the meeting, sends them to the responsible insolvency practitioner if that is someone other than himself. (Rule 8.4)

(d) Inspection

The insolvency practitioner must, as long as he holds the proxies, allow them to be inspected, at all reasonable times on a business day, by the bankrupt and by creditors who have proved their debts or persons who have submitted a written claim to be creditors, but not by those whose proofs or claims have been wholly rejected for purposes of voting, dividend or otherwise. A person attending a meeting is also entitled to inspect the proxies immediately before or in the course of the meeting. (Rule 8.5)

(e) Interest of proxy holder

A proxy holder may not vote for any resolution which would directly or indirectly place him or any associate of his in a position to receive any remuneration out of the insolvent estate, unless the proxy specifically directs him so to vote. This applies also to a person acting as chairman and using proxies in that capacity, and in this connection the proxy holder is deemed an associate of his (Rule 8.6). There is no rule against the bankrupt himself being appointed as a proxy.

(f) Chairman as proxy holder

Where the chairman holds a proxy requiring him to vote for a particular resolution and no other person proposes that resolution, the chairman must himself propose it unless he considers there is good reason for not doing so; if he does not propose it he must, immediately after the meeting, notify his principal of the reason why not (Rule 6.89).

Note also Rule 5.16 as to the restriction on the use of a proxy by the chairman to alter the remuneration of the nominee or supervisor, unless the proxy specifically directs him to vote in that way.

7. Appeal by the trustee

(a) Application for directions

The trustee may apply to the court under s 303(2) for directions in relation to any particular matter arising under the bankruptcy as to law or procedure. In a case where the creditors have by resolution at a general meeting given the trustee directions, the court has power, for just cause shown, to direct the trustee to disregard the directions of the creditors and to act in a manner contrary to them. In such a case the court ought not to order the resolution to be vacated or to declare it void, but simply to direct the trustee to disregard it; see *Re Poole ex parte Cocks* (1882) 21 ChD 397, 31 WR 105. In *Re Russell ex parte Montgomery* (1822) 1 G I&J 338 the question arose as to whether the court should interfere with the realisation of the bankrupt's estate. It was decided that the court ought not to interfere to stay a sale. The trustee and not the court is judge of the propriety and expediency of a sale.

(b) Remuneration

Where there is no committee (or where there is but it fails to determine the remuneration of the trustee), the trustee may appeal to a general meeting of creditors to have his remuneration fixed by resolution in accordance with Rule 6.138 (see page 221). If it is still not fixed then by Rule 6.138(6) it is calculated on the scale laid down for official receivers in accordance with Regulation 19 (see Appendix 5). This overcomes the problem in those cases where creditors do not come to meetings called.

(c) Disagreement as to remuneration

Where the trustee considers that the remuneration fixed by resolution of the creditors under Rule 6.138(5) or (6) (rate for official receivers) is insufficient he may apply to the court for an order increasing the amount or rate; note, however, that any creditor may, with the concurrence of one quarter in value of the creditors including himself, likewise appeal to the court for an order reducing remuneration (see page 256).

Chapter 15

Creditors' meetings - in committee

1. Introduction

The creditors' committee is appointed by the creditors in general meeting with the duty of superintending the administration of the bankrupt estate by the trustee. It comprises not more than five and not less than three members qualified as any of the following: a creditor; a holder of a proxy from a creditor or a prospective holder; or a person holding a general power of attorney from a creditor.

The committee should be appointed if at all possible by resolution at the first meeting of creditors by those qualified to vote (see page 211), but may, by general resolution, be appointed at any subsequent meeting.

It is important for the successful running of the estate that the creditors who are appointed are selected with considerable discretion. They should have a sense of business for they have important sanctions to effect and will identify particular areas where they require specific reports from the trustee. If no committee is appointed then the Secretary of State will give all necessary authorisations on application to him by the trustee.

2. Establishment

A general meeting of a bankrupt's creditors may resolve to establish a creditors' committee to exercise the functions conferred on it by the Act under s 301. It may not, however, set up such a committee where the official receiver is trustee, other than in connection with an appointment made by that meeting of a person to be trustee instead of the official receiver. Its primary function is to control the trustee and settle his remuneration (see page 221); as to his powers, exercisable with the consent of the committee, see page 251.

The committee is formally established under Rule 6.151 when the trustee issues a certificate of constitution (Form 6.52). If the chairman of the creditors' meeting which decides to set up the committee is not also the trustee, he must give the trustee immediate notice of the resolution to establish the committee, and give him the names and addresses of those elected to be members. A creditor may not act as a committee member unless he has agreed to do so, and the trustee's certificate of the due constitution of the committee may not be issued until at least three persons elected to be members have agreed to act. If others later agree to act, the trustee issues an amended certificate (Form 6.52). The certificate, and any revised certificate, is filed in court by the trustee, who must also report to the court any changes in the membership of the committee (Form 6.53).

3. Constitution

(a) Membership

Rule 6.150 provides that the committee must consist of not fewer than three and not more than five members. The members must all be creditors of the bankrupt, and any creditor may be a member of the committee provided:

(i) he is not fully secured;
(ii) he has lodged a proof of his debt; and
(iii) his proof has neither been disallowed for voting purposes nor wholly rejected for the purposes of distribution or dividend.

A creditor who has not yet rendered a proof may be qualified for appointment to the committee but cannot act until he has proved his debt and the proof has been admitted; see *Re Jones ex parte Goatly* (1911) 56 SJ 17.

A corporate body may be a member of the committee but can only act through a duly appointed representative appointed under Rule 6.156 (see below).

(b) Representatives

Under Rule 6.156, a member of the committee may be represented by another duly authorised person. The representative must have a letter of authority giving him general or particular authority to transact the business of the committee member. The letter must be signed by or on behalf of the committee member. The chairman of any committee meeting may require to see the authority, and may exclude the representative if his authority appears defective. The following may not act as a representative:

(i) a body corporate;
(ii) an undischarged bankrupt;
(iii) a person subject to a composition or arrangement with his creditors.

No person may act as representative of more than one committee member at the same time; or act both as a member of a committee and as a representative of another member of the same committee.

Where a representative signs a document on behalf of the member, that fact must be endorsed below his signature.

(c) Expenses of members

Reasonable travelling expenses incurred by members or their representative(s) in attending creditors' meetings and conducting the business of the committee may be defrayed out of the estate in the prescribed order of priority under Rule 6.224(1)(m) - see page 233 - and Rule 6.164).

(d) Dealings by committee members and others

No member may stand in any fiduciary relationship to the bankrupt's estate, being precluded on general equitable principles: see *Re Bulmer, Greaves* v *Inland Revenue Commissioners* (1937) 1 All ER 323. Rule 6.165 concerns members of the committee, their representative(s), any associate of either, and any person who has been a member of the committee within the preceding twelve months. The rule provides that such a person may not enter into any transaction by which he:

- (i) receives out of the estate any payment for goods or services supplied in connection with the administration of the estate; or
- (ii) obtains any profit from the administration; or
- (iii) acquires an asset forming part of the estate.

This rule extends to the holder of a (general) proxy from a creditor who acts in his place on the committee: see *Re Bulmer, Greaves* v *Commissioners of Inland Revenue* (above, and see page 215) as to proxies, and professional guidance note 22 (page 27).

However, such a transaction may be entered into if:

- (i) the court gives prior leave; or
- (ii) it is done as a matter of urgency or to complete a contract entered into before the commencement of the bankruptcy and the court's leave is applied for without undue delay and given; or
- (iii) the committee, having had full disclosure of the circumstances, is satisfied that the person will be giving full value in the transaction, and gives its prior sanction. No member or representative who is to participate directly or indirectly in the transaction may vote on a resolution to grant such sanction.

The costs of an application to the court for leave do not fall to the estate unless the court so orders.

On the application of an interested person, the court may order that a transaction entered into in contravention of Rule 6.165 be set aside, or make such other order as it thinks fit. In particular it may order the person concerned to account for any profit arising, and compensate the estate for any resultant loss. However, no such order may be made against an associate of a member or representative if the court is satisfied he had no reason to suppose the transaction contravened the rule. It would not, however, appear to prevent a partner of a member of the creditors' committee from purchasing on his own account, ie not as an associate (as defined): see *Re Gallard, ex parte Gallard (No 2)* [1897] 2 QB 8, which related to a similar prohibition under the old rules on purchasing from the estate.

The consent of the court cannot be given *after* the profit had been derived but has to be obtained *before* the business from which the profit was derived was undertaken: *Re Gallard, ex parte Gallard* (above).

(e) Sanction on trustee

The committee has sanction with regard to certain powers exercisable by the trustee under s 314, including carrying on the business of the bankrupt, options, arbitration, compromise and other arrangements set out in Part 1 of Sch 5 to the Act (see *(e)* below and page 153) including the duty under Rule 12.8(2) to review from time to time the adequacy of the security (see page 24).

(f) Formal defects

The acts of the creditors' committee are valid notwithstanding any defect in the appointment, election or qualifications of any member of the committee (s 377).

4. Powers of the committee

(a) Fixing of trustee's remuneration

The trustee is entitled to receive remuneration for his services, which is fixed by the creditors' committee or (where there is no committee) by a resolution of a meeting of creditors, with appeal thereafter to the court. The remuneration of the official receiver when acting as trustee is set out in Appendix 5. Under Rule 6.224(1)(o) the trustee *cannot* receive more than is authorised for the official receiver in priority; any balance over that ranks behind other expenses at (1)(q).

As a matter of practice it is a sound plan at the outset to take the meeting through every possible provision prior to fixing the remuneration, so that the resolution expresses exactly which expenses the remuneration is to cover, and to avoid a successful challenge by a creditor under Rule 6.142 that the remuneration is excessive.

Under Rule 6.138(2), the committee decides whether to fix his remuneration either:

- (i) as a percentage of the value of the assets realised or distributed, or of the one value and the other in combination; or
- (ii) by reference to the time properly spent by the trustee and his staff in dealing with the bankruptcy.

If it settles on (i) above the committee then has to determine the percentage to be applied, in which case they must have regard to:

- (i) the complexity (or otherwise) of the case,
- (ii) any respects in which, in connection with the administration of the estate, there falls on the trustee any responsibility of an exceptional kind or degree,
- (iii) the effectiveness with which the trustee appears to be carrying out, or to have carried out, his duties as trustee, and

(iv) the value and nature of the assets in the estate with which the trustee has to deal.

(Rule 6.138(4))

It is to be noted that there is no provision in the rules for the trustee to receive any percentage on assets that have been realised by the official receiver (and on which he is entitled to claim a fee under para 19 of the Regulations).

The trustee cannot receive out of the estate any additional remuneration for services rendered, for example as an accountant for assisting in the preparation of the debtor's accounts, or as a solicitor in instituting legal proceedings, other than that to which he is entitled as trustee of the estate. All fees, costs, charges and other expenses incurred in the course of the proceedings are to be regarded as expenses of the bankruptcy.

Other matters affecting remuneration are:

(i) *Secured creditors* If the trustee sells assets on behalf of a secured creditor, he is entitled to keep from the proceeds of sale a sum by way of remuneration equivalent to the sum chargeable in the like circumstances by the official receiver.

(ii) *Joint trustees* must agree between themselves the apportionment of remuneration. Any dispute may be referred to the court, to the creditors' committee or to a meeting of creditors (Rule 6.139).

(iii) *Solicitors* If the trustee is a solicitor and employs his own firm, or any partner in it, to act on behalf of the estate, profit costs are not to be paid unless this is authorised by, *inter alia*, the creditors (see also *(c)* below)

(iv) *Exemption from restrictive trade practices* By s 428, the Restrictive Trade Practices Act 1976 is not to apply to any agreement in respect of the charges to be made, quoted or paid for insolvency services supplied, offered or obtained; the terms or conditions on or subject to which they are to be supplied or obtained; the extent (if any) to which, or the scale (if any) on which, the form or manner, and the persons or classes of persons for whom or from whom, or the areas or places in or from which, insolvency services are to be made available or supplied or are to be obtained. "Insolvency services" means the services of persons acting as insolvency practitioners, and expressions used in that Act of 1976 have the same meaning in the Insolvency Act 1986.

(b) Reporting by the trustee

It is the duty of the trustee to report to the committee all matters which appear to him to concern them, or which the members have indicated are of concern to them. Where the members have themselves indicated areas of concern, the trustee need not comply with their request for information where it appears to him that the request is frivolous or unreasonable; or the costs would be out of proportion to the value of the information; or the estate cannot afford to do so (Rule 6.152).

Where the committee is established 28 days or more after the appointment of the trustee, the trustee must give the committee a summary of his actions up to the time of appointment of the committee, and give them such further information as they may request. However, a person who becomes a member of the committee other than at its first establishment, is only entitled to a summary of matters previously dealt with. These provisions do not affect the committee's right of access to the trustee's records of the bankruptcy or to seek an explanation of any matter which forms part of the committee's responsibilities.

The trustee must, as and when directed by the creditors' committee, but not more often than once every two months, send a written report to the members setting out the progress of the bankruptcy and matters arising which the trustee considers should be brought to the attention of the committee. If the committee gives no instructions as to the frequency of reports, they must be sent out not less than once every six months (Rule 6.163).

(c) Employment of others (or himself) by the trustee

The trustee is required to give notice as to the employment of others such as a solicitor. Resolutions sanctioning the employment of others should clearly specify the nature and extent of the work to be performed for the stated rate of remuneration, ie "that the amount of the costs authorised by the creditors' committee should not exceed £*x*". If members of the committee are to retain full control over all legal proceedings, then that should likewise form part of the resolution, although it need not be in any particular form. A resolution to employ a solicitor "where necessary" would appear to be too vague: see *Re Vavasour* [1900] 2 QB 309.

Where any costs, charges or expenses of any person are payable out of the estate, the trustee may agree them with the person or may have them taxed by the court, unless the committee resolves that any such costs, charges or expenses should be taxed, in which case the trustee must require taxation. The trustee may make payments on account. If he overpays, however, the recipient must repay, with interest from the date of payment to that of the repayment.

If the trustee were to attempt to proceed on the basis of employing himself as lawyer or accountant then his *locus standi* would, of course, be as associate which could be challenged by application to the court of any person interested, under Rule 6.147. At worst this could jeopardise his role as a "fit and proper" insolvency practitioner with the competent authority, and at best subject him to an order for compensation for any loss suffered in consequence. Any attempt by a creditor to so act in a consultative capacity where a fee was expected needs to receive either the prior leave of the court or the committee, under Rule 6.165.

(d) Employment of the bankrupt

The committee (or the court) may also give the trustee power to appoint the bankrupt to superintend the management of his estate or any part of it; to carry on his business (if any) for the benefit of his creditors, or otherwise to assist in administering the estate in such manner and on such terms as the trustee may direct (s 314(2)). This section is drafted in similar terms to that first found in s 26 Bankruptcy Act 1869.

In *Re Hurren (a Bankrupt) ex parte the Trustee* v *IRC* [1982] 3 All ER 982 it was held that where there could be a surplus, and where to all intents and purposes the bankrupt's only creditor was the Inland Revenue, the bankrupt was entitled to participate in the negotiations and to agree any compromise by the trustee.

(e) Confirming the trustee's powers

A number of powers are exercisable by the trustee only with the permission of the court or of the creditors' committee. This facilitates control over the costs and expenses of the bankruptcy. These powers are set out in Part I of Sch 5 to the Act:

"1. Power to carry on any business of the bankrupt so far as may be necessary for winding it up beneficially and so far as the trustee is able to do so without contravening any requirement imposed by or under any enactment.
2. Power to bring, institute or defend any action or legal proceedings relating to the property comprised in the bankrupt's estate.
3. Power to accept as the consideration for the sale of any property comprised in the bankrupt's estate a sum of money payable at a future time subject to such stipulations as to security or otherwise as the creditors' committee or the court thinks fit.
4. Power to mortgage or pledge any part of the property comprised in the bankrupt's estate for the purpose of raising money for the payment of his debts.
5. Power, where any right, option or other power forms part of the bankrupt's estate, to make payments or incur liabilities with a view to obtaining, for the benefit of creditors, any property which is the subject of the right, option or power.
6. Power to refer to arbitration, or compromise on such terms as may be agreed on, any debts, claims or liabilities subsisting or supposed to subsist between the bankrupt and any person who may have incurred any liability to the bankrupt.
7. Power to make such compromise or other arrangement as may be thought expedient with creditors, or persons claiming to be creditors, in respect of bankruptcy debts.
8. Power to make such compromise or other arrangement as may be thought expedient with respect to any claim arising out of or incidental to the bankrupt's estate made or capable of being made on the trustee by any person or by the trustee on any person."

Where the trustee has done anything without the permission required, the court or the creditors' committee may, for the purpose of enabling him to meet his expenses out of the bankrupt's estate, ratify what the trustee has done. But the committee may not do so unless satisfied that the trustee has acted in a case of urgency and has sought its ratification without undue delay.

A person dealing with the trustee is not to be concerned to enquire whether any permission required has been given. A permission granted is not a general permission, but relates to a particular proposed exercise of the power in question.

The trustee is also required to give notice where he disposes of any property comprised in the estate to an associate of the bankrupt.

(f) Administration and financial record keeping

The Regulations provide that the trustee should prepare and keep separate financial records in respect of each bankruptcy, as well as full administrative records. The financial records comprise all the receipts and payments made by him from day to day in respect of the bankruptcy, for subsequent submission to meetings of the committee. If the committee is not satisfied with their contents then the Secretary of State is requested to have an audit carried out by virtue of his controlling power. The matter of audit is covered at page 253.

The trustee is required to keep a record of all matters which may be necessary to give an accurate account of his administration, in particular the minutes of all meetings held, including the proceedings and resolutions passed together with a note that the concurrence of the committee was obtained.

Where the trustee carries on any business of the bankrupt he must keep a separate and distinct account of its trading. This will include particulars of all local bank account transactions, where appropriate, together with the total weekly amounts of receipts and payments, which will be included in the financial records referred to above. Whilst the opening of a local bank account is a matter between the trustee and the Secretary of State, who has to be satisfied that an administrative advantage will be derived from so doing, a resolution of the committee to the effect that "it would be to the advantage of the creditors that the trustee should have an account with a local bank" may help authorisation.

(g) Power to compromise

With the sanction of the committee the trustee has ample power to compromise all claims. The court will not as a general rule, in an application by the trustee for directions, express any opinion on a proposed compromise no matter how complicated the matter may be, nor interfere in any way: see *Re Pilling, ex parte Salaman* [1906] 1 KB 644. However, should a meeting of the creditors refuse to sanction a compromise, even though approved by a majority of the committee, the compromise must be abandoned: see *Re Ridgway, ex parte Hurlbatt* (1889) 61 LT 647. A future consideration, for example in respect of the sale of property, is subject to such stipulations as to security and otherwise as the committee thinks fit.

(h) Distribution of property in specie

With permission the trustee may divide among the creditors according to its estimated value any property which, from its peculiar nature or other special circumstances, cannot be readily or advantageously sold. This is not a general permission but relates to a specific proposed exercise of the power in question and is without prejudice to the right to disclaim (see page 180).

A person dealing with the trustee in good faith and for value is not to be concerned to enquire whether any permission has in fact been given. The court or the creditors' committee may, however, ratify what the trustee has done for the purpose of enabling him to meet his expenses out of the bankrupt's estate. It must not, however, do so unless it is satisfied that the trustee acted in a case of urgency and has sought its ratification without undue delay (s 326).

(i) Disbursements

The trustee shall defray out of the estate, in the prescribed order of priority, any reasonable travelling expenses directly incurred by members of the creditors' committee or their representatives in respect of their attendance at the committee's meetings, or otherwise on the committee's business (Rule 6.164). Any necessary disbursements by the trustee of approved expenses incurred by members of the committee or their representatives are paid out in the order of priority of the payment of costs etc out of the estate (see Rule 6.224(1)(m) at page 233).

5. Meetings of the committee

(a) Summoning of meetings

The place and time of meetings is a matter for the trustee. The trustee must call a first meeting of the creditors' committee within three months of his appointment, or within three months of the establishment of the committee, whichever is later. Thereafter meetings must be called:

(i) if so requested by a member or his representative, in which case the meeting must be held within 21 days of receipt by the trustee of the request; and

(ii) for a specified date, if the committee has previously resolved that a meeting is to be held on that date.

The trustee must give seven days written notice of the venue of any meeting to all members or designated representatives, unless the notice requirement has been waived by or on behalf of the member. Notice may be waived before or at the meeting. (Rule 6.153)

(b) Quorum

A committee meeting is properly constituted if all members have been given proper notice and at least two of the members are present or represented (Rule 6.155).

(c) Chairman

A meeting of the committee is chaired either by the trustee or by a person nominated by him in writing. Any person so nominated must either be qualified to act as an insolvency practitioner in relation to the bankrupt or be an employee of the trustee or his firm and experienced in insolvency matters (Rule 6.154).

(d) Voting rights and resolutions

At a meeting, each member has one vote (whether present himself or by his representative) and a simple majority is all that is required to pass a resolution. Every resolution passed must be recorded in writing, either individually or as part of the minutes of the meeting. The record must be signed by the chairman and kept with the records of the bankruptcy proceedings. Voting is *not* based on the value of the creditor's proof. (Rule 6.161)

(e) Resolutions by post

Rule 6.162 provides for the agreement of members of the creditors' committee to a resolution to be made by post. The resolution must be circulated by post. If there is more than one resolution, each resolution must be set out as a separate document. Any member of the committee may, within seven days from the date of the sending out of the resolution, require the trustee to call a meeting to consider the matter. Otherwise, the resolution is deemed to have been carried if and when the trustee receives in writing the concurrence of a majority of the members. Copies of any resolution passed in this way, and a note of the concurrences, must be kept with the bankruptcy records.

(f) Saving

The acts of the creditors' committee are valid notwithstanding any defect in the appointment, election or qualifications of any member of the committee (s 377).

6. Termination of membership

(a) Resignation

A member may resign by notice in writing delivered to the trustee. Membership is automatically terminated if the member:

- (i) becomes bankrupt (in which case his trustee replaces him as a member of the committee) or compounds or arranges with his creditors;
- (ii) fails to attend or be represented at three consecutive committee meetings, unless at the third of those meetings it is resolved that this rule should not apply; or
- (iii) ceases to be, or is found never to have been, a creditor.

(Rule 6.158)

(b) Removal

A member may be removed by resolution of a creditors' meeting providing fourteen days notice has been given of the intention to move the resolution (Rule 6.159).

(c) Filling vacancies

A vacancy on the committee need not be filled if the trustee and a majority of the remaining members agree, so long as the membership does not fall below the minimum of three. The trustee may, with the consent of the other members and the creditor concerned, appoint a different creditor to fill the vacancy.

Alternatively, the meeting of creditors may resolve that another creditor fill the vacancy, provided he agrees. In this case at least fourteen days notice must have been given of the intention to make the appointment, although the person to be appointed need not necessarily be named in the notice. If the vacancy is filled at a meeting at which the trustee is not present, the chairman of the meeting must notify the trustee of the appointment (Rule 6.160).

7. Application to insolvent partnerships

A general meeting of the creditors or any individual member may establish a committee similar to a liquidation committee established under s 141 (as amended). It would be summoned by the official receiver under s 136(4) (winding-up of a partnership as an unregistered company) as amended by the Insolvent Partnerships Order 1986 (see Cases A, E and F in Chapter 20).

A general meeting of creditors involving the winding-up of individual corporate partners, may establish a creditors' committee composed of the same persons as the liquidation committee (established under s 141) to exercise the functions conferred on it: see Case B, page 298).

A general meeting involving the creditors of any such individual member may not establish a committee, or confer any functions on such a committee, at any time when the official receiver is trustee, except in connection with an appointment made by that meeting of a person to be trustee instead of the official receiver. Likewise, where individual partners present their own petition against the partnership (see Case C, page 298), the official receiver may summon meetings of all the creditors of the partners at any time but no liquidation or creditors' committee will be appointed.

8. Vesting of functions in the Secretary of State

The creditors' committee is not to be able or required to carry out its functions at any time when the official receiver is trustee; at such a time the functions of the committee are vested in the Secretary of State and exercised by the official receiver (s 302).

Where in the case of any bankruptcy there is no creditors' committee for the time being and the trustee is a person other than the official receiver, the functions of the committee are vested in the Secretary of State but may be exercised by the official receiver.

By virtue of the vesting requirements the rules about notices to be given or reports to be made to the committee by the trustee do not apply. Nevertheless the committee may require a report on any matter.

9. Appeals by the trustee

If he wishes to appeal against a decision of the committee, the trustee may apply to the court under s 303(2) for directions in any particular matter arising as to the law or procedure.

If the matter is one of policy or administration then he should call a general meeting of the creditors under Rule 6.81 (see page 212). Resolutions of a general meeting of the creditors may clearly be made to prevail over a decision of the committee by s 301(1). Also see *Re Salmon* [1916] 2 KB 510 which was heard under the 1914 Act, but which, by s 79(1) of that Act, was specific on the point.

Where the committee has fixed his remuneration but he considers the rate or amount to be insufficient, the trustee may appeal to a general meeting of the creditors to increase its amount or rate. If it is not increased by the committee, he may then appeal to the court. The procedure in either case is laid down by Rule 6.141.

The trustee must give at least fourteen days' notice of his application to the members of the creditors' committee; and the committee may nominate one or more members to appear or be represented, and to be heard, on the application. If there is no creditors' committee, the trustee's notice of application is sent to such one or more of the bankrupt's creditors as the court may direct, and those creditors may nominate one or more of their number to appear or be represented.

The court may order the costs of the trustee's application, including the costs of any member of the creditors' committee appearing on it, or any creditor so appearing, to be paid out of the estate.

Conversely any creditor may under Rule 6.142, with the concurrence of one quarter in value of creditors including himself, apply to the court for an order reducing remuneration (see page 256).

Chapter 16

Distribution to creditors

1. Introduction

The trustee must recognise at the outset of his administration that some creditors are paid in priority to others, some debts will be the subject of disputed proofs and claims, and other creditors, perhaps by reason of distance, may not have had time to tender and establish their proofs by the time he is ready to pay the first dividend. Furthermore, the right to a dividend may be assigned.

Certain classes of creditor are preferred and have priority over others in a prescribed order; they comprise, first and with equal priority, the Inland Revenue for PAYE; Customs and Excise for VAT, car tax, betting and gaming duties; social security payments, pension contributions and remuneration of employees. Next in rank are the dividends due to the general body of ordinary creditors, followed by the payment of interest on debts due since the commencement of bankruptcy, and finally, debts due to a spouse. In addition, other payments such as costs and remuneration of the administration, take precedence for payment out of the available funds in the order prescribed by the Rules.

The trustee may also divide property which cannot be sold readily or advantageously in its existing form, known as *in specie*, among the creditors, with the permission of the creditors' committee (see page 225).

2. The order of ranking for the distribution

There is a set order of priority for distribution of the bankrupt's estate under s 328. The estate is applied to the following liabilities in the order shown, until exhausted:

(a) certain priorities under the Act and related legislation (s 328(6));

(b) the expenses of the bankruptcy (s 328(2) and Rule 6.224);

(c) preferential debts, which are paid in priority to other debts under s 328(2); they rank equally between themselves and are paid in full, or abate in equal proportions between themselves where the estate is insufficient for meeting them;

(d) subjugatable preferential debts, which rank for preferential status under (c) above unless the estate is insufficient to meet those preferential debts in full; see s 347(3) (distraint);

(e) ordinary dividends under s 328(3), being debts which are neither preferential nor debts to which (f) below applies. They rank equally between themselves and are paid in full or abate in equal proportions;
(f) interest on preferential and ordinary debts rank equally (s 328(4));
(g) creditors deferred to the above debts and expenses ((a) to (e)) and interest ((f)), together with interest payable in the same priority as the debt on which it is payable (s 329(2) (spouse));

Any surplus remaining is paid to the bankrupt.

However, should there be insufficient moneys for the distribution to pay any particular class of creditor in full, then the debts abate in equal proportions between themselves as to the amounts of their agreed proofs, that is they rank *pari passu.*

As an example of the order of ranking, suppose £5,000 remains after paying expenses and preferential creditors. Ordinary creditors X, Y and Z have proved for £6,000, £3,000 and £1,000 respectively. In the distribution X will receive £3,000, Y £1,500 and Z £500. Any claim by a spouse would be unmet and there would be no interest payable on outstanding debts either to the ordinary or preferred creditors.

3. Distribution of the bankrupt's estate

In accordance with the order of ranking set out above, the estate in distributed in the following order:

(a) In priority

(i) Expenses following the failure of a voluntary arrangement under s 276(2): Where a bankruptcy order is made on a supervisor's petition under s 264(1)(c) any expenses properly incurred as expenses of the administration of the voluntary arrangement are a first charge on the estate.

(ii) Expenses following the failure of a deed of arrangement: Where a deed of arrangement is avoided by reason of the bankruptcy of the debtor, any expenses properly incurred by the trustee under the deed in the performance of any of the duties imposed on him by the Deeds of Arrangement Act 1914 (see Chapter 23) are allowed or paid him under s 21 of that Act, by the trustee in the bankruptcy as a first charge on the estate. Such expenses are strictly limited to those sums incurred in the execution of duties imposed by the Act; see *Green* [1917] 1 KB 183. The court may permit the trustee some return for his exertions but only if it is amply satisfied that these have resulted in a real benefit to the creditors. Otherwise the trustee will be ordered to pay over all moneys collected by him as happened in *Re Zakon ex parte Trustee* v *Bushell* [1940] Ch 253.

Note, however, that this does not apply to a deed which has never become effective because a majority of the creditors has not assented to it by s 3 of that Act.

(iii) Replacement of bankrupt's excluded property under s 308(3): Before any of the

estate is distributed to any class of creditor, the trustee has a duty in priority to apply funds out of the estate to the purchase by or on behalf of the bankrupt of reasonable replacements for the exempt property of the bankrupt, namely his tools of trade and the like, which may nevertheless have been demanded by the trustee (see page 150).

(iv) Articled clerks and apprentices: A bankruptcy order against an employer has the effect of discharging any indenture of apprenticeship or articles of agreement to which he is party, with effect from the commencement of the bankruptcy. Where money has been paid by the apprentice or articled clerk the trustee may pay back a reasonable sum, having regard to the amount of the fee, the proportion of the period of apprenticeship served and the other circumstances of the case. This power has priority over the payment of ordinary debts of the estate under s 348(4). Alternatively the trustee may transfer the indenture or articles to another person, if it appears expedient to do so, on an application made by the apprentice or clerk.

Section 348 also applies to s 122(7) Employment Act with respect to reasonable payments to apprentices and articled clerks.

(v) Priority of other statutory liabilities under s 328(6): The distribution is without prejudice to any provision of the Act or any other Act under which the payment of any debt or the making of any other payment is, in the event of bankruptcy, to have a particular priority or to be postponed.

(b) Expenses of the bankruptcy

Before preferential debts or dividends are paid to creditors, the costs of the administration of the bankruptcy must first be allowed for or discharged; these costs include the remuneration of the trustee and the official receiver, costs of security and of the petitioner, and are in the order set down by Rule 6.224:

"6.224 (1) The expenses of the bankruptcy are payable out of the estate in the following order of priority -

(a) expenses properly chargeable or incurred by the official receiver [page 74 *et seq*] or the trustee [page 148 *et seq*] in preserving, realising or getting in any of the assets of the bankrupt, including those incurred in acquiring title to after-acquired property [page 161]

(b) any other expenses incurred or disbursements made by the official receiver [page 76] or under his authority, including those incurred or made in carrying on the business of a debtor or bankrupt [pages 74 and 89]:

(c) (i) the fee payable under any order made under section 415 for the performance by the official receiver of his general duties as official receiver [page 356];

(ii) any repayable deposit lodged by the petitioner under any such order as security for the fee mentioned in sub-paragraph (i) (except where the deposit is applied to the payment of the remuneration of an insolvency practitioner appointed under section 273 (debtor's petition)) [pages 33 and 47];

(d) any other fees payable under any order made under section 415, including those payable to the official receiver, and any remuneration payable to him under general regulations [pages 75 and 358];

(e) the cost of any security provided by an interim receiver [page 68], trustee [page 24] or special manager [page 91] in accordance with the Act or the Rules;

(f) the remuneration of the interim receiver (if any) [page 69];

(g) any deposit lodged on an application for the appointment of an interim receiver [page 68];

(h) the costs of the petitioner, and of any person appearing on the petition whose costs are allowed by the court [see pages 25 and 66 as to costs of security if allowed here];

(j) the remuneration of the special manager (if any) [page 90];

(k) any amount payable to a person employed or authorised, ... to assist in the preparation of a statement of affairs or of accounts [page 94];

(l) any allowance made, by order of the court, towards costs on an application for release from the obligation to submit a statement of affairs, or for an extension of time for submitting such a statement [page 94];

(m) any necessary disbursements by the trustee in the course of his administration [page 226] (including any expenses incurred by members of the creditors' committee or their representatives and allowed by the trustee under Rule 6.164 [page 219], but not including any payment of capital gains tax in circumstances referred to in sub-paragraph (p) below;

(n) the remuneration or emoluments of any person (including the bankrupt [see pages 223 and 262]) who has been employed by the trustee to perform any services for the estate, as required or authorised by or under the Act or the Rules [pages 154 and 223];

(o) the remuneration of the trustee [page 221], up to any amount not exceeding that which is payable to the official receiver under general regulations [pages 75 and 358];

(p) the amount of any capital gains tax on chargeable gains accruing on the realisation of any asset of the bankrupt (without regard to whether the realisation is effected by the trustee, a secured creditor, or a receiver or manager appointed to deal with a security) [pages 137 and 156];

(q) the balance, after payment of any sums due under sub-paragraph (o) above, of any remuneration due to the trustee [page 221].

(2) The costs of employing a shorthand writer, if appointed by an order of the court made at the instance of the official receiver in connection with an examination, rank in priority with those specified in paragraph (1)(a) [page 79]. The costs of employing a shorthand writer so appointed in any other case rank after the allowance mentioned in paragraph (1)(l) and before the disbursements mentioned in paragraph (1)(m) [page 79].

(3) Any expenses incurred in holding an examination under Rule 6.174 (examinee unfit), where the application for it is made by the official receiver [page 81], rank in priority with those specified in paragraph (1)(a)".

For the treatment of expenses in a partnership insolvency, see page 305.

By arts 4 and 5 Administration of Insolvent Estates of Deceased Persons Order, modifying s 305(4), the trustee must have regard, in priority over the preferential debtors, to any claim by the personal representative to payment of reasonable funeral, testamentary and administration expenses incurred by him (or another person incurring the expenses) provided that the trustee has sufficient funds in hand for the purpose in priority over the preferential debts (see page 312).

(c) Preferential debts

Preferential creditors are paid in priority to other debts under s 328(2); they rank equally between themselves and are paid in full, or abate in equal proportions between themselves where the estate is insufficient for meeting their claims.

Where the Secretary of State makes a payment from the redundancy fund to an employee or into the resources of an occupational pension scheme, he has rights of subrogation in priority but limited to the extent of the payment he has actually made.

The categories of preferential debt are listed in Schedule 6 to the Act. To be preferred the debt must not only fall into one of the defined categories but must have existed at a time determined by reference to the "relevant date". In relation to a debtor who is not an undischarged bankrupt, the relevant date is the date of the interim order. In relation to a debtor (where at the time the bankruptcy order was made an interim receiver was appointed), the relevant date is the date on which the interim receiver was first appointed after the presentation of the bankruptcy petition. Otherwise, it is the date of the making of the bankruptcy order (s 387).

Debts failing to qualify as preferential can be proved *pari passu* with the ordinary debts. The categories of preferential debt are:

- (i) debts due to Inland Revenue
- (ii) debts due to Customs and Excise
- (iii) Social Security contributions
- (iv) contributions to occupational pension schemes etc
- (v)
  - remuneration and holiday pay of employees
  - reserve forces.

Category 1: Debts due to Inland Revenue

With one important exception, the Inland Revenue's status under insolvency law is that of an ordinary creditor. The exception is the preferential right accorded to PAYE debts. Originally the extent of the crown's prerogative in the recovery of debt at common law was neatly summed up by Lord MacNaghton in the following terms: "The interests of individuals are to be postponed to the interests of the community", but the Crown's prerogative has since been given up in exchange for a limited preference. The general effect is to limit the priority to PAYE due under s 204 of the Income and Corporation Taxes Act 1970 and those deductions required to be made by the debtor under s 69 of the Finance No 2 Act 1975 in respect of sub-contractors in the construction industry.

The special nature of a tax debt to the Crown is thereby recognised, but partly to ameliorate the claims of the other creditors, a ceiling on the amount which may be treated as preferential is imposed; that ceiling is the amount due in the twelve months preceding the relevant date. Thus, included in the preferential debts are any sums due at the relevant date from the debtor on account of deductions of income tax from emoluments paid during the twelve months up to that date. Any balance remaining will simply rank *pari passu* with non-preferential debts.

The amount due from the bankrupt employer on account of tax deductions for any period is the amount of the deductions required to be made, less the amount of the repayments of income tax which that person was liable to make to employees during the same period.

What is not so clear is the position as to tax penalties: under ss 93 and 94 of the Taxes Management Act 1970 penalties may be imposed by the Inland Revenue in respect of the failure to make a return for either income or capital, or to notify chargeability to tax. Incorrect returns or accounts are penalised under s 95 (but see page 189).

Category 2: Debts due to Customs and Excise

The general rule is that the amount of any Value Added Tax relating to the period of six months immediately preceding the relevant date is a preferential debt, so that all other VAT due ranks with the ordinary debts. The preference period originally proposed in the Bill (for the 1985 Act) was twelve months. This was one of the relatively few clauses to be vigourously contested in both Houses of Parliament and the period of six months was only settled after the government had accepted defeat on the issue in the House of Lords.

Where the whole of the accounting period (prescribed by Regulations made by the Commissioners of Customs & Excise) to which any VAT is attributable falls within the six month period, the whole amount of that tax is referable to that period. Otherwise, the amount of any VAT which is referable to the six month period is the proportion of the tax which is equal to such proportion (if any) of the accounting reference period in question as falls within the six month period.

Where repayments which have been withheld under s 14(7) of the Value Added Tax Act 1983, pre-insolvency repayments arising from a return in the preferential period are applied wholly in reduction of the preferential debt and are not withheld or pro-rated over their preferential and unsecured claims. As to the position following distraint see *Re Memco Engineering Ltd* [1985] 3 All ER 267 (see page 175).

Trustees should also note that if, with the intention of evading VAT, any person does any act or omits to take any action so as to give rise to a charge of dishonesty, the default surcharge provisions of s 19 Finance Act 1985 come into effect, whether or not that act or omission gives rise to criminal liability. The trustee must guard against the penalty provisions of s 17 of that Act. This provides that if any person fails to comply with the requirements, he will be liable to a daily penalty at the prescribed rate for each day on which the failure continues. However, these penalties are not levied where a default surcharge is assessed.

As far as default through insolvency is concerned, it is not HM Customs and Excise's intention to levy a default surcharge in respect of either pre- or post-bankruptcy default in the submission of VAT returns. Consequently, if there is to be no default surcharge, then, as the concession is at present framed, trustees will be aware of a potential laibility.

The amount of any car tax which is due at the relevant date from the debtor and which became due within a period of twelve months next before that date is a preferential debt.

Any amount which is due from the debtor at the relevant date, under s 12(1) or 14, or Sch 2 to the Betting and Gaming Duties Act 1981, and which became due within the twelve months preceding that date, is also a preferential debt.

Category 3: social security contributions

The following debts are accorded preference:

(i) all sums which on the relevant date are due from the debtor on account of Class 1 or Class 2 contributions under the Social Security Act 1975 as amended by s 74 of the Social Security Act 1986 and which became due from the debtor in the twelve months immediately preceding the relevant date;

(ii) all sums which on the relevant date have been assessed on and are due from the debtor on account of Class 4 contributions under the above Act which are due to the Commissioners of Inland Revenue and are assessed on the debtor up to 5 April immediately preceding the relevant date but not exceeding, in the whole, any one year's assessment.

Category 4: Pension contributions

Contributions to occupational pension schemes: This provision relates to any scheme or arrangement which provides or is capable of providing, in relation to employees in any description of employment, benefits (in the form of pensions or otherwise) payable to or in respect of any such employees on the termination of their employment or on their death or retirement. These provisions are contained in Sch 3 to the Social Security Pensions Act 1975 and complement the Social Security Act 1975 as amended by the Act of 1986, whereby the Secretary of State is given power to pay out of the redundancy fund, and into an occupational pension scheme, certain unpaid contributions to that scheme which are due from the insolvent employer. Such sums must not exceed the amount deducted from the pay of the employee in respect of his contributions during the twelve months immediately preceding the date on which the employer became insolvent, and which have been designated for, but not actually paid into, the scheme.

Consequently, priority is afforded to such unpaid contributions (and state scheme premiums; see below) by bankrupt employers, employed earners and self-employed earners under the Act.

By s 58 of the Social Security Pensions Act 1975 and Sch 3(2) any sum owed on account of an employer's contributions to a contracted-out scheme has priority if the contributions are payable:

(i) in the period of twelve months immediately preceding the date of the relevant event; and
(ii) in respect of earners in contracted-out employment by reference to the scheme towards the provision for those earners of guaranteed minimum pensions under the scheme.

In so far as contributions cannot be identified as falling within the earner's contributions or payments as above, the amount of the debt having priority by virtue of Sch 3(2) is deemed to be an amount equal to:

(i) 7% of the total reckonable earnings paid or payable in the twelve month period to or for the benefit of non-contributing earners; or
(ii) 4.5% of the total reckonable earnings paid or payable in that period to or for the benefit of contributing earners. By Sch 2 to the Social Security Act 1986, this applies to any sum owed on account of an employer's minimum payments to a contracted-out scheme falling to be made in the period of twelve months immediately preceding the relevant date.

"Reckonable earnings" means the earner's earnings from that employment so far as those earnings were comprised in any payment of earnings made to him or for his benefit at a time when the employment was contracted-out employment, and exceeded the current lower earnings limit but not the current upper earnings limit. The earnings to be taken into account are those paid or payable to or for the benefit of earners in contracted-out employment by reference to the scheme, in the whole or any part of the period of twelve months.

"Earners" includes both those who, during the period in question were liable, under the terms of a contracted-out scheme, to contribute to the scheme, and those who were not so liable.

Contributions to state pension scheme: These are contributions equivalent to the premium payable on termination of contracted-out employment; or accrued rights premiums and pensioner's rights premiums; and limited revaluation premiums under the Social Security Pensions Act 1975 in respect of any sum owed on account of a state scheme premium payable at any time before, or in consequence of, a person being adjudged bankrupt.

Section 58 and Sch 3 to the 1975 Act, as amended by Sch 14 to the Insolvency Act 1986, complement the Social Security Acts of 1975 and 1986 whereby priority is extended to state pension schemes. This extension is the necessary corollary to what may be termed a partnership with the occupational schemes referred to above. Schedule 3 applies to any such sum owed.

Where any such premium is payable in respect of a period of service of more than twelve months (including that from previous employment) the amount to be paid in priority is limited to the amount of the premium that would have been payable if the service had been confined to the last twelve months taken into account in fixing the actual amount of the premium.

Where the whole or part of a premium is required to be paid in priority to other debts of the debtor or his estate, and the person liable for the payment would be entitled to recover the whole or any part of any sum paid on account from another person, then that other person is liable for any part of the premium unpaid.

Payment of any amount in respect of a premium has the same effect on the rights and liabilities of the person making it, as if it had been a payment of that amount on account of the sum recoverable from him in respect of a premium as mentioned above.

Contributions to personal pension plans: A personal pension plan is a scheme or arrangement introduced by the Social Security Act 1986 which provides benefits in the form of pensions or otherwise, payable on death or retirement to or in respect of employees who have made arrangements with the trustees or managers of the scheme for them to become members of the scheme.

The provisions of the Employment Act (referred to above) are duly amended to provide for this new scheme with the effect that any person competent to act under such a scheme has the same right to payment as a person acting under an occupational pension scheme.

Category 5: Remuneration etc of employees

An employee whose employer has been adjudged bankrupt is given the right to claim unpaid wages or salary through the Secretary of State from a redundancy fund which was established under the Redundancy Payments Act 1965 (now the Employment Protection (Consolidation) Act 1978). The right is in respect of the whole or any part of the period of four months immediately preceding the relevant date (see page 158 *et seq*).

This is designed to mitigate hardship on employees by providing speedy payment of wages etc due, and to provide machinery for the Secretary of State to reclaim moneys from the estate in priority or as the case may be. It gives recognition to an employee's rights in his job by giving some financial protection on the insolvency of his employer provided, of course, that at the relevant date the employee was entitled to be paid the whole or any part of any debt following the termination of his employment. For these purposes an employer is taken to be insolvent if he is adjudicated bankrupt, enters into a voluntary arrangement, or has died and an order is made for the administration of his estate.

The sums duly payable under the scheme are limited and conditions must be fulfilled. By paying out wages from the fund the Secretary of State becomes a preferential creditor in place of the employee for arrears of pay of up to £800, but any sum paid from the fund over and above £800 makes the Secretary of State an unsecured creditor for that sum so as to rank *pari passu* with the remainder of the creditors as a non-preferential creditor.

This right is now extended to payments in respect of certain rights arising on the insolvency of an employer, provided that on the relevant date the employee was entitled to be paid the whole or part of any debt following termination of his employment (s 122 Employment Act).

"Remuneration" includes holiday, maternity and other arrears of pay. A sum is payable by the debtor to a person by way of remuneration in respect of any period if it is paid as wages or salary in respect of services rendered to the debtor in that period or it is an amount payable by the debtor in respect of that period as:

(i) a guarantee payment under s 12(1) of the Employment Protection (Consolidation) Act 1978 in respect of an employee without work to do for a day or part of a day;
(ii) remuneration on suspension on medical grounds under s 19 of that Act;
(iii) any payment for time off under s 273 (trade union duties); s 31(3) (looking for work etc); or s 31A(4) (ante-natal care); or
(iv) remuneration under a protective award made by an industrial tribunal under s 101 of the Employment Protection Act 1975 (redundancy dismissal with compensation).

"Holiday remuneration" is the amount owed in respect of any period of employment before the relevant date to a person whose employment by the debtor has been terminated whether before, on or after that date. It is deemed to have accrued to that person by virtue of his contract of employment or by virtue of any enactment, ie that remuneration would have accrued if his employment had continued until he became entitled to be allowed the holiday (paras 10 and 14(2) of Sch 6 to the Act of 1986).

Reserve forces

The limit of £800 also applies to so much of the amount as is ordered to be paid by the debtor, whether before or after the relevant date under the Reserve Forces (Safeguard of Employment) Act 1985, ie as to the reinstatement in and employment of members of the reserve and auxiliary forces who have been called into whole-time service in the armed forces of the Crown.

(d) Subjugatable preferential debts

Preferential debts relating to distress are "subjugatable". They rank for preferential status under *(c)* above unless the estate is insufficient to meet those preferential debts in full, in which case they rank behind them, but before those debts which are not preferential as *(e)* to *(g)* below.

Landlord's preferential right to rent: The landlord's right under s 347 is limited to six months rent accrued before the commencement of the bankruptcy where he (or his managing agent) has distrained upon the goods or effects of an individual who is adjudged bankrupt before the end of three months beginning with the distraint. By subs (3) so much of those goods or effects, or of the proceeds of their sale, as is not held for the bankrupt, is charged for the benefit of the bankrupt's estate with the preferential debts (*(c)* above) to the extent that it is for the time being insufficient to meet those debts.

Where the landlord surrenders any goods or effects to the trustee of a bankrupt's estate or makes a payment to him, that person ranks as a preferential creditor of the bankrupt, except as against so much of the bankrupt's estate as is available for the payment of preferential creditors by virtue of the surrender or payment under subs (4). This could either be in respect of the amount of the proceeds of the sale of those goods or effects, or the amount of the payment; by surrendering the goods to the trustee, it appears that he would then rank as a preferential creditor by notice of the surrender under subs (4), again for a maximum of six months rent without prejudice to a landlord's right to prove for the balance (if any).

Following distraint for rates and taxes: Under s 347(8), nothing in the Act affects any right to distrain for goods and chattels by any person (subs (3)) otherwise than for rent (see above). This right is exercisable at any time against property comprised in the bankrupt's estate without restriction, for the purpose of obtaining payment of the whole of the amount due. If the distrainer surrenders the goods to the trustee, it appears that by s 347(4) he would then rank as a preferential creditor by virtue of the giving of a notice of the surrender under subs (4), except as against so much of the bankrupt's estate as is available for the payment of preferential creditors by virtue of the surrender or payment. This might also apply to the collection of rates (under s 96 General Rate Act 1967); the collection of taxes (under s 62 Taxes Management Act 1970); and the collection of sums due from a rentcharge (under the Law of Property Act 1925 s 121(3); see also page 176).

Other distraint: Where any person surrenders to the trustee any goods or effects of a bankrupt's estate or makes a payment to such a trustee, that person ranks, in respect of the amount of the proceeds of the sale of those goods or effects by the trustee or the amount of the payment, as a preferential creditor of the bankrupt, except as against so much of the bankrupt's estate as is available for the payment of preferential creditors by virtue of the surrender or payment.

(e) Ordinary dividends

Ordinary dividends under s 328(3) are those debts which are neither preferential nor debts to which *(f)* below applies. They rank equally between themselves and are paid in full or abate in equal proportions one with the other, together with the balance of those debts and expenses otherwise paid in priority (as above).

(f) Interest

Interest on preferential debts ranks equally with interest on non-preferential debts, and is payable under s 328(4). The rate of interest payable for any debt is whichever is the greater of:

(i) the rate specified in s 17 Judgments Act 1838 at the commencement of the bankruptcy;

(ii) the rate applicable to that debt apart from the bankruptcy.

Any surplus remaining after paying preferential debts is applied in paying interest on those debts in respect of the periods during which they have been outstanding since the commencement of the bankruptcy. Other creditors are not entitled to interest out of surplus funds until any creditor who has proved for a debt payable at a future time (after the declaration of dividend) has been paid the full amount of his debt (Rule 11.13).

Where there have been many years of interest to be paid (under s 33(8) of the 1914 Act) there were applications to the official receiver and the court to abate that interest so that something might arise as a "windfall" to the debtor or to his family: "it would be better than leaving the administration to be the target of this give a little comfort to the destitute attitude" (*Blagden* Minutes, HMSO, Cmnd 59944).

In the case of a partner against whom an insolvency order has *not* been made, before any part of the surplus from the insolvent partnership forms part of his own separate estate, interest on the joint debts of the partnership is paid out of his share of the estate to the creditors of the partnership (s 189).

(g) Deferred creditors

These creditors are linked in some way to the bankrupt or are "puisne partnerships" created by lending. They do not rank for payment until all the other creditors for value who can come in have been satisfied; see *Ex parte Taylor, In re Grason* (1879) 12 Ch 366. They are postponed to the above debts, expenses and interest. The common principle followed is that just as a debtor may not, when proving against the assets, compete with his own creditors, so a partner of a debtor may not compete with his own creditor so long as there are any creditors of the debtor not fully satisfied to whom the partner is under liability; see *Re Cummings and West, ex parte Neilson and Craig* [1929] 1 Ch 534.

Debts to spouse: A debt between husband and wife is deferred to the previous debts together with interest which is payable by s 329(2) in the same priority as the debt on which it is payable. Such debts rank in priority after the debts and interest required to be paid in pursuance of s 328(3) & (4) (see *(e)* and *(f)*) and are payable with interest for the period during which they have been outstanding since the commencement of the bankruptcy. This section penalises the lawfully married; the co-habitee can lend the bankrupt money on more advantageous terms than can a spouse: "It is a matter which does, of course, cause a great deal of annoyance in certain cases, because the mistress frequently adopts the name of the bankrupt and by many people she is regarded as his wife. It does leave a very nasty taste in the mouth of the creditors when a claim is lodged by a woman in these circumstances and the claim has to be admitted". (*Blagden* Minutes, HMSO, Cmnd 59944). The new Act does nothing to correct the position.

"Debts to spouse" are bankruptcy debts owed in respect of credit provided by a person who was the bankrupt's spouse at the commencement of the bankruptcy, whether or not that person was the bankrupt's spouse at the time the credit was provided.

Goodwill: Where a person has sold the goodwill of a business in consideration of a share of the profits of the business and the business subsequently fails, then the seller of the goodwill is by s 3 Partnership Act 1890 not entitled to recover. In *ex parte Sheil* (1877) 4 CD 789 a person who was being paid an annuity out of a business likewise had his claim deferred to the payment in full of all the other creditors; see also *Re Grason* (above).

Torts: Claims for damages in tort must normally be liquidated by a judgment before being admitted for proof, but for an indication as to how the law appears to be otherwise edging forward from *Re Rolls Royce Ltd* [1974] 1WLR 1584, see *Re Islington Metal & Plating Works Ltd* [1984] 1WLR 14, both cases in winding-up proceedings, and yet to be tested in a bankruptcy case.

Venture capital: Where money has been advanced by way of a loan under a contract whereby the lender obtains an interest in the profits, but the borrower is subsequently adjudged bankrupt, then under s 3 Partnership Act 1890, the lender is not entitled to recover anything from the bankrupt until the claims of the other creditors of the borrower for value in the bankruptcy have been satisfied: see *Re Meade (a Bankrupt) ex parte Humber* v *Palmer (Trustee)* [1951] Ch 774. It makes no difference whether the contract is in writing or oral: see *Re Fort, ex p Schofield* [1897] 2 QB 495.

(h) The bankrupt

Individual insolvent: If a surplus remains on the final distribution after payment of all the bankrupt's creditors in full and with interest, together with the payment of the expenses of the bankruptcy, then by s 330(5) the bankrupt is entitled to the surplus. If he is dead it would be paid to the personal representative unless the court otherwise orders.

Partnership surpluses: Any surplus remaining after the payment of the separate debts of any insolvent member out of his separate estate without the prior payment of any interest under ss 189 or 328(4) of the Act, forms part of the *joint estate* of the partnership and is applied in payment of the joint debts due to the creditors of the partnership.

Any surplus remaining after the payment of the joint debts of the partnership out of its *joint* estate forms part of the *separate* estate of each partner in proportion to the right and interest of each such partner in the joint estate. In the case of a solvent partner, before any part of the surplus forms part of his separate estate, interest is paid out of his share on the joint debts to the creditors of the partnership under s 189.

Where any surplus remains after the administration of a separate partnership, the surplus is carried over to the separate estates of the partners in that partnership according to their respective rights and interest therein.

4. Payment of dividends

Having determined the order of ranking and prepared lists of creditors, the trustee can then commence the distribution. Whenever the trustee has sufficient funds in hand to make a distribution by means of a dividend he must by virtue of s 324 declare an interim or final dividend among those creditors who have proved, and give notice of his intention to declare and distribute the dividend within four months from the last date for proving (see page 186).

(a) Declaration of dividend

The first dividend is to be declared and distributed within four months from the last date for proving, unless the trustee has reason to postpone or cancel the dividend. Subsequent dividends are paid whenever he has sufficient funds in hand. He retains out of the amount distributed such sums as may be necessary for the expenses of the bankruptcy.

Before declaring a dividend the trustee gives notice of his intention to do so to all creditors including those who have not proved their debts. The notice specifies a date, not less than 21 days from that of the notice, up to which proofs may be lodged. The notice must give details of:

- (i) the amounts realised from the sale of assets, indicating, as far as practicable, the amounts raised from particular assets;
- (ii) payments made by the trustee in the administration of the estate;
- (iii) any provision made for unsettled claims and any funds retained for particular purposes;
- (iv) the total amount to be distributed and the rate of dividend;
- (v) whether any further dividend is expected to be declared, and if so when.

The dividend may be sent out with the notice declaring it. Payment may be by post or as may be arranged with a particular creditor; or it may be held for collection by him. Where a dividend is paid on a bill of exchange or other negotiable instrument, the amount of the dividend must be endorsed on the instrument or on a certified copy of it, if required to be produced by the holder for that purpose. (Rule 11.6)

Where a dividend is to be declared for preferential creditors, a notice of intended dividend need only be given to those creditors whose debts the trustee has reason to believe are preferential.

In the calculation and distribution of a dividend the trustee must make allowance for any bankruptcy debts which appear to him to be due to persons who, because of the distance of their place of residence, may not have had sufficient time to tender and establish their proofs; for any debts which are the subject of claims yet to be determined; and for disputed proofs and claims.

However, he may not, without leave of the court, declare a dividend where an application has been made to the court to reverse or vary a decision of his on a proof, or to expunge or reduce a proof (see pages 195 and 196). If the court does give leave, he may make such provision in respect of the proof in question as the court directs.

(b) Payment of dividend

The rules for the payment of dividends to creditors are contained in Regulation 15 of the Regulations (see page 253). They are payable on application to the Department of Trade and Industry. If the amount claimed by a creditor in his proof is increased after payment of the dividend, the creditor is not entitled to disturb the distribution of the dividend. However, he is entitled to be paid the dividend which he has failed to receive out of any money available for the payment of any further dividends, before it is applied to that payment (Rule 11.8 and see page 199).

(c) Postponement or cancellation

The trustee may postpone or cancel the dividend if, within the four month period during which he must declare a dividend, an application has been made to the court to reverse or vary the trustee's decision on a proof, or for a proof to be expunged or the amount of it reduced (Rule 11.4).

(d) Notice of no, or no further, dividend

If the trustee is unable to declare a dividend or further dividend, he gives notice to the creditors. The notice must contain a statement that either:

- (i) no funds have been realised; or
- (ii) the funds realised have already been distributed, used or allocated for defraying the expenses of administration.

(Rule 11.7)

(e) Claims by unsatisfied creditors

No action lies against the trustee for a dividend, but if the trustee refuses to pay, the court may order him to do so and also to pay out of his own money interest on the dividend and the costs of the proceedings in which the order to pay is made. Interest is at the rate for the time being specified in s 17 Judgments Act 1838 from the time the dividend was withheld.

(f) Creditor proving after the declaration of a dividend

A creditor who has not proved before the declaration of any dividend is not entitled to disturb the dividend payment on the grounds that he has not participated in it. When, however, he has proved that debt he is entitled to be paid out of any money for the time being available in respect of any further dividend; ie he is entitled to be paid any dividend which he has failed to receive out of money becoming available before that money is applied to the payment of such further dividend (s 325).

(g) Assignment of right to dividend

If a person entitled gives notice that he wishes the dividend to be paid to another person, or that he has assigned his entitlement to another person, the trustee must pay the other accordingly.

(h) Disqualification

If a creditor contravenes any provision of the Act or rules relating to the valuation of securities, the court may order that the creditor be wholly or partly disqualified from participation in any dividend (Rule 11.10).

(i) Final dividend

When the trustee has realised all the bankrupt's estate, or so much of it as can in his opinion be realised without needlessly protracting the trusteeship, he either gives notice of his intention to declare a final dividend (presumably as for *(a) a*bove and see Rule 11.6), or he gives notice that no dividend, or no further dividend will be declared (see *(d)* above and Rule 11.7).

Before so doing he must give notice to creditors who have not established their claims to his satisfaction that if they do not do so by a date, the "final date", he will disregard their claim: see *Re Pavyer, Brown, Son & Vardy* v *Trustee* [1936] 1 All ER 568. Any person, presumably including the bankrupt, may, on application to the court, postpone the final date by application under s 330(3).

The trustee may not, of course, declare the dividend so long as there is an appeal outstanding to the court to reverse or vary a decision of his on a proof, or to expunge or reduce the amount claimed. But any creditor who neglects to assert his rights until after the estate has been fully administered and the trustee released comes too late to claim a dividend (see *Re Gill Ex p Barnard* (1882) 46 LT 824) provided that he had full knowledge of those rights.

5. Second and subsequent bankruptcies

Any amounts relating to an earlier bankruptcy which are provable under s 335(5) in a later bankruptcy rank in priority *after* all the other debts provable in the later bankruptcy and after interest thereon.

The cut-off point for the existing trustee is notice (Form 6.78) of the presentation of the petition for the later bankruptcy. Any subsequent distribution of the bankrupt's estate is void under s 334 except to the extent that it is made with the consent of, or is subsequently ratified by, the court.

6. Unclaimed funds and dividend

All receipts are paid by the trustee into the Insolvency Services Account kept by the Department of Trade and Industry with the Bank of England unless the trustee has been given permission to open a local bank account in the name of the estate for administrative advantage, for example where a special manager is appointed. As soon as the trustee stops carrying on the business or gives up the trusteeship that bank account is closed and the balance remitted to the Insolvency Services Account. As to accountancy control by the Secretary of State, see page 251 *et seq.*

Any person claiming to be entitled to any moneys paid into the Insolvency Services Account may apply to the Secretary of State for payment. The application should be supported by evidence for the claim, and, if dissatisfied with the decision in respect of the claim, the applicant may appeal to the court under s 378.

If a surplus remains after payment in full and with interest of all the bankrupt's creditors together with payment of the expenses of the bankruptcy, the bankrupt is entitled to the surplus.

In the matter of unclaimed funds and dividends, a trustee, as an officer of the court, may not rely on the Limitation Acts: see *Re Cornish* [1891] 1 QB 99.

For the duty of the Secretary of State to pay into the Consolidated Fund from the Insolvency Services Account, see s 407.

7. Distribution in insolvent partnerships

(a) Priority of debts

Where insolvency orders are made in relation to an insolvent partnership as well as an insolvent member the following provisions apply as regards priority of debts.

The joint estate of an insolvent partnership is applicable in the first instance in payment of the joint debts due to the creditors of the partnership other than those to be postponed under s 3 Partnership Act 1890 (or any other Act). The separate estate of each insolvent member is applicable in the first instance in payment of the separate debts of that member, other than those to be postponed as mentioned above.

(b) Surplus

Any surplus remaining after the payment of the separate debts of any insolvent member out of his separate estate without the prior payment of any interest under s 189 or 328(4) of the Act, forms part of the joint estate of the partnership and is applied in payment of the joint debts due to the creditors of the partnership.

Any surplus remaining after the payment of the joint debts of the partnership out of its joint estate forms part of the separate estate of each partner in proportion to the right and interest of each such partner in the joint estate.

(c) Claim of solvent partner

In the case of a partner against whom an insolvency order has not been made, before any part of the surplus forms part of his separate estate, interest is, by s 189, to be paid out of his share on the joint debts of the partnership to the creditors of the partnership.

All debts of the partnership other than preferential debts rank equally between themselves, subject to the Act, and the Partnerships Order. Where insolvency orders are made in relation to an insolvent partnership as well as an insolvent member the following provisions apply as regards priority of debts: the *joint* estate of an insolvent partnership is applicable in the first instance in payment of the joint debts due to the creditors of the partnership other than those to be postponed under s 3 Partnership Act 1890 (see above). The *separate* estate of each insolvent member is applicable in the first instance in payment of the separate debts of that member, other than those to be postponed as mentioned above. As to surpluses remaining see page 242.

In *Re Judd & Son Ltd* [1984] Ch 237, where two companies that had traded in partnership were both insolvent, it was held that the creditors of the *partnership* took priority over the individual creditors of the *companies* and it made no difference whether or not they ranked in priority.

Chapter 17

Controlling the trustee

The trustee's powers outside England and Wales are not restricted by the Act. Otherwise, except for the general powers set out in Part II of Sch 5 to the Act, he is bound by the creditors, and their committee if there is one, and to the court. Initially, he is responsible to his authorising body for permission to practice as an insolvency practitioner (see page 19), and to the Department of Trade and Industry in regard to records, money received and the auditing of his accounts.

1. Control by general meeting of the creditors

Creditors are always free to meet to discuss the administration of the estate outside general meetings. Their views can be given formal effect if expressed in resolutions at properly convened general meetings, thus the need for the trustee to call the creditors together to enable him to ascertain their wishes on important matters of policy or difficulty.

(a) Appointment of the trustee

The trustee may be appointed by the creditors (page 85). If the official receiver fails to hold a general meeting of creditors under s 293, they may request a meeting under s 294 (see page 85).

A general meeting of creditors summoned specially for the purpose under s 298 may remove the trustee provided that a certificate for the summary administration of the estate is not in force. The notice should draw the attention of creditors to s 299(3) of the Act with respect to the trustee's release. A copy of the notice is sent to the official receiver.

However, where the trustee was appointed otherwise than by the creditors, a general meeting of creditors is summoned for the purpose of replacing him only if the trustee thinks fit, the court so directs, or the meeting is requested by one of the bankrupt's creditors with the concurrence of not less than one quarter in value of the creditors including the creditor making the request (see page 206).

Where the appointment fails to take effect the official receiver is trustee until the vacancy is filled. He may summon a general meeting of the creditors for the purpose of filling the vacancy and must do so if the creditors so require under s 314(7) (creditors' requisition). "Vacancy" here includes the case where it is necessary to revive the trusteeship (ie after holding a final meeting under s 331 or the giving of a notice by the official receiver under s 299(2)) in relation to any property which is or may be comprised in a bankrupt's estate.

(b) Right to call meetings

The trustee may summon a general meeting of the bankrupt's creditors at any time if he wishes, but he must summon a meeting if he is requested to do so by a creditor of the bankrupt, and the request is made with the concurrence of not less than one tenth in value of the bankrupt's creditors (including the creditor making the request). Rule 6.83 provides the procedure for calling a requisitioned meeting; see page 213. If the meeting is for the appointment or removal of the trustee then the concurrence of at least one quarter in value of the creditors is required.

(c) Right to have a list of creditors

A creditor who (under the rules) has the right to inspect documents on the court file, also has the right to require the trustee to send him (for the appropriate fee) a list of creditors and the amounts of their respective debts, unless either a statement of affairs has already been filed in the bankruptcy court, or the trustee declines on the basis that the list is confidential or of such a nature that its disclosure would be calculated to be injurious to the interests of the other creditors.

(d) Remuneration

If there is no creditors' committee, or if there is a committee but it does not make the requisite determination, the trustee's remuneration may be fixed by a resolution of a meeting of creditors to which Rule 6.138 (see page 250) applies.

(e) Withdrawal of authorisation

The individual creditor, or the body of creditors in general meeting, are at liberty to express their views to the competent authority and to be a local "watchdog" to ensure proper administration by, and the competence of, the appointed trustee.

A licence for an insolvency practitioner to practice may be withdrawn by the competent authority under s 393(4) where it appears that he is no longer a fit and proper person or has failed to comply with the Act or the regulations. Supplying false, inaccurate or misleading information is included as a ground for withdrawal of the licence.

(f) Release

Where it appears to the trustee that the administration of the bankrupt's estate is for practical purposes complete, he summons a final general meeting of the creditors (see page 214). Failure by him to give due notice to a creditor (not merely his solicitor) was held to revoke his release in a case under similar, old, rules: see *Singer v Munro's Trustee* [1981] 3All ER 215.

2. Control by the creditors' committee

Control of the trustee by the creditors is more specifically exercised by his reporting to the creditors' committee, discussed in Chapter 15. This comprises a small representative group of creditors usually elected at the first general meeting of the creditors, principally to settle the trustee's remuneration and to give approval to those powers exercisable by him but only with their permission (or that of the court).

(a) Remuneration

The trustee is entitled to receive remuneration for his services, fixed by the committee. If there is no committee then it may be fixed by a resolution of a meeting of creditors on the same basis (as above).

The remuneration of the trustee is either based on a percentage of the value of the assets realised or distributed, or fixed by reference to the time taken (see page 221 and Appendix 5). Where the trustee is not the official receiver, the creditors' committee, if there is one, determines the basis of remuneration, and, in determining any percentage of assets to be applied, must, under Rule 6.138, have regard to:

(i) the complexity or otherwise of the case;
(ii) any exceptional responsibility falling to the trustee;
(iii) the effectiveness with the trustee appears to be carrying out, or to have carried out, his duties; and
(iv) the value and nature of the assets in the estate with which the trustee has to deal.

If not fixed as above, the trustee's remuneration is on the scale laid down for the official receiver (see Appendix 5).

As to the eligibility of a trustee to receive legal aid, see: *Re A Debtor (No 26A of 1975)* [1985] 1 WLR 6, the Legal Aid (General) Regulations 1980 and Regulations 34, 124 & 128.

The Act prohibits trustees from retaining any money or other estate property.

(b) Record keeping by the trustee

Under the Insolvency Practitioners Regulations the trustee is required to prepare and keep administrative records in relation to each separate bankrupt, containing the minutes of the proceedings at any meeting of the committee and the record of every resolution passed, including resolutions by post. He should submit financial records to the committee when required. If they are not satisfied with the contents they inform the Secretary of State giving reasons for the dissatisfaction and request an audit of the relevant account.

He may refuse inspection of confidential records or where disclosure would be calculated to be injurious to the interests of the insolvent creditors (Rule 12.13).

(c) Powers exercisable with sanction

A number of powers are exercisable by the trustee only with the permission of the court or the committee. This is to facilitate control over the costs and expenses of the administration. Thus, under s 314(1) he may exercise any of the powers specified in Sch 5, Part 1 of the Act subject to the sanction of the committee (see page 224).

3. Duty to the official receiver

It is the duty of the trustee to assist the official receiver to carry out his functions in relation to the bankruptcy by producing to him and permitting him to inspect books, papers and other records, and giving him such other assistance as he may reasonably require.

The official receiver has power to call a meeting at any time to ascertain the wishes of the creditors. The detailed provisions for the calling and chairmanship of such a meeting are contained in Rules 6.81 and 6.82; see page 212.

4. Accounting control by the Secretary of State

(a) Local bank account

Where the trustee intends to carry on the business of the bankrupt, he may apply to the Secretary of State for authorisation to open a current account with a local bank, subject to a limit. The Secretary of State may authorise him to make payments into and out of such an account, instead of into and out of the Insolvency Services Account, if satisfied that an administrative advantage will be derived from having such an account.

The account should be opened and maintained in a clearly named local bank account in the name of the individual bankrupt so that where money is provided for a specific purpose it is clearly identifiable in a separate account. Money received which relates to the purpose for which the account was opened is paid to the credit of the bankrupt's account.

It is up to the trustee to keep records, including documentary evidence, of all money paid into and out of every local bank account so opened, and to pay any surplus above his authorised limit into the Insolvency Services Account (see below).

The account is closed as soon as the trustee ceases to carry on the business of the bankrupt, vacates office, or his authorisation is withdrawn. The balance is then remitted to the Insolvency Services Account.

(b) Insolvency Services Account

Subject to the provisions for local bank accounts, the trustee must pay all money received by him into the Insolvency Services Accounts kept by the Secretary of State with the Bank of England. More particularly:

"(2) Every responsible insolvency practitioner shall remit the money ..... once every 14 days, or forthwith if £5,000 or more has been received.

(3) Every remittance of money .... shall be;

(a) paid in through Bank Giro system; or

(b) sent direct to the Bank of England, Threadneedle Street, London EC2R 8AH, by cheque drawn in favour of the "Insolvency Services Account" and crossed "A/C payee only" "Bank of England" and the responsible insolvency practitioner shall on request be given by the Department a receipt for the money so paid.

(4) Every remittance of money ..... shall be accompanied by forms obtainable on application from the Department for the purpose or by forms which are substantially similar". (Reg 4).

If the trustee fails to pay over any money, then unless he explains that failure to the satisfaction of the Secretary of State, he pays interest at the rate of 20% pa together with expenses occasioned by reason of his default.

Regulation 5 regulates payments out of the Insolvency Services Account:

"(1) Every responsible insolvency practitioner shall, on application to the Department on a requisition form obtainable on application from the Department or on a form which is substantially similar, be repaid all necessary disbursements by him, and expenses properly incurred by him, in the course of his administration to the date of his vacation of office out of any moneys standing to the credit of the insolvent in the Insolvency Services Account.

(2) Every application under paragraph (1) above shall give details of all disbursements and expenses claimed.

(3) Every responsible insolvency practitioner who vacates office shall be repaid by any succeeding responsible insolvency practitioner, or if none by the official receiver, out of any funds available for the purpose any necessary disbursements made by him and any expenses properly incurred by him but not repaid before he vacates office.

(4) Every responsible insolvency practitioner shall, on application on a requisition form obtainable from the Department or on a form which is substantially similar, obtain cheques, money orders or payable orders to the order of the payee for sums which become payable on account of the insolvent for delivery by the responsible insolvency practitioner to the persons to whom the payments are to be made."

A certificate of the balance standing to the credit of the bankrupt is available on written application to the Secretary of State.

(c) Payment of dividends

The manner of the distribution of the bankrupt's estate is by application to the Department of Trade and Industry by the trustee and is controlled by Regulation 15:

"(1) A responsible insolvency practitioner shall pay every dividend by payable order on HM Paymaster General which will be prepared by the Department on the application of the responsible insolvency practitioner and transmitted to him for distribution amongst the creditors.

(2) The application for a payable order for a payment of dividend shall be made in Form 2 and shall be accompanied by a certified list of all proofs of debts admitted for dividend in whole or in part and, at the request of the Secretary of State, by the said proofs.

(4) The responsible insolvency practitioner shall enter the total amount of every dividend ......, that he desires to pay .... in the records to be kept .... in one sum.

(5) The responsible insolvency practitioner, on the expiration of six months from the last day of the month of issue, shall destroy any lapsed payable orders which have become invalid after first preparing a list of their numbers, names of payees and amounts,

(6) The responsible insolvency practitioner shall send the list mentioned in paragraph (5) above to the Department.

(7) On the responsible insolvency practitioner vacating office he shall send to the Department any unclaimed payable orders for dividends ..... after defacing them by cutting off the bottom right hand corner."

(d) Audit

The trustee must, in each year during which he acts as trustee, send to the Secretary of State an account setting out all receipts and payments. The account must be in Form 1 prescribed by the Regulations and accompanied by bank statements relating to any local bank account.

The first such account submitted must be accompanied by a summary of the insolvent's statement of affairs (if any) submitted under the Act, showing the amounts of assets realised and explaining the reasons for any non-realisation of any assets. Where no such statement of affairs has been submitted, the account must be accompanied by a summary of all known assets and the amounts actually realised, and a summary of all known assets not realised and their value, with reasons for any non-realisation.

The accounts in respect of the first year must be sent within 30 days of the expiration of twelve months from the date of the bankruptcy; later accounts should be sent within 30 days of the expiration of every twelve month period thereafter until the trustee vacates office.

Within fourteen days of vacating office the trustee must submit an account covering the period since the last account. If no account has been submitted, then an account in respect of the whole period of his trusteeship must be sent, together with the summaries mentioned above.

Any account submitted may be audited. Whether or not it is audited, the trustee must send to the Secretary of State on demand any vouchers and information relating to the account, and produce on demand and allow inspection of any accounts, books or other records.

Where the creditors have resolved to remove the trustee, the Secretary of State must first certify that the trustee has reconciled his account with that held by him in respect of the bankruptcy.

5. Control by the bankruptcy court

Every bankruptcy is by s 363 under the general control of the court which has full power to decide all questions of priorities and all other questions arising, whether of law or fact.

(a) As to conduct

The trustee is an officer of the court and as such the highest standard of conduct is imposed on him. It is not easy to define the exact extent of the disciplinary control the court exercises over its officers, although there are some indicators; see *Re Killmier* [1966] ALR 906.

In *Re Condon, ex parte James* (1874) LR 9 Ch 609; 22 WR 937 the Court of Appeal held that a trustee in bankruptcy, to whom an execution creditor had paid over the fruits of his execution under a view of the law which a decision of the Court of Appeal given shortly afterwards showed to have been wrong, must refund the money so paid under a mistake of law to the creditor. He is to hold money in his hands upon trust for its equitable distribution among the creditors: "the Court of Bankruptcy ought to be as honest as other people". See also *Re Cornish* [1891] 1 QB 99.

This should, however, be distinguished from the case where a bank had inadvertently paid creditors on the instruction of the bankrupt and not the trustee: Goulding J in *Re Byfield* [1982] 1 Ch @ 271: "To my mind there is nothing offensive either to commercial or to general morality in the general body of creditors receiving a benefit - a windfall, if you will - from the bank's unfortunate payment in the present case ...... I do not think that the ethical addition to the ordinary rules allowed by the principle of *Ex p James* can properly have an application in the present case". Note however, the position of the bank under the new Act with regard to "after acquired property" under s 307(4) (see page 161).

As to the general power of inquiry by the court into the conduct of a trustee, in a Commonwealth case, *Re Gault; Gault* v *Law* [1982] 57 FLR 165, it was held that in considering whether or not to order an inquiry:

(i) a court is not obliged to order an inquiry unless it is satisfied that sufficient grounds in support have been made out;

(ii) it may take into account whether substantial allegations are made of misconduct in the administration of the trustee;

(iii) it should consider whether the applicant has other remedies which are open to him to pursue;

(iv) it should consider the extent of any delay and the effect of such delay upon any inquiry.

(b) Setting aside

If a bankrupt, any of his creditors or any other person is dissatisfied by any act, omission or decision of a trustee, he may apply to the court under s 303. On such an application the court may confirm, reverse or modify any act or decision of the trustee, may give him directions or may make such other order as it thinks fit.

Under Rule 6.147, the court may, on the application of any person interested, set aside a transaction and order the trustee to compensate the estate for loss suffered in consequence if the trustee enters into a transaction with a person who is an associate of his. However, this power does not apply if the transaction had the prior consent of the court or if it is shown to the satisfaction of the court that the transaction was for value or was entered into by the trustee without knowing or having any reason to know that the person concerned was an associate as defined by s 435. The Rule does not affect any rule of law or equity relating to a trustee's dealings with trust property or the fiduciary obligations of any person.

(c) Discovery

Under Rule 7.60 any party to insolvency proceedings may, with the leave of the court, administer interrogatories to, or obtain discovery from, any other party. An application for such leave may be made *ex parte*.

(d) Restitution

Where, on an application under s 304, the court is satisfied that the trustee has misapplied, retained, or become accountable for any money or other property comprised in the bankrupt's estate, or that the estate has suffered any loss in consequence of any misfeasance or breach of fiduciary or other duty by a trustee of the estate in the carrying out of his functions, the court may order the trustee to repay, restore or account for money or other property. For example, the trustee may be personally liable for the return of premiums illegally charged under the Rent Act 1977: see *Adair* v *Murrell* (1981) 263 EG 66. He is also liable to pay interest at such rate as the court thinks just and to pay compensation for misfeasance or breach of a fiduciary or other duty.

The application may be made by the official receiver, the Secretary of State, a creditor, or the bankrupt himself. An application may be made in respect of a trustee who has been released only with the leave of the court.

(e) Applications concerning trustee's remuneration

A creditor may, with the concurrence of at least one quarter in value of the creditors (including himself), apply to the court for an order that the trustee's remuneration be reduced on the grounds that, in the circumstances, it is excessive. The court may dismiss the application if it thinks no sufficient cause is shown, but shall not do so unless the applicant has had an opportunity to attend the court for an *ex parte* hearing and has had seven days notice of such a hearing. If the application is not dismissed, the applicant must, at least fourteen days before the day fixed for the hearing, send to the trustee a notice stating the venue fixed and accompanied by a copy of the application and any evidence which it is intended shall be adduced in support. The court may make an order fixing a reduced amount of remuneration. The costs of the application are to be paid by the applicant unless the court otherwise orders (Rule 6.142).

Notwithstanding any resolution of the creditors' committee or the creditors, the court may order that no remuneration should be allowed out of the estate in the event of any improper solicitation by, or on behalf of, the trustee in obtaining proxies or procuring his appointment.

Furthermore the court has residual powers under the umbrella of s 363(1) to fix the trustee's remuneration; see generally *Re Colgate (A Bankrupt) ex parte the Trustee* [1986] 1 All ER 419, in which Lloyd LJ confirmed that where the machinery for fixing the trustee's remuneration was available, it must be used.

(f) Where permission required

The trustee may, with the sanction of the court or the creditors' committee, exercise any of the powers set out in Sch 5 Part I (see page 224), including the power to appoint the bankrupt to carry on the business. The court may also ratify any unauthorised expenditure (s 314(4)). To justify the retrospective sanction for the employment of a solicitor, see *Re A Debtor (No 26A of 1975)*[1985] 1 WLR 6.

(g) Rule against solicitation

If the court is satisfied that the trustee, or anyone on his behalf, has improperly solicited his appointment as trustee, or improperly solicited proxies, it may order than no remuneration be paid from the estate to that person. Any such order of the court takes precedence over any resolution of the creditors, the creditors' committee, or any other provision of the rules governing remuneration (Rule 6.148).

(h) Enforcement of trustee's obligations to official receiver

The court may, on the application of the official receiver, make such order(s) as it thinks fit for the the enforcement of the duties of the trustee under s 305(3). Section 305(3) concerns information and assistance to be given and the production and inspection of books and records; see page 251. Such an order may provide for the costs of the application therefor to be met by the trustee. (Rule 6.149)

(i) Bankrupt's letters

On application, the court may order (by Form 6.80) the Post Office to re-direct and send or deliver to the official receiver or trustee (or otherwise) any postal packet, ie letters, postcards and parcels, which would otherwise be sent or delivered to the bankrupt. An order only has effect for a period not exceeding three months (s 371). If the trustee refuses to apply for such an order, or to appeal from an order made on his application, the petitioning creditor has no *locus standi* to apply to the court himself; see *Re Halberstanm ex parte Lister* (1881) 17 Ch 518.

(j) Co-operation between courts

An order made by a court in any part of the UK is enforceable in any other part of the UK as if it were made by a court exercising the corresponding jurisdiction in that other part.

The Secretary of State, with the concurrence of the Lord Chancellor, may by order make provision for securing that a trustee or assignee has, with such modifications as may be specified in the order, the same rights in relation to any property situated in another part of the UK as he would have in the corresponding circumstances if he were a trustee or assignee under the insolvency law of that part.

(k) Liability notwithstanding release

The trustee vacates office on giving notice to the court that a final meeting of creditors has been held (Rule 6.137), but he remains liable after his release for general maladministration. The same applies to a trusteeship in respect of a person adjudged bankrupt *before* the appointed day, or adjudged bankrupt on or after 29 December 1986 on a petition presented before that day; see page 314.

(l) Extra benefit

The Act prohibits trustees from retaining any money or other estate property.

(m) Unpaid dividends

No action lies against the trustee for a dividend but if he refuses to pay, the court may order him to do so and also to pay, out of his own money, interest from the time it was withheld and the costs of the proceedings in which the order to pay is made.

6. Taxation of costs

Rules 7.34 provides for the taxation of costs, charges or expenses payable out of the bankrupt's estate. The trustee may agree such costs, charges or expenses with the person entitled to receive them, or may require them to be taxed by the court. Likewise, a creditors' committee may resolve that any such costs be taxed. Where the costs to be taxed are those of any person employed by the trustee, the requirement to tax does not preclude the making of payments on account if the recipient undertakes to repay, immediately and with interest, any money which may transpire to be an overpayment.

The court may order the costs of any proceedings before the court, including proceedings on a petition, to be taxed. Unless otherwise directed or authorised, the costs of a trustee are to be allowed on the standard basis. Rule 7.34 applies to proceedings commenced before 29 December 1986.

Order 38 of the County Court Rules applies to insolvency proceedings in a county court and O 62 of the Rules of the Supreme Court to proceedings in the High Court.

(a) Procedure where taxation required

In the case of the costs of any person employed in insolvency proceedings by a trustee, the taxing officer must require a certificate of employment to be endorsed on the bill and signed by the insolvency practitioner. The certificate must show the name and address of the person employed; details of the functions to be carried out under the employment and any special terms of remuneration which have been agreed.

A person whose costs are to be taxed must deliver his bill of costs to the taxing officer when required to do in writing by the trustee. If he fails to do so within three months, or within such further time as the court may allow, the trustee may deal with the estate without regard to the claim of the person who has not delivered his bill of costs. If that person also had a claim against the trustee personally, that claim is likewise forefeited. (Rule 7.35)

(b) Costs paid otherwise than out of the estate

Where a bill of costs is taxed under an order of the court directing that the costs are to be paid otherwise than out of the estate, the taxing officer notes by whom or the manner in which they are to be paid, on the certificate of taxation (Rule 7.38).

(c) Award of costs against official receiver or trustee

Where the official receiver or trustee is made a party to any proceedings he is not personally liable for costs unless the court otherwise directs. This is without prejudice to any provision of the Act or the Rules to the effect that the official receiver is not in any event to be liable for costs and expenses (Rule 7.39).

(d) Application for costs

A party to, or any person affected by, any proceedings, may apply to the court for an order allowing his costs, or part of them incidental to the proceedings, after they are concluded. He should serve a sealed copy of his application on the responsible insolvency practitioner, who may appear on the application. No costs of or incidental to the application may be allowed unless the court is satisfied that it could not have been made at the time of the proceedings.

(e) Witness costs

No allowance may be made to the bankrupt or an officer of the insolvent company to which the proceedings relate. A petitioner is *not* regarded as a witness although the taxing officer may allow his expenses of travelling and subsistence.

(f) Certificate of taxation

A certificate of taxation of the taxing officer, which includes an order of the registrar in a county court, is final and conclusive as to all matters which have not been objected to in the manner provided for under the rules of the court. Where the certificate has been lost or destroyed the taxing officer may issue a duplicate (Rule 7.42).

(g) Employment of others by the trustee

Where any costs, charges or expenses of any person are payable out of the estate, the trustee may agree them with the person or may have them taxed by the court, unless the committee resolves that such costs, charges or expenses should be taxed, in which case the trustee must require taxation.

The trustee may make payments on account, but then if he overpays, the recipient must repay, with interest from the date of payment to that of repayment.

Chapter 18

The bankrupt

1. Introduction

A bankrupt is an individual who has been adjudged bankrupt, and in relation to a bankruptcy order is the individual adjudged bankrupt by that order (s 381).

This chapter concerns the position of the debtor after the making of the bankruptcy order against his property (including his duty to declare any property or income that comes into his hands after adjudication) for the benefit of his bankruptcy estate, and the ensuing disqualification and disabilities to which he is subject. He has access to the courts with or without legal advisers. He may appeal, and he retains a number of rights including the right to receive full information from his trustee so that he can make the judgements set out below; he might also be required to manage his property or business.

The first step is for him to prepare his statement of affairs which contains particulars of his creditors and debts, other liabilities and assets (see Chapters 8 & 9). In the case of his own petition the debtor is required to submit the statement of affairs (Form 6.28) at the same time as the petition. In the case of a petition by a creditor the statement of affairs follows that event (Form 6.33).

Rule 6.62 concerns the power of the official receiver to release the bankrupt from the duty to submit a statement of affairs or to extend the time for so doing. For the provisions concerning assistance in preparing the statement, see page 94, but as to the official receiver's duty to investigate further, see page 74.

If without reasonable excuse, the bankrupt fails to submit a statement of affairs or submits one that does not comply with the prescribed requirements, he is guilty of contempt of court and liable to be punished accordingly.

2. Applications to the court on or before bankruptcy

"Bankruptcy is a technical subject and a technical point may be a good point on appeal" (*Re a Debtor (No 26 of 83)* [1984] 2 All ER @ 262).

Where the statutory demand in respect of which the petition is presented is for a liquidated sum payable at some future time, the debtor may apply to the court to order the petitioning creditor to give security for costs. The nature and amount of the security is at the court's discretion.

The bankrupt may apply to the court to order the official receiver to suspend action following the making of a bankruptcy order on a creditor's petition, ie to suspend advertising the order and giving notice to the Land Registry, pending a further order of the court. Such application should be supported by an affidavit stating the grounds on which it is made.

In a case involving a voluntary arrangement, the debtor may appeal to the court within 28 days following the creditors' meeting summoned to decide whether or not to approve the proposed voluntary arrangement, on one or both of the grounds that it unfairly prejudices the interests of a creditor, and/or that there has been some material irregularity at or in relation to such a meeting.

Appeals in bankruptcy lie to a single judge of the High Court from a county court or from a High Court registrar. From a High Court judge, with the leave of that judge or of the Court of Appeal, appeal is to the Court of Appeal. The normal rules of the Supreme Court apply, except that in an appeal to a single judge of the High Court, any reference in the Rules of the Supreme Court to the Court of Appeal is replaced by a reference to that judge; and the procedure under Order 59 (application to the Court of Appeal) is by application not by summons.

Any appeal against a decision of the Secretary of State or the official receiver must be brought within 28 days of the notification of the decision (Rule 7.50).

It is also to be noted that insolvency proceedings are not invalidated by any formal defect or irregularity unless the court before which objection is made considers that substantial injustice has been caused and that it cannot be remedied by any order of the court (Rule 7.55).

3. Rights retained

The bankrupt retains a number of rights, among which are those set out in *(a)* to *(s)* below.

(a) Rights of action

The bankrupt retains certain rights of action which do not therefore pass to the trustee. Thus, a right of action resulting in injuries wholly to the person or personal feelings of the bankrupt remains the right of the bankrupt; see *Stanton* v *Collier* (1854) 2 WR 197. Likewise, the trustee is not entitled to the damages recovered by the bankrupt in an action for tort for personal injuries brought by him before discharge: see *Re Wilson ex parte Vane* (1878) 26 WR 534.

However, should the bankrupt have accumulated the money and invested it in property, the trustee might be entitled to the property, but he may not intercept the damages or prevent the bankrupt from expending them in the maintenance of himself and his family.

The position with regard to other causes of action is now less clear. Under the old law, the bankrupt was entitled to pursue in his own name any action started by him before his bankruptcy if the trustee had assigned or purported to assign to him all rights to the action: see *Ramsey* v *Hartley and Others* [1977] 2 All ER 673. However, it is doubtful that this is now possible because the power of the trustee to make a transfer of a cause of action to "any person" has not been brought forward from s 55(1) of the Act of 1914. Therefore the fundamental rule in *Kitson* v *Hardwick* (1872) LR 7 CP 473 that property and rights over may be assigned by the trustee to his bankrupt would now appear not to assist the litigious bankrupt. There is, however, an exception: property which is considered "onerous" by the trustee could in theory be assigned back to the bankrupt.

Alternatively, the trustee has, by s 314 and Sch 5 to the Act, the general power to sell "any part of the property". It is submitted that this would not, *prima facie,* be a bar to the bankrupt purchasing the right to an action, either outright or by option, against the benefit of the proceeds, or possibly better, by shares therein *pari passu* with the estate. Such sales are not impeachable on grounds of champerty or maintenance: see *Trendex Trading Corp* v *Credit Suisse* [1982] AC 679 (HL).

In the case of a contract involving personal skill or labour on the bankrupt's part, the trustee cannot sue for a breach committed after bankruptcy proceedings have commenced. The bankrupt himself may sue and retain the amount recovered but only in so far as it is required for the support of himself and his dependants: see *Bailey* v *Thurston* [1903] 1 KB 137.

Finally, bankruptcy is not a ground for an order for security of costs in an action: see *Ramsey* v *Hartley* (above).

(b) To assist in the administration

With the permission of the committee or the court the bankrupt may be appointed by the trustee to assist him in the administration of the estate. The trustee will grant the bankrupt an allowance for the support of himself and his family in consideration of his services, unless the creditors by resolution otherwise determine. Such an allowance is payable as an expense of the bankruptcy in priority; see Rule 6.224(1)(n), page 233.

(c) On annulment

On annulment of a bankruptcy order, the bankrupt, or his personal representative, can require the Secretary of State to advertise the making of the order of annulment, at the bankrupt's cost. He must also give security where a debt is disputed or a creditor who has proved can no longer be traced. This is held for no more than twelve months following which the court must, on application, order it to be released.

(d) Attendance at creditors' meetings

Whenever a meeting of creditors is summoned or adjourned, the convener is required to give 21 days' notice of the meeting to the bankrupt whether or not he is required to be present or in attendance. In the case of any meeting, the bankrupt or any other person, for example his lawyer, may be admitted if he has given reasonable notice of his wish to be present. It is, however, for the chairman to decide what intervention if any they may make. See further page 208.

(e) To carry on the business

With the permission of the creditors' committee or the court, the trustee may appoint the bankrupt to carry on his business for the benefit of his creditors (s 314(2)(b)). The relationship of the trustee with the bankrupt in this connection has been recognised by the courts and Parliament to be of importance, but not without its dangers.

(f) Church benefice

A bankrupt retains the right of nomination to a vacant ecclestiastical benefice.

(g) Diplomatic immunity

Diplomatic immunity applies to those persons in the foreign, commonwealth and international diplomatic corps who are entitled to exemption from the ordinary law. The main enactments providing for diplomatic immunity are the International Organisation (Immunity and Privileges) Act 1952, the Diplomatic Immunities (Commonwealth Countries and Republic of Ireland) Act 1961, the European Communities Act 1972, the State Immunity Act 1978, the International Organisation Acts 1968 & 1981, and the Diplomatic and Consular Premises Act 1987.

(h) On discharge

In connection with a suspension from automatic discharge (see page 282) the bankrupt has the right, seven days before the hearing, to file in court a notice specifying any statements in the official receiver's report which he intends to deny or dispute. He is then required to send copies of his notice not less than four days before the date of the hearing to the official receiver and trustee. Where the discharge is suspended he is sent a copy of the order by the court.

(i) Inspections

The bankrupt, and his solicitor, have a right to inspect the court files, and to require the court to provide an office copy of any document from the file. The copy is in such form as the registrar thinks appropriate and should bear the court seal. The trustee may also allow them to inspect the creditors' proofs so long as they are lodged with him, at all reasonable times on any business day. If the bankrupt is attending a creditors' meeting he also has the right to inspect the proxies and associated documents to be used in connection with that meeting, and, on payment, to take office copies of those documents.

(j) Insurance

Where under any contract of insurance a person is insured against liability to third parties, in the event of his becoming bankrupt his rights are transferred to and vest in the third party to whom the liability was so incurred, and the trustee cannot receive payment from or settle with the insurer (s 1 Third Parties (Rights Against Insurers) Act 1930).

(k) To manage his estate

A permission by the court or the creditors' committee given to enable the bankrupt to manage his estate (see page 223) is not a general permission, but relates to a particular proposed exercise of the power in question. A person dealing with the trustee in good faith and for value need not enquire whether any permission required has been given under s 314(2)(a).

(l) Medical examination

There is no jurisdiction to compel a bankrupt to submit to a medical examination so as to enable the trustee to effect an insurance on his life with a view to increasing the realisable value of the bankrupt's life in a property: see *Garnett ex parte Bullock* (1885) 34 WR 79.

(m) Rights of occupation

The bankrupt, with or without his spouse, has certain rights of occupation of a dwelling-house which he is entitled to occupy by virtue of a beneficial estate or interest (see page 126). He has the right, if in occupation, not to be evicted or excluded from the dwelling-house or any part of it except with the leave of the court; if not in occupation, he has a right with the leave of the court to enter into and occupy it. This applies whether or not the bankrupt's spouse (if any) has rights of occupation under the Matrimonial Homes Act 1983.

The bankrupt's rights are a charge, having the like priority as an equitable interest created immediately before the commencement of the bankruptcy, on so much of his estate or interest in the dwelling-house as vests in the trustee. Such rights appear conclusive where the trustee has successfully applied to the court for an order imposing a charge on the property, which effectively takes it out of the estate.

The position appears not so secure for the bankrupt where a charge has neither been made on the property, nor application made to the court under s 1 of the Matrimonial Homes Act 1983 for possession until at least a year after it was first vested in the trustee; for then the court is bound to assume that unless the circumstances of the case are exceptional, the interests of the bankrupt's creditors outweigh all other considerations. The position of the bankrupt who is trustee for sale is not so straightforward. Application through the court is subject to, *inter alia*, all the circumstances of the case, excluding his needs.

(n) Postal packets

The bankrupt has a right to receive any letters and parcels unless the court has made an order for re-direction to the trustee (Form 6.80). This has effect for a maximum period of three months (unless renewed from time to time), after which the entitlement reverts to the bankrupt.

(o) Appeal against decision on a proof

If the bankrupt is dissatisfied with the trustee's decision admitting or rejecting the whole or any part of a proof, he has the right, within 21 days of becoming aware of the trustee's decision, to make application to the court for the decision to be reversed or varied. The trustee is not liable for the costs of the hearing unless the court makes an order to that effect. (Rule 6.105).

(p) Exempt property

Exempt property comprises such tools, books, vehicles and other items of equipment as are necessary to the bankrupt for use personally by him in his employment, business or vocation; and such clothing, bedding, furniture, household equipment and provisions as are necessary for satisfying the basic domestic needs of the bankrupt and his family.

The value of the exemption was set at £250 in 1976, and before that at £20 for the previous 106 years, but is now subject only to the discretion of the trustee by reference to the cost of a "reasonable replacement". Where it appears to the trustee that the realisable value of the whole or any part of the exempt property exceeds the cost of a reasonable replacement, the trustee may by notice in writing under s 308 claim it, or part of it, for the bankrupt's estate (see page 150). It is to be noted that, similarly, the minimum value of property with which the bankrupt could abscond without incurring criminal liability was also set in 1976 at £250 (previously £20). This has now been doubled to £500. This suggests that £500 may be a suitable cut-off point, in that the trustee might exercise his powers over exempt property only if their value appears to exceed £500.

As an alternative to the trustee's replacing the exempt property, a third party may provide the estate with a sum of money equivalent to the difference between the realisable value and the cost of reasonable replacement, so that the bankrupt can be left in possession of the property.

(q) Surplus

The bankrupt is entitled to any surplus remaining from the administration after payment in full to all creditors with interest and payment of the expenses of the bankruptcy (s 330(5)). As to partnerships and personal representatives of deceased estates, see page 242.

(r) Property held on trust

Property held on trust by the bankrupt for any other person or for a specific purpose is not included in the estate and he retains control of it (s 283(3)(a)). This anticipates the Convention on the Law Applicable to Trusts whereby under article 11 personal creditors of a trustee have no recourse against the trust assets and they do not form part of the trustee's estate in the event of his bankruptcy (now enacted in s 1 of the schedule to the Recognition of Trusts Act 1987).

However, if the bankrupt has a beneficial interest, then it may be argued that the trust has ended and all legal and equitable interests vest in the trustee in bankruptcy; see *In Re McCarthy* [1975] 1 WLR @ 809. On the other hand, where a bankrupt had agreed to repay his friend's payment to a creditor, that money was held to be a loan to the bankrupt which was not impressed with a trust and therefore a disposition of property void as against the trustee: see *Re Salamon (A Bankrupt)* (1983) 127 SJ 763.

(s) Against the trustee

The bankrupt has the right under s 303(1) to apply to the court if he is dissatisfied by any act, omission or decision of his trustee. On such an application, the court may confirm, reverse or modify any act or decision of the trustee, including directions, or make such other order as it thinks fit.

This section replaces the old s 80 of the 1914 Act by introducing the word "omission" and replacing "aggrieved" by "dissatisfied". It seems that this right does not arise until the trustee has concluded his administration. The bankrupt may request a copy of the receipts and payments accounts for any period, including future periods, from the trustee free of charge.

Where there is likely to be a surplus for the bankrupt himself, he may, with the leave of the court, make an application under s 304(2) for the trustee to repay, restore or account for money or other property together with interest, or to pay such sum by way of compensation in respect of the misfeasance or breach of fiduciary or other duty as the court thinks just (see page 255 - "restitution").

If in the administration of his estate the trustee enters into any transaction with a person who is an associate of the trustee, the bankrupt may apply to the court to have the transaction set aside. This does not apply where the court gave its prior consent and, where the transaction was for value, it was entered into without the trustee knowing, or having any reason to suppose, that the person concerned was an associate. The trustee may also be required to compensate the estate for any loss suffered (see also pages 254-255).

As to the revesting of property in the bankrupt following the trustee's disclaimer under s 315, see page 182.

4. Disqualification

There are several activities from which the bankrupt is disqualified. These are examined in *(a)* to *(j)* below.

(a) Directorships

An undischarged bankrupt is disqualified from acting as a company director other than by leave of the court. The application by the bankrupt is under s 11 of the Company Directors Disqualification Act 1986 to "act as director of, or directly or indirectly to take part or be concerned in the promotion, formation or management of a company". It must be supported by affidavit identifying the company and specifying (by Rule 6.203):

(i) the nature of its business or intended business and the place(s) where the business is or is to be carried on;
(ii) whether it is or will be a private or public company;
(iii) the persons who are, or are to be, principally responsible for the conduct of its affairs in whatever capacity;
(iv) the manner and capacity in which the applicant intends to be involved in the company's business (ie promotion, formation, management);
(v) the emoluments and other benefits to be derived from the directorship;
(vi) if the company already exists:
  - the date of incorporation;
  - the amount of the nominal and issued share capital;

  if the company does not already exist:
  - the amount or approximate amount of the proposed commencing share capital and the sources from which it has been raised;

(vii) where the bankrupt intends to take part or be concerned in the promotion or formation of a company, an undertaking by him that he will, not later than seven days after the incorporation of the company, file in court a copy of its Memorandum (and Articles) of Association and certificate of incorporation.

The words "being concerned in the management of a company" have been held to include being a management consultant advising on the financial management and the restructuring of a company; see *R* v *Campbell* (1984) BCLC 83.

The court fixes a venue for the hearing of the application and notifies the bankrupt accordingly. Not less than 28 days before the date so fixed, the bankrupt must give to the official receiver and the trustee notice of the venue and copies of the application and supporting affidavit. Not less than fourteen days before that date, the official receiver may file in court a report on any matters he considers should be brought to the court's attention. He must send a copy of that report to the bankrupt and to the trustee.

Not later than seven days before the date fixed for the hearing the bankrupt may file in court a statement specifying any aspects of the official receiver's report he intends to deny or dispute; he must send copies of any such statement to the official receiver and the trustee not less than four days before the date fixed for hearing. The official receiver and the trustee may appear on the hearing of the application (which is heard in open court if it is opposed), make representations and question the bankrupt (Rule 6.204).

If the court grants the application, its order must specify what it is the bankrupt is thereby entitled to do. At the same time the court may also vary any income payments order (see page 272) already in force in respect of the bankrupt, or make one if none already exists. Whatever the outcome of the hearing, copies of the court's order are sent by the court to the bankrupt, the trustee and the official receiver (Rule 6.205).

If a county court administration order is revoked (see page 340) the court may make a disqualification order under s 429 of the Act. The disabilities pursuant to s 12 of the Company Directors Disqualification Act 1986 apply for not more than two years.

Special rules apply to partnerships; for the disqualification of partners see page 304.

(b) Estate agency

By s 23 of the Estate Agents Act 1979, a bankrupt may not engage in estate agency work of any description except as an employee of another person, which does not include a directorship. This prohibition ceases to have effect if and when he is discharged from bankruptcy.

"Estate agency work" comprises things done by any person in the course of a business pursuant to instructions received from a client who wishes to dispose of or acquire an interest in land for the purpose of, or with a view to, effecting the introduction to the client of a third person who wishes to acquire or, as the case may be, dispose of such an interest; and after such an introduction has been effected in the course of that business, securing the disposal or acquisition of that interest. It does not therefore, *prima facie* include work of managing or letting property, surveying or valuation.

(c) Justices' liquor licences

Where the holder of a justices' licence has been adjudged bankrupt, or a voluntary arrangement proposed by the holder of the licence has been approved under the Act, or a trustee has been appointed under a deed of arrangement for the benefit of the creditors of the holder of the licence, then the justices' licence is transferred to the insolvency practitioner. He is in the same position as regards carrying on the business under the licence as a person to whom a protection order had been validly granted, on the date on which he became trustee or supervisor, under the Licensing Act 1964.

The justices may grant him the licence if they are satisfied that the trustee applicant is a person to whom the licensing justices could grant a transfer of the licence.

(d) Justice of the peace

A bankrupt is disqualified from being appointed or acting as a justice of the peace by virtue of s 32(1)(c) of the Bankruptcy Act 1883. Disqualification ceases if and when the bankruptcy order is annulled or the bankrupt is discharged.

(e) Land drainage committee

A bankrupt is disqualified from membership of a land drainage committee, as is a person who has made a composition or arrangement with his creditors. The disqualification ceases on discharge unless the bankruptcy order made against him is previously annulled, in which case it ceases on the date of the annulment.

By s 8(3) of the Land Drainage Act 1976, where a person is disqualified by reason of his having made a compromise or arrangement and he pays his debts in full, the disqualification ceases on the date the payment is completed, and in any other case on the expiration of five years from the date on which the terms of the deed of composition or arrangement are fulfilled.

(f) Local government

By s 80 of the Local Government Act 1972, where a person is disqualified from membership of a local authority by reason of having been adjudged bankrupt, or by reason of having made a composition or arrangement with his creditors, the disqualification ceases after his discharge from bankruptcy. If the bankruptcy is annulled then the disqualification ceases on that day. The making of a deed of arrangement is likewise a disqualification under this Act.

When he is disqualified by virtue of having made a composition or arrangement and he pays his debt in full, the disqualification ceases on the date on which the payment is completed, and in any other case not until five years from the date on which the terms of the deed of composition or arrangement are fulfilled. These penal terms (which are not in step with other disqualifications) appear to have inadvertently spilled over without amendment from the old legislation.

(g) Local valuation panel

A bankrupt is disqualified from membership of a local valuation panel under the General Rate Act Act 1967. The disqualification ceases on his discharge from the bankruptcy unless the bankruptcy order was previously annulled. If the order was so annulled the disqualification ceases on the date of annulment.

(h) Parliament

A bankrupt is disqualified by s 427 of the Act for sitting or voting in the House of Lords, from being elected to, sitting or voting in the House of Commons, and for sitting or voting in a committee of either House. He must vacate his seat at the end of the period of six months from the date of the bankruptcy order. Disqualification continues until such time as the bankruptcy order is annulled or discharged.

Where the court has certified an adjudication to the Speaker of the House of Commons, then immediately after it becomes apparent which of the following certificates is available, the court must certify to the Speaker either:

- (i) that the period of six months beginning with the day of the adjudication has expired without it having been annulled, in which case the member must vacate his seat; or
- (ii) that the adjudication has been annulled before the end of that period, in which case the disqualification ceases.

No writ of summons may be issued to any Lord of Parliament who is for the time being disqualified under this section.

(i) Public service vehicle operator's road service licence

These licences terminate on bankruptcy under s 57 Public Passenger Vehicles Act 1981. The traffic commissioners by whom a PSV operator's licence, or road service licence, was granted may direct that its termination be deferred for a period not exceeding twelve months, or eighteen months in special circumstances, and that otherwise the business of the licence holder be carried on under the licence by some other person during the period of deferment, subject to such conditions as the commissioners may impose.

(j) Solicitors

A bankrupt may not practise as a solicitor after having been adjudged bankrupt or having entered into a composition with his creditors or a deed of arrangement for the benefit of his creditors. Where a bankruptcy order is made against a solicitor, or such an order made against a solicitor is rescinded or anulled, the court gives immediate notice to the Secretary of The Law Society of the order that it has made.

An adjudication in bankruptcy operates immediately to suspend any practising certificate of that solicitor for the time being in force. The suspension continues until the certificate expires or the adjudication is annulled. The solicitor may at any time before the certificate expires and while the adjudication remains unannulled, apply to The Law Society to terminate the suspension. On such an application under the Solicitors Act 1974 the Society may by order terminate the suspension either unconditionally or subject to such conditions as it thinks fit, or refuse the application.

Appeal then lies to the Master of the Rolls who may affirm the decision or terminate the suspension either unconditionally or subject to such conditions as he thinks fit. When he is discharged, he may apply for a practising certificate under the Practising Certificate Regulations 1976 as amended by SI 1986 No 2001. He must give The Law Society not less than six weeks notice of his intention to apply.

5. Duty to the insolvency practitioner

(a) To deliver up

The bankrupt should give the trustee such information as to his affairs, attend on him at such times, and do all such things as the trustee may, for the purpose of carrying out his functions, reasonably require. If the bankrupt fails, without reasonable excuse, to comply he is guilty of a contempt of court and liable to be punished accordingly.

(b) Notice by the bankrupt as to after-acquired property

The trustee has a discretion whether or not to claim any property which has been acquired by, or has devolved upon, the bankrupt since the bankruptcy (see page 161). This, however, does not apply to excluded property such as tools, vehicles, household goods or property held on trust. For these purposes "property" does not include income, although income may be subject to an income payments order (see below).

The bankrupt is required to give the trustee notice under s 333(2), within 21 days of the bankrupt's becoming aware of the acquisition or devolution of property, or of an increase in income. The bankrupt may not, without the trustee's written consent, dispose of such property within 42 days from the date of the notice.

If he disposes of the property before giving the required notice to the trustee, or within the 42 day limit, he must inform the trustee immediately of the name and address of the person to whom it has been transferred, the "disponee", and provide any other information necessary to trace and recover the property. These requirements do not, however, apply to property acquired in the ordinary course of a business being carried on by the bankrupt, or acquired after discharge.

If the bankrupt carries on a business he must, at intervals of not less than six months, give the trustee information about the business, showing the total of goods bought and sold, or services supplied, and the profit or loss arising. The trustee may call for such fuller details as he may require (Rule 6.200). If the bankrupt fails to comply with his obligations without reasonable excuse, he is guilty of contempt of court.

(c) General control by the court

Whether discharged or undischarged, where the estate is still being administered, the bankrupt must follow the directions of the court for the purposes of his bankruptcy or the administration of his estate. The official receiver or trustee may apply to the court for a direction, with which the bankrupt must comply or be guilty of a contempt of court and liable to be punished accordingly in addition to any other punishment to which he may be subject (s 363).

6. Duty to the official receiver

Where a bankruptcy order has been made the bankrupt is under a duty to deliver possession of his estate to the official receiver unless a trustee has been appointed, and to deliver up to him all books, papers and other records of which he has possession or control and which relate to his estate and affairs, including any which would be privileged from disclosure in any proceedings.

Where any part of the estate consists of things which cannot be delivered up then it is up to him to do all that may reasonably be required by the official receiver for the protection of those things or that property. This does not apply when, by virtue of s 297, the bankrupt's estate vests in a trustee immediately on the making of the bankruptcy order.

The bankrupt is also under a duty, by s 291, to attend on the official receiver at such times as he may reasonably require and to give him an inventory of his estate and such other information as he may reasonbly require (see page 74).

7. Income payments orders (s 310)

This is the only method by which the trustee's claim to income for the bankrupt's estate may proceed. Income does not vest in him until there is an order under s 310 for the payment by the bankrupt of his income subsequent to the bankruptcy.

For the purposes of an income payments order the "income" of the bankrupt comprises every payment in the nature of income from time to time made to him or to which he from time to time becomes entitled. "Income" includes payment in respect of the carrying on of any business or in respect of any office or employment (s 310(7)).

(a) The order

The court may make an income payments order claiming for the bankrupt's estate so much of the income of the bankrupt during the period for which the order is in force as may be specified (s 310(3)(a)). But it cannot make an order which would have the effect of reducing his income below what appears necessary for meeting the reasonable domestic needs of the bankrupt and his family. Nor should an order be made after discharge, and if made before, should not have effect after discharge other than as a discharge with a condition, requiring it to continue in force for no later than three years after the making of the order, not the date of discharge.

The order will be addressed either to the bankrupt (Form 6.65) or to his employer (Form 6.66) (Rule 6.190(1)). Sums received by the trustee under the order form part of the bankrupt's estate.

(b) Application for order

An application to the court is made by the trustee on Form 6.64. Notice of the application and of the venue is sent by the trustee to the bankrupt at least 28 days before the day fixed for the hearing, together with a copy of the trustee's application and a short statement of the grounds. The notice informs that bankrupt that:

(i) unless at least seven days before the date fixed for the hearing he sends to the court and to the trustee written consent to an order in the terms of the application, he must attend the hearing; and

(ii) if he attends he will be given an opportunity to show cause why the order should not be made, or why an order should be made otherwise than as applied for by the trustee. (Rule 6.189).

(c) Procedure following order

If the court makes an order, the trustee must send a sealed copy of it to the bankrupt immediately (Form 6.65). Where the order is made under s 310 (3)(b) (Form 6.66) (requiring the person making the payment to the bankrupt to pay it to the trustee instead), the trustee must also send a sealed copy of the order to that person. The payer must then make the necessary arrangements to comply with the order. When making payment to the trustee, he may deduct the appropriate fee towards the administrative costs of complying with the order. He must also give the bankrupt a written statement of any amount so deducted.

If, at the time the payer receives notice of the order, he is no longer liable to pay the bankrupt any income, or if he later ceases to be so liable, he must give immediate notice to the trustee. (Rules 6.191 and 6.192)

(d) Variation

If the bankrupt does not comply with an income payments order, the trustee may apply to the court for it to be varied so as to take effect as an order to the payor of the relevant income. Such application may be made *ex parte* and sealed copies of any order made (on Form 6.67) must be sent by the court to the trustee and the bankrupt, and, where appropriate, to the payor of the relevant income. (Rule 6.191)

(e) Review

The trustee or the bankrupt may apply to the court for variation or discharge of an income payments order while it is in force. Rule 6.189 (application for income payments order) applies with any necessary modification if the applicant is the trustee. Where the bankrupt is the applicant the application must be accompanied by a short statement of the grounds.

The court may dismiss the application if it thinks that no sufficient cause is shown. However, it may not dismiss the application unless the applicant has had the opportunity to attend court for an *ex parte* hearing of which he had at least seven days notice. If the application is not dismissed, the court must fix a venue for hearing. The trustee or the bankrupt, whichever of them is the applicant, must give to the other of them at least 28 days notice of the hearing, and that notice must be accompanied by a copy of the application and, if the bankrupt is applicant, a copy of the statement of grounds.

If he thinks fit the trustee may appear and be heard on the application. Whether or not he intends to appear he may, not less than seven days before the hearing date, file a written report on any matters he thinks should be brought to the court's attention. Sealed copies of any order made (Form 6.66) on the application must be sent forthwith by the court to the trustee, the bankrupt and the payor (if other than the bankrupt). (Rule 6.193)

(f) Attachment of earnings

Where the court makes an income payments order, it may discharge or vary any attachment of earnings order that is for the the time being in force to secure payments by the bankrupt. Note, however, *Re Green (a Bankrupt)* [1979] 1 WLR 211, when such moneys paid into court by a debtor were held to belong to the creditors, notwithstanding the subsequent making of the then receiving order.

(g) Effect of discharge

An income payments order may not be made following a bankrupt's discharge. If made before discharge, it may not have effect after discharge save under a condition imposed by the court or provision in the order to that effect.

Such a condition may be imposed, firstly, under s 310(6) in a case of discharge by order of the court under s 279(1)(a) imposing the condition; secondly, in the case of a discharge at the expiration of the relevant period of two or three years, under s 279(1)(b), the order may include a provision requiring the income payments order to continue in force for a period ending after the discharge but no later than three years after the making of the order.

This would apply to those cases of severe deficiency where there is a surplus of income in excess of the immediate requirements of the bankrupt's family. As the order might not be made for some time after the adjudication, and indeed not until discharge, the court has the flexibility to make the order most appropriate to the circumstances of each case, provided that it does not continue for more than three years overall. See also the comments of the *Review Committee*, at para 1158 *et seq.*

(h) Following second bankruptcy

Any sums which remain payable are paid to the existing trustee, after the commencement of the later bankruptcy, but form part of the second bankruptcy. The court may give consequential directions modifying the income payments order.

8. Contracts with bankrupts

Where a contract has been made with a person who is subsequently adjudged bankrupt, the court may, on the application of any other party to the contract, make an order under s 345. That order may discharge obligations under the contract, on such terms as to payment by the applicant or the bankrupt of damages for non-performance or otherwise, as appear to the court to be equitable. Any damages payable by the bankrupt by virtue of an order of the court are provable as a bankruptcy debt.

9. Incapacitated persons

Special provisions (Rules 7.43 to 7.46) apply where it appears to the court that a person affected by the proceedings is one who is incapable of managing and administering his property and affairs either by reason of mental disorder under the Mental Health Act 1983 or because of physical affliction or disability.

The court may appoint such person as it thinks fit to represent the incapacitated person, either generally or for a specific purpose. The court may make the appointment either of its own motion or on the application of:

(a) a person who has been appointed by a court in the UK or elsewhere to manage the affairs of, or represent, the incapacitated person; or
(b) a relative or friend of the incapacitated person who appears to the court to be a proper person to make the application; or
(c) the official receiver; or
(d) the trustee.

Application may be made *ex parte*. The court may require such notice as it thinks reasonable to be given to the incapacitated person and any other person, and may adjourn hearing the application to enable notice to be given. The application must be supported by an affidavit of a registered medical practitioner as to the condition of the person concerned, unless the application is made by the official receiver, in which case his report is sufficient. Any notice served on a person appointed under these provisions has the same effect as if it had been served on the incapacitated person (Form 7.19).

See also the Court of Protection Rules 1984 made under the Act of 1983. They provide generally for the protection and management of the property and affairs of persons under mental disability.

10. Summary of the bankruptcy offences

The provisions of the Act rendering certain matters an offence apply where the court has made a bankruptcy order, and, by s 350, whether or not it is annulled. However, proceedings for an offence under the Act cannot be instituted after annulment. A bankrupt is not guilty of an offence in respect of anything done after his discharge, although proceedings may be begun against a discharged bankrupt for an offence committed before his discharge.

Section 352 provides the defence of innocent intention: a person is not guilty of the offence if he proves that, at the time of the conduct constituting the offence, he had no intent to defraud or to conceal the state of his affairs. This defence applies to the offences in *(a)* to *(g)* below, but not those in *(h)* and *(i)*. The Act applies to persons having privilege of Parliament or peerage as it applies to persons not having such privilege.

Schedule 10 to the Act under s 430 sets out the punishments for offences under the Act, together with the mode of prosecution and, where applicable, the daily default fine.

(a) Obtaining credit or engaging in business in another name

Where an undischarged bankrupt, either alone or jointly with any other person, obtains credit to the extent of £250 or more from any person without informing him that he is an undischarged bankrupt; or engages directly or indirectly in any business under a name other than that in which he was adjudged bankrupt, without disclosing to all persons with whom he enters into any business transaction the name under which he was adjudged bankrupt, he is guilty of an offence.

The "whether directly or indirectly" provision brings bankruptcy into line with the corresponding winding-up offence in s 302(1) Companies Act 1985 to prevent control of the business from behind the scenes, for example, through relatives. The maximum punishment is, on indictment, imprisonment for two years, a fine or both; or on summary conviction imprisonment for six months or a fine up to the statutory maximum, or both (s 360).

A bankrupt may be convicted if he has actually obtained credit, it not being necessary to show that there was any express stipulation between the parties to grant him credit: see *R* v *Juby* (1887) 35 WR 168: nor is an intent to defraud a necessary ingredient of the offence: see *R* v *Duke of Leinster* [1924] 1 KB 311.

"Obtaining credit" means obtaining some benefit from another under an agreement which postpones payment of the consideration for the benefit. It includes the case where goods are bailed to the bankrupt under a hire purchase agreement (reversing the decision in *R* v *Miller* [1977] 3 All ER 986) or agreed to be sold to him under a conditional sale agreement, and where the bankrupt himself is paid in advance (whether in money or otherwise) for the supply of goods and services.

If the facts disclose that credit was not obtained for the undischarged bankrupt but for another person, then there is no offence; see *Re Godwin* (1980) 71 Crim App R 97. The critical question is whether on the evidence the bankrupt held himself out as as the person for whom credit was sought, or whether it was for a genuine and separate business and not a charade to disguise the fact that he was the person seeking credit.

(b) Acting as a director

It is an offence for a person who is an undischarged bankrupt to act as director of, or directly or indirectly to take part in or be concerned in the promotion, formation or management of, a company except with the leave of the court. If a person acts in contravention of a disqualification order he is liable on conviction or indictment to imprisonment for not more than two years or a fine or both, and on summary conviction to imprisonment for not more than six months or a fine not exceeding the statutory maximum or both. See page 267 for the procedure for applying for the leave of the court to act as a director. See ss 11 and 13 Company Directors Disqualification Act 1986.

(c) Disposal of property

The bankrupt is also guilty of an offence if, in the twelve months before the petition is presented or in the initial period before adjudication (s 351), he disposes of any property which he had obtained on credit and had not paid for at the time he disposed of it. In this instance it is a defence if he can prove that at the time of the conduct he had no intent to defraud or to conceal the state of his affairs. "Disposing" of property includes pawning or pledging it, and in determining whether any property is disposed of, acquired, or received in the ordinary course of a business carried on by the bankrupt, regard may be had, in particular, to the price paid for the property (s 359).

The maximum punishment on indictment is imprisonment for seven years or a fine or both; on summary conviction, imprisonment for six months or the statutory maximum fine, or both.

(d) False statements

The bankrupt must not make false statements, or make any material omission in any statement made under the Act relating to his affairs. In particular he is guilty of an offence if:

(i) knowing or believing that a false debt has been proved by any person under the bankruptcy he fails to inform the trustee as soon as practicable: or

(ii) he attempts to account for any part of his property by fictitious losses or expenses; or

(iii) at any meeting of his creditors in the twelve months before petition or at any time in the initial period he did anything which would have been an offence under (ii) if the bankruptcy order has been made before he did it; or

(iv) he is, or at any time has been, guilty of any false representation or other fraud for the purpose of obtaining the consent of his creditors, or any of them, to an agreement with reference to his affairs or to his bankruptcy. (s 356)

(e) Non-disclosure

The bankrupt is guilty of an offence if he does not, to the best of his knowledge and belief, disclose all the property comprised in his estate to the official receiver or the trustee. He is likewise guilty if he does not inform the official receiver or the trustee of any disposal of any property which, but for the disposal, would be so comprised, giving full details of the disposal. This does not, however, apply to any disposal in the ordinary course of business carried on by the bankrupt, or to any payment of the ordinary expenses of the bankrupt or his family. (s 353)

(f) Concealment

The test here is non-cooperation, so that the bankrupt is guilty of an offence if, for example, he does not deliver up possession, or removes (including during the initial period) property in his possession or under his control to a value of £500 or more, as set out in s 354. He is likewise guilty of an offence if he conceals or falsifies books and papers as set out in s 355.

(g) Fraudulent disposal of property

The bankrupt is guilty of an offence if he makes or causes to be made, or has in the period of five years ending with the commencement of the bankruptcy made or caused to be made, any gift or transfer of, or charge on, his property. This includes causing, or conniving at, the levying of any execution against that property (s 357).

(h) Absconding

It is an offence to leave, attempt, or make preparations to leave the country with property he is required to deliver up to a value of £500 or more. It is also an offence, in the six months before petition or in the initial period, to do anything which would have been an offence if the bankruptcy order had been made immediately before the thing is done (s 358).

(i) Accounts

Where the bankrupt has been engaged in any business for any of the period of two years before petition, he is guilty of an offence if he failed to keep proper accounting records throughout the period - or has not preserved all the accounting records which he has kept.

However, no offence is committed if the unsecured liabilities at the commencement of the bankruptcy were below £20,000, or if the bankrupt proves that in the circumstances in which he carried on business the omission was honest and excusable (s 361).

Nevertheless, when a business is transferred as a going concern, the VAT records are also required to be preserved by the transferee, unless HM Customs & Excise otherwise directs at the request of the transferor under s 331(1) (b) of the Value Added Tax Act 1983. Failure under that Act to observe this requirement may lead to a penalty of £500 being imposed on the transferee for failure to preserve such records.

(j) Gambling

It is an offence to materially contribute to or increase the extent of insolvency by gambling, either in the initial period, or during the two years before petition, as well as by rash and hazardous speculations, but subject to consideration of the bankrupt's financial position at that time (s 362).

Chapter 19

Discharge and annulment

1. Introduction

A bankrupt is discharged either automatically or by order of the court.

The bankruptcy of an individual against whom a bankruptcy order has been made, commences with the day on which the order is made and continues until the individual is discharged or the bankruptcy is annulled. Discharge normally happens automatically, as of right, in two years where a certificate of summary administration was issued, or in three years under the provisions contained in s 279 of the Act.

If the bankruptcy is earlier annulled because of formal approval of a voluntary arrangement, where the court decides that the order should never have been made, or where the debts and expenses of the bankruptcy have been paid in full, then the effect of annulment is the same as discharge. Where payment is made in full it is extremely difficult for the court to refuse an annulment.

Unless it is a second bankruptcy the court cannot refuse to discharge the bankrupt and cannot impose conditions as to his discharge.

Personal application by the bankrupt for discharge now only arises in cases where discharge has previously been suspended or where it is a second or subsequent bankruptcy, provided that five years have elapsed from the commencement of the bankruptcy.

The court may annul a bankruptcy order whether or not the bankrupt has been discharged from the bankruptcy.

2. The effect of discharge

(a) Release from debts

Basically discharge releases the bankrupt from all provable bankruptcy debts other than those specified in s 281 (see *(b)* below), but it has no effect on the functions or operation of the trustee of his estate. Neither does it affect the right of any secured creditor to enforce his security for the payment of a debt from which the bankrupt is released, for secured debts cannot found a bankruptcy petition. It is therefore essential to note the debts and liabilities which survive the order of discharge.

"The overriding intention of the legislature in all Bankruptcy Acts is that the debtor on giving up the whole of his property shall be a free man again, able to earn his livelihood, and having the ordinary inducements to industry." (*Re Gaskell* [1904] 2 KB 476).

In addition, it is important for the debtor to note that debts contracted with him by a person having notice of the bankruptcy (expressed in the old law as having "notice" of an available act of bankruptcy) are not provable. What may be deemed to be sufficient notice of the bankruptcy under the new Act depends on the circumstances. Nevertheless the discharge completely frees the debtor from such a debt since the debt is in itself provable even though the creditor is precluded from proving for it; see *Buckwell* v *Norman* [1898] 1 QB 622.

A promise to pay a debt after discharge which was provable in the bankruptcy is *nudum pactum* and no action will lie on it unless there is some new consideration: see *Re Andrews ex parte Barrow* (1881) 45 LT 97. Thus where there is fresh consideration the promise is binding, even though it was made before the discharge: see *Wild* v *Tucker* [1914] 3 KB 36.

Even after his discharge the bankrupt remains under such duties to the trustee for the purpose of carrying out his functions as he may reasonably require.

(b) Debts surviving discharge

Discharge does not, except to such extent and on such conditions as the court may direct, release the bankrupt from any bankruptcy debt which consists in a liability to pay damages for negligence, nuisance or breach of a statutory, contractual or other duty or to pay damages by virtue of Part I of the Consumer Protection Act 1987, being in all such cases damages in respect of personal injuries to any person, or which arises under any order made in family or domestic proceedings (s 218(5) of that Act).

As has already been noted, discharge does not affect the right of any secured creditor to enforce his security for the payment of a debt from which the bankrupt is released. Neither does it release the bankrupt from any fraud or fraudulent breach of trust to which he was a party. He remains liable for any fine imposed for an offence and in respect of any liability under a recognisance, except with the consent of the Treasury, in the case of a penalty imposed for an offence under an enactment relating to the public revenue or of a recognisance.

Discharge does not release the bankrupt from any obligation arising under a confiscation order made under s 1 of the Drug Trafficking Offences Act 1986 (Rule 6.223).

Discharge does not release any person other than the bankrupt (for example, a partner or co-trustee) from any liability from which the bankrupt is released by the discharge, or from any liability as surety for the bankrupt or as a person in the nature of such a surety (s 281 (7)).

A landlord or other person to whom rent is payable is not, at any time after the discharge, entitled to distrain upon any goods or effects comprised in the bankrupt's estate (s 347(5)).

(c) Effect on public examination

Discharge of the bankrupt proceeds whether or not a public examination has been carried out, but any application for a public examination of the bankrupt must be made by the official receiver before the discharge takes effect.

(d) Income payments order

No income payments order for recovery by the estate of the income of the bankrupt received after discharge may be made unless it has been provided for. See page 275.

3. Automatic discharge

Where a certificate for the summary administration of the bankrupt's estate (see page 44) has been issued and is not revoked before the bankrupt's discharge, then he is automatically discharged two years after the commencement of the bankruptcy. In any other case the period for automatic discharge is three years (s 279).

The periods run from the commencement of the bankruptcy, unless the official receiver reports to the court that the bankrupt has failed or is failing to comply with his obligations, in which case the court may order that the period shall cease to run for such period, or until the fulfilment of such conditions, as may be specified (see below).

The bankrupt may apply to the court for a certificate of discharge (Form 6.77) on the expiration of the time or otherwise, which the court must then issue. He is asked if he wishes the notice of discharge to be Gazetted, or advertised in any newspaper in which the bankruptcy was advertised, or both. If so he must pay the cost of the advertisement, and the Secretary of State is under no obligation to advertise until that sum has been paid.

4. Suspension of automatic discharge

(a) Section 279(3) application

Automatic discharge may be suspended where the court is satisfied, on an application by the official receiver under s 279(3), that an undischarged bankrupt has failed or is failing to comply with any of his obligations. "We see any attempt to bring before the court what might be described as the bankrupt's civil conduct, rather than his criminal conduct. as the erection of a barrier against the rehabilitation of bankrupts." (*Hansard: Standing Committee E* Col 370 18 June 1985).

Thus a bankrupt who fails to surrender to the proceedings could effectively be prevented from being discharged. Where his public examination has been adjourned generally, the official receiver may, there and then, make application. Time will start to run again only when the court is satisfied with the bankrupt's conduct.

Section 279 is without prejudice to any power of the court to annul a bankruptcy order.

(b) Report of the official receiver

Where the official receiver applies to the court for an order he must file a report setting out the reasons why it appears to him that such an order should be made. The court fixes a venue for the hearing of the application and gives notice of it to the official receiver, the trustee and the bankrupt. Copies of the report are sent by the official receiver to the trustee and the bankrupt so as to reach them at least 21 days before the date fixed for the hearing.

Not later than seven days before the date of the hearing, the bankrupt may file in court a notice specifying any statements which he intends to deny or dispute, sending copies of his notice, not less than four days before the date of the hearing, to the official receiver and trustee. If, on hearing the application, the court makes an order suspending the bankrupt's discharge, copies of the order (Form 6.72) are sent by the court to the official receiver, trustee and bankrupt. (Rule 6.215)

(c) Application by bankrupt to lift suspension

The bankrupt may apply for the discharge of the order of suspension. The court fixes a venue for the hearing of the application and the bankrupt must, not less than 28 days before the date fixed for the hearing, notify the official receiver and the trustee of that venue; the notice must be accompanied by a copy of the application.

Both the official receiver and the trustee may appear and be heard in open court at the hearing and, regardless of whether or not he appears, the official receiver may file in court a report of any matters which he considers should be brought to the court's attention. If the court's order suspending automatic discharge was on the basis that conditions were to be fulfilled, it may request a report from the official receiver as to whether or not the conditions have been fulfilled.

Copies of any report of the official receiver must be sent by him to both the bankrupt and the trustee not later than fourteen days before the hearing. Not later than seven days before the date fixed for the hearing, the bankrupt may file in court a notice specifying any statements in the official receiver's report which he intends to deny or dispute. Copies of any such notice must be sent to the official receiver and the trustee at least four days before the hearing. If the court discharges the suspension order (Form 6.73), it issues a certificate to that effect (Form 6.74) to the bankrupt. (Rule 6.216)

5. Discharge by order of the court

The first-time bankrupt has no need to apply to the court for his discharge; either the bankruptcy will be annulled or the automatic discharge procedure will, normally, be available. An order of the court is therefore only required for a discharge in the following circumstances:

- (a) in the case of an individual who has been an undischarged bankrupt at any time in the last fifteen years (s 279(1)(a));
- (b) where the bankrupt has failed or is failing to comply with any of his obligations as a bankrupt (s 279(3), above);
- (iii) in the case of an individual who had a criminal bankruptcy order made against him.

(a) A section 279(1)(a) case

An application for an order discharging an individual in a case involving a second or subsequent bankruptcy may be made by the bankrupt at any time after five years from the commencement of the earlier bankruptcy. Any time spent as a bankrupt by virtue of an order that was subsequently annulled is disregarded.

(b) Application for discharge

The bankrupt must give the official receiver notice of his application for discharge and deposit with him such sum as the official receiver may require to cover his costs of the application. The court fixes a venue for hearing the application and gives at least 42 days notice thereof to the official receiver and the bankrupt. The official receiver then gives notice, not later than fourteen days before the hearing date, to the trustee and to every creditor who, to the official receiver's knowledge, has a claim outstanding against the estate which has not been satisfied (Rule 6.217). The bankrupt may, with the leave of the court, withdraw such an application.

(c) Report of the official receiver

The court first considers a report by the official receiver before determining what order (if any) to make. Rule 6.218 provides that the official receiver must, at least twelve days before the hearing date, file in court a report indicating:

- (i) any failure by the bankrupt to comply with his obligations under Parts VIII to XI of the Act;
- (ii) the circumstances surrounding the present bankruptcy, and any previous bankruptcy;
- (iii) the extent to which, in the current and any previous bankruptcy, his liabilities have exceeded his assets; and
- (iv) particulars of any distribution which has been or is expected to be made to

creditors in the present bankruptcy, or, if it is the case, that there has been and is to be no distribution;

(v) any other matter(s) which the official receiver considers should be before the court.

Such a report is *prima facie* evidence of the facts stated in it. The official receiver sends a copy of the report to the bankrupt and the trustee, so as to reach them at least fourteen days before the date of the hearing. Not later than seven days before that date, the bankrupt may file a notice identifying any statements in the report which he intends to deny or dispute (Form 6.75); if he does so he must send a copy to the official receiver and trustee at least four days before the hearing date. The official receiver, the trustee and any creditor may appear at the hearing and may make representations and put to the bankrupt such questions as the court may allow.

(d) Order of the court

On an application the court may, under s 280(2):

(i) refuse the discharge:

(ii) make an order discharging the bankrupt absolutely: or

(iii) make an order discharging him subject to conditions. These conditions apply in respect of any income which may subsequently become due to him, or with respect to property devolving upon him, or acquired by him, after his discharge, as may be specified in the order.

An order under (ii) or (iii) may have immediate effect or be suspended until the fulfilment of such conditions, including a condition requiring the court to be satisfied as to any matter as may be specified in the order. The order is not issued or Gazetted until the time allowed for appealing has expired or, if an appeal is entered, until the appeal has been determined.

The order of discharge is dated with the date on which it was made, but does not take effect until it has been drawn up by the court. It is then effective retrospectively to the date on which it was made. Copies of the order are sent by the court to the bankrupt, the trustee and the official receiver. (Rule 6.219 and Form 6.76)

Section 280 repeats those powers given to the courts under the 1914 Act, but with one exception, to enable them to discharge those difficult cases that fall within s 280. Other than an outright refusal or absolute discharge, the court has a discretion in every case to suspend the discharge for a period without condition, or to make an order for discharge subject to the bankrupt agreeing to an income payments order (see above and page 275).

However, it appears that the discretion for the court to both suspend *and* to attach conditions to a bankrupt's discharge which was to be found under s 26(8) of the Act of 1914 has been lost; the drafting of s 280(3) suggests that the court does not have the option of granting a suspension concurrently with conditions attached. The court is therefore left with a choice, to

(i) refuse the discharge; or

(ii) give an absolute discharge; or
(iii) suspend discharge; or
(iv) require the bankrupt to consent to conditions.

(e) Appeals

An appeal lies at the instance of the Secretary of State from any order of the court made on an application for a bankrupt's discharge. See page 292.

6. Transitional arrangements for discharge

(a) General position under the 1914 and 1976 Act

Where a person was adjudged bankrupt before the appointed day for the coming into force of the 1986 Act (29 December 1986), or is adjudged bankrupt on or after that day on a petition presented *before* that day, and he was not an undischarged bankrupt at any time in the period of fifteen years ending with the adjudication, that person is deemed (if not previously discharged) to be discharged from his bankruptcy for the purposes of the 1914 Act at the end of the discharge period. The "discharge period" is three years in the case of a person adjudged bankrupt *before* 29 December 1986, and three years in the case of a person who is adjudged bankrupt *on or after that day* on a petition presented before that day, in both cases beginning with the date of adjudication.

(b) Effect on second and subsequent bankruptcies within the previous fifteen years where the bankrupt has not applied for discharge

Where the bankrupt has *not* previously applied for discharge under s 26 of the Act of 1914, he may apply at any time, or wait for a review of the case under s 8 of the Act of 1976. Application "under s 8 of the Act of 1976" means that within twelve months of the fifth anniversary of the date of adjudication, ie the sixth year, the official receiver makes application to the court for a review of the bankrupt's conduct and affairs, including a report on his conduct during the proceedings under his bankruptcy. Where his discharge has already been reviewed under the latter procedure on the application of the official receiver, he may apply for a further review under s 108 of the Act of 1914.

(c) Effect on second and subsequent bankruptcies within the previous fifteen years where the bankrupt has applied for discharge under s 26 of the Act of 1914

Where the discharge is due to take place on or *before* 29 December 1989, the bankrupt will be discharged in accordance with the terms of the order of the court. Where the discharge is due to take place *after* 29 December 1989 then the conditional discharge will be effective either on that day or in the sixth year of bankruptcy, whichever is the later.

Where application is refused, or discharge has already been turned down on review by application of the official receiver, the bankrupt may apply for a further review under s 108. Applications under this section do not qualify for automatic discharge under s 7 of the Act of 1976 except that the court may, on the application of the official receiver or the trustee, rescind the order at any time before the fifth anniversary of the date of adjudication. All bankruptcy courts may, of course, review, rescind or vary any order made.

(d) Automatic discharge for first time bankruptcies under s 7 of the Act of 1976

For those with no previous bankruptcy at any time in the fifteen years before the present proceedings, if the receiving order was made before 29 December 1984, automatic discharge will be effective under s 7 of the Act of 1976 from the fifth anniversary of the bankruptcy. If the receiving order was made on or after 29 December 1984, automatic discharge will take effect automatically on 29 December 1989 under the 1976 Act, or three years from the date of bankruptcy under the 1986 Act, whichever is the later.

It was not the intention of Parliament that the court should make an order s 7(1) as a mere formality. If the official receiver was in any real doubt about the matter the court should *not* grant an automatic discharge. It should leave it to the bankrupt to make his own application in due course for discharge under s 26(1) of the 1914 Act; *or* if he did not do so, for the official receiver to apply in the sixth year of the adjudication as required by s 8(2) of the 1976 Act; see *Re Reed (a Debtor)* [1979] 2 All ER 22.

(e) Order of the court for first time bankruptcies (non-automatic cases)

Where the bankrupt has made application under s 26 of the Act of 1914, the court may refuse to make an order of discharge, in which case discharge will take effect from 29 December 1989 or three years after the date of the bankruptcy (under the new Act), whichever is the later. If the court had made an order of discharge, the discharge would be effective on the date stated in the order provided that the date was on or *before* 29 December 1989; if the order is to take effect after that date then the discharge will be three years after bankruptcy, provided that the order was not a suspension order.

Where the bankrupt has not made application to the court for a review of his conduct and affairs within twelve months of the fifth anniversary of the date of adjudication, the official receiver applies to the court under s 8 of the Act of 1976 with a report on the bankrupt's conduct during the proceedings under his bankruptcy. The effect of the application is the same as on the bankrupt's application subject to suspension or conditions.

If at any time after two years from the date of the order, the bankrupt satisfies the court that there is no reasonable probability of his being in a position to comply with any conditions in the order, for example as to payment of capital or income, it may modify the order.

(f) Suspension of the discharge

If the court is satisfied, on the application of the official receiver, that the bankrupt has failed or is failing to comply with any of his obligations under the Act of 1914, any rules made under that Act or any transitional provisions in connection with the coming into force of the new rules, the court may order that the discharge period shall cease to run for such period, or until the fulfilment of such conditions, as may be specified in the order, including a condition requiring the court to be satisfied as to any matter. The discharge is then proceeded with under the suspension procedures for the new Act (above).

7. Annulment by order of the court

The court may under s 282, annul a bankruptcy order, whether or not the bankrupt has been discharged from it, because it ought not to have been made, or the debts have been paid up or secured to the satisfaction of the court. By s 262, it may give effect to a voluntary arrangement.

(a) Application to the court under s 282(1)(a)

The court may annul a bankruptcy order if at any time it appears to the court that:

(i) on any grounds existing at the time the order was made, the order ought not to have been made (s 282(1)(a)); or

(ii) to the extent required by the rules (see below), the bankruptcy debts and the expenses of the bankruptcy have all, since the making of the order, been either paid or secured for to the satisfaction of the court (s 282(1)(b)).

An application to the court must specify under which of the above it is made, and in either case be supported by affidavit stating the grounds on which it is made, including all the facts by reference to which, in the case of subsection (ii), the court is required to be satisfied before annulling the order. The applicant must, not less than 28 days before the hearing, give to the official receiver, the trustee and the applicant notice of the venue fixed. (Rule 6.206)

The court may, before the hearing takes place, make an interim order staying any proceedings which it thinks ought, in the circumstances of the case, to be stayed. Application for such an order may be made *ex parte*. (Rule 6.208)

"Ought not to have been made" is relevant particularly where the presentation of the petition was an abuse of the legal process. An adjudication obtained on a debtor's petition to evade his long term liabilities, where he is in fact able to meet his obligations as they fall due, may be annulled on the application of the trustee; see *Re Betts, ex parte Official Receiver* (1901) 84 LT 427; and *Re A Debtor* [1967] 1 All ER 668. It will not, however, be annulled where the bankrupt has clearly sought to defeat an attachment for non payment of instalments under a judgment summons; see *Re Painter ex parte Painter* [1895] 1 QB 85, or where he honestly believed that he was unable to pay his debts; see *Re Dunn* [1949] 1 Ch 640.

Subsection (1)(b), referring to "paid or secured" is a departure from the previous requirement that debts be paid "in full". The test now appears to be satisfied by not necessarily paying debts in full or in cash (contrary to, for example *Re Keet ex parte Offical Receiver* [1905] 2 KB 666), provided that the settlement is to the satisfaction of the court, normally on hearing from the official receiver for the creditors. Nevertheless, in a Commonwealth case involving an absent bankrupt subject to offences for fraud, his subsequent application for annulment based on payment in full after seven years, was not accepted by the court on the grounds that it had no information about how he had come by the funds to pay off his creditors; see *Re Gray* (1960) 19 ABC 29. On the other hand, if the bankrupt can use the security of property or other assets owned by him, friends or family, for example by means of a deed of assignment in favour of the creditors (see page 326) or by raising cash against the security, this would now appear to be sufficient to satisfy the court, and provide a further real opportunity for an alternative to longer term bankruptcy.

(b) Debts and expenses paid or secured (s 282(l)(b))

There are further preconditions for annulment under s 282(1)(b). Obviously, all bankruptcy debts which have been proved must have been paid in full. But if a debt is disputed, or a creditor who has proved can no longer be traced, the bankrupt must give security, ie pay money into court or provide a bond with approved securities, as the court considers adequate. In the case of an untraced creditor an advertisement may be required; in that event the security is released on application after twelve months. (Rule 6.211).

Where a discharged bankrupt does succeed in paying his bankruptcy debts, payment is usually made out of taxed income. There is an argument that some tax concession, especially in respect of payments in full of debts which did not rank for full dividend, would encourage more ex-bankrupts to do what some term "the honourable thing" and seek an eventual annulment to the benefit of the community as a whole. However, no such allowance has been introduced.

(c) Report by trustee

Not less than 21 days before the date fixed for hearing the application for annulment, the trustee, or, if no trustee has been appointed, the official receiver, must file in court a report giving:

- (i) the circumstances leading to the bankruptcy;
- (ii) a summary of the extent of the bankrupt's assets and liabilities at the date of the bankruptcy order and at the date of the present application;
- (iii) details of any creditors known to him to have claims but who have not proved;
- (iv) particulars of the extent, if any, to which and the manner in which, the debts and expenses of the bankruptcy have been paid or secured. If debts and expenses are unpaid but secured, the report must state whether and to what extent the security is considered satisfactory;
- (iv) such other matters as he considers are necessary for the information of the court.

A copy of the report is sent to the applicant at least fourteen days before the hearing date and he may file further affidavits in answer to any statements made in the report. Copies of such affidavits must be sent by the applicant to the official receiver and trustee. If the trustee is someone other than the official receiver, he must send a copy of his report to the official receiver at least 21 days before the hearing. The official receiver may then file an additional report, a copy of which is sent to the applicant at least seven days before the hearing (Rule 6.207)

Where it has been reported to the court that there are known creditors of the bankrupt who have not proved, the court may:

- (i) direct the trustee to send notice of the application to those creditors whom the court thinks ought to be informed of it so that they may prove their debts within 21 days; and
- (ii) direct the trustee to advertise the fact that the application has been made, so that creditors who have not proved may do so within a specified time;
- (iii) adjourn the application meanwhile for a minimum period of 35 days.

(Rule 6.209)

(d) Notice to creditors

Where the official receiver has notified creditors of the debtor's bankruptcy, and the bankruptcy order is later annulled, he must forthwith notify the creditors of the annulment. The expenses of so doing are a charge in favour of the official receiver on the property of the former bankrupt, whether or not in his hands. Where any property is in the hands of a trustee or person other than the former bankrupt himself, the official receiver's charge is valid subject only to any costs that may be incurred by that person in realising the property for the purpose of satisfying the charge. (Rule 6.212)

The duty of the official receiver to send reports to creditors ceases on annulment.

(e) The order

The trustee must attend the hearing of the application. The official receiver, if he is not the trustee, may attend but is not obliged to do so unless he has filed a report in the matter. If the court makes an order on the application, it must send copies to the applicant, the official receiver and the trustee. (Rule 6.210; Form 6.71)

The court must give notice of the making of the order to the Secretary of State. Where an order relates to a petition as a pending action, the court must include provision permitting vacation of its registration and of the bankruptcy order in the register of writs and orders affecting land.

The former bankrupt may require the Secretary of State to give notice of the making of the order in the London Gazette or in any newspaper in which the bankruptcy order was advertised, or both. The Secretary of State notifies him forthwith as to the cost of the advertisement, and is under no obligation to advertise until that sum has been paid.

Where the former bankrupt has died (see Chapter 21) or is a person incapable of managing his affairs (see page 275), then his personal representative or a person appointed by the court represents or acts for him as the case may be.

(f) Trustee's final account

Where a bankruptcy order is annulled under s 282, the trustee is not automatically released from any duty or obligation under the Act or Rules to account for all his dealings in the estate. He must submit his final account to the Secretary of State as soon as practicable after the order of annulment and must also file a copy of the final account in court. The account must include a summary of the trustee's receipts and payments and a statement to the effect that he has reconciled his account with that of the Secretary of State. The trustee is released from such time as the court may determine having regard to whether or not the final account has been submitted and whether or not any security under Rule 6.211(3) has been, or will be, released. (Rule 6.214)

8. Part VIII annulment

The court may annul the bankruptcy order by which the debtor was adjudged bankrupt where the creditors accept a proposed voluntary arrangement under s 261(1)(a), effectively in place of the bankruptcy proceedings. Such an annulment takes effect at the end of 28 days beginning with the day on which the report of the creditors' meeting was made to the court, unless an appeal is pending. See page 12.

9. Annulment of an insolvency administration order

The court may annul an insolvency administration order under s 282(1) for a deceased debtor, if at any time it appears to the court that, on grounds existing at the time the order was made, the order ought not to have been made, or that the insolvency debts and expenses have all, since the making of the order, either been paid or secured to the satisfaction of the court.

10. Effect of annulment

Where the court annuls a bankruptcy order any sale or other disposition of property, payment made or other thing duly done by or under the authority of the official receiver, trustee or the court is valid, but if any of the estate is vested in the trustee, it vests in a court appointee or in default reverts to the bankrupt or the deceased debtor's estate as the case may be, on such terms, if any, as the court may direct. See *Re a Debtor (No 37 of 1976)* [1980] Ch 565.

The trustee at the time of the annulment has his release with effect from such time as the court may determine.

In determining whether a person was an undischarged bankrupt at any time, s 282(5) provides that any time when he was a bankrupt by virtue of an order that was subsequently annulled is to be disregarded.

Where a proof has been rejected by the trustee and his decision has not been appealed from, such rejection remains valid even after annulment, and a future claim for the amount sought to be proved would be barred; see *Brandon* v *McHenry* [1891] 1 QB 538. Otherwise the person whose bankruptcy has been annulled is returned to the position he was in prior to the making of the bankruptcy order. He is once again liable for all debts not otherwise paid off or discharged in the meanwhile, which would not have been the position had he been discharged from the bankruptcy; see *Re More* v *More* [1962] Ch 424

The deposit paid on presentation of the petition is repaid to the extent that it is not required for payment to an insolvency practitioner appointed under s 273 (to submit a report under s 274 with a view to a voluntary arrangement).

11. Appeals

An appeal lies at the instance of the Secretary of State from any order of the court made on an application for the rescission or annulment of a bankruptcy order or an order of discharge. The appeal must be brought within 28 days beginning with the day on which the report of the creditors' meeting was made to the court. In the case of an order made by a county court or by a registrar of the High Court, appeal lies to a single judge of the High Court and an appeal from a decision of that judge on such an appeal lies, with the leave of that judge or of the Court of Appeal, to the Court of Appeal.

Chapter 20

Partnerships and unregistered companies

1. Introduction

A partnership is that relationship which subsists between persons carrying on business in common with a view to profit. The rights of the partners between themselves are governed by the partnership agreement if there is one, the Partnership Act 1890 or the Companies Act.

For larger firms, the Companies Act 1985 perpetuates the earlier pre-Partnership Act meaning of a partnership as an "unregistered company" provided that it is neither a foreign partnership, association or company, nor registered under that Act as a limited company; and it is this procedure that is now adopted by the first group of Parts of the Insolvency Act (not otherwise discussed in this volume) for the compulsory winding-up of *all* insolvent "partnerships" with not fewer than eight members as an unregistered company under Parts IV and V. This applies whether or not any of the partners is solvent or insolvent provided that the partnership is at least three years old.

However, for the smaller and/or younger firm with two to eight partners (and none corporate) the bankruptcy provisions apply. A petition may be presented jointly by the partners under s 264 (ie as for the debtor's petition but adapted by the Insolvent Partnerships Order 1986) *without* the partnership being wound up as an unregistered company so as effectively to cease trading.

The law of bankruptcy applies only to insolvent members of the partnership and no longer to the firm (as under the old law). The bankruptcy court may make bankruptcy orders against any individual partner under Part IX of the Insolvency Act or an interim order under Part VIII, whether or not a winding-up order is made against the partnership as an unregistered company.

Where a partner, or more than one of them, is itself a firm or corporate entity under the Companies Act then the court may either order that the partnership be wound up (and it would then be up to the liquidator to pursue separate remedies against the individual partners of the particular corporation) or for an administration order to be made in respect of the corporate partner(s).

This chapter covers all other than the corporate cases of the winding-up of partnerships as unregistered companies. References to "the Order" in this chapter are to the Insolvent Partnerships Order 1986 which modifies the Act (s 420). Forms with single digit references are prescribed by the Insolvent Partnerships Order. Other forms mentioned are prescribed by the Insolvency Rules 1986.

An "insolvency petition" in the case of a petition presented against a corporate member, is a petition for its winding-up by the court, and in the case of an individual member, is a petition to the court for a bankruptcy order to be made against the individual. An "insolvency order" means, in the case of an insolvent partnership or a corporate member, a winding-up order, and in the case of an individual member, a bankruptcy order.

2. Termination

(a) How terminated in insolvency

The manner in which a partnership may be terminated following insolvency are as follows:

(i) by petition in bankruptcy against individual partners under Part IX of the Act (see Chapters 3 or 5) or for winding-up against corporate partners (under the first group of Parts of the Act);

(ii) by petitioning for an insolvency order against the partnership under the corporate winding-up provisions of Part IV in relation to the partnership as an unregistered company by Part V of the Act as amended by the Order.

In addition there are transitional provisions to allow for bankruptcy proceedings pending on 29 December 1986.

(b) Conditions to be satisfied by a debtor

A bankruptcy petition may not be presented to the court by the creditor or the debtor unless the debtor is domiciled in England and Wales on the day the petition is presented, or at any time in the previous three years has been ordinarily resident, had a place of residence or has carried on business in England and Wales (s 265). "Business" includes the carrying on of business by a firm or partnership of which the individual is a member, and the carrying on of business by an agent or manager for the individual or for such a firm or partnership.

(c) Checklist: petition and winding-up

The following summarises the "Case" numbers allocated in the next section of this chapter (page 298 *et seq*) to different sets of circumstances and the forms to be used in the various proceedings appropriate to those circumstances:

(i) in respect of the individual member of the partnership -

- *bankruptcy of individual partners (Case A)* -
  - by the debtor: bankruptcy petition Form 6.27 and statement of affairs Form 6.28;

- by creditor: bankruptcy petition Form 6.7, 6.8 or 6.9 and statutory demand Form 6.1 or 6.2;
- *winding-up of individual corporate partners (Case B)* - company petition Form 4.2; advertisement Form 4.6 and affidavit Form 4.3;

(ii) in respect of the insolvent partnership -

- *individual partners presenting their joint bankruptcy petition against all members of the partnership (Case C)* - petition Form 8 and affidavit Form 6.13;
- *winding-up of partnership not involving insolvency of partners (Case D)* - petition Form 1 and demand Form 2;

(iii) in respect of the insolvent partnership and its partners:

- *bankruptcy of individual member with petition against partnership (Case E)* -
  - as to debtor's petition, Form 7
  - as to creditor's petition, Form 7, demand Form 3 and bankruptcy demand Form 6.1 or 6.2
- *winding-up of partnership involving insolvency of two or more partners (Case F)* - petition Form 4 (for the firm) or petition as Case A and/or Case G for the individual and/or corporate partner respectively, demand Form 3 and advertisement Form 5;
- *winding-up of individual corporate partners (Case G)* - petition Form 6, demand Form 3 and advertisement Form 5;

(iv) Continuation of the business following application for a voluntary arrangement (see page 308):

- *individual interim order:* Bankruptcy petition Form 6.27 or affidavit under Rule 5.5
- *company administration order* - company petition for an administration order Form 2.1.

(d) Forms of petition

Under the Insolvent Partnerships Order, the following forms (see Appendix 6) are set down for use in petitioning for the an insolvency order:

Form 1: Liquidator's or trustee's petition to wind up partnership
Form 4: Petition to wind up partnership presented in conjunction with petitions against members
Form 6: Petition to wind up corporate member presented in conjunction with petition againt partnership
Form 7: Bankruptcy petition against individual member presented in conjunction with petition against partnership
Form 8: Joint bankruptcy petition against individual members.

Use of these forms is appropriate only where an insolvent partnership is being wound up and not in the winding-up of corporate partners, or the making of a bankruptcy order against individual partners in other cases, the latter taking place under the bankruptcy provisions of Part IX of the Act, as described in Chapter 6.

(e) The written demand

The written demand (Form 2 (by partner), Form 3 (by creditor) - see Appendix 6) must state the amount of the debt and the consideration for it , or, if there is no consideration, the way in which it arises. If the amount claimed includes any charge by way of interest not previously notified to the debtor, or any other charge accruing from time to time, the amount or rate of charge must be separately identified and the ground on which it is claimed must be stated. In any event the amount claimed must be limited to that which has accrued due at the date of the demand. (Rule 4.5)

The written demand must also include an explanation of:

(i) the purpose of the demand and the fact that, if it is not complied with, proceedings may be instituted for winding-up;

(ii) the time within which it must be complied with to avoid that consequence; and

(iii) the methods of compliance open.

The demand must state how the company can communicate with one or more named individuals with a view to securing or compounding for the debt. The address and telephone number (if any) of any named individual must also be given. (Rule 4.6)

(f) The advertisement

In Cases F and G below the petition is advertised once in the London Gazette unless the court otherwise directs (Form 5).

If the petitioner is the company itself, the advertisement must appear not less than seven business days before the day appointed for the hearing; otherwise it must appear not less than seven business days after service of the petition on the company and not less than seven business days before the day fixed for the hearing. However, if it appears to the court not reasonably practicable to comply with these time limits, it may direct that the petition be advertised in a specified London morning newspaper or other newspaper instead of the Gazette. The advertisement must state:

(i) the address of the company's principal place of business;

(ii) the name and address of the petitioner;

(iii) where the petitioner is not the company itself, the address of its principal place of business;

(iv) the date on which the petition was presented;

(v) the venue fixed for the hearing of the petition;

(vi) the name and address of the petitioner's solicitor (if any); and

(vii) that any person intending to appear at the hearing, whether in support of or in opposition to the petition, must give notice of his intention so to do.

The form of advertisment is prescribed by the Order (Form 5). If the advertising rules are not complied with, the court may dismiss the petition. (Rule 4.11)

(g) Deposits

The appropriate deposit set out in the Fees Order is as follows: In relation to a winding-up petition it is £200; a bankruptcy petition presented by an individual, £100; and by a creditor or supervisor of a voluntary arrangement, £200.

Where a winding-up or bankruptcy petition is dismissed or withdrawn the deposit is repaid in full unless a winding-up or bankruptcy order has been made, or a fee has become payable to an insolvency practitioner under s 273(2) following a debtor's petition to prepare a report.

It the assets of the company being wound up, or the bankrupt's estate, are sufficient to pay the whole or part of the relevant administration fee, then the deposit is repaid to the extent that it is not required for payment of that fee.

(h) Joint debtor's petition

A joint debtor's petition may be presented to the court by individual members only on the grounds that the partnership is unable to pay its debts. If petitions are at the same time presented for insolvency orders against the partnership and every other member, each member must be willing for an insolvency order to be made against him. The petition should contain a statement to this effect.

(i) Disputes

If an individual partner claims that he is solvent and should therefore not be made bankrupt, it will be up to him to pay off the debt. There is no question of an order not being made against him if orders are made against all the others involved. If a petitioner is paid off, the substitution of another petitioner will only be allowed if he takes over the whole petition and not, for example, against one only of the partners. To ensure that a creditor of an individual partner is not deprived of an effective remedy it is possible for a non-partnership creditor to present a petition against a partner at the same time as a partnership petition is pending.

(j) Right of the firm to prove against a partner

For the purpose of proving a debt a partnership is treated as an entity distinct from its members. The general rule is that a partnership may not prove upon the insolvent estates of its members. The exceptions are as follows:

(i) where the debt has been incurred by fraud;

(ii) where goods were supplied to the partner in a separate trade. For example, where the bankrupt has taken property from the partnership fund and applied it to his own use without the knowledge of the other partners;

(iii) when the conduct of the parties signifies their acquiescence.

As for the order of priority in the distribution, including surplus funds, see page 246.

3. Bankruptcy petitions and winding-up: the cases

Case A: Bankruptcy of individual partners

Proceedings are begun by the debtor with bankruptcy petition Form 6.27 and statement of affairs Form 6.28; by a creditor on petition Form 6.7, 6.8 or 6.9 and statutory demand Form 6.1 or 6.2. The procedure for the petition in bankruptcy is as set out in Chapters 3 (debtor's) and 5 (creditor's), and is unaffected by the Order.

Case B: Winding-up of individual corporate partners

The appropriate forms are petition Form 4.2, advertisement Form 4.6 and affidavit Form 4.3. The order does not affect the winding-up of corporate partners under Part IV of the Act. The matter of the winding-up of corporate partnerships under the Companies Act is not a matter properly for this book and will therefore only be referred to in context.

Case C: Individual partners presenting their joint bankruptcy petition against all members of the partnership

The requisite forms are petition Form 8, and affidavit Form 6.13.

Where all the members of an insolvent partnership are individual members and none of them is a limited partner, a petition for bankruptcy orders to be made against all of them may be presented to the court (Form 8) by the individual members jointly under s 264 of the Act. The partnership itself need not be wound up as an unregistered company. However, this procedure is only available on the grounds that the partnership is unable to pay its debts.

If petitions are at the same time presented for insolvency orders against the partnership and every other member, each member must be willing for an insolvency order to be made against him. The petition should contain a statement to this effect.

The petition contains a request that the trustee shall wind up the partnership business and administer the partnership property. It is accompanied by an affidavit made by the partner who signs the petition showing that all the partners concur in the presentation of the petition, ie the petitioner names all known partners as well as the partnership so that it will be effective against partners served. It will not, as previously, be effective against all the partners if served only on the partnership. But if served on the partnership it will, of course, be effective against the partnership as an entity and the court will thereafter be able to make a winding-up order against the partnership.

At any time the official receiver may summon meetings of all the creditors of the partners. No liquidation or creditors' committee is appointed.

Case D: Winding-up of partnership not involving insolvency of partners

The forms are Petition Form 1 and demand Form 2. An insolvent partnership may be wound up under Part V of the Act as an unregistered company, only by the court, without involving the insolvency of its partners. The provisions of Part V that apply with modifications are specified in Sch 1 to the Order (art 7). Where the partnership is a company it may also be wound up by the court following a special resolution under s 124 of the Act.

The circumstances in which an unregistered company may be wound up are as follows:

(i) if the company is dissolved, or has ceased to carry on business, or is carrying on business only for the purpose of winding-up its affairs;
(ii) if the company is unable to pay its debts;
(iii) if the court is of opinion that it is just and equitable that the company should be wound up.

No unregistered company can be wound up voluntarily.

An unregistered company is unable to pay its debts in the following circumstances:

(i) if there is a creditor, by assignment or otherwise, to whom the company is indebted in a sum exceeding £750 then due; and the creditor has served on the company a written demand (Form 2) requiring the company to pay the sum due; and the company has for three weeks after service neglected to pay the sum or to secure or compound for it to the creditor's satisfaction;
(ii) if an action or other proceeding has been instituted against any member for any debt or demand due, or claimed to be due, from the company, or from him as a member and notice has been served; and the company has not within three weeks after service of the notice paid, secured or compounded for the debt or demand, or procured the action or proceeding to be stayed or sisted, or indemnified the defendant or defender to his reasonable satisfaction against the action or proceeding, and against all costs, damages and expenses to be incurred by him because of it;
(iii) if execution or other process issued on a judgment, decree or order obtained in any court in favour of a creditor against the company, or any member of it as such, or any person authorised to be sued as nominal defendant on behalf of the company, is returned unsatisfied;
(iv) if it is otherwise proved to the satisfaction of the court that the company is unable to pay its debts as they fall due;
(v) if it is proved to the satisfaction of the court that the value of the company's assets is less than the amount of its liabilities, taking into account its contingent and prospective liabilities.

A petition (Form l) may be presented:

(i) for winding-up an unregistered company, by the liquidator of a corporate partner, or the trustee of a bankrupt partner, on the grounds that:
   - the company is dissolved or has ceased to carry on business, or is carrying on business only for the purpose of winding-up its affairs;

- the company is unable to pay its debts;
- the court is of the opinion that it is just and equitable that the company should be wound up;

(ii) by the partnership or any member of it, if the partnership consists of not less than eight members.

The partner applies to the court for leave to present the petition after the written demand (Form 2) has been served in respect of a joint debt or debts exceeding £750 then due by the partnership but paid by the member personally. The court must be satisfied when granting leave to present the petition that he has obtained a judgment, decree or order of any court against the partnership for reimbursement to him of the amount of the joint debt or debts so paid, and all reasonable steps (other than insolvency proceedings) have been taken by the member to enforce that judgment, decree or order.

Under (i) above the court may appoint as liquidator or trustee the person who is the liquidator of the corporate partner (or former corporate partner) or the trustee of the bankrupt partner's (or former bankrupt partner's) estate who presented the petition. There is no duty on the official receiver to summon a creditors' meeting.

If the partnership assets are insufficient to satisfy the costs of the liquidator or trustee as petitioner the costs may be paid out of the assets of the corporate or individual member in the same order of priority as expenses properly chargeable or incurred by the liquidator or trustee in getting in any of the assets of the member.

Case E: Bankruptcy of individual member with petition against partnership

For a debtor's petition, Form 7 is needed; for a creditor's petition, Form 7, demand Form 3 and bankruptcy demand Form 6.1 or 6.2.

Article 8(2) of the Order provides for the bankruptcy of individual partners of an insolvent partnership in conjunction with the winding-up of the partnership as an unregistered company under Part V of the Act. The provisions of the Insolvency Act 1986 relating to bankruptcy apply, with the modifications specified in Part III of Sch 2 to the Order.

By s 264 (as amended) a petition in Form 7 for a bankruptcy order to be made against a partner of an insolvent partnership may be presented to the court by one of the individual's creditors, or jointly by more than one of them.

A petition against the partnership as such or against the partners in the name of the firm cannot be presented under the bankruptcy provisions of Part IX.

The petition against the individual partner must be presented at the same time and to the same court as the petition for winding-up the partnership. At any time after presentation of the petition, the petitioner may add other partners as parties to the proceedings in relation to the insolvent partnership, with the leave of the court.

The petition against the individual must also contain particulars of other petitions being presented in relation to the partnership, identifying the partnership and the members concerned.

The petitioner may, on three days notice to the court before the date appointed for the hearing of the petition, withdraw the petition if he also withdraws at the same time every other petition which he has presented against the partnership and any other insolvent partner. The court may substitute any creditor of the partnership as petitioner.

A debtor's petition (also in Form 7) may be presented to the court by a partner only on the grounds that the partnership is unable to pay its debts. If petitions are at the same time presented for bankruptcy orders against the partnership and every other member, then each member must be willing for a bankruptcy order to be made against him; the petition should contain a statement to this effect.

The petitioning creditor to whom the insolvent partnership owes a joint debt should serve on the individual member a "statutory demand" in Form 6.1 (liquidated sum payable immediately) or 6.2 (following a judgment), and on the partnership a "written demand" in Form 3 requiring the member and the partnership to pay the debt or to secure or compound for it to the reasonable satisfaction of the creditor. Three weeks should have elapsed since the relevant demand was served and not been complied with (or not set aside).

Case F: Winding-up of partnership involving insolvency of two or more partners

The forms are petition Form 4 (for the firm) or a petition as in Case A and/or Case G for individuals and/or corporate partners, demand Form 3 and advertisement Form 5.

Any insolvent partnership may be wound up as an unregistered company under Part V of the Act involving the insolvency of two or more partners. This is subject to all the provisions of the Act and the Companies Act 1985 about winding-up by the court with modifications in Sch 2 Part I of the Order (art 8(1)(b)).

By s 124 as amended, application to the court for the winding-up of an insolvent partnership is by petition (Form 4) presented by any creditor(s) to whom the partnership is indebted in respect of a liquidated sum payable immediately. It should be presented at the same time and to the same court as any insolvency petition against an insolvent member and advertised (Form 5). The petition must contain particulars of other petitions being presented in relation to the partnership against insolvent partners, identifying the members concerned. At any time after presentation, the petitioner may, with the leave of the court, add other partners as parties to the proceedings in relation to the insolvent partnership.

Any partner or person against whom a winding-up or bankruptcy petition has been presented is entitled to appear and to be heard on any petition for the winding-up of the partnership.

The court fixes a venue for the hearing of the petition in advance of that fixed for the hearing of any petition against an insolvent member.

The court only has jurisdiction if the partnership has carried on business at any time in the period of three years ending with the day on which the petition for winding it up was presented.

The petitioner may withdraw the petition if at the same time he withdraws every petition which he has presented against any insolvent member, and he gives notice to the court at least three days before the date appointed for the hearing of the petition of his intention.

Where notice is given the court may substitute as petitioner any creditor of the partnership who in its opinion would have a right to present the petition, and at the same time substitute him as petitioner in respect of every petition which the petitioner has presented against an insolvent member. If the court makes such a substitution the petition is not withdrawn.

Case G: winding-up of individual corporate partner

The forms are petition Form 6, demand Form 3 and advertisement Form 5. All the provisions of the Insolvency Act 1986 and the Companies Act 1985 about the winding-up of companies by the court apply to the winding-up of a corporate partner, with the modifications contained in Part II of Sch 2 to the Order. Likewise, where an insolvent partnership or other body is itself a member of an insolvent partnership the Act applies as though the former body were a corporate member of that partnership (art 8(2)).

For the purposes of a creditor's petition the partner "appears to be unable to pay a debt exceeding £750" if, but only if, the debt is payable immediately, a written demand (Form 3) has been served and the court has made a winding-up order against the principal partnership.

Where the petitioning creditor has obtained judgment, decree or order of any court against the partner or partnership, the written demand may be served at the principal place of business. Such service is not effective service unless the creditor was entitled to issue execution or other process against the property of the member or of the partnership.

A petition by a corporate member may be presented only on the grounds that the partnership is unable to pay its debts, and provided that petitions are at the same time presented for insolvency orders against the partnership and every other member. Each partner must be willing for an insolvency order to be made against him and the petition must contain a statement to this effect. The petition must also contain particulars of the other petitions being presented in relation to the partnership, identifying the partnership and members concerned.

At any time after presentation of the petition, the petitioner may, with the leave of the court obtained on application and on such terms as it thinks just, add other partners as parties to the proceedings in relation to the insolvent partnership.

An application to the court for the winding-up of a corporate partner is by petition (Form 6) presented by that member, or any creditor or creditors, to whom the partnership is indebted in respect of a liquidated sum payable immediately. The petition must be presented at the same time and to the same court as the petition for the winding-up of the principal insolvent partnership and advertised (Form 5).

Petitions cannot be presented under Part IX of the Act against the partnership or against the individual partners in the name of the firm. There are also special provisions about priority of expenses and debts (see page 305).

The petitioner may withdraw his petition if, at the same time, he withdraws every petition which he has presented against the partnership and any other insolvent member (unless the court is satisfied that it would be likely to prejudice or delay the other), and he gives notice to the court at least three days before the date appointed for the hearing of the petition.

Where notice is given, the court may substitute as petitioner any creditor of the individual corporate partner who in its opinion would have a right to present the petition and who has been substituted by the court in the winding-up of the principal partnership. At the same time the court may substitute him as petitioner in respect of every petition which has been presented against other corporate members, and if it makes such a substitution, the petition in question will not be withdrawn.

4. Appointment and release of the liquidator/trustee

(a) General meeting of creditors

A general meeting involving the creditors of any individual member summoned under s 136(4) of the Act (as amended in relation to insolvent partnerships) to choose a person to be liquidator in place of the official receiver, may establish a committee, the creditors' committee, composed of the same persons as the liquidation committee established under s 141 (as amended). However, it may not set up a committee where the official receiver is trustee, except in connection with an appointment of a person to be trustee instead of the official receiver. See page 218 for the establishment of the creditors' committee.

(b) Appointment of the liquidator/trustee

The same person or persons (in the case of a joint appointment), will normally be appointed to act as liquidator of the partnership estate and the estate of the corporate partner(s), and as trustee of the individual partner. One meeting of the creditors' committee will determine the appointment, and the meeting thereafter will be run on normal lines.

If one of the partners is already subject to formal insolvency proceedings then it is submitted that the Secretary of State should be asked to appoint the practitioner already dealing with the connected estate. However, in the unusual event that two or more partners were already subject to insolvency proceedings, then this procedure may produce problems if different trustees have already been appointed. Where there is an existing insolvency it may be possible for the meeting of the creditors to appoint an insolvency practitioner to act jointly with the one dealing with the existing case, although again this is more difficult if there is more than one practitioner in office.

(c) Removal and release of the liquidator/trustee

The liquidator (or provisional liquidator) of a corporate member may be removed from office only by an order of the court. This is to ensure that he cannot vacate office, either by removal or otherwise, unless he also vacates office in the connected estates.

5. Disqualification of partners

Where an insolvent partnership is wound up as an unregistered company under Part V the provisions of ss 6 - 10, 15, 19(c) and 20 of, and Sch 1 to the Company Directors Disqualification Act 1986 apply in relation to the partnership as if any member of the partnership were a director of a company, and the partnership were a company as defined by that Act. The duty of the court to disqualify a director of an insolvent company for unfitness is set out in ss 6 to 9 and Sch 1 to that Act. These provisions allow for disqualification from acting as a director of any other company for a minimum period of two and a maximum of fifteen years. The director would be personally liable under s 15 for the relevant debts of a company if he acts in contravention of such an order.

By s 10 the court may make a declaration that the director is liable to make a personal contribution to the company's assets where he has participated in "fraudulent" and "wrongful" trading under ss 213 and 214 of the Insolvency Act.

Any member or former member of the partnership, as well as any other person who has or has had control or management is deemed to be an officer and director of the company. Thus all those who may be connected with the company have responsibility under the Act of 1986.

6. Limited partnerships

A "limited partnership" under the Limited Partnership Act 1907 is one in which there may be one or more partners who are not under any liability in respect of the debts or day to day obligations of the firm beyond the amount of capital they contribute, except that there must be one or more partners responsible for all the liabilities. The limited partner is unaffected by the insolvency of the firm beyond his contribution.

Where there is a limited partner he will be able to avoid having an order made against him personally, provided that he is able to lodge in court a sufficient sum or security to cover the limit of his liability. This sum is then available to the partnership liquidator should the partnership be wound up. The court may also dismiss a petition against him if he satisfies the court that he is no longer under any liability in respect of the debts and obligations of the partnership.

By s 6 of the 1907 Act the bankruptcy of a limited partner does not dissolve the limited partnership, but if all the general partners are adjudged bankrupt then the assets vest in the trustee and the winding-up is conducted by the court in accordance with the provisions relating to the winding-up of unregistered companies.

7. Treatment of expenses in the distribution

The joint estate of an insolvent partnership must be applied first in payment of the joint expenses of the insolvency proceedings in winding-up the partnership.

The separate estate of each insolvent member is used first to pay the separate expenses of the insolvency proceedings relating to that member.

Where the joint estate of the partnership is insufficient for the payment in full of the joint expenses of the insolvency proceedings in winding-up the partnership incurred up to and including the date of appointment of the insolvency practitioner, the unpaid balance is apportioned equally between the separate estates of the insolvent members and forms part of the expenses to be paid out of those estates.

Where any separate estate of an insolvent member is insufficient for the payment in full of the expenses of the insolvency proceedings to be paid out of that estate, the unpaid balance forms part of the expenses to be paid out of the joint estate of the partnership.

If any estate is insufficient for the payment in full of the expenses to be paid out of that estate, the balance then remaining unpaid is apportioned equally between the other estates. If, after such an apportionment, one or more estates are insufficient for the payment in full of the expenses to be paid out of those estates, the total of the unpaid balances continues to be apportioned equally between the other estates until full provision is made or there is no estate available for the payment of the balance finally remaining unpaid, in which case it abates in equal proportions between the estates which are then insufficient.

Where the joint estate of the partnership is insufficient for the payment in full of the joint expenses of the insolvency proceedings in winding-up the partnership incurred *after* the date of appointment of the insolvency practitioner, the unpaid balance is apportioned between the separate estates of the insolvent members and forms part of the expenses to be paid out of those estates in such proportions as the liquidation committee sanctions, or the court, on application by the liquidator or any person interested, orders.

With the sanction of the liquidation committee established for the partnership and any corporate member, or with the leave of the court obtained on application, the responsible insolvency practitioner may either pay out of the joint estate of the partnership as part of the expenses to be paid out of that estate any expenses so incurred for any separate estate of an insolvent member, or pay out of any separate estate of an insolvent member any part of the expenses so incurred for the joint estate of the partnership which affects that separate estate.

8. Transitional provisions

Where a petition for a winding-up order or a bankruptcy petition was presented against a partnership or a member of a partnership under the law in force immediately before 29 December 1986, then that law continues to have effect. This also applies to a case in which bankruptcy proceedings under the Act of 1914 were pending against a partner and whether or not in the name of the partnership. Where the new law does not apply then the law in force immediately before 29 December 1986 continues to have effect.

"Pending" bankruptcy proceedings includes any case in which a bankruptcy notice against the partnership or a member of it was served under s 2 of the 1914 Act.

9. Sections of the Act included by the order

The provisions of Part V and IX of the Act are applied by the Order to the winding-up of insolvent partnerships and the bankruptcy of the individual partner(s) as follows:

(a) Application of the Act to individual members of the partnership

The following provisions of Part IX of the Act, together with the relevant subordinate legislation, apply to individual partners, subject to modifications set out in the Order:

- debtor's bankruptcy petition (s 272)
- creditor's bankruptcy petition (ss 264, 265, 267, 268 and 271)
- bankruptcy order (ss 278 - 282)
- protection of bankrupt's estate (ss 283(1), (3) - (6) - 285 and 291)
- appointment of interim receiver (s 286)
- appointment of receiver and manager (s 287)
- statement of affairs (s 288)
- investigation by official receiver (ss 289 and 290)
- appointment and control of trustee (ss 292, 295, 296, 301-304)
- release of trustee (s 298(1), (2), (5) - (8) - 300(1), (2), (6) - (8))
- administration by trustee (ss 305-349)

- bankruptcy offences (ss 350 - 362)
- power of court and general provisions (ss 363 - 379)
- interpretation (ss 380 - 387)
- insolvency practitioners (ss 388 - 398)
- official receivers (ss 399 - 401)
- insolvency service finance etc (ss 403 - 410)

(b) Application to insolvent partnerships in a winding-up by the court

The following provisions of Part IV and V of the Act, together with subordinate legislation, apply to partnerships subject to the modifications set out in the Order:

- jurisdiction (ss 117 - 119)
- grounds, effect and commencment of winding-up petition (ss 112 - 130)
- investigation procedures (ss 131-134)
- appointment of liquidator and functions (ss 135 - 139, 143 - 146)
- liquidation committee (s 141)
- general powers of the court (ss 147-160)
- liquidator's powers and duties (ss 163-170)
- release of liquidator (ss 171 - 174)
- administration (ss 175 - 200)
- dissolution after winding-up (ss 201 - 205)
- malpractice (ss 206 - 219)
- winding-up of unregistered companies (ss 220 - 222, 225 - 229)

(c) Application to insolvent corporate partners in a winding-up by the court

The following provisions of Parts IV and V of the Act, and the relevant subordinate legislation, apply to the winding-up of a corporate member of the partnership where the insolvent partnership is wound up as an unregistered company, subject to the modifications set out in the Order:

- alternative modes of winding-up (s 73)
- jurisdiction (ss 117-119)
- grounds, effect and commencement of winding-up petition (ss 122 - 130)
- investigation procedures (ss 131 - 134)
- appointment of liquidator and functions (ss 135 - 139, 143 - 146)
- liquidation committee (s 141)
- general powers of the court (ss 147 - 160)
- liquidator's powers and duties (ss 163 - 170)
- release of liquidator (ss 171 - 174)
- administration (ss 175 - 200)
- dissolution after winding-up (ss 201 - 205)
- malpractice (ss 206 - 219)
- winding-up of unregistered companies (ss 220 - 229).

10. Individual voluntary arrangements

Part VIII of the Act (individual voluntary arrangements - see Chapter 1) applies to a partner or partners where insolvency orders are made against the partnership and that partner or partners, with the modification that any reference to the creditors of the company or of the debtor includes a reference to the creditors of the partnership.

11. Company voluntary arrangements

Part I of the Act applies to corporate partners where insolvency orders are made against the partnership and an insolvent partner, with the modification that any reference to the creditors of the company or of the debtor includes a reference to the creditors of the partnership.

Chapter 21

The deceased bankrupt

1. Introduction

The estate of a deceased person is insolvent if, when realised, it is insufficient to meet in full all the debts and other liabilities to which it is subject.

However, when a debtor by or against whom a bankruptcy petition has been presented, dies, the proceedings continue as if he were alive but with certain modifications, unless the court otherwise orders (s 421).

A bankruptcy debt in relation to a deceased debtor or his personal representative (or if there is no personal representative such person as the court may elect), means, *inter alia,* any debt or liability to which he was subject at the date of death. "The court" means the court within the jurisdiction of which the debtor resided or carried on business for the greater part of the six months immediately prior to his death.

References in this chapter to "the Order" are to The Administration of Insolvent Estates of Deceased Persons Order 1986 (SI 1986 No 1999) and include forms (see Appendix 6). The following provisions of the Act and subordinate legislation apply, subject to the modifications set out in the Order:

- approval of voluntary arrangements, provided that the individual has not died before the creditors' meeting has been held (ss 257 - 263)
- debtor's bankruptcy petition (ss 272 and 273)
- creditor's bankruptcy petition (ss 264, 266, 267, 269 and 271)
- supervisor's petition (s 276(2))
- bankruptcy order (ss 278, 282(1) and (4))
- protection of the bankrupt's estate (ss 283 - 285 and 291)
- appointment of interim recevier (s 286(1), (3) - (8))
- appointment of receiver and manager (s 287)
- statement of affairs (s 288)
- investigation by official receiver (s 289)
- appointment and control of trustee (ss 292 - 297(1) - (3), (5) - (8), 301 - 304)
- release of trustee (ss 298 - 300)
- administration by trustee (ss 305 - 349)
- bankruptcy offences (ss 350(1), (2), (4) - (6), 351(c) and 359)
- power of court and general provisions (ss 363, 365 - 379)

- interpretation (ss 380 - 387(1), (5), (6))
- insolvency practitioners (ss 388 - 398)
- official receivers (ss 399 - 401)
- insolvency service finance etc (ss 403 - 410)

An "insolvency administration order" means an order for the administration in bankruptcy of the insolvent estate of a deceased debtor (art 2).

2. Personal representative's petition

The petition (Form 6) is presented by the personal representative of a deceased debtor and is for an insolvency administration order. It is followed by a statement of affairs (Form 7) which contains particulars of the deceased's creditors, debts, liabilities, assets etc.

Whereas a debtor's petition is usually presented on the grounds that the debtor is unable to pay his debts, in the case of a deceased debtor, it is *always* on the specific ground that the estate is insufficient to pay his debts.

The court makes an insolvency administration order (Form 4) if it is satisfied that the deceased debtor's estate is insolvent and without regard to a minimum amount of indebtedness.

3. Death of a debtor before presentation of a bankruptcy petition by a creditor

Where the debtor dies before presentation of a bankruptcy petition by a creditor, a creditor's petition for an insolvency adminstration order (Form 1) may be presented to the court in the circumstances where, had the debtor been alive:

(a) the amount of the debt or the aggregate amount of the debts owed by the debtor would have been equal to or exceeded the bankruptcy level of £750; or

(b) the debt or each of the debts owed by the debtor would have been for a liquidated sum payable to the petitioning creditor or one or more of the petitioning creditors, either immediately or at some certain future time, and would have been unsecured.

The court may make an insolvency administration order (Form 4) on a creditors' petition for such an order under s 271(1) as amended if it is satisfied that the debt (or one of them) in respect of which the petition was presented, is a debt which, having been payable at the date of the petition or having since become payable, has neither been paid nor secured or compounded for, nor has any reasonable prospect of being able to be paid when it falls due. There should also be a *reasonable probability* that the estate will be insolvent.

A petition for an insolvency administration order should not be presented to the court after proceedings have been commenced in any court for the administration of the deceased debtor's estate. However, where proceedings have already commenced in another court, then that court may, if satisfied that the estate is insolvent, transfer the proceedings to the court exercising bankruptcy jurisdiction, which may then make an insolvency administration order (Form 5) as if a petition for such an order had been presented.

If it appears that there has been a contravention of the rules - or for any other reason - the court may dismiss a petition for an insolvency administration order with or without costs or stay proceedings on such a petition.

An insolvency administration order has effect from the day on which it is made. Any expenses properly incurred as expenses of the administration of the insolvent estate are a first charge on the estate.

4. Power to appoint interim receiver

If it is shown to be necessary for the protection of the property after the presentation of a petition to the court and before making an insolvency administration order, the court may appoint the official receiver to be interim recever of all the debtor's property under s 286. He then has all the usual rights, powers, duties and immunities under the Act unless his powers are limited in any way by the court.

The estate comprises all property belonging to or vested in the debtor on the date of death, excluding tools of his trade etc. and such clothing, bedding, furniture, household equipment and provisions as are necessary for satisfying the basic domestic needs of the family of the deceased debtor. "Property" here includes the capacity to exercise and take proceedings for exercising all such powers over or in respect of property as might have been exercised by the debtor's personal representative for the benefit of the estate on the date of the insolvency administration order and exercisable over or in respect of property not for the time being comprised in the estate.

5. Receivership pending appointment of the trustee

The official receiver remains the receiver and manager of the estate between the making of an insolvency administration order and the time at which the deceased debtor's estate is vested in a trustee, and is under a duty to act as such.

6. Investigation of affairs

Where an insolvency administration order has been made, the personal representative, or if there is no personal representative such person as the court may direct on the application of the official receiver, must submit a statement of the deceased debtor's affairs to the official receiver. Under s 288 as amended, the statement must be submitted within 56 days beginning with the date of a request by the official receiver, or such longer period as the official receiver or the court may allow. It contains particulars of the assets and liabilities of the estate as at the date of the insolvency administration order, together with other particulars of the affairs of the deceased debtor as is set out (Form 7) (see page 120).

Contrary to his usual role, the official receiver is not under any duty to investigate the affairs and conduct of the deceased debtor unless he thinks fit, and there will naturally be no public examination in any form.

7. Trustees in bankruptcy

The deceased debtor's estate vests in the trustee immediately on his appointment taking effect or, in the case of the official receiver, on his becoming trustee. Property vests in him under s 306 without any conveyance, assignment or transfer and he may claim for the estate anything which has been acquired by, or has devolved upon the estate since the date of death of the deceased debtor.

By Sch 1 para 18 under art 3, the functions and duties of the trustee under the Act remain for the deceased's estate with the modification that, where a meeting of creditors is summoned the rules regarding the trustee in bankruptcy and the creditor's committee continue to apply.

Under the Agricultural Holdings Act 1986 an agricultural tenancy is not transferred to his trustee or other person deriving title from a tenant by operation of law.

The trustee remains fully liable in respect of misfeasance or breach of fiduciary or other duty in the carrying out of his functions. If the personal representative, creditor or any other person is dissatisfied by any act, omission or decision of a trustee of the deceased debtor's estate, he may apply to the court, which has power to confirm, reverse or modify any act or decision of the trustee, give directions or make such other order as it thinks fit.

The trustee must have regard to any claim by the personal representative, or if there is no personal representative, by any other person, to payment of reasonable funeral, testamentary and administration expenses incurred by him in respect of the deceased debtor's estate. Such claims have priority over preferential debts, the categories of which otherwise remain unchanged (see page 233).

Assets vesting in the trustee after the death of the bankrupt are for the purposes of the Capital Gains Tax Act 1979 regarded as held by a personal representative of the deceased by s 61(3) of that Act, so that capital gains tax is not assessable on or recoverable from the trustee in this instance.

When he has realised all the deceased debtor's estate, or so much of it as he can, if a surplus remains after payment in full (and with interest) of all the deceased debtor's creditors and the payment of the expenses of the bankruptcy, the surplus is paid to the personal representative unless the court otherwise orders.

8. Death of a debtor after presentation of a bankruptcy petition

By art 5 and Sch 2 to the Order, if the debtor dies after presentation of a bankruptcy petition, the personal representative usually submits a statement of the deceased debtor's affairs within 56 days (beginning with the date of a request by the official receiver), or such longer period as the court may allow. It contains the particulars of the assets and liabilities of the estate as at the date of the bankruptcy order together with other particulars of his affairs (Form 7).

It is also up to the personal representative to give the trustee notice of the reasonable funeral and testamentary expenses so that they can be paid out of the estate before the final distribution. These expenses have priority over preferential debts.

If a debtor dies after presentation of a bankruptcy petition but before service, the court may order service to be effected on his personal representative or such other person as it thinks fit.

9. The moratorium for the insolvent debtor who subsequently dies

There are special rules where the court has made an interim order under s 252 of the Act (see page 6) in respect of an individual who subsequently dies.

By Part III of the Order, where he dies before the nominee has submitted his document and statement the nominee gives the court notice that the individual has died and the court must then discharge the interim order.

Where a creditors' meeting was to be summoned but the debtor dies before it has been held, then the meeting is cancelled. If he was at the date of death an undischarged bankrupt, the personal representative must give notice of his death to the trustee of his estate and to the official receiver.

Where a creditors' meeting has been held and its result reported to the court then that meeting is effectively valid and the later death of the individual cannot affect its result even although the voluntary arrangement then ceases to apply. If it has taken effect, the personal representative of the deceased debtor together with the deceased debtor's creditors or any other person may apply to the court if they are dissatisfied by any act, omission or decision of the supervisor. He is required to give notice to the court that the individual has died.

The supervisor may still present a petition for an insolvency administration order by serving Form 2 where it is not practical to continue with the voluntary arrangement.

Chapter 22

Releasing the trustee

1. Introduction

The trustee has his release on:

- completion of his administration
- removal from office
- resignation
- vacating office
- death
- annulment of the bankruptcy.

The word "release" can be misleading for the trustee is not always freed for all time at the conclusion of his trusteeship. While s 299(5) of the Act discharges his liability "both in respect of acts or omissions of his in the administration of the estate" his conduct nevertheless remains exposed to challenge by application to the court under s 304(2) *after* he has had his release and whether or not there is, or is likely to be, a surplus. The circumstances in which he remains liable are set out in s 304(1):

(a) that the trustee of a bankrupt's estate has misapplied or retained or become accountable for, any money or other property comprised in the bankrupt's estate, or

(b) that a bankrupt's estate has suffered any loss in consequence of any misfeasance or breach of fiduciary or other duty by a trustee in the carrying out of his functions.

Likewise, in this new era of accountability, the practitioner will find that the powers of the court and the creditors as to his release have considerably increased under the new legislation.

2. Release on completion of administration

Where it appears to the trustee that the administration of the bankrupt's estate is for practical purposes complete and the trustee is not the official receiver, he summons a final general meeting of creditors to receive the trustee's report of his administration and determine whether he should have his release under s 331. The procedure is set out in Rules 6.136 and 6.137; see page 214.

(a) Notice

Where the trustee is not the official receiver, he must give 28 days notice of the final meeting of creditors to be held under s 331(2). The notice must go to all creditors who have proved and to the bankrupt. He has a discretion whether or not to give the notice summoning the general meeting at the same time as giving notice of the final distribution (s 330 - page 245). However, if the meeting is summoned for an earlier date, the meeting must be adjourned (and, if necessary, further adjourned) until he is able to report that the administration of the bankrupt's estate is for practical purposes complete.

It is also the trustee's duty to retain sufficient sums from the estate to cover the expenses of summoning and holding the final meeting.

(b) Final meeting of creditors

The final meeting of creditors receives the trustee's report of his administration and determines whether he should have his release. The trustee presents the meeting a report including a summary of his receipts and payments and a statement by him that he has reconciled his account with that of the Secretary of State in respect of the bankruptcy. The creditors may question the trustee on any matter arising out of the report, and may resolve against him having his release. See page 214 for the procedure.

The trustee must notify the court that the final meeting has been held (on Form 6.50), stating whether or not he has been given his release. The notice must be accompanied by a copy of the report which was put to the meeting. The trustee also sends a copy of his notice to the official receiver (Rule 6.137).

If there is no quorum at the final meeting, the trustee must report to the court that the meeting was summoned but that there was no quorum. The final meeting is deemed to have been held and the creditors not to have resolved against the trustee's being released. By this means the trustee is able to obtain his release.

If the creditors at the final meeting do not resolve that the trustee should have his release, he must obtain it from the Secretary of State; if the meeting does not resolve against his release, he has it when he notifies the court that the final meeting has been held.

(c) Where the official receiver is trustee

Where the official receiver is the trustee then, before giving notice to the Secretary of State that the administration of the estate is for all practical purposes complete, he sends notice of his intention to do so to all creditors who have proved their debts, and to the bankrupt. The notice is accompanied by a summary of the official receiver's receipts and payments as trustee. The Secretary of State, when he has determined the date from which the official receiver is to have his release, notifies the court that he has done so, and that notice is also accompanied by a copy of the receipts and payments.

(d) Vacating office

The trustee vacates office on giving notice to the court that a final meeting has been held under s 331 and of the decision (if any) of that meeting.

3. Removal of the trustee before completion of the administration

Generally, the trustee may be removed from office before completion of his administration only by an order of the court or by a general meeting of the bankrupt's creditors summoned specially for that purpose, except when a certificate for the summary administration of the estate is in force in which case removal is a matter for the court.

(a) Removal by the court

It will be up to the court to remove the trustee, where he has not previously resigned, in those cases where it is brought to its notice that his practising licence as an insolvency practitioner has been withdrawn or not renewed; where he has for whatever reason lost his professional qualification; been adjudged bankrupt; become a company or otherwise become unfit, eg as a mental health patient.

The official receiver then takes over as trustee until the vacancy is again filled (see page 88), and he is also registered as proprietor under the Land Registration Rules 1986 (see page 143).

The court may dismiss an application for the removal of the trustee if it thinks insufficient cause is shown, but may only do this where the applicant has had the opportunity, on seven days notice, to attend the court for an *ex parte* hearing. If the application is not dismissed, the court fixes a venue for hearing. At least fourteen days before the date fixed for hearing, the applicant must send notice thereof to the trustee and the official receiver, accompanied by a copy of the application and of any evidence which the applicant intends to adduce in support. The costs of the application do not fall to the estate unless the court so orders. If the court orders that the trustee be removed, it must send copies of the order to him and to the official receiver (Form 6.48). The order may include such provision as the court thinks fit concerning matters consequential on the removal, and if a new trustee is appointed, to which the provisions of Rule 6.121 (see page 86) apply. (Rule 6.132)

(b) Removal by the creditors

The trustee may be removed from office by a general meeting of the bankrupt's creditors, provided that they are summoned especially for that purpose, and provided that a certificate for the summary administration of the estate is not in force. The meeting should be summoned using Form 6.35 which should indicate that the removal of the trustee is the purpose, or one of the purposes, of the meeting. It should draw the attention of creditors to s 299(3) of the Act with respect to the trustee's release. A copy of the notice is sent to the official receiver.

However, where the trustee was appointed otherwise than by the creditors, a general meeting of creditors for the purpose of replacing him may be summoned only if:

(i) the trustee thinks fit; or
(ii) the court so directs; or
(iii) the meeting is requested by one of the bankrupt's creditors with the concurrence of not less than one quarter in value of the creditors including the creditor making the request.

At the meeting, a person other than the trustee or his nominee may be elected to act as chairman; but if the trustee or his nominee *is* chairman and a resolution has been proposed for his removal, the chairman may not adjourn the meeting without the consent of at least one half in value of the creditors present in person or by proxy and entitled to vote.

Where the chairman is someone other than the official receiver and the meeting resolves:

(i) to remove the trustee; or
(ii) that a new trustee should be appointed; or
(iii) that the removed trustee should not be given his release,

the chairman must send a copy of the resolution to the official receiver within three days. If it is resolved to remove the trustee, the chairman of the meeting (when not himself the official receiver) must send to the official receiver a "certificate of removal" (Form 6.47). If the creditors resolve to appoint a new trustee, a certificate of his appointment must also be sent to the official receiver within the three day period (Rule 6.129).

Where the creditors have resolved to remove the trustee, the Secretary of State must first certify that the trustee has reconciled his account with that held by him in respect of the bankruptcy. When that has been done, the official receiver files a certificate of removal in court. The resolution removing the trustee is effective from the date on which the certificate of removal is filed in court, and that date is endorsed on the certificate. A copy of the certificate is sent by the official receiver to the trustee thereby removed and, if a new trustee has been appointed, to him. (Rule 6.131).

The court may, on the application of any creditor, give directions as to the mode of summoning a meeting of creditors to remove the trustee, including the sending out and return of forms of proxy (Form 8.4), the conduct of the meeting, and any other matter which appears to the court to require regulation or control. (Rule 6.130)

Where the general meeting of creditors has not resolved against his release, a person who has ceased to be trustee has his release at the time at which notice that that person has ceased to hold office is given to the court. The fact of his release is stated in the certificate of removal (Form 6.47).

Where the general meeting of creditors resolves against his release, the person has his release at such time as the Secretary of State may determine on an application by that person in Form 6.49.

(c) Removal by the Secretary of State

If the trustee was appointed by the Secretary of State, he may be removed by a direction from him under s 298(5), but before doing so, the Secretary of State notifies the trustee and the official receiver of his decision and the grounds of it, specifying a period within which the trustee may make representations against implementation of the decision. If the Secretary of State directs the removal of the trustee he must forthwith file notice of that decision in court and notify the trustee and the official receiver. The court may then make such order as it could have done had the trustee been removed by the court (see *(a)* above). (Rule 6.133)

(d) Where the official receiver is trustee

Where the official receiver has ceased to be the trustee of a bankrupt's estate and a person is appointed in his stead, the official receiver has his release by s 299(1) with effect from:

- (i) where that person is appointed by a general meeting of the bankrupt's creditors or by the Secretary of State, the time at which the official receiver gives notice to the court that he has been replaced; or
- (ii) where that person is appointed by the court, at such time as the court may determine.

On his release he is discharged from all liability for the administration of the estate and otherwise in relation to his conduct as trustee, save for the provisions of s 304 (continuing personal liability of the trustee notwithstanding his release).

4. Resignation of the trustee

The trustee's resignation is effective from the date on which the official receiver files the copy notice in court with the date endorsed on the copy notice (Form 6.44; Rule 6.127(7)).

(a) Creditors' meeting to receive resignation

A trustee may resign by giving notice to the court under s 298(7). The procedure in Rule 6.126 applies where:

- (i) the trustee resigns on grounds of ill health; or
- (ii) the trustee intends ceasing to practice as an insolvency practitioner; or
- (iii) there is a conflict of interest or change of personal circumstances which

makes it impracticable for him to continue as trustee.

Where there are joint trustees, any one may proceed under these provisions if he and the other joint trustee(s) are of the opinion that it is no longer expedient for there to continue to be the present number of joint trustees.

The trustee resigning must first call a meeting of creditors to receive his resignation. Notice of the meeting is sent simultaneously to the official receiver and to the creditors. The notice must indicate that the purpose, or one of the purposes, of the meeting is to receive the resignation. It must draw attention to the provisions of Rule 6.135 as to the release of the resigning trustee.

(b) Procedure following acceptance of resignation

Where the chairman of the meeting is not the official receiver, and the meeting passes a resolution that:

(i) the trustee's resignation be accepted; or
(ii) that a new trustee be appointed; or
(iii) that the resigning trustee not be released,

then the chairman must send the official receiver a copy of the resolution within three days. If the resignation is accepted, the chairman sends to the official receiver a certificate to that effect (Form 6.44); the trustee must give notice to the court immediately as required by s 298(7). That notice must be accompanied by a copy of his account to the creditors, and a copy of the notice must be sent to the official receiver. The official receiver files a copy of that notice in court. The trustee's resignation takes effect from the date the official receiver files the copy notice in court. (Rule 6.127)

If the meeting resolves to appoint a new trustee, the certificate of his appointment is also sent to the official receiver within the three days and the usual procedure on the appointment of a trustee applies (see Rule 6.120, page 85; Form 6.40 or 6.41).

(c) Resignation not accepted

If the meeting does not accept the resignation, the trustee may apply to the court for leave to resign; notice is in Form 6.46. If the court gives leave, its order may make such provision as appears fit for matters arising in connection with the resignation. The trustee's release is effective from such date as the court may determine. The court sends two sealed copies of the order to the trustee, who must immediately send one of those copies to the official receiver. (Form 6.45). On sending notice of his resignation to the court, the trustee also sends a copy of it to the official receiver.

5. Vacation of office

The trustee, not being the official receiver, must vacate office if he ceases to be qualified as an insolvency practitioner in relation to the bankrupt. He has his release at such time as the Secretary of State may determine following notice by him (Form

6.51) filed in court (Rule 6.144), to which Rule 6.135 applies (s 390).

6. Death of the trustee

Where the trustee other than the official receiver has died, it is the duty of his personal representatives to give notice of the fact to the official receiver, specifying the date of death. Alternatively, where he was a partner in a firm, notice may be given to the official receiver by a partner in the firm who is qualified to act as an insolvency practitioner, or is a member of any body recognised by the Secretary of State for the authorisation of insolvency practitioners, or by anyone producing the relevant death certificate or a copy of it. The official receiver gives notice to the court for the purpose of fixing the date of the deceased trustee's release.

7. Annulment of the bankruptcy order

The trustee vacates office if the bankruptcy order is annulled by order of the court under s 298(9) (see page 288), but the annulment does not of itself release him from his duties and obligations to account for his administration of the estate. He must send a copy of his final account to the Secretary of State as soon as practicable after the order of annulment, and file a copy in the court. The account must include a summary of the trustee's receipts and payments in the administration and contain a statement that he has reconciled his account with that held by the Secretary of State. The trustee is then released at such time as the court determines, having regard to whether the requirement to file an account has been met; and whether any security (see page 24) has been, or will be, released. (Rule 6.214)

8. Trustee's duties on vacating office

(a) Notice of intention to vacate office

Where the trustee intends to vacate office, whether by resignation or otherwise and there are still unrealised assets in the estate, he must give notice of his intention to the official receiver, advising him of the nature, value and whereabouts of the assets in question. Where there is to be a creditors' meeting in connection with the trustee's vacating office, the notice to the official receiver must be given at least 21 days before that meeting. (Rule 6.145)

(b) Vacating office before completion of administration

On vacating office before the administration of the bankrupt's estate is complete, the trustee must hand over to the person succeeding him as trustee:

- (i) the assets of the estate, after deducting any expenses properly incurred and distributions made by him;
- (ii) the bankruptcy records including correspondence, proofs and the like;
- (iii) the bankrupt's books, papers and other records.

Otherwise, when the administration of the estate is for all practical purposes complete, the trustee files in court all proofs remaining with him.

When a new trustee is appointed he states in his advertisement of his appointment that his predecessor has resigned or been removed and has been given his release if that is the case.

9. Transitional arrangements

Where a trustee had been appointed before 29 December 1986 and had not made application for release under s 93 of the 1914 Act, then except where the Secretary of State otherwise directs, s 93 will not apply to any trustee who holds office on or at any time after the appointed day and is not the official receiver. This applies as regards the trustee to the case of a person adjudged bankrupt before the appointed day, or adjudged bankrupt on or after that day but on a petition presented before that day.

10. Second and subsequent bankruptcies

In a second or subsequent bankruptcy, the trustee's trusteeship becomes inoperative upon service of notice on him (Form 6.78) of the presentation of a petition for a later bankruptcy under s 334(2), although his ability to prove in the later bankruptcy (see page 200) is not affected. His release from the earlier bankruptcy is not otherwise provided for.

Chapter 23

Voluntary arrangements outside bankruptcy

Depending upon the size and extent of his debt, the debtor has two further useful options open to him:

I the deed of arrangement, without limit on size, provided that it can be anchored to security on property; and

II the administration order procedure, which is normally available where he has been unable to pay the amount of a judgment obtained against him in the county court and provided that his total indebtedness does not exceed £5,000.

Both procedures, although not amounting to bankruptcy and thereby avoiding the stigma remaining with the debtor, are nevertheless related to bankruptcy through the Insolvency Act. The connecting features are the licensing of the trustee (in I) and the possible effect of failure of either arrangement.

One further matter concludes the chapter, that is the procedure whereby the deceased's estate is administered otherwise than in bankruptcy (see III). However, for the living debtor seeking life after debt, there may yet be further options, not within the ambit of this volume, namely the debt counsellors' service in cases where the debtor has been neither reckless nor fraudulent. Through advice centres, their difficult task is to get the agreement of creditors to a schedule of repayment either outside or within the control of the court (under II) but avoiding the control of either the 1914 or 1986 Acts.

I. DEEDS OF ARRANGEMENT

1. Introduction

References in this chapter to the 1914 Act are to the Deeds of Arrangement Act 1914; "Rules" refer to the Deeds of Arrangement Rules 1925 and forms (Nos 1 to 20) are those prescribed pursuant to r 4, and reproduced in Appendix 6.

A deed of arrangement takes various forms to allow for the liquidation of liabilities as an alternative to bankruptcy. It is a product of early consumer law which, initially under an Amendment Act of 1882, required the deed to be registered as a bill of sale, without which any attempt to enter into an arrangement was void. That early law first introduced registration of matters which were previously private arrangements between the debtor and his creditors, outside public record.

The Deeds of Arrangement Act 1914 consolidated the then law by regularising private arrangements, which could be made either before or after an adjudication in bankruptcy. Provided the instrument of arrangement was capable of being registered as a bill of sale by the county court registrar under s 2 and thereby fell within the Act, the Act afforded any interested person the opportunity of searching the register.

It is perhaps more by luck than judgement that the procedures have not fallen into total disuse over the years. Until the 1985 Act abolished the concept of the act of bankruptcy, the making of an assignment for the benefit of the creditors was the quintessential event upon which a bankruptcy petition could be founded, and had been a convenient method for even a minority creditor to avoid the arrangement and put the debtor into bankruptcy straightaway. With the obstacle removed by the repeal of s 24(1) and (2) of the 1914 Act, there is now a real opportunity for a resurgence of professional interest in the deed as an alternative to bankruptcy or the Part VIII arrangement (to which by s 260(3), it bears no relation). It should particularly appeal to the debtor who is not under pressure from his creditors and who does not need the protection of the moratorium provided by an interim order (see Chapter 1).

Nevertheless it is obviously important that all creditors with debts of at least £750, ie capable of supporting a petition in bankruptcy, should be marshalled into the deed to prevent it being subsequently scuppered, and that provided it is properly drawn, clear in its intent, and quickly registered, such a course is barred to those creditors who might otherwise raise a petition against the debtor in bankruptcy. Arrangements made before a bankruptcy order are binding, without the approval of the court, only on creditors who assent; arrangements made after adjudication generally bind all creditors entitled to prove in the bankruptcy and then require the approval of the court. Nevertheless the making of such a registrable "arrangement" with creditors is still, for the debtor, a tightrope between debt, disability, a diminished credit rating as well as, for example, disqualification from local government elections, all of which will probably tend to keep it less popular than the Part VIII arrangement, although it provides more alternatives honed to the needs of the debtor and his creditors.

Although the procedure for registering the deed is basically unaltered by the Act of 1986, in a sense it effectively merges the existing requirements under the 1914 Act for the trustee under the deed, with those for the licensed practitioner under the Act of 1986. Thus the accountancy and auditing procedures, including the right of creditors to investigate the trustee's accounts and the requirement for security in the form of a general penalty bond for £250,000 and a specific penalty bond (see page 24), all apply. Otherwise the insolvency practitioner, in his capacity as trustee of the deed, remains free from official check.

Jurisdiction remains in the bankruptcy court but there is no official investigation into the debtor's conduct. In this respect the deeds of arrangement procedure is now similar to that where a voluntary arrangement has been entered into under Part VIII of the Act or where a certificate of summary administration has been issued under s 275. By s 24, nothing in the Act of 1914 is to be construed as repealing or affecting any provision of insolvency law or giving validity to any deed or instrument which by law is void or voidable. The practitioner should, however, keep a weather eye open for amendments to the 1914 Act, in particular for those to be found in the Administration of Justice Act 1925 and the Finance Act 1949, together with the amendments in the Insolvency Acts of 1985 and 1986 (see 7 below).

2. Deeds to which the Act applies

Every deed of arrangement is a contract and its effect depends entirely upon its own terms. Thus there is no prescribed form or any proposal to introduce one, so that the deed stands or falls by itself subject only to the Deeds of Arrangement Act 1914 as amended and the rules made thereunder. If it is for the benefit of the creditors generally, it will also be void unless it receives the assent of a majority in number and value of the creditors before or within 21 days after registration or within such extended time as the court may allow.

(a) General application

The Act will apply to written instruments for an arrangement made by three or more individual creditors, not companies, and will not apply to oral agreements. The term "arrangement" has a wide connotation and includes any of the instruments outlined in s 1 (see *(c)* below). For the purpose of determining the number of "creditors" for whose benefit a deed is made, any two or more joint creditors are treated as a single creditor.

(b) Form and content

The most usual form of deed will comprise the following:

- (i) *instrument* - the deed will be expressed to be an instrument to which s1 of the Act of 1914 applies;
- (ii) *insolvency practitioner* - it will make provision for the powers and remuneration of a licensed trustee under the deed;
- (iii) *property* - it will provide for the assignment of all property of the debtor within the meaning given by s 436 Insolvency Act (see 6 below) pursuant to s 30, and will not include "after-acquired" property, although unlike bankruptcy it may automatically make provision for income accruing to the debtor;
- (iv) *real estate* - the trustee to hold in fee simple;
- (v) *creditors* - all to be bound by the terms of the deed without initiating or continuing bankruptcy or other proceedings (discontinuation of a petition

is with the permission of the court) and representation by committee (of inspection);

(vi) *running the business* - provision re secured creditors to enable satisfactory continuation of trading.

(c) Class of instrument

A deed of arrangement to which s1(1) Deeds of Arrangement Act 1914 applies includes any instrument of the following classes whether or not under seal:

(i) made by for or in respect of the affairs of a debtor for the benefit of his creditors generally;

(ii) made by, for or in respect of the affairs of a debtor who was insolvent at the date of the execution of the instrument for the benefit of any three or more of his creditors otherwise than in pursuance of the law for the time being in force relating to bankruptcy by s 1(1).

The classes of instrument referred to in s 1(2), which are discussed in the next part, are as follows:

(i) an assignment of property;

(ii) a deed of, or agreement for, a composition;

(iii) a deed of inspectorship entered into for the purpose of carrying on or winding up a business;

(iv) a letter of licence;

(v) any agreement or instrument.

In cases (iii), (iv) and (v), creditors of the debtor obtain control over the property or business of the debtor.

(d) Creditors

As to the assent of the majority (on Form 2), a deed which is either expressed to be or is in fact for the benefit of a debtor's creditors generally will by s 3 be void unless within 21 days (unless extended) it has received the assent of a majority in number and value of the creditors. A deed for the benefit of particular creditors only is not for the "benefit of creditors generally" (as for s 1(1) above) and comes neither within the letter or spirit of the Act; see *Re Samson and Schreiber's Contract* (1895) 39 SJ 504. If the creditors assent they cannot succeed in an action for the balance of the price of the goods sold beforehand; see *Victor Weston (Fabrics) Ltd* v *Morgensreons* [1937] 3 All ER 769.

In calculating a majority of creditors, a creditor holding security upon the property of the debtor is reckoned as a creditor only in respect of the balance, if any, due to him after deducting the value of his security. Creditors whose debts amount to sums exceeding £10 are reckoned in the majority in value but not in the majority in number. Those for less than £10 are eliminated from the voting, ie from the total of creditors as well as those whose votes form a majority; see *Re Wilson* [1916] 1 KB 382.

(e) Inconsistency with the Act

The deed cannot be inconsistent with the provisions of s 1; in *Gee* v *Schmutter* (1971) 123 CLR 503 (a Commonwealth case but on similar principles) it was held that the deed was not necessarily void because of the provisions written into it: "It may be that any such provision being in conflict with the statute may be inoperative or it may be that because of provisions of that kind, the court of bankruptcy in the particular circumstances of the case may be disposed in the exercise of a discretion to declare the deed void." In the event it may only be necessary to make the particular provision inoperative.

3. The typical deed

The most important of the instruments that give rise to a deed of arrangement are described below:

(a) Assignment of property

The most common form of deed of arrangement is the deed of assignment whereby the debtor assigns his property to a trustee or assignee for the benefit of his creditors with a view to sale of the property. Conveyances of this kind comprise the whole, or substantially the whole, of the debtor's property to trustees for the benefit of all his creditors, not a particular class only; see *Re Saumarez ex parte Salaman* [1907] 2 KB 170, where the alleged assignment was for the benefit of certain named creditors only and therefore did not require registration.

Likewise a letter signed by the debtor in the following terms is not an assignment of property within s 1(2), nor a deed of arrangement within s 1(1):

> "I hereby authorise you to realise my estate including stock-in-trade, book debts, furniture and all other assets and to apply the proceeds first in payment of the costs, charges and preferential claims etc and secondly to pay the balance to my creditors *pro rata.*"

If the arrangement purports to be an assignment it must be shown that it is in fact an "assignment" effecting a passing of title, and not a mere authority to deal with property by way of control and realisation as agent for the true owner; see *Lipton Ltd* v *Bell* [1924] 1 KB 701. Contrast this with a document for the settlement of all debts in the following terms:

> "(1) all the goods which have been removed from M's office & given to M & Co in trust on behalf of creditors, should be handed over to the creditors.
> (2) M undertakes to pay to the above trustee for the creditors £80 payable
> (3) M also undertakes to pay on his own account (certain named creditors) who shall be excluded from the list of the general creditors. I agree to these terms".

This document was accepted as an agreement for the benefit of three or more creditors (to take it within s 1(1)) made by a debtor who was insolvent at the date of the execution of the deed, and would therefore have been a deed of arrangement within s 1 (had it not been void because it was not registered): see *Landsberg* v *Mendel* (1924) WN 46.

An assignment is not registered unless it appears that it has been or purports to have been executed, or (if not made by deed) signed by the trustee or assignee. It is the duty of the registrar to satisfy himself that the assignment purports to have been duly executed or signed by the trustee or assignee before registering it. A deed of assignment executed by a foreign debtor in his own country does not require registration so that the trustee under such a deed is entitled to goods in this country belonging to the debtor as against an execution creditor at the date of the assignment: see *Dulaney* v *Merry & Sons* [1901] 1 KB 536.

An example of a deed of assignment is given below:

> DEEDS OF ARRANGEMENT ACT 1914
> In the matter of a Deed of Assignment
> BETWEEN
> of *(add description)*
> (hereinafter called "the Debtor" of the one part and his creditors dated the .... day of 19
> (and registered under the Deeds of Arrangement Act 1914, on the .... day of ....19..) *[Strike out if deed has not already been registered]*
> TRUSTEE [AB] of
> (hereinafter called "the Trustee") of the other part:
> WITNESSETH THAT
> (a) the Debtor conveys and assigns to the Trustee all his property within the meaning of section 30 of the Deeds of Arrangement Act 1914 UPON TRUST to deal with the same in accordance with Part IV of that Act for the benefit of the creditors of the Debtor and as to any surplus after paying in full the several debts and liabilities of the debtor proved under this Deed together with costs charges and expenses of or incidental to the execution of the trusts of this Deed (including the remuneration and expenses of the Trustee) UPON TRUST for the Debtor his executors administrators or assigns; and
> (b) the Trustee accepts appointment as trustee of this Deed and the conveyance and assignment of the said property upon the trusts hereinbefore set out.
> IN WITNESS whereof the parties have hereunto set their hands and seals. Signed, sealed and delivered (by Debtor and Trustee in the presence of witnesses)"

This short form of assignment is an example of a statutory form, taken from Form 36A of Sch 1 to the Bankruptcy Rules (Statutory Rules No 2 of 1968, as amended) under the Australian Bankruptcy Act 1966 (as amended), and modified to suit the English Deeds of Arrangement Act 1914 and the Rules thereunder (see Form 1). This is a rare example of such a deed for which there is a singular lack of statutory direction. However, other and longer forms of assignment to suit differing circumstances are available from law stationers, and are in occasional use by institutions such as the London Stock Exchange for cases of default.

(b) Deed of or agreement for a composition

The effect of a composition is that the debtor deprives himself of the power to carry on his business with a view to making a different distribution of his property from that which the bankruptcy laws prescribe for the insolvent individual. Effectively it is an alternative way of distributing his assets without the safeguards which those laws provide.

Cave J: "Where the debtor makes over his assets to be administered by a trustee, that is a scheme; where the debtor keeps his assets and undertakes to pay over to the creditors a certain sum, that is a composition." (*Re Griffith* (1886) 3 Mor 111)

The fact that the composition is not secured in any way is a circumstance which will generally lead to the inference that the composition has not been *bona fide* accepted for the benefit of creditors, and especially so when the debtor has scant assets: see *Re Walton ex parte Hudson* (1883) 22 CD 773.

The effect of this form of deed is that the creditors accept less than the full amount of the debt or payment: "to each of the creditors a composition of ....p in the £" by regular instalments. The payments may be secured by guarantors, or by conveying the debtor's property to a trustee or by promissory note.

(c) A deed of inspectorship entered into for the purpose of carrying on or winding-up a business

These may also involve the assignment of the property of the debtor to the "inspector" who is also the trustee, with a view to carrying on or winding-up the business under the supervision of a committee of inspection appointed by the creditors.

In *Redpath* v *Wigg* (1866) 14 WR 866 the debtor carried on business as C J M & Co. Goods were ordered by the debtor before the deed, and delivery was requested by the inspectors in writing, signed "For C J M & Co". It was held that the deed of inspectorship did not in fact constitute the Inspectors as principals of the debtor and accordingly in default the plaintiff could only look to the debtor (who was C J M & Co) for payment as well as to the trust which the deed contained as to payment of the current expenses.

(d) A letter of licence

This is an agreement authorising the debtor, or any other person, to manage, carry on realise or dispose of a business, for a stated period, with a view to the payment of his debts, at the end of which he undertakes to pay his debts in full.

(e) Any other agreement or instrument

Where any other form of arrangement is entered into its purpose is for the carrying on or winding-up the debtor's business, or authorising the debtor or any other person to manage, carry on, or realise or dispose of the debtor's business with a view to the payment of his debts. A receipt stating the terms of a composition does not come within the Act although it is a record of an oral agreement; see *Hughes* v *Newton* [1939] 3 All ER 869.

4. Registration

(a) Execution

Before the deed can be registered, it must be executed by the trustee or assignee, but it may be executed by the creditors after registration (Form 5). It must also be executed by the debtor or his solicitor.

(b) Mode of registration

The registration of a deed of arrangement is effected by presenting to and filing with the Registrar of Bills of Sale at the Department of Trade and Industry copies of the deed within seven clear days after the first execution by the debtor or any creditor (unless it is executed out of England) together with any schedules or inventory annexed thereto (s 22 Administration of Justice Act 1922; Form 6). The number of copies required is as the registrar deems necessary for the purpose of carrying out the requirements of the Act (s 5 Act of 1914).

An affidavit (Forms 4, 5 or 6) is also submitted, which verifies the time of execution and contains a description of the residence and occupation of the debtor, the place or places where his business is carried on. An affidavit (Form 6) by the debtor states the total estimated amount of property and liabilities included under the deed, the total amount of the composition (if any) payable thereunder, and the names and addresses of his creditors.

Every copy of the deed is endorsed with the name of the debtor, the date of the deed and the date of filing, the total amount of duty and a certificate signed either by the solicitor of the debtor or the person who presents the copy for filing certifying that the copy is a correct copy of the deed (r 6).

If the deed concerns land, it must be registered at the Land Registry. For a case where a deed of assignment was registered under the 1914 Act but not under the Land Charges Act 1925, see *Veitch* v *Caldicott* (1945) 173 LT 30.

As for fees taken in respect of registration, see Appendix 5 (s 26).

(c) Certificate of registration

When a deed is registered a certificate is written on the original deed stating that it has been duly registered as prescribed by the Act, together with the date of registration (r 8). The certificate is sealed by the registrar. For the form of register to be kept by the registrar see Form 7.

(d) Local register

Within three days after registration the registrar should transmit a copy of the deed to the registrar of the county court in the district of which the place of business or residence of the debtor is situate where he lives outside London (s 10).

Any person is entitled to search the register of deeds on payment of 50p and make extracts from any registered deed of arrangement without being required to make written application or to specify any particulars in reference thereto also upon payment of 50p for each name inspected (s 9).

(e) Void deeds

The deed is void unless registered within seven clear days after first execution by the debtor or any creditor (s 2). If the instrument is void it cannot create a trust for the benefit of creditors and the trustee is bound to repay any moneys to the debtor (or to the official receiver where a bankruptcy order has been made).

Where it is either expressed to be or is in fact for the benefit of a debtor's creditors generally, the deed is void unless, before or within 21 days after registration (unless extended by the High Court or the court having jurisdiction in individual insolvency) it has received the assent of a majority in number and value of the creditors of the debtor (s 3).

The trustee is liable where the deed has to his knowledge become void by reason of non-compliance with any of the requirements of the Deeds of Arrangement Act or after he has failed to give security within the time and in the manner provided for by the Act (s 12). In the latter case he is liable thereunder to a fine of £5 per day.

Where the deed is, *inter alia,* void because the requisite majority of creditors has not assented to it, the trustee is not liable if he proves that at the time he did not know, and had no reason to suspect, that the deed was void (s 19).

Where a deed is void for any reason other than that it has not been registered the trustee must give notice to each creditor whose name and address he knows and file a copy of the notice with the Registrar of Bills of Sale. If he fails to do so he commits an offence (s 20). The registrar issues an order declaring the deed void or appointing a new trustee (Form 12).

5. Duty of the trustee

(a) *Role as insolvency practitioner*

A person acts as an insolvency practitioner in relation to an individual by acting as trustee under a deed which is a deed of arrangement made for the benefit of his creditors by virtue of s 388(2)(b) of the Act of 1986. The "trustee under a deed" is treated as a trust corporation; even though he is sole trustee for the sale of land he alone can give a receipt for the purchase money (s 3 Law of Property (Amendment) Act 1926).

(b) *Remuneration*

There is no statutory reference to remuneration payable, which is therefore a matter for the trustee to arrange between the debtor and creditors. In *Re Zakon* [1940] 1 All ER 263 the deed never became effective by reason of the failure of the creditors to assent to it. The court however expressed an opinion that even in such a case, the trustee might be entitled to remuneration if he could show that his labours for the creditors had not been in vain. "Generally speaking, if a person chooses to come in and chooses to put his hand in his pocket and expend money in the matter, he is doing it entirely at his own risk."

The position as to remuneration is precarious since for the first three months from the execution of the deed it is always liable to be superseded by bankruptcy (s 19); except that in those circumstances under s 21, any expenses properly incurred by the trustee under the deed in the performance of any of the duties imposed on him are allowed or paid him by the trustee in the bankruptcy as a first charge on the estate (see page 231).

(c) *Security*

Within seven days from the date in which the statutory declaration (Form 3) certifying the assent of creditors is filed, the trustee must give security, ie as applicable to the individual arrangement, to the registrar in a sum equal to the estimated assets available for distribution amongst the unsecured creditors as is shown by the filed affidavits (s 11).

Before taking up any appointment, the practitioner who has been appointed to act as a trustee for an arrangement on behalf of the creditors, is required to have in force a specific penalty bond of up to £5m under regulation 10(1) (b) of the Insolvency Practitioners Regulations 1986 (see page 24). The trustee appears to come within the regulation by virtue of Sch 2, para 1(a)(x) as being a trustee under a trust deed. However, this interpretation would not appear to be the considered view of the Department of Trade and Industry who have written an opinion in reply to the author that that regulation and part II of Sch 2 do *not* in fact apply to such trustees.

If that were so, then the onus for the specific penalty bond is upon the Registrar of Bills of Sale under s 11, rather than the recognised professional body or the competent authority. Responsibility for the issue of a certificate that the security has been given (Form 11) would continue to be that of the registrar following filing of the statutory declaration certifying the assent of the creditors (Form 8) and the form of bond (Form 9). In addition, the general penalty bond is now also required in respect of such deeds by virtue of the deed trustee's inclusion as an insolvency practitioner under s 388(2)(b). By reg 10(1)(a) of the Insolvency Practitioners Regulations the bond must be in the sum of £250,000 to bring that trustee into line with his bankruptcy counterpart, thus overriding the provisions of the Deeds of Arrangement Act 1914 and the rules of 1925 (paras 24 - 42 as to security, audit and accounts).

(d) Accounting

The trustee must administer the deed properly and account fully for the assets which come into his hands. All moneys received are banked in an account opened in the name of the debtor's estate.

If a trustee under a deed fails to comply with these requirements the court may declare the deed void or may make an order appointing another trustee in the place of the trustee appointed by the deed. This may happen on the application of any creditor and after hearing such persons as the court may think fit.

There is an obligation by s 14 upon the trustee under a deed to send all the creditors a summary account (Form 13) of his receipts and payments every six months from the date of registration of the deed under s 14. The affidavit (Form 17) verifying his formal yearly accounts (on Form 15), lodged with the registrar, and sent to the Department of Trade and Industry, contains a clause whereby the trustee declares that he has duly carried out this obligation, setting out the dates when he did so. Failure to do so puts him in contempt of court and liable to be punished accordingly.

When the trustee carries on a business, he is personally liable for materials supplied to complete houses forming part of the debtor's estate; see *Hunt Bros* v *Colwell* [1939] 4 All ER 406). A trading account must be forwarded as a distinct account and the totals of receipts and payments are alone set out in the yearly account. (The trading account in Form 18 is to be on sheets size 13" x 16", the metric system not having yet arrived, by r 33).

(e) Audit

This is required where a majority of the creditors (who have assented to the deed) in number and value apply to the Department of Trade and Industry for an official audit of the trustee's accounts and in respect of which all the provisions of the Insolvency Act apply (see below).

The Department has power on the audit to require production of a certificate for the taxed costs of any solicitor whose costs have been paid or charged by the trustee, and to disallow the whole or any part of any costs in respect of which no certificate is produced.

Rules made under s 412 of the Insolvency Act 1986 relating to the institution and enforcement of an audit of the accounts of a trustee in bankruptcy (including the provisions as to fees) apply to the trustee's accounts, subject to any necessary modifications.

(f) Distribution

Once the costs of the realisations have been paid, the proceeds are divided among the creditors in accordance with the terms of the deed of arrangement (see r 36) and a list (Form 19) is sent to the Department of Trade and Industry.

If a trustee pays any creditor a larger sum in proportion to his claim than that paid to other creditors entitled to the benefit of the deed, then, unless the deed so authorises, or unless such payments are either made to a creditor entitled to enforce his claim by distress or are such as would be lawful in bankruptcy, he is guilty of an offence (s 17).

(g) Undistributed moneys

At any time after two years from the date of registration of the deed, the court may, on the application of the trustee or a creditor, or on the application of the debtor, order that all moneys representing unclaimed dividends and undistributed funds then in the hands of the trustee or under his control be paid into the Supreme Court or, if a county court has jurisdiction in the matter, into that court (s 16).

(h) Final account

When the trustee has fulfilled his obligations, and as soon as he has realised all the property included in any deed or so much as can probably be realised, and has distributed a final dividend, or final instalment of a composition, he transmits his final account to the Department of Trade and Industry together with an affidavit (Form 20) verifying the account (r 40).

(i) Release of the trustee

Unlike a trustee in bankruptcy, the trustee under a deed has no formal release and is automatically discharged from his duties when he has carried out the terms of the deed or is replaced.

6. Appointment of new trustee

(a) The power

By virtue of s 41(2) Trustee Act 1925 (replacing s 18 of the 1914 Act) the court has power to appoint a new trustee(s) whenever it is found expedient, difficult or impracticable to do so without the assistance of the court, in substitution for, or in addition to, any existing trustee, or where there is no trustee.

Section 36 of the 1925 Act gives wide power to appoint new or additional trustees subject to any contrary provisions in the trust deed (s 69(2)). A new trustee(s) may be appointed in place of a trustee who:

- seeks discharge
- dies
- remains outside the UK for a continuous period of twelve months
- refuses to act
- is unfit to act, eg becomes bankrupt
- is incapable of acting, eg because of age and mental disability
- is a minor
- is removed under a power of the trust instrument.

Further assistance may be obtained under s 363 (general control of the court) or s 375 Insolvency Act (power to review, rescind or vary any order).

(b) Applications for appointment

Applications for the appointment of a new trustee may be made by any creditor or trustee under s 58 of the 1925 Act. The appointment may be made by the person nominated by the trust instrument; by the surviving or continuing trustee, eg where retiring; by the personal representative; or by the court under s 41 of the 1925 Act. That section does not, however, operate to discharge any former or continuing trustee. Where an existing trustee is replaced, there does not seem to be any legal obligation to advise anyone other than the registrar of the new appointment. However, the creditors who are parties to the deed should clearly be informed at the same time.

It is also provided by s 36 of the 1925 Act that the person making the appointment may appoint himself and also that if he appoints someone whom the court would not appoint that appointment is not thereby invalidated nor is it a breach of trust where he is trustee: see *Briggs* v *Parsloe* [1937] 3 All ER 831.

7. Relationship with bankruptcy

The Act of 1914 now has to be considered alongside the Insolvency Act 1986 and its subordinate legislation. A summary of amendments to the 1914 Act effected by the 1986 Act is given below:

(a) Jurisdiction

By s 23 of the Act of 1914 jurisdiction is in the bankruptcy court in the district in which the debtor resided or carried on business at the date of the execution of the deed. By r 17 all applications (other than those under s 7 - rectification of register) are deemed to be proceedings in bankruptcy in accordance with the Insolvency Act and rules thereunder, but with such variations as the circumstances may require, and should be supported by affidavit.

(b) Accounts, audit and security

Rules 24 - 42 are now governed by the Insolvency Act, and the various rules and regulations made thereunder, pursuant to the incorporation into the 1914 Act of the requirement that the trustee be a licensed insolvency practitioner (s 388(2)(b)).

(c) Audit of trustee's accounts

By s 15 of the Act of 1914, the Insolvency Rules 1986 apply to the audit of the accounts (Deeds of Arrangement Rules 29 and 30), provisions as to fees, and certificate for the taxed costs of any solicitor where costs have been paid or charged by the trustee.

(d) Property

By s 30 of the Act of 1914 the meaning of property is as given by s 436, to include money, goods, things in action, land and every description of property wherever situated and also obligations and every description of interest, whether present or future or vested or contingent, arising out of, or incidental to, property. A right to litigation by deed of assignment is a properly constituted action: see *Ramsey* v *Hartley and others* [1977] 2 All ER 673.

Both contingent and future claims which before the Act were only provable in bankruptcy may now therefore benefit automatically under the deed. As to a discussion on future rent payable see *Re Casse, Robinson* v *Grigg* [1937] 2 All ER 710 (but which would otherwise have now been decided differently). For the rights of third parties against insurers, see page 73.

(e) Surety

The provisions of the law of bankruptcy were not, expressly or by implication imported into the terms of the covenant not to sue, and the express reservation of the rights and remedies of creditors against any surety, upon its proper construction, preserved the surety's consequential rights against the debtor: see *Cole and Another* v *Lynn* [1941] 3 All ER 502.

(f) Voluntary arrangements

The 1914 Act does not apply to approved voluntary arrangements under part VIII of the Insolvency Act for which no instrument, assignment or registration is *prima facie* required. It therefore provides the debtor with a clear alternative to the deed (s 260(3) 1986 Act.

II. THE ADMINISTRATION ORDER

1. Introduction

By Part VI of the County Courts Act 1984 ("CCA"), where a judgment has been obtained in a county court and the debtor is unable to pay the amount forthwith and alleges that his whole indebtedness - not just the unsecured debts - amounts to a sum not exceeding the county court limit (presently £5,000), inclusive of the debt for which the judgment was obtained, that court may make an order for the administration of his estate, by the county court.

2. Nature of the order

The order (Form N94) is made under Order 39 of the County Court Rules 1981, and provides for payment of the debts by instalments or otherwise, either in full or to such extent as appears practicable to the court in the circumstances of the case. It is also subject to any conditions as to future earnings or income which the court may think just.

The effect of the order is to protect the debtor and to allow the orderly collection of instalments from him, with a view to distribution *pari passu* amongst the creditors whose names appear in the schedule to the order. Creditors whose debts are proved after the order has been made (see 5 below) rank equally among themselves but behind the debtors whose debts were admitted or proved before the date of the order (r 18).

The *Cork Report* highlighted a crucial distinction between the administration order debtor and the bankruptcy debtor by pointing out that the former usually has few, if any, tangible assets but has earning capacity out of which he can pay, and can be ordered to pay, periodical sums for the benefit of his creditors.

Another distinction is that the administration order is administered and supervised by the county court and its staff; the debtor's estate is not, in fact, administered in the same sense as it would be in bankruptcy. However, the substantial purpose of an administration order is to ascertain details of the debtor's creditors; to give the debtor protection against further legal proceedings for the recovery and enforcement of those debts, and to arrange for the total or partial liquidation of all the debts by reasonable instalments out of earnings. As to the meaning of "debtor" see *Shah* v *Barnet LBC* [1983] 1 All ER 226 (HL).

Administration orders are not orders in bankruptcy and cannot *ipso facto* give rise to the making of a bankruptcy order. Application for an order can be made to any county court, not merely those having bankruptcy jurisdiction. However, disabilities on the revocation of an order are provided for by insolvency legislation. Where administration order proceedings have begun a bankruptcy petition cannot be presented, although the court may transfer the proceedings to bankruptcy jurisdiction.

3. Origination of the order

The debtor may file a request himself. The order may alternatively originate under the Attachment of Earnings Act 1971 or by virtue of the oral examination under O 25 r

2 of the County Court Rules, and the court must give leave to file such a petition.

(a) Debtor's request

The debtor files his own request (Form N 92) in the court for the district in which he resides or carries on business. The :equest states that a judgment was obtained against him for a certain sum and that he is unable to pay forthwith; he requests that an order (Form N94) be made for the administration of his estate under s 112 CCA providing for the payment of his debts in full (or to the extent of *x*p in the £) by instalments of £*y* for every month. A list of all creditors is appended. The statement must be verified on oath.

(b) Attachment of Earnings

By s 4 of the Attachment of Earnings Act 1971, where it appears to the court on an application for an attachment of earnings order (Form N93), that the debtor also has other debts, the court considers whether the case may be one in which all the debtor's liabilities should be dealt with together and that therefore an administration order should be made.

If the court is of the opinion that it may be such a case it has power, whether or not it makes the order applied for, to order the debtor to list all his creditors and the amounts owing to them respectively, with a view to making an administration order. If, on receipt of this list, it appears that his whole indebtedness amounts to not more than the £5,000 limit, the court may make the administration order in respect of the debtor's estate.

This is however subject to s 20(3) of the Administration of Justice Act 1965 which requires that before an administration order is made, notice is to be given to all the creditors, and thereafter restricts the right of any creditor to institute bankruptcy proceedings. It does not, however, prejudice the right of a debtor to apply for an administration order.

(c) Oral examination of judgment debtor

If, on examination under O 25 r 2 or otherwise, a debtor furnishes a list of his creditors and the respective amounts owed to them, the court may proceed as if the debtor had filed a request for an administration order (O 39 r 2(1).

4. Procedure

(a) Appointment

On the filing of a request for an administration order, or on the filing of a list where the administration order procedure derives from an oral examination or attachment of earnings application, the court appoints a day for hearing and gives at least fourteen days notice of it to the debtor and to each creditor named by the debtor (r 5).

Any creditor receiving such a notice from the court may object to any of the debts listed by the debtor. He must do so not less than seven days before the hearing date, stating the grounds of objection. The notice must be sent to the court, the debtor and the creditor to whose debt he objects. If notice is not given in this way, the leave of the court is needed to raise an objection (r 6).

(b) Procedure on day of hearing

At the hearing, any creditor, whether listed by the debtor or not, may attend and prove his debt. He may also object to another creditor's debt, provided he has given notice or has the leave of the court as described above. Every debt is taken to be proved unless objected to, or disallowed by the court, or required by the court to be supported by evidence. The court may adjourn proof of any debt. When doing so, it may also adjourn the decision whether or not to make the order, or may determine that question and if an order is made, any debt later proved may at that time be added to the debts scheduled in the order. Any creditor whose debt is admitted, and (with the leave of the court) any creditor whose debt has been adjourned for proof, may address the court on the question of whether or not the order should be made (r 7).

(c) The order

The order, if made, requires the debtor to pay the debts scheduled and all other debts then due and afterwards proved under the order in full (or to the extent of *x*p in the £) by instalments to the court.

When making an order, the court may require that it be subject to review at such intervals as may be specified. In such a case the court gives seven days notice of any date fixed for such a review, to the debtor and to every creditor who appeared on the making of the order (r 8). Order 39 r 14 provides that on such a review the court may vary, suspend or revoke the order. If after the making of the order, the debts are found to exceed £5,000 the administration order is not invalid, but may be set aside.

(d) Service of the order

Whether or not a review is ordered, notice of the order is sent by the court to the debtor; every creditor named by the debtor; any other creditor who has proved his debt; and any other court in which, to the knowledge of the registrar, judgment has been obtained against the debtor or in which proceedings are pending in respect of any debt scheduled to the order (r 9).

Order 39 contains provisions whereby creditors who did not have notice of the hearing may subsequently prove a debt or raise objections to the debts scheduled to the order.

Where an order has been made, notice of it is:

- (i) sent to the registry of county court judgments;
- (ii) posted in the office of the county court for the district in which the debtor resides, and

(iii) sent to every person whose name the debtor has notified to the court as being a creditor of his, or who has proved.

Where, in the opinion of the court in which the judgment was obtained, it would be convenient that the county court for the district in which the debtor resides or the majority of the creditors reside should administer the order, it causes a certificate for the judgment to be forwarded to that court, which then administers the order.

5. Effect of the order

The effect of an administration order is to protect the debtor from his creditors and to enable him to become discharged from his debts. Creditors may prove their debts before the registrar and so become scheduled creditors. Those that become creditors after the date of the order may also be scheduled as creditors for the amount of their proofs, but they receive no dividend until the creditors originally scheduled have been paid to the extent provided by the order.

An officer of the court has the conduct of the order and takes steps to enforce it, and to bring to the court's attention any matter which may make it desirable to review the order (r 13). From time to time he declares and distributes dividends among the creditors entitled (r 17) who are to rank equally (r 18).

So long as an administration order is in force a scheduled creditor may not, without leave of the court making the order, present or join in a bankruptcy petition against the debtor unless he was, within 28 days immediately preceding the petition, notified to the court as a creditor by the debtor, and unless the debt by virtue of which he presents, or joins in the petition, exceeds £1,500 (s 220(2) Act of 1985 amending s 112(4) CCA).

After the order is made, no creditor has any other remedy against the debtor in respect of any debt which the debtor has notified to the court or which has been scheduled, except by leave of the court and on such terms as the court may impose.

Any county court in which proceedings are pending against the debtor in respect of any debt so notified or scheduled must stay the proceedings but may allow costs already incurred. This requirement to stay proceedings does not, however, affect proceedings in bankruptcy against the debtor.

Where it appears to the registrar that the property of the debtor exceeds the minimum amount, presently £50 in value, at any time while the order is in force he must on request of any creditor and without fee, issue execution against the debtor's goods (s 115(1) & (1A) CCA, by virtue of s 220(4) of the 1985 Act).

A landlord or other person to whom any rent is due has a limited right at any time, either before or after the date of the order, to distrain upon the goods or effects of the debtor for the rent due to him. There is a limitation in that if the distress is levied after the date of the order, it is available only for six months' rent accrued due prior to the date of the order, and is not available for rent payable in respect of any period subsequent to the date when distress was levied. The landlord may, however, prove under the order for the surplus due for which the distress is not available.

6. Discharge

Money paid into court is applied in satisfying first the cost of administration (not to exceed 10p in the £ on the total amount of the debts) and then in payment of debts in accordance with the order.

Where the amount received is sufficient to pay each scheduled creditor to the extent provided by the order, the costs of the plaintiff in the action in respect of which the order was made, and the costs of administration, the order is superseded and the debtor is discharged from his debts to the scheduled creditors.

7. Disabilities on revocation

Where a person fails to make a payment under an administration order the court which is administering that person's estate may revoke the order by serving Form N95 on the debtor (s 429 Insolvency Act). He may not then, either alone or jointly with another person, obtain credit of £250 or more or enter into any transaction in the course of or for the purpose of any business in which he is directly or indirectly engaged without disclosing the fact that s 429 applies to him. "Obtaining credit" includes the case where goods are bailed or hired to a person under a hire-purchase agreement or agreed to be sold to him under a conditional sale agreement, and the case where he is paid in advance, whether in money or otherwise, for the supply of goods or services.

The court may also make an order directing that s 429 of the 1986 Act and s 12 of the Company Directors Disqualification Act 1986 apply to the person for such period not exceeding two years as may be specified in the order.

A person who contravenes s 429 is guilty of an offence and liable to imprisonment on indictment for two years or a fine or both, and in summary proceedings to imprisonment for six months or the statutory maximum, or both.

III DECEASED'S ESTATE BEING ADMINISTERED OTHERWISE THAN IN BANKRUPTCY

Section 115(1) Supreme Court Act allows the High Court to grant administration to a trust corporation either solely or jointly with another person and that corporation may act accordingly as administrator. A "trust corporation" in relation to a bankrupt's property (or property the subject of a deed of arrangement) is the respective trustees thereof (s 128).

Section 113 enables the court to issue a grant of representation in respect of part of the deceased's estate, but such a grant may not sever the estate where part is known to be insolvent, except in the case of a trust estate in which the deceased had no beneficial interest. An order is required to apply for a grant limited to part of the estate. Application is made *ex parte* on affidavit to the registry to which the application for the grant will be made. The affidavit must state:

(i) whether the grant is to be in respect of real or personal estate only or any part thereof, or in respect of a trust estate only;
(ii) that the estate is insolvent;
(iii) that all persons entitled to a grant in respect of the whole estate in priority to the applicant have been settled.

So far as the respective rights of the secured and unsecured creditors are concerned, however, the law of bankruptcy does apply to debts and liabilities provable, to the valuation of future and contingent liabilities and to the priorities of debts and other payments including the reasonable funeral, testamentary and administration expenses which have priority over the preferential debts listed in Sch 6 to the Act (see page 233).

Where an administration is operative outside insolvency law, it follows that there is no requirement to appoint a qualified insolvency practitioner as administrator or executor.

Appendix 1

Insolvency practitioners

1. Records

Schedule 3 of The Insolvency Practitioners Regulations 1986 (SI 1986 No 1995) sets out the form of record to be kept by the insolvency practitioner in respect of the estate. This applies to an insolvency practitioner acting, *inter alia*, as:

- (a) trustee in bankruptcy (see Chapter 11);
- (b) interim receiver (see Chapter 6);
- (c) trustee under a deed of arrangement (see Chapter 23);
- (d) supervisor of a voluntary arrangement (see Chapter 1);
- (e) administrator of the estate of a deceased person (see Chapter 21);

(s 388); and in respect of any security required under s 390 (3) (see Chapter 2).

The "form of record" prescribed in Schedule 3 is as follows:

"Insolvency Practitioner No.
NAME OF PRACTITIONER:
PRINCIPAL BUSINESS ADDRESS:
AUTHORISING BODY (INCLUDING COMPETENT AUTHORITY):

1. NAME OF PERSON IN RELATION TO WHOM THE PRACTITIONER IS ACTING
2. NATURE OF INSOLVENCY PROCEEDING
3. PROGRESS OF ADMINISTRATION

   (entries should be made in respect of all matters applicable to the particular case)

   - (i) Date of commencement of insolvency proceeding
   - (ii) Date of Appointment as insolvency practitioner in insolvency proceeding
   - (iii) Date of Appointment notified to
     - (a) Registrar of Companies
     - (b) Accountant in Bankruptcy
   - (iv) (a) Date of issue of certificate of specific cover under security requirements
     - (b) Amount of specific cover (£)
     - (c) Name of surety/cautioner
     - (d) Date of certificate of cover filed/delivered
   - (v) (a) Date of increase in amount of specific cover
     - (b) Revised amount (£) of cover
     - (c) Date further certificate of cover filed/delivered
   - (vi) Date surety/cautioner notified of termination of office
   - (vii) (a) Date of Meeting of Members
     - (b) Date of First Meeting of Creditors or of statutory meeting in sequestration
       - (i) to consider an administrator's proposals

(ii) to consider an administrative receiver's report
(iii) in liquidation or bankruptcy
(iv) to consider a voluntary arrangement proposal
(v) in sequestration of creditors according to a trust deed for creditors

(viii) Date(s) and purpose of any subsequent Meeting(s)
.... (1)
.... (2)
.... (3) et seq

(ix) Disqualification of directors - performance of practitioner's duty under section 7 of the Company Directors' Disqualification Act 1986 to report the conduct of directors:-
(a) Date conduct report submitted to Secretary of State
(b) (i) Date return due
(ii) Date return submitted to Secretary of State
(c) Date further report (s) submitted, if any

(x) Date of Vacation of Office

(xi) Date of Release or Discharge (including date of certificate granted by the Accountant in Bankruptcy)

(xii) Final Notice to, or Meeting of, Creditors

4. DISTRIBUTION TO CREDITORS AND OTHERS
(i) For each payment to Preferential/Preferred Creditors
- Date
- Amount (p in £)
(ii) For each payment to Unsecured Creditors
- Date
- Amount (p in £)
(iii) For each Return of Capital
- Date

5. FILING OF STATUTORY RETURNS AND ACCOUNTS
(Secretary of State, Registrar of Companies, Accountant in Bankruptcy)
(i) In respect of each interim return/abstract of receipts and payments
Date Due
Date Filed
(ii) Final return/abstract of accounts
Date Due
Date Filed"

2. Academic qualifications

The academic requirements which an unqualified insolvency practitioner must have under s 393(2)(b) (see Chapter 2) are set out in Schedule 1 to the Regulations. The Schedule applies only to an applicant who is aged less than 35 on or before 15 December 1986 and who has not held an authorisation under s 393 of the Insolvency Act 1986 or s 5 of the Insolvency Act 1985:

"PART I

1. A degree (other than an honorary degree) conferred by a University in the United Kingdom or Republic of Ireland or by the Council for National Academic Awards.

2. A General Certificate of Education or a Senior Certificate from a Secondary Education Board listed in Part II of this Schedule, in five subjects which must

include:-

(a) English Language:

(b) 2 Advanced level passes or Higher grade passes obtained in one sitting in subjects included in the list in Part III of this Schedule ("acceptable subjects"):

(c) 2 other Ordinary level or Ordinary grade passes at appropriate grades (see note 1) in acceptable subjects or Advanced level or Higher grade passes in acceptable subjects.

NOTE 1: The appropriate grades are grades A, B and C at the Ordinary level of the GCE or where relevant Grades 1 to 6 at that level.

PART II

Associated Examining Board
University of Cambridge Local Examination Syndicate
University of Durham
Joint Matriculation Board
University of London
Department of Education or Ministry of Education, Northern Ireland
Northern Ireland General Certificate of Education Examinations Board
Oxford and Cambridge Schools Examination Board
University of Oxford Delegacy of Local Examinations
Southern Universities' Joint Board for Schools Examinations
Welsh Joint Education Committee
Scottish Examination Board

PART III

Mathematics; Sciences; Modern Languages; Welsh; Gaelic; Classics; History; Geography; Economics and Politics; English Literature; Law; Music; Religious Knowledge; Modern Studies; General Studies; Principles of Accounts; Theatre Studies; Design; Home Economics"

3. Requirements for security or caution

For the purposes of s 390(3)(b) (see page 24) the requirements for security for the proper performance of an insolvency practitioner are that:

(a) there is in force a bond complying with Sch 2 Part I of the Regulations in the general penalty sum of £250,000;

(b) there is issued under that bond a certificate of specific penalty to a value not less than the value of the assets calculated in accordance with Sch 2 Part II; and

(c) a further certificate is issued should it later appear that the assets were under-valued.

The provisions of Sch 2 are as follows:

PART I

The bond referred to in Regulation 10 shall be a bond in a form approved by the Secretary of State which contains provision whereby:-

(i) a surety or cautioner undertakes to be jointly and severally liable with the insolvency practitioner for the proper performance by the practitioner of the duties and obligations imposed upon the practitioner by the [Insolvency Act 1986] ...... and the subordinate legislation made under the [Insolvency Act 1986] ....

(ii) the liability of the surety or cautioner and the practitioner is in both a general penalty sum and a specific penalty sum in respect of each person in respect of whom the practitioner acts and is limited to a sum equivalent to the losses caused by the fraud and dishonesty of the practitioner.

(iii) a certificate is issued by the surety accepting liability in respect of the practitioner acting in relation to a particular person in the amount of the specific penalty, and

(iv) any claims made under the bond are made firstly in respect of the specific penalty sum.

PART II

1. Subject to paragraph 3 below for the purposes of Regulation 10(1)(b) the value of a person's assets shall be:-

(a) where the practitioner is appointed to act as:-

(i) an interim receiver;

(ii) a trustee in bankruptcy;

(iii) an administrator of the estate of a deceased individual;

(iv) a supervisor of a voluntary arrangement approved by a company under Part I of the Act;

(v) a supervisor of a voluntary arrangement proposed by an individual and approved under Part VIII of the Act;

(vi) a provisional liquidator;

(vii) a liquidator;

(viii)an administrator appointed under Part II of the Act;

(ix) an interim or permanent trustee in sequestration;

(x) a trustee under a trust deed for creditors;

the value at the date of the appointment of the practitioner estimated by him having regard (where appropriate) to paragraph 2 of this Part of the Schedule;

(b) where the practitioner is appointed to act as an administrative receiver an amount equivalent to that part of the assets of the company to which the practitioner is appointed which at the date of the appointment would appear to be available for the unsecured creditors of the company, whether in respect of the preferential debts of the company or otherwise, were the company to go into liquidation at the date of the appointment.

2. In estimating the value of a person's assets, the practitioner shall have regard to:-

(a) in a case specified in subparagraphs 1(a)(i) - (vii) and (x) above, the estimated value of those assets disclosed in any statement of affairs in respect of such cases and any comments of creditors or the official receiver on that statement; and

(b) in a case specified in subparagraph 1(a)(viii), the estimated value of the assets of the company as disclosed in any report on the company's affairs prepared pursuant to Rule 2.2 of the Insolvency Rules 1986 or, as the case may be, pursuant to Rule 2.1 of the Insolvency (Scotland) Rules 1986;

(c) in a case specified in subparagraph 1(a)(ix) the estimated value of those assets disclosed, as the case may be, by the most recently available of -

(i) the debtor's list of assets and liabilities under section 19 of the Bankruptcy Act;

(ii) the preliminary statement under section 20 of that Act; or

(iii) the final statement of the debtor's affairs by the interim trustee under section 23 of that Act.

3. In any case where the value of a person's assets estimated in accordance with paragraphs 1 and 2 above is less than £5,000 the value of those assets shall for the purposes of this Part of the Schedule, be deemed to be £5,000.

4. In any case where the value of a person's assets estimated in accordance with paragraph 1 and 2 above is less than £5m the value of those assets shall, for the purposes of this Part of the Schedule, be deemed to be £5m."

Appendix 2

Practice Direction: Bankruptcy Practice

10 December 1986 [1987] 2 All ER 1000

1. As from 29 December 1986 (the appointed day) and until further notice, the order of Cave J dated 1 January 1884 as amended shall cease to have effect, and the following directions shall apply to insolvency proceedings in relation to individuals:
2. The following applications shall be made direct to the judge and unless otherwise ordered shall be heard in open court: (i) applications for the committal of any person to prison for contempt; (ii) applications for an extension of time to apply to set aside a statutory demand served under s 268 of the Insolvency Act 1986 and to restrain presentation of the petition in the meantime; (iii) other applications for injunctions or for the modification or discharge of injunctions; (iv) applications for interlocutory relief or directions after the matter has been referred to the judge.
3. All other applications shall be made to the registrar in the first instance. He shall give any necessary directions and may, if the application is within his jurisdiction to determine, in his discretion hear and determine it himself or refer it to the judge.
4. The following matters shall be heard in open court: (i) the public examination of debtors; (ii) opposed applications for discharge or for the suspension or the lifting of the suspension of discharge; (iii) opposed applications for leave to be a director; (iv) in any case where the petition was presented or the receiving order or order for adjudication was made before the appointed day, those matters and applications specified in r 8 of the Bankruptcy Rules 1952 SI 1952/2113; (v) all matters and applications heard by the judge, except matters and applications referred by the registrar to be heard by the judge in chambers or directed by the judge to be so heard.
5. All cases where the petition is presented on or after the appointed day shall be listed under the name of the debtor, and all adjourned applications for leave to withdraw a petition presented on or after the appointed day on the ground that the debt has been paid or compounded shall be heard in chambers and shall be listed so as to indicate the nature of the application.
6. All appeals and applications to the Divisional Court in cases where the petition was presented or the receiving order or order for adjudication was made before the appointed day shall be listed for hearing on Mondays or so soon thereafter as the case can be heard.
7. Each term two judges of the division will sit to hear insolvency cases. One of them will be primarily concerned to hear cases affecting individual debtors (the bankruptcy judge). As often as may be necessary he will sit with another judge of the division to hear appeals and applications to the Divisional Court. Subject thereto, the bankruptcy judge will sit alone to hear (i) applications

made to him direct, (ii) applications and matters referred to him by the registrar in bankruptcy of the High Court and (iii) appeals from county courts or registrars in bankruptcy of the High Court under s 375(2) of the Insolvency Act 1986.

8. Applications to extend the time to apply to set aside a statutory demand and to restrain presentation of a bankruptcy petition, and other ex parte applications to the judge, should be made to the bankruptcy judge, but in cases of urgency and where the bankruptcy judge is not available they may be made to the judge hearing ordinary motions, who will hear them for the bankruptcy judge.

Note: Other Practice Directions appear in the relevant parts of the text.

Appendix 3

Bankruptcy courts

Bankruptcy county courts by circuits and groups

Midland & Oxford Circuit

Birmingham	-	Banbury, Birmingham, Coventry, Northampton, Oxford, Peterborough, Warwick
Nottingham	-	Boston, Chesterfield, Derby, Grimsby, Leicester, Lincoln, Nottingham, Scunthorpe
Stafford	-	Burton-on-Trent, Dudley, Hereford, Kidderminster, Shrewsbury, Stafford, Stoke-on-Trent, Stourbridge, Walsall, Wolverhampton, Worcester
North Eastern Circuit		
Leeds	-	Bradford, Dewsbury, Halifax, Harrogate, Huddersfield, Leeds, Wakefield, York
Newcastle-upon-Tyne		Darlington, Durham, Middlesbrough, Newcastle-upon-Tyne, Stockton-on-Tees, Sunderland
Sheffield	-	Barnsley, Doncaster, Kingston-upon-Hull, Scarborough, Sheffield
Northern Circuit		
Liverpool	-	Birkenhead, Liverpool
Manchester	-	Ashton-under-Lyne, Bolton, Manchester, Oldham, Rochdale, Salford, Stockport, Wigan
Preston	-	Barrow, Blackburn, Blackpool, Burnley, Carlisle, Kendal, Lancaster, Preston, Whitehaven, Workington
South Eastern Circuit		
Chelmsford	-	Bedford, Cambridge, Chelmsford, Colchester and Clacton, Great Yarmouth, Hertford, Ipswich, King's Lynn, Luton, Norwich, Southend
Kingston-upon-Thames	-	Aylesbury, Kingston-upon-Thames, Newbury, Reading, St Albans, Slough
Greater London	-	Croydon
Maidstone	-	Brighton, Canterbury, Chichester, Croydon, Eastbourne, Hastings, Maidstone, Tunbridge Wells
Wales & Chester Circuit		
Cardiff	-	Aberdare, Aberystwyth, Blackwood, Bridgend, Cardiff, Carmarthen, Haverfordwest, Merthyr Tydfil, Neath, Newport, Pontypridd, Swansea
Chester/Mold	-	Bangor, Chester, Crewe, Macclesfield, Welshpool and Newtown, Portmadoc, Rhyl, Warrington, Wrexham

Western Circuit

Bristol	-	Bath, Bristol, Cheltenham, Gloucester, Swindon, Thornbury
Exeter	-	Barnstaple, Bridgwater, Exeter, Plymouth, Taunton, Torquay, Truro, Yeovil
Winchester	-	Bournemouth, Newport (IoW), Portsmouth, Salisbury, Southampton, Winchester

Alternative courts for presentation of petitions

See page 36 for the rules as to venue for the presentation of a debtor's petition. Rule 6.40(3) provides that, in a county court case, the petition may be presented to the debtor's nearest full-time court if that is more expedient. Schedule 2 to the Rules identifies nearest full-time courts as follows:

Debtor's own county court	*Nearest full-time court*
ABERDARE	CARDIFF
ABERYSTWYTH	CARDIFF
ASHTON -U- LYNE & STALYBRIDGE	MANCHESTER
AYLESBURY	LUTON
BANBURY	LUTON or GLOUCESTER
BANGOR	BIRKENHEAD
BARNSLEY	SHEFFIELD
BARNSTAPLE	EXETER
BARROW-IN-FURNESS	BLACKPOOL
BATH	BRISTOL
BEDFORD	LUTON
BLACKBURN	PRESTON
BLACKWOOD	CARDIFF
BOSTON	NOTTINGHAM
BRIDGEND	CARDIFF
BRIDGWATER	BRISTOL
BURNLEY	BOLTON or PRESTON
BURTON-ON-TRENT	LEICESTER
BURY ST EDMUNDS	CAMBRIDGE
CANTERBURY	CROYDON or ROMFORD
CARLISLE	PRESTON or BLACKPOOL
CARMARTHEN	CARDIFF
CHELMSFORD	SOUTHEND
CHELTENHAM	GLOUCESTER
CHESTER	BIRKENHEAD
CHESTERFIELD	SHEFFIELD
COLCHESTER	SOUTHEND
COVENTRY	BIRMINGHAM
CREWE	STOKE
DARLINGTON	MIDDLESBROUGH
DERBY	NOTTINGHAM
DEWSBURY	LEEDS
DONCASTER	SHEFFIELD
DUDLEY	BIRMINGHAM
DURHAM	NEWCASTLE
EASTBOURNE	BRIGHTON
GREAT GRIMSBY	HULL

GREAT YARMOUTH	NORWICH
GUILDFORD	CROYDON
HALIFAX	LEEDS
HARROGATE	LEEDS
HASTINGS	BRIGHTON
HAVERFORDWEST	CARDIFF
HEREFORD	GLOUCESTER
HERTFORD	LUTON
HUDDERSFIELD	LEEDS
IPSWICH	NORWICH or SOUTHEND
KENDAL	BLACKPOOL
KIDDERMINSTER	BIRMINGHAM
KING'S LYNN	NORWICH
LANCASTER	BLACKPOOL
LEOMINSTER	GLOUCESTER
LINCOLN	NOTTINGHAM
MACCLESFIELD	STOKE
MAIDSTONE	CROYDON
MEDWAY	CROYDON
MERTHYR TYDFIL	CARDIFF
MILTON KEYNES	LUTON
NEATH	CARDIFF
NEWBURY	READING
NEWPORT (GWENT)	CARDIFF
NEWPORT (I.O.W.)	SOUTHAMPTON
NORTHAMPTON	LUTON
OXFORD	READING
PETERBOROUGH	CAMBRIDGE
PONTYPRIDD	CARDIFF
PORTMADOC	BIRKENHEAD or STOKE
ROCHDALE	BOLTON
RHYL	BIRMINGHAM
SALISBURY	BOURNEMOUTH or SOUTHAMPTON
SCARBOROUGH	YORK, HULL or MIDDLESBROUGH
SCUNTHORPE	HULL
SHREWSBURY	STOKE
ST ALBANS	LUTON
STAFFORD	STOKE
STOCKTON-ON-TEES	MIDDLESBROUGH
STOCKPORT	MANCHESTER
STOURBRIDGE	BIRMINGHAM
SUNDERLAND	NEWCASTLE
SWANSEA	CARDIFF
SWINDON	GLOUCESTER
TAUNTON	EXETER
TORQUAY	EXETER
TRURO	PLYMOUTH
TUNBRIDGE WELLS	CROYDON
WAKEFIELD	LEEDS
WARRINGTON	SALFORD
WARWICK	BIRMINGHAM
WELSHPOOL	STOKE

WEST BROMWICH	BIRMINGHAM
WEYMOUTH	BOURNEMOUTH
WIGAN	BOLTON
WINCHESTER	SOUTHAMPTON
WORCESTER	GLOUCESTER
WORKINGTON	PRESTON
WREXHAM	BIRKENHEAD or STOKE
YEOVIL	EXETER or BRISTOL

Appendix 4

Statutory Instruments related to individual insolvency

SR&O/SI No	*Title*	*Date in force*
1925 No 795	The Deeds of Arrangement Rules 1925	1 October 1925
1981 No 1687	The County Court Rules 1981	1 September 1982
1982 No 586	The County Court (Forms) Rules 1982	1 September 1982
1984 No 887	The Deeds of Arrangement Fees Order 1984	1 August 1984
1986 No 952	The Insolvency Practitioners Tribunal (Conduct of Investigations) Rules 1986	10 June 1986
1986 No 1764	The Insolvency Practitioners (Recognised Professional Bodies) Order 1986	10 November 1986
1986 No 1924	The Insolvency Act 1985 (Commencement No 5) Order 1986	29 December 1986
1986 No 1925	The Insolvency Rules 1986	29 December 1986
1986 No 1994	The Insolvency Regulations 1986	29 December 1986
1986 No 1995	The Insolvency Practitioners Regulations 1986	29 December 1986
1986 No 1996	The Insolvency Proceedings (Monetary Limits) Order 1986	29 December 1986
1986 No 1999	The Administration of Insolvent Estates of Deceased Persons Order 1986	29 December 1986
1986 No 2001	The Insolvency (Amendment of Subordinate Legislation) Order 1986	29 December 1986
1986 No 2030	The Insolvency Fees Order 1986	29 December 1986
1986 No 2116	The Land Registration (Companies & Insolvency) Rules 1986	29 December 1986
1986 No 2123	The Co-operation of Insolvency Courts (Designation of Relevant Countries and Territories) Order 1986	29 December 1986
1986 No 2142	The Insolvent Partnerships Order 1986	29 December 1986
1986 No 2143	The County Court Fees (Amendment No 2) Order 1986	29 December 1986
1986 No 2144	The Supreme Court Fees (Amendment No 2) Order 1986	29 December 1986
1986 No 2245	The Insolvency (Land Registration Rules) Order 1986	28 December 1986
1986 No 2247	The Insolvency Practitioners (Amendment) Regulations 1986	29 December 1986

1986 No 2283	Employment Protection (Variation of Limits) Order 1986	1 April 1987
1987 No 1398	The Insolvency (Amendment of Subordinate Legislation) Order 1987 (provides that the legislation as amended by SI 1986 No 2001 will only affect new Act cases).	1 September 1987
1987 Draft	The Insolvency (Amendment) Rules 1987 (minor corrections to rules and forms arising from practical difficulties)	December 1987
1987 Draft	The Insolvency (Amendment) Regulations 1987 (minor amendments to the 1986 Regulations)	December 1987

Appendix 5

Fees and remuneration

The fees shown in this Appendix are correct as at September 1987

1. Fees payable in individual insolvency
(The Insolvency Fees Order 1986 (SI 1986 No 2030)

VAT is payable on the following fees

"*Fee no.*	*Description of proceedings*	*Amount - £*
1.	On registration with the Secretary of State of an individual voluntary arrangement under Part VIII of the Act	27.50
2.	For the performance by the official receiver of his general duties as official receiver on the making of a bankruptcy order	245.00
3.	For all official stationery, printing, postage and telephone charges, including notices to creditors in respect of the first meeting of creditors and of sittings of the court -	
	(i) for a number of creditors not exceeding 25	135.00
	(ii) for every additional 10 creditors or part thereof	30.00
4.	(a) Where the official receiver decides to summon a meeting of creditors under section 293(1), for the holding of that meeting	50.00
	(b) Where any other meeting of creditors is held by the official receiver, for summoning and holding the meeting -	
	(i) for a number of creditors not exceeding 25	120.00
	(ii) for every additional 10 creditors or part thereof	15.00
5.	On the payments made by the official receiver into the Insolvency Services Account as a result of the performance of his functions as receiver and manager under section 287 (after deducting any sums paid to secured creditors in respect of their securities and any sums spent in carrying on the business of the debtor) a fee in accordance with the following scale -	
	(i) on the first £5,000 or fraction thereof	per cent 20.00
	(ii) on the next £5,000 or fraction thereof	per cent 15.00
	(iii) on the next £90,000 or fraction thereof	per cent 10.00
	(iv) on all further sums	per cent 5.00
6.	Where the official receiver, acting as receiver and manager under section 287, makes any payment to creditors, a fee of one-half the scale fee calculated under Fee No. 5 on the amount of the payment.	
7.	On any application to the court for the rescission or annulment of a bankruptcy order or relating to the discharge	

	of a bankrupt, where the official receiver attends or makes a report to the court	67.00
	for each further attendance or report	35.00
8.	Where the official receiver supervises a special manager or the carrying on of a debtor's business - for each week or part thereof	67.00
9.	For taking an affidavit, affirmation or declaration, except affidavits of debt -	
	(i) for each person making the same	3.00
	(ii) for each exhibit or schedule to be marked	0.75
10.	On the insertion in the Gazette by the Secretary of State or the official receiver of any notice authorised by the Act or the Rules	16.25
11.	On each application by a trustee to the Secretary of State or to the official receiver to exercise the powers of a creditors' committee by virtue of section 302 or rule 6.166	21.00
12.	On an application to the Secretary of State under regulation 5 and 15 for a payment from the Insolvency Services Account or for the re-issue of a cheque, money order or payable order in respect of moneys standing to the credit of the Insolvency Services Account, for each cheque, money order or payable order issued or re-issued	0.50
13.	For the performance by the Secretary of State of his general duties under the Act, the Rules and the Regulations in relation to the administration of the estates of individuals, a fee in accordance with the following scale, calculated on the amount paid into the Insolvency Services Account by trustees under regulation 4 and by the official receiver as receiver and manager under section 287 (after deducting any sums paid to secured creditors in respect of their securities and any sums spent out of money received in carrying on the business of the debtor):-	
	(a) on the first £50,000 or fraction thereof	per cent 10.00
	(b) on the next £50,000 or fraction thereof	per cent 7.50
	(c) on the next £400,000 or fraction thereof	per cent 6.50
	(d) on the next £500,000 or fraction thereof	per cent 3.75
	(e) on the next £4,000,000 or fraction thereof	per cent 2.00
	(f) on all further amounts	per cent 1.00"

2. County Court fees

(The County Court Fees (Amendment No 2) Order 1986, SI 1986 No 2143)

No & Description of fee	*Amount*
"9. COMPANIES ACT 1985 & INSOLVENCY ACT 1986	
(i) On entering a bankruptcy petition -	
(a) if presented by a debtor or the personal representative of a deceased debtor	£15
(b) if presented by a creditor or other person	£45
(ii) On entering any other petition One fee only is payable where more than one petition is presented in relation to a partnership	£40
(iii) On an application to the Court (except by the Official Receiver	

when applying only in that capacity or on an application to set aside a statutory demand)-

	(a) for hearing before a registrar	£10
	(b) for hearing before a judge	£15
(iv)	On the hearing of a public examination This fee is not payable until after a hearing on which the debtor has appeared and has been examined."	£15

3. Remuneration of the official receiver as trustee

(The Insolvency Regulations 1986, SI 1986 No 1994, Regulations 19, 20 & 21)

"*Official receiver's remuneration while acting as liquidator or trustee calculated as a percentage of the value of assets realised or distributed*

19. Subject to Regulation 22 below, when he is the liquidator or trustee of the insolvent, the official receiver's remuneration for his services as such shall be calculated on the scales in the Table below, as a percentage of the value of the assets of the insolvent realised (after deducting any sums paid to secured creditors in respect of their securities and any sums spent out of money received in carrying on the business of the insolvent) and of the assets distributed to the insolvent's creditors (including payments made in respect of preferential debts) and, in the case of a company, to contributories.

TABLE

The realisation scale		
i.	on the first £5,000 or fraction thereof	20%
ii.	on the next £5,000 or fraction thereof	15%
iii.	on the next £90,000 or fraction thereof	10%
iv.	on all further sums realised	5%
The distribution scale		
i.	on the first £5,000 or fraction thereof	10%
ii.	on the next £5,000 or fraction thereof	7.5%
iii.	on the next £90,000 or fraction thereof	5%
iv.	on all further sums distributed	2.5%

Official receiver's general remuneration while acting as interim receiver, provisional liquidator, liquidator or trustee

20. ....

(2) Table 1 shall be used when calculating the remuneration of the official receiver of the London insolvency district and Table 2 shall be used when calculating the remuneration of the official receiver of any other district.

(3) The Tables referred to .... above are:

TABLE 1

Official	*Total hourly rate in £*
Official receiver	33
Deputy/Assistant Official Receiver	26
Senior Examiner	22
Examiner	18

TABLE 2

Official	*Total hourly rate in £*
Official receiver	24
Deputy/Assistant Official Receiver	19
Senior Examiner	16
Examiner	13

Official receiver's remuneration while acting as liquidator, provisional liquidator, trustee or interim receiver for the transfer or conveyance of property subject to a charge

21. When he is a liquidator, provisional liquidator, trustee or interim receiver appointed under section 286, the official receiver's remuneration for the transfer or conveyance at the request of a secured creditor or a receiver appointed by such a creditor of property subject to any charge over the property created by the insolvent shall be 0.5 per cent of the sale price of the property or £110, whichever is the greater."

Appendix 6

Forms

Bankruptcy forms under the Insolvency Rules 1986

(SI 1986 No 1925)

The forms are for use in either High Court or county court, and by Rule 12.7(2) they should be used with such variations, if any, as the circumstances may require.

General forms under The Insolvency Rules 1986

Forms under The Insolvency Regulations 1986
(SI 1986 No 1994)

Forms under The Insolvent Partnerships Order 1986
(SI 1986 No 2142)

Forms under the Administration of Insolvent Estates of Deceased Persons Order 1986
(SI 1986 No 1999)

Forms under the Deeds of Arrangement Rules 1925
(SR&O 1925 No 795)

Rule 6.1 **Form 6.1**

Statistical Demand under section 268(1)(a) of the Insolvency Act 1986

Debt for Liquidated Sum Payable Immediately

In Bankruptcy

Warning:

- This is an important document. You **must** deal with this demand within 21 days of its service upon you or you could be made bankrupt and your property and goods taken away from you. Please read this demand and notes carefully.
- If you are in any doubt about your position, you should seek advice **immediately** from a solicitor or your nearest Citizens Advice Bureau.
- There are additional notes overleaf.

Demand

To ______________________________

Address ______________________________

____

This demand is served on you by the creditor:

Name ______________________________

Address ______________________________

____

The creditor claims that you owe the following debt and that it is payable immediately and, to the extent of the sum demanded, is unsecured:

When Incurred (1)	Description of Debt (2)	Amount due as at the date of this demand (3)

Amount of Debt £ [ ]

If creditor issuing this demand is a Minister of the Crown or a Government Department, is it intended to present a bankruptcy petition in the High Court?

- Yes/No

The creditor demands that you pay the above debt or secure or compound for it to the creditor's satisfaction

Signature ______________________________

Name (BLOCK LETTERS) ______________________________

Date ______________________________

Position with or relationship to creditor: ______________________________

______________________________ duly authorised

Address ______________________________

Tel. No. ______________________________

Ref. ______________________________

N.B. The person making this demand must complete the whole of this page and parts A, B and C on page 2

Notes for Creditor

- If the creditor is entitled to the debt by way of assignment, details of the original creditor and any intermediary assignees should be given in part C on page 2.
- If the amount of debt includes interest, details should be given in column (2), including the grounds upon which interest is charged. The amount of interest must be shown separately in column (3).
- Any other charge accruing due from time to time may be claimed. The amount **or** rate of the charge must be identified and the grounds on which it is claimed must be stated.
- In either case the amount claimed must be limited to that which has accrued due at the date of the demand.
- If the creditor holds any security the amount of debt should be the sum the creditor is prepared to regard as unsecured for the purposes of this demand. Brief details of the total debt should be included in column (2), and the nature of the security and the value put upon it by the creditor, as at the date of the demand, must be specified.
- If signatory is a solicitor or other agent of the creditor the name of his/her firm should be given.

Part A

Appropriate Court for setting aside demand

Rule 6.4(2) of the Insolvency Rules 1986 states that the appropriate court is the court to which you would have to present your own bankruptcy petition in accordance with Rule 6.40(1) and (2). In accordance with these rules on present information the appropriate Court is [the High Court of Justice] [court] (address)

Any application by you to set aside this demand should be made to that court.

Part B

The person or persons to whom any communication regarding this demand may be addressed is/are:

____

Address ________________________________

____

Tel. No. ________________________________

Part C

For completion if the creditor is entitled to the debt by way of assignment

	Name	Date(s) of Assignment
Original creditor		
Assignees		

How to comply with a statutory demand or have it set aside

If you wish to avoid a bankruptcy petition being presented against you, you must pay the debt set out on page 1 of this notice within the period of 21 days of service upon you. Alternatively, you can attempt to come to a settlement with the creditor. To do this you should:

- inform the person or persons (or one of the persons) named in part B above immediately that you are willing and able to offer security for the debt to the creditor's satisfaction; or
- inform the person or persons (or one of the persons) named in part B immediately that you are willing and able to compound for the debt to the creditor's satisfaction.

If you dispute the demand in whole or in part you should:

- contact the person or persons (or one of the persons) named in part B immediately

If you consider that you have grounds to have this notice set aside or if you do not receive a satisfactory written reply from the person or persons (or one of the persons) named in part B before the expiration of 18 days after the service you should:

- apply without delay to the appropriate court shown in part A above to have the notice set aside.

Remember: You have only 21 days from the date of service on you of this document before the creditor may present a bankruptcy petition.

Rule 6.1 **Form 6.2**

Statutory Demand under section 268(1)(a) of the Insolvency Act 1986
Debt for Liquidated Sum Payable Immediately Following a Judgment or Order of the Court

In Bankruptcy

Warning

- This is an important document. You **must** deal with this demand within 21 days of the service upon you or you could be made bankrupt and your property and goods taken away from you. Please read this demand and notes carefully.
- If you are in any doubt about your position, you should seek advice **immediately** from a solicitor or your nearest Citizens Advice Bureau
- There are additional notes overleaf

Demand

To ______________________________

Address ______________________________

____

This demand is served on you by the creditor:

Name ______________________________

Address ______________________________

____

The creditor claims that you owe the following debt and that it is payable immediately and, to the extent of the sum demanded, is unsecured:

When Incurred (1)	Description of Debt (2)	Amount due as at the date of this demand (3)

Amount of Debt £ [ ]

*By a Judgment/Order of the ____________ Court in proceedings entitled (Plaint) Number ______ between Plaintiff and ____________ Defendant it was adjudged/ordered that you pay to the Plaintiff creditor the sum of £ ______ and £ ______ for costs

If creditor issuing this demand is a Minister of the Crown or a Government Department, is it intended to present a bankruptcy petition in the High Court?

- Yes/No

The creditor demands that you pay the above debt or compound for it to the creditor's satisfaction.

Signature ______________________________

Name (BLOCK LETTERS) ______________________________

Date ______________________________

Position with or relationship to creditor: ______________________________

____

Address ______________________________

____

Tel. No. ______________________________

Ref. No. ______________________________

NB. The person making this demand must complete the whole of this page and parts A, B and C on page 2

Notes for Creditor

- If the creditor is entitled to the debt by way of assignment, details of the original creditor and any intermediary assignees should be given in part C on page 2.
- If the amount of debt includes interest, details should be given in column (2), including the grounds upon which interest is charged. The amount of interest must be shown separately in column (3).
- Any other charge accruing due from time to time may be claimed. The amount **or** rate of the charge must be identified and the grounds on which it is claimed must be stated.
- In either case the amount claimed must be limited to that which has accrued due at the end of the demand.
- If the creditor holds any security the amount of debt should be the sum the creditor is prepared to regard as unsecured for the purposes of this demand. Brief details of the total debt should be included in column (2), and the nature of the security and the value put upon it by the creditor, as at the date of the demand, must be specified.
- *Here set out details of Judgement
- If signatory is a solicitor or other agent of the creditor the name of his/her firm should be given.

Part A
Appropriate Court for setting aside demand

Rule 6.4(2) of the Insolvency Rules 1986 states that the appropriate court is the court to which you would have to present your own bankruptcy petition in accordance with Rule 6.40(1) and (2). In accordance with these rules on present information the appropriate Court is [the High Court of Justice] [court] (address)

Any application by you to set aside this demand should be made to that court, or, if this demand is issued by a Minister of the Crown or a Government Department, you **must** apply to the High Court to set aside if it is intended to present a bankruptcy petition against you in the High Court.

Part B

The person or persons to whom any communication regarding this demand may be addressed is/are:

____

Address ________________________________

____

Tel. No. ________________________________

Part C

For completion if the creditor is entitled to the debt by way of assignment

	Name	Date(s) of Assignment
Original creditor		
Assignees		

How to comply with a statutory demand or have it set aside

If you wish to avoid a bankruptcy petition being presented against you, you must pay the debt set out on page 1 of this notice within the period of 21 days of service upon you. However if the demand follows a Judgement or order of a County Court any payment must be made to that County Court. Alternatively, you can attempt to come to a settlement with the creditor. To do this you should:

- inform the person or persons (or one of the persons) named in part B above immediately that you are willing and able to offer security for the debt to the creditor's satisfaction; or
- inform the person or persons (or one of the persons) named in part B immediately that you are willing and able to compound for the debt to the creditor's satisfaction.

If you dispute the demand in whole or in part you should:

- Contact the person or persons (or one of the persons) named in part B immediately

If you consider that you have grounds to have this notice set aside or if you do not receive a satisfactory written reply from the person or persons (or one of the persons) named in part B before the expiration of 18 days after the service you should:

- apply without delay to the appropriate court shown in part A above to have the notice set aside.

Remember: You have only 21 days from the date of service on you of this document before the creditor may present a bankruptcy petition.

Rule 6.1 **Form 6.3**

Statistical Demand under section 268(2) of the Insolvency Act 1986
Debt Payable at Future Date

In Bankruptcy

Warning

- This is an important document. You **must** deal with this demand within 21 days of its service upon you or you could be made bankrupt and your property and goods taken away from you. Please read this demand and notes carefully.
- If you are in any doubt about your position, you should seek advice **immediately** from a solicitor or your nearest Citizens Advice Bureau.
- There are additional notes overleaf.

Demand

To ______________________________

Address ______________________________

____

This demand is served on you by the creditor:

Name ______________________________

Address ______________________________

____

The creditor claims that you will owe the following when payment falls due on ______________________________

When Incurred (1)	Description of Debt (2)	Amount of future debt (3)
		£

The creditor is of the opinion that you have no reasonable prospect of paying this debt when it falls due because*

____

____

____

If creditor issuing this demand is a Minister of the Crown or a Government Department, is it intended to present a bankruptcy petition in the High Court?

- Yes/No

Signature ______________________________

Name ______________________________

Date ______________________________

Position with or relationship to creditor ______________________________

____

Address ______________________________

Tel. No. ______________________________

Ref. No. ______________________________

NB The person making the demand must complete the whole of this page and parts A, B and C on page 2.

Notes for Creditor.

- If the creditor is entitled to the debt by way of assignment, details of the original creditor and any assignees should be given in part C on page 2.
- If the amount of debt when due will include interest, details should be given in column (2), including the grounds upon which interest is charged.
- Any other charge accruing due from time to time may be claimed. The amount **or** rate of the charge must be identified and the grounds on which it is claimed must be stated.
- In either case the amount claimed must be limited to that which will have accrued due when payment falls due on the date specified.
- If the creditor holds any security the amount of debt should be the sum the creditor is prepared to regard as unsecured for the purposes of this demand. Brief details of the total debt should be included in column (2), and the nature of the security and the value put upon it by the creditor, as at the date of the demand, must be specified.
- *Here set out the grounds for this opinion.
- If signatory is a solicitor or other agent of the creditor the name of his/her firm should be given.

Part A

Appropriate Court for setting aside demand

Rule 6.4(2) of the Insolvency Rules 1986 states that the appropriate court is the court to which you would have to present your own bankruptcy petition in accordance with Rule 6.40 (1) and (2). In accordance with these rules on present information the appropriate court is [the High Court of Justice] [court] (address).

Any application by you to set aside this demand should be made to that court.

Part B

The person or persons to whom any communication regarding the demand may be addressed is/are:

____

Address ____________________

____

Tel. No. ____________________

Part C

For completion if the creditor is entitled to the debt by way of assignment

	Name	Date(s) of Assignment
Original creditor		
Assignees		

How to comply with a statutory demand or have it set aside

If you wish to avoid a bankruptcy petition being presented against you, you must within the period of 21 days of service upon you, satisfy the creditor that you are able to meet the debt demanded when it is due.

If you dispute that the debt will be due in whole or in part or if you dispute the allegation that you will be unable to pay the debt when it falls due or if you consider that you may be able to offer security for the debt or to compound for it you should:

- contact the person or persons (or one of the persons) named in part B immediately.

If you consider that you have grounds to have this notice set aside or if you do not receive a satisfactory written reply from the person or persons (or one of the persons) in part B before the expiration of 18 days after service you should

- apply without delay to the appropriate court shown in part A above to have the notice set aside.

Remember: You have only 21 days from the date of service on you of this document before the creditor may present a bankruptcy petition.

 Fourmat Publishing 27 & 28 St Albans Place Islington Green London N1 ONX

In the

In Bankruptcy No of 19

Re

Let [(a)]

attend before the Registrar as follows:-

Date: ____________________

Time: ____________________ hours

Place: ____________________

on the hearing of an application by [(b)]

the applicant for an order that the statutory demand dated
be set aside.

The grounds on which the applicant claims to be entitled to the order are set out in the affidavit of the applicant sworn on [(c)]
a copy of which accompanies this application.

The names and addresses of the persons upon whom this application should be served are [(d)]

The applicant's address for service is [(e)]

Dated: ____________________

Signed: ____________________

[Solicitor for the] Applicant

If you do not attend, the Court may make such order as it thinks fit.

(a) Insert name and address of person to attend hearing (b) Insert name of debtor (c) Insert date (d) State the names and addresses of the persons to be served (e) State the applicant's address for service

In the

In Bankruptcy No of 19

Re

I[(a)] ____

____

____

____

make oath and say as follows:-

1. That on [(b)] ______________________ the statutory demand exhibited hereto and marked "A" came into my hands.

2. That I [(c)]

[3. That to the best of my knowledge and belief the creditor[s] named in the demand [has] [have] not presented a petition against me.

4. That reasons for my failure to apply to set aside the demand within 18 days after service are as follows:

5. Unless restrained by injunction the creditor[s] may present a bankruptcy petition against me.]

Sworn at

this day of

Before me,

(a) Insert name address and description of person making the oath (b) Insert date (c) Insert one of the following alternatives; or if none of them are applicable state grounds on which you consider the statutory demand should be set aside: (1) "Do not admit the debt because ...." [here state grounds] *or* (2) "Admit the debt but not that it is payable immediately" [state reason]; *or* (3) "Admit the debt as to £ ....., and that this is payable but that the remainder is not immediately payable. I am prepared to pay the amount of £ ..... immediately" [State reason]; *or* (4) "Admit the debt and am prepared to secure or compound for it to the creditor's satisfaction by ..... " [State nature of satisfaction]; *or* (5) "Say that the debt is a secured debt" [give full details of security and its value]; *or* (6) "Have a counterclaim (or set-off or cross demand) for £ ..... being a sum equal to (or exceeding) the claim in respect of" [here state grounds of counterclaim etc]; *or* (7) "Say that execution on the judgment of the court has been stayed [give details] *or* (8) "Say that the demand does not comply with the Insolvency Rules in that" [State reason]

In the

In Bankruptcy No of 19

Re

Upon the application of [(a)] ______________________________

____

____

and upon hearing

and upon reading the evidence

IT IS ORDERED that the statutory demand dated
be set aside.

AND IT IS ORDERED THAT [(b)]

Dated: ______________________________

(a) Insert name and address of applicant (b) Insert details of any further order in the matter

 Fourmat Publishing 27 & 28 St Albans Place Islington Green London N1 ONX

Creditor's Bankruptcy Petition on Failure to Comply with a Statutory Demand for a Liquidated Sum Payable Immediately

In the

In Bankruptcy No of 19

(a) Insert full name(s) and address(es) of petitioner(s).

I/We (a) ______________________________

____

____

(b) Insert full name, place of residence and occupation (if any) of debtor

petition the court that a bankruptcy order may be made against (b) ______________

____

(c) Insert in full any other name(s) by which the debtor is or has been known

[also known as (c) ______________________________]

(d) Insert trading name (adding "with another or others", if this is so), business address and nature of business

[and carrying on business as (d) ______________________________

____

______________________________]

(e) Insert any other address or addresses at which the debtor has resided at or after the time the petition debt was incurred

[and lately residing at (e) ______________________________

____

______________________________]

(f) Give the same details as specified in note (d) above for any other businesses which have been carried on at or after the time the petition debt was incurred

[and lately carrying on business as (f) ______________________________

____

______________________________]

and say as follows:—

1. The debtor has for the greater part of six months immediately preceding

(g) Delete as applicable

the presentation of this petition (g) [resided at] [carried on business at]

____

(h) Or as the case may be following the terms of Rule 6.9.

within the district of this court (h)

2. The debtor is justly and truly indebted to me[us] in the aggregate sum of

(j) Please give the amount of debt(s), what they relate to and when they were incurred. Please show separately the amount or rate of any interest or other charge not previously notified to the debtor **and the reasons why you are claiming it**

£(j)

3. The above-mentioned debt is for a liquidated sum payable immediately and the debtor appears to be unable to pay it.

(k) Insert date of service of a statutory demand

4. On (k) ______________________ a statutory demand was served upon the debtor by

(l) State manner of service of demand

(l) ______________________
in respect of the above-mentioned debt. To the best of my knowledge and belief the demand has neither been complied with nor set aside in accordance with the Rules and no application to set it aside is outstanding

(m) If 3 weeks have not elapsed since service of statutory demand give reasons for earlier presentation of petition

(m)

5. I/We do not, nor does any person on my/our behalf, hold any security on the debtor's estate, or any part thereof, for the payment of the above-mentioned sum

OR

(n) Delete as applicable

I/We hold security for the payment of (n) [part of] the above-mentioned sum. I/We will give up such security for the benefit of all the creditors in the event of a bankruptcy order being made.

OR

I/We hold security for the payment of part of the above-mentioned sum and I/we estimate the value of such security to be £ This petition is not made in respect of the secured part of my/our debt.

Endorsement

This petition having been presented to the court on ______________________ it is ordered that the petition shall be heard as follows:—

Date ______________________

Time ______________________ hours

Place ______________________

(p) Insert name of debtor

and you, the above-named (p) ______________________, are to take notice that if you intend to oppose the petition you must not later than 7 days before the day fixed for the hearing:

(i) file in court a notice (in Form 6.19) specifying the grounds on which you object to the making of a bankruptcy order; and

(ii) send a copy of the notice to the petitioner or his solicitor.

(q) Only to be completed where the petitioning creditor is represented by a solicitor

The solicitor to the petitioning creditor is:— (q)

Name ______________________

Address ______________________

____

Telephone Number ______________________

Reference ______________________

Fourmat Publishing 27 & 28 St Albans Place Islington Green London N1 ONX

Creditor's Bankruptcy Petition on Failure to Comply with a Statutory Demand for a Liquidated Sum Payable at a Future Date

In the

In Bankruptcy No of 19

(a) Insert full name(s) and address(es) of petitioner(s).

I/We (a) ______________________________

____

____

(b) Insert full name, place of residence and occupation (if any) of debtor

petition the court that a bankruptcy order may be made against (b) ______________

____

____

(c) Insert in full any other name(s) by which the debtor is or has been known

[also known as (c) ______________________________]

____

(d) Insert trading name (adding "with another or others", if this is so), business address and nature of business

[and carrying on business as (d)

____

______________________________]

(e) Insert any other address or addresses at which the debtor has resided at or after the time the petition debt was incurred.

[and lately residing at (e) ______________________________

______________________________]

(f) Give the same details as specified in note (d) above for any other businesses which have been carried on at or after the time the petition debt was incurred.

[and lately carrying on business as (f) ______________________________

______________________________]

and say as follows:—

(g) Delete as applicable

1. The debtor has for the greater part of six months immediately preceding the presentation of this petition (g) [resided at] [carried on business at] ______________

____

(h) Or as the case may be following the terms of Rule 6.9.

within the district of this court (h)

(j) Please give the amount of debt(s), what they relate to and when they were incurred. Please show separately the amount or rate of any interest or other charge not previously notified to the debtor **and the reasons why you are claiming it.**

2. The debtor is justly and truly indebted to me[us] in the aggregate sum of £(j) ______

(k) Insert date or dates when the debt becomes payable.

3. The above-mentioned debt is for a liquidated sum payable on (k) ______________________________ and the debtor appears to have no reasonable prospect of being able to pay it.

(l) Insert date of service of statutory demand

4. On (l) ______________________________ a statutory demand was served upon the debtor by

(m) State manner of service of the demand

(m) ______________________________ in respect of the above-mentioned debt. To the best of my knowledge and belief the demand has neither been complied with nor set aside in accordance with the Rules and no application to set it aside is outstanding.

(n) If 3 weeks have not elapsed since service of statutory demand give reasons for earlier presentation of petition

(n)

5. I/We do not, nor does any person on my/our behalf, hold any security on the debtor's estate, or any part thereof, for the payment of the above-mentioned sum.

OR

(p) Delete as applicable

I/We hold security for the payment of (p) [part of] the above-mentioned sum. I/We will give up such security for the benefit of all the creditors in the event of a bankruptcy order being made.

OR

I/We hold security for the payment of part of the above-mentioned sum and I/we estimate the value of such security to be £ This petition is not made in respect of the secured part of my/our debt.

Endorsement

This petition having been presented to the court on ______________________________

it is ordered that the petition shall be heard as follows:—

Date ______________________________

Time ______________________________ hours

Place ______________________________

(q) Insert name of debtor

and you, the above-named (q) ______________________________ are to take notice that if you intend to oppose the petition you must not later than 7 days before the day fixed for the hearing:

(i) file in court a notice (in Form 6.19) specifying the grounds on which you object to the making of a bankruptcy order; and

(ii) send a copy of the notice to the petitioner or his solicitor.

(r) Only to be completed where the petitioning creditor is represented by a solicitor.

The solicitor to the petitioning creditor is:— (r)

Name ______________________________

Address ______________________________

____

Telephone Number ______________________________

Reference ______________________________

Fourmat Publishing 27 & 28 St Albans Place Islington Green London N1 ONX

Creditor's Bankruptcy Petition Where Execution or Other Process on a Judgment has been Returned in Whole or Part

In the

In Bankruptcy No of 19

(a) Insert full name(s) and address(es) of petitioner(s).

I/We (a) ______________________________

____

(b) Insert full name, place of residence and occupation (if any) of debtor

petition the court that a bankruptcy order may be made against (b) __________

____

____

(c) Insert in full any other name(s) by which the debtor is or has been known

(d) Insert trading name (adding "with another or others", if this is so), business address and nature of business

(e) Insert any other address or addresses at which the debtor has resided at or after the time the petition debt was incurred

(f) Give the same details as specified in note (d) above for any other businesses which have been carried on at or after the time the petition debt was incurred

(g) Delete as applicable

(h) Or as the case may be following the terms of Rule 6.9.

[also known as (c) ______________________________]

[and carrying on business as (d) ______________________________

______________________________]

[and lately residing at (e) ______________________________

______________________________]

[and lately carrying on business as (f) ______________________________

____

______________________________]

and say as follows:—

1. The debtor has for the greater part of six months immediately preceding the presentation of this petition (g) [resided at] [carried on business at] _

____

within the district of this court (h)

2. The debtor is justly and truly indebted to me[us] in the aggregate sum of

(j) Please give the amount of debt(s), what they relate to and when they were incurred. Please show separately the amount or rate of any interest or other charge not previously notified to the debtor **and the reasons why you are claiming it.**

£(j) ______

3. The above mentioned debt is for a liquidated sum payable immediately and the debtor appears to be unable to pay it.

(k) Insert date on which judgment was obtained

4. On (k) ____________________ judgment was obtained in (g) [the High Court of Justice ____________ Division] [____________________ County Court]. [or as the case may be] on an action the short title and reference to the record whereof is "A " V. "B " Number ______ in the sum of £ __________ following which execution was issued at the ______________ court in respect of the debt and on (l) ____________ the sheriff/county court (g) [made a return] [endorsed upon the writ a statement] to the effect that the execution was unsatisfied (g) [as to the whole] [as to part] and the above-mentioned debt represents the amount by which the execution was returned unsatisified.

(l) Insert date of execution

5. I/We do not, nor does any person on my/our behalf, hold any security on the debtor's estate, or any part thereof, for the payment of the above-mentioned sum.

OR

I/We hold security for the payment of (g) [part of] the above-mentioned sum. I/We will give up such security for the benefit of all the creditors in the event of a bankruptcy order being made

OR

I/We hold security for the payment of part of the above-mentioned sum and I/we estimate the value of such security to be £ This petition is not made in respect of the secured part of my/our debt.

Endorsement

This petition having been presented to the court on ____________________

it is ordered that the petition shall be heard as follows:—

Date ____

Time ______________________________ hours

Place ____

(m) Insert name of debtor

and you, the above-named (m) ____________________ are to take notice that if you intend to oppose the petition you must not later than 7 days before the day fixed for the hearing:

(i) file in court a notice (in Form 6.19) specifying the grounds on which you object to the making of a bankruptcy order; and

(ii) send a copy of the notice to the petitioner or his solicitor.

(n) Only to be completed where the petitioning creditor is represented by a solicitor.

The solicitor to the petitioning creditor is:— (n)

Name ____

Address ____

____

Telephone Number ______________________________

Reference ____

Fourmat Publishing 27 & 28 St Albans Place Islington Green London N1 ONX

Rule 6.6 **Form 6.10**

Bankruptcy Petition for Default in Connection with Voluntary Arrangement

In the

In Bankruptcy No of 19

(a) Insert full name(s) and address(es) of petitioner(s).	I/We (a) ____________________ ____________________ ____________________
(b) Insert full name, place of residence and occupation (if any) of debtor	petition the court that a bankruptcy order may be made against (b) ____________________ ____________________ ____________________
(c) Insert in full any other name(s) by which the debtor is or has been known	[also known as (c) ____________________ ____________________ ____________________]
(d) Insert trading name (adding "with another or others", if this is so), business address and nature of business	[and carrying on business as (d) ____________________ ____________________ ____________________]
(e) Insert any other address or addresses at which the debtor has resided at or after the time the petition debt was incurred	[and lately residing at (e) ____________________ ____________________ ____________________]
(f) Give the same details as specified in note (d) above for any other businesses which have been carried on at or after the time the petition debt was incurred	[and lately carrying on business as (f) ____________________ ____________________ ____________________]
	and say as follows:—
(g) Delete as applicable	1. That the debtor has for the greater part of six months immediately preceding the presentation of this petition (g) [resided at] [carried on business at] ____________________ ____________________
(h) Or as the case may be following the terms of Rule 6.9.	within the district of this court (h)
(j) Insert date the debtor entered into voluntary arrangement	2. On (j) ____________ a voluntary arrangement proposed by the debtor was approved by his creditors and I am (g) [a person who is for the time being
(k) Insert name of supervisor.	bound by the said voluntary arrangement and (k) ____________________ is the supervisor] [(k) ____________________ the supervisor of the said voluntary arrangement]

(l) Give details of the default in connection with the composition or scheme, being the grounds under section 276(1) IA86 upon which the bankruptcy order is sought

3. (l)

Endorsement

This petition having been presented to the court on ______________________

it is ordered that the petition shall be heard as follows:—

Date ______________________

Time ______________________ hours

Place ______________________

(m) Insert name of debtor

and you, the above-named (m) ______________ are to take notice that if you intend to oppose the petition you must not later than 7 days before the day fixed for the hearing:

(i) file in court a notice (in Form 6.19) specifying the grounds on which you object to the making of a bankruptcy order; and

(ii) send a copy of the notice to the petitioner or his solicitor.

(n) Only to be completed where the petitioning creditor is represented by a solicitor.

The solicitor to the petitioning creditor is:— (n)

Name ______________________

Address ______________________

____

Telephone Number ______________________

Reference ______________________

Fourmat Publishing 27 & 28 St Albans Place Islington Green London N1 ONX

In the

In Bankruptcy No of 19

Re

Date of statutory demand: ______________________________

I [(a)] ______________________________

____

make oath and say as follows:-

1. [(b)] [I] [______________________________]
   did on [(c)] ______________ at [(d)] ______________
   ____
   personally serve the above named debtor with the demand dated ______________
   ____

[(e)] [2. That on [(c)] ______________ the debtor acknowledged service of the demand by [(f)] ______________
   ____
   ______________________________]

3. A copy of the demand marked "A" [(e)] [and the acknowledgement of service marked "B"] is [(e)] [are] exhibited hereto.

Sworn at

this day of

Before me,

(a) Insert name address and description of person making the oath and whether the creditor or a person acting on his behalf. (b) Delete "I" and insert name and address of person who effected service, as applicable (c) Insert date (d) Insert address (e) Delete words in [ ] if no acknowledgement of service has been received (f) Give particulars of the way in which the debtor acknowledged service of the demand

In the

In Bankruptcy No of 19

Re

Date of statutory demand: ____________________

I [(a)] ____________________

____

make oath and say as follows:-

1. That on [(b)] ____________________ an attempt was made to serve the demand on the above named debtor by [(c)]

2. That on [(b)] ____________________ substituted service of the demand was effected in the following way:-

3. That to the best of my knowledge, information and belief the demand will have come to the attention of the above named debtor by [(b)] ____________

[(d)] [4. That on [(b)] ____________________ the debtor acknowledged service of the demand by [(e)]

]

5. A copy of the demand marked "A" [(d)] [and the acknowledgement of service marked "B"] [(f)] [is] [are] exhibited hereto.

Sworn at

this day of

Before me,

(a) Insert name address and description of person making the oath (b) Insert date (c) Give particulars of the steps taken with a view to serving the demand and why they were ineffective and if the creditor has taken advantage of Rule 6.3(3) (newspaper advertisement) state the means of the creditor's knowledge for the purposes of that Rule and the date or dates on which, and the newspaper in which, the demand was advertised. (d) Delete words in [ ] if no acknowledgement of service has been received. (e) Give particulars of the way in which the debtor acknowledged service of the demand (f) Delete as applicable

In the

In Bankruptcy No of 19

Re

I [(a)] ____

____

____

make oath and say as follows:-

[1. I am the petitioner. The statements in the petition now produced and shown to me marked "A" are true to the best of my knowledge, information and belief.

2. [(b)]

]

OR

[1. I am [(c)] ____
of the petitioner; or

2. I am duly authorised by the petitioner to make this affidavit on [(d)] [its] [his] behalf.

3. I have been concerned in the matters giving rise to the presentation of the petition and I have the requisite knowledge of the matters referred to in the petition because [(e)]

4. The statements in the petition now produced and shown to me marked "A" are true to the best of my knowledge, information and belief.

5. [(b)]

]

Sworn at

this day of

Before me,

(a) Insert name address and description of person making oath (b) If petition is based upon a statutory demand, and more than 4 months have elapsed between service of the demand and presentation of the petition, give reason(s) for delay and explanation of circumstances which have contributed to the late presentation of the petition (c) State the capacity, eg director, secretary, solicitor etc. (d) Delete as applicable (e) State means of knowledge of matters sworn to in the affidavit

Rule 6.13, 6.43

Form 6.14

Application for Registration of Petition in Bankruptcy against an Individual under Land Charges Act 1972

In the
In Bankruptcy No of 19
Re

Notes		Official Use Only
This form should be completed in typescript or BLOCK LETTERS in black ink.	Application is made for Registration of a petition in bankruptcy presented this day as a pending action under section 5 of the Land Charges Act 1972 in respect of the following particulars.	Seal of Court
A separate form should be completed for each debtor and for any alternative name (other than trading name(s)) referred to in the petition. Please tick correct box. Insert initials if full forename(s) not known	**Particulars of Debtor:** Mr ☐ Mrs ☐ Miss ☐ Ms ☐ Other ______ Forename(s) ______ Surname ______	Land Charges Use PAB BANKS
Give details of trade, profession or occupation including any trading name(s)	Occupation ______	
Include debtor's business address(es) if appropriate. Where there are more than 2 addresses enter the additional addresses on the back page.	Address(es) 1 ______ 2 ______	
Enter the key number allocated to the court by the Land Charges Department	Key Number ☐☐☐☐☐☐☐	1 C / 2 F / 3
Enter Name of Court	High Court of Justice ______ County Court } in Bankruptcy	4 / 5 / 6
Number of petition	No. ______ of 19___	
Please give the full name and address of petitioner, unless the petition is presented by the debtor in which case insert 'the debtor'	**Particulars of Petitioner** Name ______ Address ______	

Signature of Registrar ______ Date ______

Additional Addresses of Debtor

1.

2.

3.

The Superintendent
Land Charges Department
Registration (Bankruptcy) Section
Burrington Way
PLYMOUTH PL5 3LP

Fourmat Publishing 27 & 28 St Albans Place Islington Green London N1 ONX

In the

In Bankruptcy No of 19

Re

Mr Registrar in Chambers

In the matter of a bankruptcy petition filed on [(a)]

Upon the application of [(b)]

And upon reading the affidavit of [(c)]

IT IS ORDERED that the sending of a sealed copy of the above-mentioned petition together with a sealed copy of this order by [(d)] prepaid post addressed to

at

and/or by publication in the London Gazette and/or in the newspaper of the presentation of such petition and the time and place fixed for hearing the petition shall be deemed to be good and sufficient service of the said peition on the above-named debtor on the day after completing such posting and/or publication as aforesaid.

Dated ____________________________________

(a) Insert date (b) Insert full name, address and description of applicant (c) State name, address and description of person making oath (d) State class of postage to be used

In the [a] [High Court of Justice]
[________________________________ County Court]

In Bankruptcy No of 19

To [b] ____

____

TAKE NOTICE that a bankruptcy petition has been presented against you in this court by [c] ____

____

____

____

and the court has ordered that [d] ____

____

____

shall be deemed to be service of the petition upon you.

The said petition will be heard at this court on:
Date ____
Time ____ hours
Place ____

Important
If you do not attend the hearing of the petition the court may make a bankruptcy order against you in your absence.

The petition can be inspected by you on application at this court, whose offices are at [e] ____

____

____

Dated ________________________________

(a) Delete as applicable (b) Insert full particulars of debtor as in petition (c) Insert name(s) and address(es) of petitioner(s) (d) Insert terms of order of substituted service (e) Insert address

 Fourmat Publishing 27 & 28 St Albans Place Islington Green London N1 ONX

In the

In Bankruptcy No of 19

Re

In the matter of a bankruptcy petition filed on [(a)]

I [(b)]

and for the purpose of service instructed by [(c)]

[(d)] [Solicitor(s) for] the

make oath and say as follows:-

1. That I did on [(a)] serve the above-named debtor with a copy of the above-mentioned petition, duly sealed with the seal of the court by delivering the same personally to the said [(e)]

   at [(f)]

2. A sealed copy of the said petition is now produced and shown to me marked "A" [(g)]

Sworn at

this day of
Before me,

Note: This affidavit and exhibit should be filed in court immediately after service (Rule 6.15(2))

(a) Insert date (b) Insert full name, address and description of person making oath (c) Insert name and address (d) Delete as applicable (e) Insert name of debtor as in title (f) State exact place of service (g) Sealed copy must be marked as an exhibit

In the

In Bankruptcy No of 19

Re

In the matter of a bankruptcy petition filed on [(a)]

I [(b)]

and for the purpose of service instructed by [(c)]

[(d)] [Solicitor(s) for] the

make oath and say as follows:-

1. That I did on [(a)] serve the above-named debtor with a sealed copy of the above-mentioned petition, together with a sealed copy of the order for substituted service thereof, by [(e)]

2. A sealed copy of the said petition is now produced and shown to me marked "A" [(f)]

3. A sealed copy of the said order is now produced and shown to me marked "B" [(f)]

Sworn at

this day of

Before me,

Note: This affidavit and exhibits should be filed in court immediately after service (Rule 6.15(2))

(a) Insert date (b) Insert full name, address and description of person making oath (c) Insert name and address (d) Delete as applicable (e) Set out terms of order for substituted service (f) Sealed copy must be marked as an exhibit

 Fourmat Publishing 27 & 28 St Albans Place Islington Green London N1 ONX

In the

In Bankruptcy No of 19

Re

Take note that I [(a)] ____________________

intend to oppose the application to make a bankruptcy order on the following grounds:-

Dated ____________________

To the Court

and to the [solicitors for] the petitioner

(a) Insert name

 Fourmat Publishing 27 & 28 St Albans Place Islington Green London N1 ONX

In the

In Bankruptcy No of 19

Re

In the matter of a bankruptcy petition filed on [(a)] ______________________
to be heard on [(a)] ______________________
I [(b)] ______________________
____
____
a creditor of the above-named debtor in respect of [(c)] ______________________
____
intend to appear on the hearing of the above-mentioned petition and to [(d)] [support] [oppose] the petition.

Signed: ______________________
Dated: ______________________
Name in BLOCK LETTERS ______________________

Position with or relationship to creditor [(e)] ______________________
____
____
____
Telephone no: ______________________
Reference no: ______________________

To [(f)] ______________________
____
____
____

(a) Insert date (b) Insert full name and address, or if a firm, the name of the firm and address (c) State amount and nature of debt, eg goods supplied (d) Delete as applicable (e) If creditor's solicitor or other agent please give name and address of firm (f) Insert name(s) and address(es) of petitioner(s)

In the

In Bankruptcy **No** **of 19**

Re

In the matter of a bankruptcy petition filed on [(a)] ______________________

The following creditors have given notice that they intend to appear on the hearing of the above-mentioned petiton on [(a)] ______________________.

Name of creditor	Address of creditor	Amount owed to creditor	Creditor's Solicitors (if any)	Whether intending to support or oppose the petition

[Solicitors for the] Petitioning creditor[(b)]

(a) Insert date (b) Insert name and address

 Fourmat Publishing 27 & 28 St Albans Place Islington Green London N1 ONX

In the

In Bankruptcy No of 19

Re

Mr Registrar in Chambers

In the matter of a bankruptcy petition filed on [(a)]

Upon the application of [(b)]

And upon hearing

And upon reading the evidence

IT IS ORDERED that [(c)] [this petition be dismissed] [the petitioner has leave to withdraw this petition]
[and that [(d)]

]

AND IT IS ORDERED that the registration of the petition as a pending action at the Land Charges Department or Land Registry on [(e)]
under Reference No. be vacated upon the application of the debtor under the Land Charges Rules.

Dated ____________________

Notice to debtor

It is your responsibility and is in your interest to ensure that the registration of the petition as an entry, both in the Land Charges register and your registered titles, is cancelled.

(a) Insert date (b) Insert full name, address and description of applicant (c) Delete as applicable (d) Insert any further terms of the order, eg as to costs (e) Insert date of registration

 Fourmat Publishing 27 & 28 St Albans Place Islington Green London N1 ONX

In the

In Bankruptcy No of 19

Re

In the matter of a bankruptcy petition filed on [(a)]

Upon the [(b)][adjourned] hearing of the petition today

And upon hearing

And upon reading the evidence

IT IS ORDERED that the further hearing of this petition be adjourned to:

Date ______________________________

Time ______________________________ hours

Place ______________________________

Dated ______________________________

(a) Insert date (b) Delete as applicable

In the

In Bankruptcy No of 19

Re

In the matter of a bankruptcy petition filed on [(a)]

TAKE NOTICE that by order of the court dated ______________________________
the further hearing of the petition has been adjourned to:

Date ______________________________

Time ______________________________ hours

Place ______________________________

Signed ______________________________

Dated ______________________________

Name in BLOCK LETTERS ______________________________

To [(b)]

(a) Insert date (b) Insert name and address of debtor and creditors

In the

In Bankruptcy No of 19

Re

Upon the petition of [(a)]

a creditor, which was presented on
and upon hearing

and upon reading the evidence

IT IS ORDERED that [(b)]

be adjudged bankrupt

Dated ____________________

Time ____________________ hours

Important Notice to Bankrupt

*[The] [One of the] official receiver(s) attached to the court is by virtue of this order receiver and manager of the bankrupt's estate. You are required to attend upon the Official Receiver of the court at [(c)] ____________________

____

____

____

immediately after you have received this order.

The Official Receiver's offices are open Monday to Friday (except on Holidays) from 10.00 to 16.00 hours.

Endorsement on Order [(d)]

The solicitor to the petitioning creditor is:

Name ____________________

Address ____________________

____

Telephone no ____________________

Reference ____________________

(a) Insert name and address of petitioning creditor (b) Insert full description of debtor as set out in the petition (c) Insert address of Official Receiver's office (d) Order to be endorsed where petitioning creditor is represented by a solicitor
* Delete as appropriate

Rule 6.34, 6.46

Form 6.26

Application for Registration of a Bankruptcy Order against an Individual under Land Charges Act 1972

In the

In Bankruptcy No of 19

Re

Notes	Form	Land Charges Use
This form should be completed in typescript or BLOCK LETTERS in black ink.	Application is made for Registration of a bankruptcy order presented this day as a pending action under section 6 of the Land Charges Act 1972 in respect of the following particulars.	
A separate form should be completed for each bankrupt and for any alternative name (other than trading name(s)) referred to in the bankruptcy order.	Particulars of Bankrupt:	**Land Charges Use** **WOB**
Please tick correct box	Mr ☐ Mrs ☐ Miss ☐ Ms ☐ Other ______	
Insert initials if full forename(s) not known	Forename(s) ______	**BANKS**
	Surname ______	
Give details of trade, profession or occupation including any trading name(s)	Occupation ______ ______ ______ ______	
Include bankrupt's business address(es) if appropriate. Where there are more than 2 addresses enter the additional addresses on the back page.	Address(es) 1. ______ ______ ______ 2. ______ ______ ______	
Enter the key number allocated to the Court by the Land Charges Department	Key Number ☐☐☐☐☐☐☐	1: C; 2: F; 3: —
Enter name of Court	High Court of Justice / ______ County Court } in Bankruptcy	4: —; 5: —; 6: —
Number of petition	No. ______ of 19______	
Please give the full name and address of petitioner, unless the petition is presented by the bankrupt in which case insert 'the bankrupt'	Particulars of Petitioner Name ______ Address ______	

Signature of Official Receiver ______ Date ______

Address ______

______

Additional Addresses of Bankrupt

1. ____

____

2. ____

____

3. ____

____

The Superintendent
Land Charges Department
Registration (Bankruptcy) Section
Burrington Way
Plymouth PL5 3LP

 Fourmat Publishing 27 & 28 St Albans Place Islington Green London N1 ONX

Debtor's Bankruptcy Petition

In the

In Bankruptcy No of 19

(a) Insert full name, address and occupation (if any) of debtor

I (a) ____

____

____]

(b) Insert in full any other name(s) by which the debtor is or has been known

also known as (b) ____

[lately residing at (c) ____]

(c) Insert former address or addresses at which the debtor may have incurred debts or liabilities still unpaid or unsatisfied

[and carrying on business as (d) ____

____

____]

(d) Insert trading name (adding "with another or others", if this is so), business address and nature of the business.

[and lately carrying on business as (e) ____

____

____

(e) Insert any former trading names (adding "with another or others", if this is so), business address and nature of the business in respect of which the debtor may have incurred debts or liabilities still unpaid or unsatisfied

____

____]

request the court that a bankruptcy order be made against me and say as follows:—

(f) Delete as applicable

1. I have for the greater part of six months immediately preceding the presentation of this petition (f) [resided at] [carried on business at] ______________

____

within the district of (f) [this court] [(j) county court. I am presenting my petition to this court, as it is the nearest full-time county court to (j) county court, for the following reasons:

(g) State reasons

(g)

]

2. I am unable to pay my debts.

3. (f) That within the period of five years ending with the date of this petition:—

(i) I have not been adjudged bankrupt

OR

(h) Insert date

(j) Insert name of court

I was adjudged bankrupt on (h) in the (j)

(k) Insert number of bankruptcy proceedings

Court No. (k)

(ii) I have not (f) [made a composition with my creditors in satisfaction of my (S.16 debts] or (f) [entered into a scheme of arrangement with creditors] BA 1914)

OR

On (h) I (f) [made a composition] [entered into a scheme of arrangement] with my creditors.

(iii) I have not entered into a voluntary arrangement

OR

On (h) I entered into a voluntary arrangement

(iv) I have not been subject to an administration order under Part VI of the County Courts Act 1984

OR

On (h) an administration order was made against me in the (j) county court.

4. A statement of my affairs is filed with this petition.

Date ______________________________

Signature ______________________________

Complete only if petition not heard immediately

Endorsement

This petition having been presented to the court on ______________________ it is ordered that the petition shall be heard as follows:—

Date ______________________________

Time ____________________ hours

Place ______________________________

 Fourmat Publishing 27 & 28 St Albans Place Islington Green London N1 ONX

Statement of Affairs (Debtor's Petition)

Insolvency Act 1986

NOTE:
These details will be the same as those shown at the top of your petition

In the ______________________

In Bankruptcy No __________ of 19______

Re ______________________

The 'Guidance Notes' Booklet tells you how to complete this form easily and correctly

Show your current financial position by completing all the pages of this form which will then be your Statement of Affairs.

AFFIDAVIT

This Affidavit must be sworn before a Solicitor or Commissioner of Oaths or an officer of the court duly authorised to administer oaths when you have completed the rest of this form

(a) Insert full name and occupation

I (a) ______________________

(b) Insert full address

of (b) ______________________

Make oath and say that the several pages exhibited hereto and marked ______ are to the best of my knowledge and belief a full, true and complete statement of my affairs at today's date.

Sworn at ______________________

Date ______________________ Signature(s) ______________________

Before me ______________________

A Solicitor or Commissioner of Oaths or Duly authorised officer

Before swearing the affidavit, the Solicitor or Commissioner is particularly requested to make sure that the full name, address and description of the deponent are stated, and to initial any crossings-out or other alterations in the printed form. A deficiency in the affidavit in any of the above respects will mean that it will be refused by the court, and will need to be re-sworn.

 Fourmat Publishing 27 & 28 St Albans Place Islington Green London N1 ONX

A

LIST OF SECURED CREDITORS

Tick Box
YES ☐ NO ☐

Is anyone claiming something of yours to clear or reduce their claim?

If **'YES'** give details below:

	Name of creditor	Address (with postcode)	Amount owed to creditor £	What of yours is claimed and what is it worth?
1.				
2.				
3.				
4.				

Signature ______________________

Date ______________________

Fourmat Publishing 27 & 28 St Albans Place Islington Green London N1 ONX

B

LIST OF UNSECURED CREDITORS

1. No.	2 Name of creditor or claimant	3 Address (with postcode)	4 Amount the creditor says you owe him/her £	5 Amount you think you owe £

Signature ______________________ Date ______________________

 Fourmat Publishing 27 & 28 St Albans Place Islington Green London N1 ONX

C1

ASSETS

Tick Box

Do you have any bank accounts or an interest in one? Yes ☐ No ☐
If **'YES'** state where they are, how much is in them and how much is your share.

Do you have any business bank accounts, including joint accounts? Yes ☐ No ☐
If **'YES'** state the name of the accounts, where they are and how much is in them.

Do you have any building society accounts or an interest in one? Yes ☐ No ☐
If **'YES'** state where they are and how much is in them and how much is your share.

Signature ______________________ Date ______________

 Fourmat Publishing 27 & 28 St Albans Place Islington Green London N1 ONX

C2

ASSETS

	Tick Box Yes	No
Do you have any other savings? If **'YES'** give details	☐	☐

____

____

____

____

____

	Yes	No
Do you use a motor vehicle? If **'YES'** who owns it and what is it worth?	☐	☐

____

____

____

____

	Yes	No
Have you an interest in any other motor vehicles? If **'YES'** give details and their value.	☐	☐

____

____

____

____

____

Signature ____________________ Date ____________________

C3

ASSETS

Now show anything else of yours which may be of value:

	£
a) Household furniture and belongings	
b) Life policies	
c) Money owed to you	
d) Stock in trade	
e) Other property (see Guidance Notes):—	
TOTAL	

Signature ______________ Date ______________

1. State the name, age (if under 18), and relationship to you of your dependants

1 ____	6 ____
2 ____	7 ____
3 ____	8 ____
4 ____	9 ____
5 ____	10 ____

Tick Box
Yes ☐ No ☐

2. Has distress been levied against you by or on behalf of any creditor?
If **'YES'** give details below:—

Name of creditor	Amount of claim £	Date Distress levied	Description and estimated value of property seized

Signature ____ Date ____

Fourmat Publishing 27 & 28 St Albans Place Islington Green London N1 ONX

Tick Box

3. At the date you present your bankruptcy petition, is any court judgment or other legal process outstanding against you that has been made by any court in England and Wales? Yes ☐ No ☐
If **'YES'** give details below:—

Name of creditor	Amount of claim £	Type and date of process issued	Description and estimated value of any property involved

Tick Box

4. At the date you present your bankruptcy petition, is any attachment of earnings order in force against you? Yes ☐ No ☐
If **'YES'** give details below:—

Name of creditor	Date of order	Court	Amount of instalment payable under order (per month/week) £	Total amount paid under order £	Date order expires (if applicable)

Signature ______________________ Date ______________________

 Fourmat Publishing 27 & 28 St Albans Place Islington Green London N1 ONX

5(a) Have you, before you presented your petition, tried to come to any agreement with your creditors generally for payment of your debts? Tick Box Yes ☐ No ☐

(b) If the answer to 5(a) is **'YES'**, what terms were offered to the creditors:—

(1) Time for repayment ______

(2) Total pence in £ ______ receivable by creditors ______

(3) When was the offer made? ______

(c) Did the attempt fail because the creditors refused to accept the terms offered? Tick Box Yes ☐ No ☐

If **'NO'** why did it fail? ______

6. Do you think that you will be able to introduce a voluntary arrangement for your creditors under Part VIII of the Insolvency Act 1986, which is likely to be acceptable to them? Tick Box Yes ☐ No ☐

If **'YES'**, give brief details ______

Signature ______ Date ______

Fourmat Publishing 27 & 28 St Albans Place Islington Green London N1 ONX

G

STATEMENT OF MEANS

(List below all items of regular "monthly" income and expenditure)

Items of income	£	Items of expenditure	£

This page shows that I will now be able to pay creditors £ ______ a month.

Signature ______________ Date ______________

Fourmat Publishing 27 & 28 St Albans Place Islington Green London N1 ONX

Form 6.29: Order of appointment of insolvency practitioner to prepare a report under section 274(1) of the Insolvency Act 1986

In the

In Bankruptcy No of 19

Re

Upon hearing the petition of [(a)]

the above named debtor, which was presented on[(b)]
and upon hearing

and upon reading the evidence

IT IS ORDERED that [(c)]

a person who is qualified to act as an insolvency practitioner in relation to the above-named debtor, be appointed to prepare and submit a report to the court by [(b)]

as to whether the above-named debtor is willing to make a proposal for a voluntary arrangement.

AND IT IS ORDERED that the court will consider the report on:-

Date ____________________
Time ____________________ hours
Place ____________________

[(d)] [And the debtor is [(d)] [directed to] [may] attend that hearing]

Dated ____________________

(a) Insert full name and address of debtor (b) Insert date (c) Insert name and address of insolvency practitioner to be appointed (d) Delete as applicable

 Fourmat Publishing 27 & 28 St Albans Place Islington Green London N1 ONX

In the

In Bankruptcy No of 19

Re

Upon the petition of the above named debtor, which was presented on (a)

And upon hearing

(b) [and upon considering the report of (c)

appointed under section 273 (2) of the Insolvency Act 1986]

And upon the petition and statement of affairs

IT IS ORDERED that (d)

be adjudged bankrupt.

(e) [And it is certified that the estate of the bankrupt be administered in a summary manner]
[AND IT IS ORDERED that (f)
be appointed trustee of the bankrupt's estate].
[AND IT IS ALSO ORDERED that

]

Date ____________________

Time ____________________ hours

Important Notice to Bankrupt

*[The] [One of the] official receiver(s) attached to the court is by virtue of this order receiver and manager of the bankrupt's estate. You are required to attend upon the Official Receiver of the court at (c)

immediately after you have received this order.
The Official Receiver's offices are open Monday to Friday (except on Holidays) from 10.00 to 16.00 hours.

Endorsement on Order (h)

The solicitor to the debtor is:

Name ____________________

Address ____________________

____

Telephone no ____________________

Reference ____________________

(a) Insert date (b) Delete words in square brackets if no appointment made under s.273(2) (c) Insert name of insolvency practitioner appointed under s.273(2) (d) Insert full description of debtor as set out in the petition (e) Delete if no certificate of summary administration is issued under s.275 (f) Only to be completed where a trustee is appointed on the making of the bankruptcy order under s.297(4) (g) Insert address of official receiver's office (h) Order to be endorsed where debtor is represented by a solicitor * Delete as appropriate

 Fourmat Publishing 27 & 28 St Albans Place Islington Green London N1 ONX

In the

In Bankruptcy No of 19

Re

Mr Registrar in Chambers

[a] [Upon the application of [b]

And upon hearing

and upon reading the evidence]

IT IS ORDERED that the Certificate for the Summary Administration of the above-named bankrupt's estate [a] [contained in the order of the Court] dated ______________________________ be revoked.

Dated ______________________________

(a) Delete if necessary (b) Insert full name, address and description of applicant

 Fourmat Publishing 27 & 28 St Albans Place Islington Green London N1 ONX

In the

In Bankruptcy No of 19

Re

Mr Registrar in Chambers

Upon the application of [(a)]

And upon hearing

And upon reading the evidence

IT IS ORDERED that [(b)] [upon the sum of £ ________________ being deposited by the applicant with the official receiver] the following person is appointed interim receiver of the property of the above-named debtor:

Name of interim receiver [(c)] ______________________________

Address (if applicable) ______________________________

____

____

AND IT IS ORDERED that:[(d)]

Dated ______________________________

Notice to Debtor

You must give the interim receiver all the information he may require relating to your property and affairs in order for him to carry out the functions imposed on him by the terms of the above order.

(a) Insert full name and address of applicant (b) If a person other than the official receiver is to be appointed delete the words in [ ]; otherwise insert the amount to be deposited (c) Insert either "the official receiver" or, if an insolvency practitioner is to be appointed, his full name and address (d) Insert nature and short description of property of which the interim receiver is to take possession, and the duties to be performed by him in relation to the debtor's affairs

 Fourmat Publishing 27 & 28 St Albans Place Islington Green London N1 ONX

Form 6.33

Rule 6.59

Statement of Affairs (Creditor's Petition)

Insolvency Act 1986

NOTE: These details will be the same as those shown at the top of your petition

In the ______________________

In Bankruptcy No ________ of 19 ______

Re ______________________

The 'Guidance Notes' Booklet tells you how to complete this form easily and correctly

Show your current financial position by completing all the pages of this form which will then be your Statement of Affairs.

Affidavit

This Affidavit must be sworn before a Solicitor or Commissioner of Oaths or an officer of the court duly authorised to administer oaths when you have completed the rest of this form

(a) Insert full name and occupation

I (a) ______________________

(b) Insert full address

of (b) ______________________

Make oath and say that the attached pages exhibited hereto and marked __________ are to the best of my knowledge and belief a full, true and complete statement of my affairs as at ______________ the date of the bankruptcy order made against me.

Sworn at ______________________

Date ______________________ Signature(s) ______________

Before me ______________________

A Solicitor or Commissioner of Oaths or Duly authorised officer

Before swearing the affidavit the Solicitor or Commissioner is particularly requested to make sure that the full name, address and description of the Deponent are stated, and to initial any crossings-out or other alterations in the printed form. A deficiency in the affidavit in any of the above respects will mean that it is refused by the court, and will need to be re-sworn.

A

List of Secured Creditors

Tick Box: Yes ☐ No ☐

Is anyone claiming something of yours to clear or reduce their claim?

If **'YES'** give details below:

	Name of creditor	Address (with postcode)	Amount owed to creditor £	What of yours is claimed and what is it worth?
1.				
2.				
3.				
4.				

Signature ______________________

Date ______________________

B

List of Unsecured Creditors

1. No.	2 Name of creditor or claimant	3 Address (with postcode)	4 Amount the creditor says you owe him/her £	5 Amount you think you owe £

Signature ______________________ Date ______________________

C

Assets

Now show anything else of yours which may be of value:

	£
a) Cash at bank or building society ______	
b) Household furniture and belongings ______	
c) Life policies ______	
d) Money owed to you ______	
e) Stock in trade ______	
f) Motor vehicles ______	
g) Other property (see Guidance Notes):— ______	
______	
______	
______	
______	
______	
______	
______	
______	
______	
______	
______	
______	
______	
______	
TOTAL	

Signature ______ Date ______

Fourmat Publishing 27 & 28 St Albans Place Islington Green London N1 ONX

In the

In Bankruptcy No of 19

Re

I/We,[a]

a creditor of the above-named bankrupt request you to summon a meeting of the bankrupt's creditors under section [b] ______________ of the Insolvency Act 1986 for the purpose of:

My/Our claim in the bankruptcy is £________________ and attached is a list of other creditors who concur in this request, together with confirmation of their concurrence. Their claims total £________________ which, together with my/our claim, makes a total of £________________ and which, it is believed, represents not less than [c] in value of the debts of the above named bankrupt.

I/We understand that I/we will be required to deposit with you such sum as you may determine to be appropriate by way of security for the expenses of summoning and holding the meeting.

Dated: ________________________________

Signed: ________________________________

Name in BLOCK LETTERS: ________________________________

To: [d] ________________________________

(a) Give full name and address of creditor making the request, whether an individual, firm or company
(b) Insert relevant section
(c) Insert relevant proportion of creditors
(d) State name and address of trustee or official receiver as applicable

In the

In Bankruptcy No of 19

Re

A meeting of creditors has been summoned by the [a] [official receiver] [trustee]

[a] [at the request of a creditor, under section [b]] of the Insolvency Act 1986] for the purpose of:

The meeting will be held as follows:

Date: ____________________

Time: ____________________ hours

Place: ____________________

A proxy form is enclosed which must be lodged with me not later than [c]

to entitle you to vote by proxy at the meeting (together with a completed proof of debt form if you have not already lodged one).

Dated: ____________________

Official Receiver/Trustee

[address]

Note: Insert any further details which by the nature of the meeting need to be stated

(a) Delete as applicable
(b) Insert relevant section
(c) Insert date and time by which proxy is to be lodged which should be not be more than 4 days before the date fixed for the meeting

 Fourmat Publishing 27 & 28 St Albans Place Islington Green London N1 ONX

In the

In Bankruptcy No of 19

Re

A [(a)] [first] [general] [final] meeting of your creditors will be held as follows:-

Date: ______________________________

Time: ______________________________ hours

Place: ______________________________

____

You **are required** to be (a) [present] [in attendance] at the above meeting and to be prepared to give information regarding your affairs. If you fail to comply with these requirements and do not provide an acceptable explanation you will be guilty of a contempt of court, and may be liable to be committed to prison or fined.

OR

You **are not required** to be present or in attendance at the above meeting but if you wish to be present you should advise me immediately.

Your right to be admitted will be at the discretion of the chairman, whose decision as to what intervention, if any, you may make will be final.

Dated: ______________________________
Official Receiver/Trustee

Address:

(a) Delete as applicable

 Fourmat Publishing 27 & 28 St Albans Place Islington Green London N1 ONX

Rule 6.96

Proof of Debt–General Form

In the

In Bankruptcy No of 19

Date of Bankruptcy Order No

1	Name of Creditor	
2	Address of Creditor	
3	Total amount of claim, including any Value Added Tax and outstanding uncapitalised interest as at the date of the bankruptcy order	£
4	Details of any documents by reference to which the debt can be substantiated. [Note: the official receiver or trustee may call for any document or evidence to substantiate the claim at his discretion]	
5	If the total amount shown above includes Value Added Tax, please show:— (a) amount of Value Added Tax (b) amount of claim NET of Value Added Tax	 £ £
6	If total amount above includes outstanding uncapitalised interest please state amount	£
7	If you have filled in both box 3 and box 5, please state whether you are claiming the amount shown in box 3 or the amount shown in box 5(b)	
8	Give details of whether the whole or any part of the debt falls within any (and if so which) of the categories of preferential debts under section 386 of, and schedule 6 to, the Insolvency Act 1986 (as read with schedule 3 to the Social Security Pensions Act 1975)	Category Amount(s) claimed as preferential £

9	Particulars of how and when debt incurred	
10	Particulars of any security held, the value of the security, and the date it was given	
11	Signature of creditor or person authorised to act on his behalf	
	Name in BLOCK LETTERS	
	Position with or relation to creditor	

Admitted to vote for

£

Date

Official Receiver/Trustee

Admitted preferentially for

£

Date

Trustee

Admitted non-preferentially for

£

Date

Trustee

Fourmat Publishing 27 & 28 St Albans Place Islington Green London N1 ONX

In the

In Bankruptcy No of 19

Re

I [(a)]

state as follows:-

(1) A bankruptcy order was made against the above-named bankrupt on [(b)]

and I am the trustee under that earlier bankruptcy

(2) As at [(c)] ______________________ the date of the later bankruptcy order, the following balance of debts provable against the above-named bankrupt's estate in the earlier bankruptcy of which I am trustee was outstanding as shown in the statement below:

	£
Unsatisfied balance of debts including debts due under Section 335 Insolvency Act 1986	
Interest payable thereon	
Unpaid expenses of the earlier bankruptcy	
TOTAL £	

(3) I claim in the later bankruptcy proceedings for the said amount

Dated: ______________________

Signed: ______________________

Name in BLOCK LETTERS ______________________

Admitted to vote for £	Admitted to rank for dividend but postponed pursuant to s.335(6) for £
Date ______________	Date ______________

(a) Insert name and address of trustee of earlier bankruptcy (b) Insert date of present bankruptcy order (c) Insert date of later bankruptcy order

 Fourmat Publishing 27 & 28 St Albans Place Islington Green London N1 ONX

In the

In Bankruptcy No of 19

Re

I [a]

make oath and say:

(1) That [b] [I am a creditor of the above-named bankrupt] [I am [c]

of [d]

a creditor of the above-named bankrupt.

I have been concerned in this matter[e]

and am authorised by the creditor to make this affidavit on its/his behalf]

(2) That the said [f]

on[g]

the date of the bankruptcy order, was and still is justly and truly indebted [b] [to me] [to the said creditor] in the sum of £ as shown in the proof of debt exhibited hereto marked "A".

Sworn at

this day of

Before me,

(a) Insert full name, address and description of person making oath (b) Delete as applicable (c) State capacity, eg director, secretary, solicitor, etc (d) Insert full name and address of creditor (e) State means of knowledge of matters sworn to in affidavit (f) Insert name of bankrupt (g) Insert date

 Fourmat Publishing 27 & 28 St Albans Place Islington Green London N1 ONX

In the

In Bankruptcy No of 19

Re

This is to certify that at a meeting of the creditors of the above-named bankrupt held on [(a)] ________________

[(b)] ________________

____

____

having provided a written statement that he is qualified to act as an insolvency practitioner in relation to the above-named bankrupt under the provisions of the Insolvency Act 1986 and that he consents so to act, was appointed trustee of the above-named bankrupt's estate.

Dated ________________

Signed ________________

Chairman

Name in BLOCK LETTERS ________________

(a) Insert date (b) Insert full name and address of trustee

 Fourmat Publishing 27 & 28 St Albans Place Islington Green London N1 ONX

In the

In Bankruptcy No of 19

Re

This is to certify that at a meeting of the creditors of the above-named bankrupt held on [(a)] ______________________________

[(b)] ______________________________

____

____

____

____

having provided written statements that they are qualified to act as insolvency practitioners in relation to the above-named bankrupt under the provisions of the Insolvency Act 1986, and that they consent so to act, were appointed joint trustees of the above-named bankrupt's estate.

The joint trustees are to act [(c)]

Dated ______________________________

Signed ______________________________

Chairman

Name in BLOCK LETTERS ______________________________

(a) Insert date (b) Insert full names and addresses of joint trustees (c) Specify circumstances (if any) in which the joint trustees must act together or whether one or more of them may act for the other(s)

 Fourmat Publishing 27 & 28 St Albans Place Islington Green London N1 ONX

In the

In Bankruptcy No of 19

Re

Mr Registrar in Chambers

Upon the application of [(a)] ______________________________

____

____

And upon hearing

And upon reading the evidence

IT IS ORDERED that [(b)] ______________________________

____

having filed a statement that he is qualified to act as an insolvency practitioner in relation to the above-named bankrupt under the provisions of the Insolvency Act 1986 and that he consents so to act is appointed trustee of the above-named bankrupt's estate.

Dated ______________________________

(a) Insert full name(s), address(es) and description(s) of applicant(s) (b) Insert full name and address of trustee

 Fourmat Publishing 27 & 28 St Albans Place Islington Green London N1 ONX

In the

In Bankruptcy No of 19

Re

Mr Registrar in Chambers

Upon the application of [a] ______________________________

____

____

And upon hearing

And upon reading the evidence

IT IS ORDERED that [b] ______________________________

____

____

____

having filed statements that they are qualified to act as insolvency practitioners in relation to the above-named bankrupt under the provisions of the Insolvency Act 1986, and that they consent so to act, are appointed joint trustees of the above-named bankrupt's estate.

The joint trustees are to act [c]

Dated ______________________________

(a) Insert full name(s), address(es) and description(s) of applicant(s) (b) Insert full names and addresses of joint trustees (c) Specify circumstances (if any) in which the joint trustees must act together or whether one or more of them may act for the other(s)

In the

In Bankruptcy No of 19

Re

I [(a)]

the trustee of the above-named bankrupt's estate report as follows:-

My resignation as trustee was accepted by a meeting of the bankrupt's creditors on [(b)]

The meeting [(c)] [did not pass any resolution against my being given my release as trustee] [resolved that I should not be given my release as trustee]

Dated ______________________________

Signed ______________________________

Trustee

Name in BLOCK LETTERS ______________________________

(a) Insert full name and address of trustee (b) Insert date (c) Delete as applicable

In the

In Bankruptcy No of 19

Re

Mr Registrar in Chambers

Upon the application of [a]

And upon hearing

And upon reading the evidence

IT IS ORDERED that [b]

the trustee of the above-named bankrupt's estate be at liberty to resign from office.

[AND IT IS ORDERED that [c]

]

AND IT IS ORDERED that the release of [b]

as trustee of the above-named bankrupt's estate shall be effective from [d]

Dated ______________________________

(a) Insert full name, address and description of applicant (b) Insert full name and address of trustee (c) Insert details of any further order in the matter (d) State the date from which the trustee's release is effective

In the

In Bankruptcy No of 19

Re

I [(a)]

the trustee of the above-named bankrupt's estate report as follows:-

I hereby resign from office as trustee pursuant to an order of the court dated ______________________________ giving me leave to do so.

Dated ______________________________

Signed ______________________________
Trustee

Name in BLOCK LETTERS ______________________________

(a) Insert full name and address of trustee

 Fourmat Publishing 27 & 28 St Albans Place Islington Green London N1 ONX

In the

In Bankruptcy No of 19

Re

This is to certify that at a meeting of creditors of the above-named bankrupt held on [(a)]

it was resolved that [(b)]

be removed from office as trustee of the above-named bankrupt's estate

and that the meeting [(c)] [did not pass any resolution against the trustee being given his release] [resolved that the trustee be not given his release].

Dated ______________________________

Signed ______________________________
Chairman

Name in BLOCK LETTERS ______________________________

(a) Insert date (b) Insert full name and address of trustee (c) Delete as applicable

 Fourmat Publishing 27 & 28 St Albans Place Islington Green London N1 ONX

In the

In Bankruptcy No of 19

Re

Mr Registrar in Chambers

Upon the application of [(a)]

And upon hearing

And upon reading the evidence

IT IS ORDERED that [(b)]

the trustee of the above-named bankrupt's estate be removed from office.

OR

IT IS ORDERED that [(b)]

the trustee of the above-named bankrupt's estate do summon a meeting of the above-named bankrupt's creditors on or before [(c)]
for the purpose of considering his removal from office.

[(d)] [AND IT IS ORDERED [(e)]

]

Dated ______________________________

(a) Insert full name, address and description of applicant (b) Insert full name and address of present trustee (c) Insert date (d) Delete as applicable (e) Insert details of any further order in the matter

 Fourmat Publishing 27 & 28 St Albans Place Islington Green London N1 ONX

In the

In Bankruptcy No of 19

Re

I [(a)]

the trustee of the above-named bankrupt's estate, apply to the Secretary of State to grant me a certificate of my release as trustee as a result of [(b)]

Dated ______________________________

Signed ______________________________
Trustee

Name in BLOCK LETTERS ______________________________

(a) Insert full name and address of trustee (b) Insert details of circumstances under which you have ceased to act as trustee

 Fourmat Publishing 27 & 28 St Albans Place Islington Green London N1 ONX

In the

In Bankruptcy No of 19

Re

I (a)

the trustee of the above-named bankrupt's estate, give notice that the final general meeting of creditors under Section 331 of the Insolvency Act 1986 , was summoned as follows:

Date ______________________________

Time ______________________________ hours

Place ______________________________

At the meeting the creditors did not pass any resolution against my being given my release as trustee

OR

At the meeting the creditors resolved that I should not be given my release as trustee

OR

No quorum was present at the meeting

Dated ______________________________

Signed ______________________________

Trustee

Name in BLOCK LETTERS ______________________________

(a) Insert full name and address of trustee

In the

In Bankruptcy No of 19

Re

I [(a)]

the trustee of the above-named bankrupt's estate, ceased to be an insolvency practitioner qualified to act in relation to the above-named bankrupt with effect from [(b)]

Dated __________

Signed __________

Trustee

Name in BLOCK LETTERS __________

To [(c)] __________

(a) Insert full name and address of trustee (b) Insert date (c) Insert name and address of official receiver

In the

In Bankruptcy No of 19

Re

I [a]

the trustee of the above-named bankrupt's estate, certify that a creditors' committee has been duly constituted and that the membership is as follows: [b]

[c] [This certificate amends the certificate issued by me on [d]

]

Dated ______________________________

Signed ______________________________

Trustee

Name in BLOCK LETTERS ______________________________

(a) Insert name and address of trustee (b) Insert details of members of committee (c) Delete as necessary (d) Insert date

In the

In Bankruptcy No of 19

Re

I [(a)]

the trustee of the above-named bankrupt's estate, report that the membership of the creditors' committee has altered since the last certificate dated

as follows: [(b)]

Dated ______________________________

Signed ______________________________

Trustee

Name in BLOCK LETTERS ______________________________

(a) Insert name and address of trustee (b) Insert details of changes in membership

In the

In Bankruptcy No of 19

Re

Mr Registrar in Chambers

Upon the application of [(a)]

And upon hearing

And upon reading the evidence
IT IS ORDERED that [(b)]

be appointed special manager of [(c)]

Dated ______________________________

(a) Insert full name and address of applicant (b) Insert full name and address of person to be appointed as special manager (c) Give details of the following: (i) the special manager's responsibility over the debtor's property [bankrupt's estate]; [ii] the powers entrusted to the special manager under s.370(4) of the Insolvency Act 1986; (iii) the period of the special manager's appointment; and (iv) the special manager's remuneration

In the

In Bankruptcy No of 19

Re

Mr Registrar in Chambers

Upon the application of the official receiver

And upon hearing

And upon reading the evidence

IT IS ORDERED that the above-named bankrupt do attend on:
Date ____________________
Time ____________________ hours
Place ____________________

for the purpose of being publicly examined.

Dated ____________________

Warning to bankrupt

If you fail without reasonable excuse to attend your public examination at the time and place set out in the order above, you will be guilty of contempt of court and liable to be committed to prison or fined. You will also be liable to be arrested without further notice.

 Fourmat Publishing 27 & 28 St Albans Place Islington Green London N1 ONX

In the

In Bankruptcy No of 19

Re

I/We[(a)]

of the above-named bankrupt request that you apply to the court for the holding of a public examination of the bankrupt under Section 290 of the Insolvency Act 1986.

My/Our claim in the bankruptcy is £ __________________ and attached is a list of other creditors who concur in this request together with confirmation by them of their concurrence. Their claims total £ __________________ which together with my/our claim makes a total of £ __________________, and which, it is believed, represents not less than one half in value of the debts of the above-named bankrupt.

I/We understand that I/we will be required to deposit with you such sum as you may determine to be appropriate by way of security for the expenses of holding a public examination.

I/We believe that a public examination is required because [(b)]

Signed ______________________________

Dated ______________________________

To [(c)] ______________________________

____

(a) Insert full name(s) and address(es) of creditor(s) making the request, whether an individual, firm or company (b) Insert reason why public examination required (c) Insert name and address of official receiver

 Fourmat Publishing 27 & 28 St Albans Place Islington Green London N1 ONX

Form 6.57: Order as to examination of bankrupt who is suffering from mental disorder or physical affliction or disability

In the

In Bankruptcy No of 19

Re

Mr Registrar in Chambers

Upon the application of [(a)]

And upon hearing

And upon reading the evidence

And the court being satisfied that the bankrupt is suffering from mental disorder or physical affliction or disability and

[is unfit to undergo a public examination, IT IS ORDERED that the order dated be stayed]

OR

[is unfit to attend the public examination fixed by the order dated IT IS ORDERED that the said order be varied as follows:

]

[AND IT IS ORDERED [(b)]

]

Dated ____

Warning to bankrupt[(c)]

If you fail without reasonable excuse to attend your public examination at the time and place set out in the order above, you will be guilty of contempt of court and liable to be committed to prison or fined. You will also be liable to be arrested without further notice.

(a) "The official receiver" or insert name and address of applicant and the capacity in which he makes the application
(b) Insert details of any further order in the matter (c) Delete warning where the order for public examination is stayed

In the

In Bankruptcy No of 19

Re

I [(a)]

make oath and say as follows:-

1. That I, the above-named bankrupt, [(b)] [have read over the record of my public examination] [have had the record of my public examination read over to me] and agree that it is correct.

2. A copy of the said record signed by me and marked "A" is exhibited hereto.

Sworn at

this day of

Before me,

(a) Insert name and address of bankrupt (b) Delete as applicable

 Fourmat Publishing 27 & 28 St Albans Place Islington Green London N1 ONX

In the

In Bankruptcy No of 19

Re

Mr Registrar in Chambers

This being the day appointed for the [a] [further] public examination of the above-named bankrupt and the above-named bankrupt having submitted himself for such examination:

Now upon hearing Mr the official receiver in the above matter, and upon hearing

and it appearing that

IT IS ORDERED that the public examination be adjourned to:

Date ______________________________

Time ______________________________hours

Place ______________________________

AND IT IS ORDERED that the above-named bankrupt shall attend at the above mentioned time and place, for the purpose of being further examined as to his affairs, dealings and property.

OR

IT IS ORDERED that the public examination be adjourned generally

[AND IT IS FURTHER ORDERED that the said [b]

]

Dated ______________________________

Warning to bankrupt

If you fail without reasonable excuse to attend your public examination at the time and place set out in the order above, you will be guilty of contempt of court and liable to be committed to prison or fined. You will also be liable to be arrested without further notice.

(a) Delete as applicable (b) Set out any further order or direction of the court (c) Delete warning where the public examination is not adjourned to a fixed date

 Fourmat Publishing 27 & 28 St Albans Place Islington Green London N1 ONX

In the

In Bankruptcy No of 19

Re

Mr Registrar in Chambers

Upon the application to the [a] [official receiver] [above-named bankrupt]

And upon hearing

IT IS ORDERED that the public examination of the above-named bankrupt which was adjourned generally by order of the court dated ____________________
will be held on:

Date ____
Time _______________________________________ hours
Place _______________________________________

AND IT IS ORDERED that the above-named bankrupt shall attend at this time and place.

[AND IT IS FURTHER ORDERED that the said [b]

]

Dated _______________________________________

Warning to bankrupt
If you fail without reasonable excuse to attend your public examination at the time and place set out in the order above, you will be guilty of contempt of court and liable to be committed to prison or fined. You will also be liable to be arrested without further notice.

(a) Delete as applicable (b) Set out any further order or direction of the court

In the

In Bankruptcy No of 19

Re

Part 1
On [(a)]

I [(b)], ______________________________

the trustee of the above named bankrupt's estate disclaimed all my interest in: [(c)]

Dated: ______________________________
Signed: ______________________________
Address: ______________________________
____
Name in BLOCK LETTERS: ______________________________

Part 2
This is a copy of a notice filed at the [(d)]
Court on [(a)]

Seal of the Court

Part 3
This is a copy of a notice of disclaimer filed by me at the [(d)]

Court

Signed: ______________________________
(Trustee)

Note: 1. Part 1 is to be completed by the trustee and filed in court with a copy. Part 2 is to be completed by the court and returned to the trustee. Part 3 is to be completed by the trustee when sending out copy notice under Rule 6.179 or 6.180
2. The attention of a recipient of this notice is drawn to sections 315 - 321 of the Insolvency Act 1986.

(a) Insert date (b) Insert name of trustee (c) Insert full particulars of property (d) Insert name of court

In the

In Bankruptcy No of 19

Re

I [(a)],

of property comprising [(b)]

require the trustee to decide within 28 days of receiving this notice whether he will disclaim the above property or not and to notify me of his decision.

Dated: ______________________________

Signed: ______________________________

Name in BLOCK LETTERS: ______________________________

To the trustee of the above named company

Address

(a) Insert name, address and particulars of interest in property (eg landlord etc) (b) Insert details

 Fourmat Publishing 27 & 28 St Albans Place Islington Green London N1 ONX

In the

In Bankruptcy No of 19

Re

I intend to disclaim [(a)]

If you claim an interest in this property, you must declare to me the nature and extent of your claim within 14 days of receiving this notice.

If you fail to do so, I am entitled to assume that you do not have any interest in the property which will prevent or impede my disclaimer.

Dated: ________________________________

Signed: ________________________________

(Trustee)

Address: ________________________________

____

Name in BLOCK LETTERS: ________________________________

(a) Insert full particulars of property

 Fourmat Publishing 27 & 28 St Albans Place Islington Green London N1 ONX

Form 6.64: Notice to bankrupt of application under section 310 of the Insolvency Act 1986 for income payments order

In the

In Bankruptcy No of 19

Re

To[(a)]

TAKE NOTICE that I intend to apply to this court as follows:
Date ______
Time ______ hours
Place ______

______

for an order under Section 310 of the Insolvency Act 1986 for the [payment from your income to me as your trustee in bankruptcy of [(b)] £ ______ by [(c)]

______

[(d)] [which it is intended will be paid to me by [(e)]

]

or such other order as the court thinks fit.
Attached is a statement of the grounds for this application. You are required to attend the hearing of my application unless by [(f)] ______ you send to the court and to me, using the tear-off forms below, written consent to the making of such order.
If you attend the hearing, you will be given an opportunity to show why the order should not be made, or why it should be in different terms.

Dated ______ Signed ______ Trustee
Name in BLOCK LETTERS ______
Address of trustee ______

______

(a) Insert full name of bankrupt (b) Insert total amount to be paid (c) Insert intervals at which instalments are to be paid, eg weekly/monthly and amount to be paid in each instalment (d) Delete as applicable (e) Insert name, address and description of person who will make payments, eg bankrupt's employer etc. (f) Insert date not less than 7 days before hearing

Detach here --

Notice to Court. Consent of Bankrupt to Order under Section 310 of the Insolvency Act 1986

In the

In Bankruptcy No of 19

Re

I [(a)]

the above-named bankrupt, consent to the making of an order under the terms of the application of [(b)]

Dated ______ Signed ______
Name in BLOCK LETTERS ______
(a) Insert full name and address of bankrupt (b) Insert name of trustee

Detach here --

Notice to Trustee. Consent of Bankrupt to Order under Section 310 of the Insolvency Act 1986

I [(a)]

the above-named bankrupt, consent to the making of an order under the terms of your application dated

Dated ______ Signed ______
Name in BLOCK LETTERS ______
(a) Insert full name and address of bankrupt

 Fourmat Publishing 27 & 28 St Albans Place Islington Green London N1 ONX

In the

In Bankruptcy No of 19

Re

Mr Registrar in Chambers

Upon the application of [(a)]

And upon hearing

[(b)] [And upon the consent of the above-named bankrupt] and it appearing to the court that the sum of [(c)] £ ______________________ be paid by the above-named bankrupt by [(d)]

to the trustee until [(e)]

IT IS ORDERED that the above-named bankrupt do pay [(d)]

out of his income, the first of such instalments to be made on or before [(f)]

AND IT IS ORDERED that the above-named bankrupt do send the payments to [(g)]

Dated: ____

(a) Insert full name and address of applicant (b) Delete as applicable (c) Insert total amount to be paid (d) Insert intervals at which instalments are to be paid, eg weekly/monthly and amount to be paid in each instalment (e) Insert date to which order is to remain in force (f) Insert date of first payment (g) Insert name and address of trustee to whom payments are to be sent

 Fourmat Publishing 27 & 28 St Albans Place Islington Green London N1 ONX

In the

In Bankruptcy No of 19

Re

Mr Registrar in Chambers

Upon the application of [(a)]

And upon hearing

[(b)] [And upon the consent of the above-named bankrupt] it appears to the court that the sum of [(c)] £ ______________________ be paid by the above-named bankrupt by [(d)]

to the trustee until [(e)]

IT IS ORDERED that [(f)]

do take [(d)]

out of the above-named bankrupt's income, the first of such instalments to be paid on or before [(g)]

AND IT IS ORDERED that [(f)]

do send the sums deducted to [(h)]

Dated: ____

Note:
Under Rules 6.192(2) and 13.11 you are entitled to deduct the sum of 50p for each payment sent to the trustee, from the bankrupt's income towards the clerical and administrative costs of compliance with this order

(a) Insert full name and address of applicant (b) Delete as applicable (c) Insert total amount to be paid (d) Insert intervals at which instalments are to be paid, eg weekly/monthly and amount to be paid in each instalment (e) Insert date to which order is to remain in force (f) Insert full name of payer (g) Insert date of first payment (h) Insert name and address of trustee to whom payments are to be sent

 Fourmat Publishing 27 & 28 St Albans Place Islington Green London N1 ONX

In the

In Bankruptcy No of 19

Re

Mr Registrar in Chambers

Upon the application of [(a)]

the trustee of the above-named bankrupt

And upon reading the order dated

And it appearing to the court that the above-named bankrupt has failed to comply with the above-mentioned order

IT IS ORDERED that the above-mentioned order dated be varied as follows:
(b)

do take [(c)]

out of the above-named bankrupt's income, the first of such instalments to be paid on [(d)]

IT IS ORDERED that [(b)]

do send the sums deducted to [(e)]

Dated: ______________________________

By the Court

Note:
Under Rules 6.192(2) and 13.11 you are entitled to deduct the sum of 50p for each payment sent to the trustee, from the bankrupt's income towards the clerical and administrative costs of compliance with this order

(a) Insert full name and address of applicant (b) Insert full name and address of payer (c) Insert intervals at which instalments are to be paid, eg weekly/monthly and amount to be paid in each instalment (d) Insert date of first payment (e) Insert name and address of trustee to whom payments are to be sent

 Fourmat Publishing 27 & 28 St Albans Place Islington Green London N1 ONX

In the

In Bankruptcy No of 19

Re

Mr Registrar in Chambers

Upon the application of [(a)]

[(b)] [the above-named bankrupt] [the trustee of the above-named bankrupt's estate]

And upon hearing

And upon reading the evidence

IT IS ORDERED that the order for income claimed under Section 310 of the Insolvency Act 1986 dated ______________________________

[(b)] [be discharged] [be varied as follows:

]

Dated: ______________________________

(a) Insert full name and address of applicant (b) Delete as applicable

 Fourmat Publishing 27 & 28 St Albans Place Islington Green London N1 ONX

In the

In Bankruptcy No of 19

Re

Mr Registrar in Chambers

Upon the application of [(a)]

And upon hearing

And upon reading the evidence filed

IT IS ORDERED that [(b)]

do produce to the court [(c)] [the following documents [(d)]

]

[the documents set out in the Schedule to this Order]

[(c)] [by[(e)]

]

within [(f)]

Dated: ______________________________

(a) Insert name, address and description of applicant (b) Insert name and address of Inland Revenue Official who is to produce the documents (c) Delete as applicable (d) Insert description of documents to be produced (e) Insert any requirements as to the manner in which the documents are to be produced (f) Insert time within which production required (not less than 28 days after service of order)

In the

In Bankruptcy No of 19

Re

Mr Registrar in Chambers

Upon the application of [(a)]

And upon hearing

And upon reading the evidence filed

IT IS ORDERED that [(b)]

which were produced to this court in compliance with an order dated [(c)] under section 369(1) of the Insolvency Act 1986 be disclosed to: [(d)]

AND IT IS ORDERED that the above-named be at liberty to inspect and peruse the documents so produced and to make notes of the contents thereof and to be entitled to be supplied with copies thereof on payment of the proper charges
(e)

Dated: ______________________________

(a) Insert name, address and description of applicant (b) Insert details of documents to be disclosed (c) Insert date of order under Section 369(1) (d) Insert details of persons to whom the documents may be disclosed as applicable. These persons can only be the Official Receiver, the Trustee and any of the bankrupt's creditors; see Section 369(2) (e) Insert any further order regarding means of disclosure

In the

In Bankruptcy No of 19

Re

Mr Registrar in Chambers

Upon the application of [(a)]

And upon hearing

And upon reading the evidence filed

And it appearing that [(b)] [the bankruptcy order ought not to have been made] [the bankruptcy debts and the expenses of the bankruptcy have all been paid or secured to the satisfaction of the court] [under Section 282(2) of the Insolvency Act 1986 the bankruptcy order ought to be annulled].

IT IS ORDERED that the bankruptcy order dated
against [(c)]
is hereby annulled.

AND IT IS ORDERED that the petition filed on [(d)]
be dismissed.

AND IT IS ORDERED that the registration of the petition as a pending action at the Land Charges Department of HM Land Registry on [(e)]
under reference number [(e)] and of the bankruptcy order on the register of writs and orders affecting land at that department on [(e)]
under reference number [(e)]
be vacated upon application made by the bankrupt.

Dated: ______________________________

Notice to bankrupt

1. Should you, the bankrupt, require advertisement of this order in a local newspaper and/or the Gazette, you should, within ________________ days, notify the Secretary of State, enclosing the prescribed fee, details of which can be obtained by contacting the official receiver.
2. It is your responsibility and it is in your interest to ensure that the registration of the petition and of the bankruptcy order at HM Land Registry is cancelled.

(a) Insert name, address and description of applicant (b) Delete as applicable (c) Insert bankrupt's full title as set out in the bankruptcy order (d) Insert date (e) Insert date of registration/reference number

In the

In Bankruptcy No of 19

Re

Mr Registrar in Chambers

Upon the application of the official receiver and after taking into consideration his report filed on [(a)] as to the above-named bankrupt's conduct during the proceedings under the bankruptcy

And upon hearing

And upon reading the evidence

And a bankruptcy order having been made against the above-named bankrupt on [(a)]

And it appearing to the court that the bankrupt [(b)] [has failed] [is failing] to comply with his obligations under the Insolvency Act 1986 namely [(c)]

IT IS ORDERED that the relevant period for the purposes of section 279 of the Insolvency Act 1986 shall cease to run [(b)]
[for a period of[(d)]]
[until the following condition(s) [(b)] [has] [have] been fulfilled[(e)]

]

Dated: ______________________________

(a) Insert date (b) Delete as applicable (c) State briefly in what respect the bankrupt has failed to comply with his obligations (d) Insert period for which discharge is to be suspended (e) Insert conditions to be fulfilled

 Fourmat Publishing 27 & 28 St Albans Place Islington Green London N1 ONX

In the

In Bankruptcy No of 19

Re

Mr Registrar in Chambers

Upon the application of [a]

the above-named bankrupt [b] [and after taking into consideration the report of [c]

the official receiver in this matter]

And upon hearing

And upon reading the evidence

IT IS ORDERED that the order made on [d]
whereby it was ordered that[e]

be discharged

Dated: ______________________________

(a) Insert full name and address of bankrupt (b) Delete as applicable (c) Insert name of official receiver (d) Insert date (e) Insert terms of previous order

In the

In Bankruptcy No of 19

Re

A bankruptcy order having been made by this court against [(a)]

on [(b)] and an order suspending the above-named bankrupt's discharge having been made on [(b)]

It is certified that the said order of suspension of discharge was lifted on [(b)]

Dated: ______________________________

(a) Insert full name and address of bankrupt (b) Insert date

 Fourmat Publishing 27 & 28 St Albans Place Islington Green London N1 ONX

Form 6.75: Notice to court by bankrupt that he intends to dispute statements made by official receiver in his report under section 289(2) of the Insolvency Act 1986

In the

In Bankruptcy No of 19

Re

TAKE NOTICE that I deny or dispute the following statements in the official receiver's report dated

Dated: ____________________

Signed: ____________________

Address: ____________________

____

To the Court

Notice to Bankrupt

Copies of this notice must be forwarded to the Official Receiver and your Trustee at least 7 days before the hearing of your application

 Fourmat Publishing 27 & 28 St Albans Place Islington Green London N1 ONX

In the

In Bankruptcy No of 19

Re

Mr Registrar in Chambers

Upon the application of [(a)]

against whom a bankruptcy order was made on [(b)]

and after taking into consideration the report of the official receiver dated as to the above-named bankrupt's conduct and affairs, including the above-named bankrupt's conduct during his bankruptcy

And upon reading the evidence

And upon hearing

IT IS ORDERED that the bankrupt be discharged absolutely

OR

IT IS ORDERED that the bankrupt be discharged but that his discharge be suspended until [(c)]

Dated: ____________________

Notice to Bankrupt

Should you, the bankrupt, require advertisement of this order in a local newspaper and/or the Gazette, you should, within ____________ days, notify the Secretary of State, enclosing the prescribed fee, details of which can be obtained by contacting the official receiver

(a) Insert full name and address of bankrupt (b) Insert date of bankruptcy order (c) Insert conditions to be fulfilled before discharge date can become effective

In the

In Bankruptcy No of 19

Re

A bankruptcy order having been made by this court against [(a)]

on[(b)]

It is certified that the said [(c)]

was discharged from his bankruptcy on[(d)]

Dated: ______________________________

Notice to Bankrupt

Should you, the bankrupt, require advertisement of this order in a local newspaper and/or the Gazette, you should, within ______________ days, notify the Secretary of State, enclosing the prescribed fee, details of which can be obtained by contacting the official receiver

(a) Insert full name and address of bankrupt (b) Insert date of bankruptcy order (c) Insert full name of bankrupt (d) Insert effective date of discharge

In the

In Bankruptcy No of 19

Re

To(a)

Please note that a bankruptcy petition was presented to the court on (b)

against (c)

who was previously adjudged bankrupt on (b)

and of whose estate you are trustee.

Any property covered by section 334(4) Insolvency Act 1986 which you have not yet distributed, should now be retained by you pending:-

(a) The dismissal of the above petition; or
(b) The making of a further bankruptcy order.

If a bankruptcy order is made, the trustee appointed will contact you in due course, with regard to the recovery of such property, any distribution or disposition of which shall, from the giving of this notice, be void, unless made with the consent of the court.

Dated: ______________________________

Signed: ______________________________

Name in BLOCK LETTERS: ______________________________

Description and address: ______________________________

____

____

(a) Insert name and address of existing trustee (b) Insert date (c) Insert bankrupt's full title as appearing in the petition

Form 6.79

Rule 6.229

Criminal Bankruptcy Petition

In the

In Bankruptcy No of 19

(a) Insert full name(s) and address(es) of petitioner(s) if other than the Official Petitioner

I, the Official Petitioner of __________ [or I/We (a)] __________

____

____

____

(b) Insert full name, place of residence and occupation (if any) of debtor

petition the court that a bankruptcy order be made against (b) __________

____

____

(c) Insert in full any other name(s) by which the debtor is or has been known

[also known as (c) __________]

and carrying on business as (d) __________

(d) Insert trading name (adding "with another or others", if this is so), business address and nature of business

____

______________________________]

[and lately residing at (e) __________]

(e) Insert any other address or addresses at which the debtor has resided at or after the time the petition debt was incurred

____

____

[and lately carrying on business as (f) __________

(f) Give the same details as specified in note (d) above for any other businesses which have been carried on at or after the time the petition debt was incurred

______________________________]

and say as follows:—

1. A criminal bankruptcy order was made against the said (b) __________

____

(g) Insert name of the court at which the Criminal Bankruptcy Order was made

at the (g) __________ court on (h)

and that an office copy of the order is annexed to this petition.

2. That the said order remains in force

OR

(h) Insert date

The said order was amended by the Court of Appeal on (h)
that an office copy of the order of the Court of Appeal is annexed to this petition and that the order as amended by the Court of Appeal remains in force.

3. According to the said criminal bankruptcy order the said (b) ________________

____

(j) Insert name(s) and address(es) of the person(s) specified in the order as having suffered loss or damage

is indebted to (j) ____

____

in the aggregate sum of (k) ____

____

____

(k) State the amount of loss or damage suffered as specified in the order

____

Endorsement

This petition having been presented to the court on ____________________ it is ordered that the petition shall be heard as follows:—

Date ____

Time ____________________ hours

Place ____

(l) Insert name of debtor

and you, the above-named (l) ____________________ are to take notice that if you intend to oppose the petition you must not later than 7 days before the day fixed for the hearing

(i) file in court a notice [in Form 6.19] specifying the grounds on which you object to the making of a bankruptcy order; and

(ii) send a copy of the notice to the petitioner or his solicitor.

(m) Only to be completed where the petitioning creditor is represented by a solicitor

The Solicitor to the petitioning creditor is:— (m)

Name ____

Address ____

____

Telephone Number ____

Reference ____

In the

In Bankruptcy No of 19

Re

Mr Registrar in Chambers

Upon the application of [(a)]

the [(b)] [official receiver] [trustee] of the above-named bankrupt's property, IT IS ORDERED that for a period of three months from [(c)]

all postal packets (as defined by Section 83 of the Post Office Act 1953) directed or addressed to the bankrupt at [(d)]

shall be re-directed, sent or delivered by the Post Office to [(e)]

EXCEPT any letter on which there is a specific direction signed by the[(b)] [official receiver] [trustee] that it is be delivered as addressed, if possible.

A sealed copy of this order is to be forthwith sent by the [(b)] [official receiver] [trustee] to the Post Office.

Dated: ______________________________

(a) Insert full name (b) Delete as applicable (c) Insert date (d) Insert full address(es) (e) Insert name and address of person to whom post is to be re-addressed

In the

No of 19

[In Bankruptcy
Re]

[In the matter of
and in the matter of the Insolvency Act 1986]

Mr Registrar in Chambers

Upon the application of [(a)]

And upon hearing

And upon reading the evidence

And it appearing that [(b)]

is incapable of managing and administering his property and affairs

IT IS ORDERED that [(c)]

be appointed to [(d)] [appear for] [represent] [act for] [(e)]

[(d)] [for the purpose of

]

[generally in the proceedings]

Dated: ______________________________

(a) "The Official Receiver" or insert full name and address of the applicant and the capacity in which he makes the application (b) Insert name and description of incapacitated person (c) Insert name and address of incapacitated person's representative (d) Delete as applicable (e) Insert name of incapacitated person

 Fourmat Publishing 27 & 28 St Albans Place Islington Green London N1 ONX

Insolvency Act 1986
Proxy (Company or Individual Voluntary Arrangements)

In the matter of

and in the matter of the Insolvency Act 1986

Notes to help completion of the form

Please give full name & address for communication

Name of creditor/member ______________________
Address ______________________

Please insert name of person (who must be 18 or over) or the "Chairman of the meeting" (see note below). If you wish to provide for alternative proxy-holders in the circumstances that your first choice is unable to attend please state the name(s) of the alternatives as well.

Name of proxy-holder ______________________
1 ______________________
2 ______________________
3 ______________________

Please delete words in brackets if the proxy-holder is only to vote as directed, ie he has no discretion

I appoint the above person to be my/the creditor's/member's proxy-holder at the meeting of creditors/members to be held on ______________________, or at any adjournment of that meeting. The proxy-holder is to propose or vote as instructed below [and in respect of any resolution for which no specific instruction is given, may vote or abstain at his/her discretion].

Voting instructions for resolutions

* Please delete as appropriate

1. For the acceptance/rejection* of the proposed voluntary arrangement [with the following modifications:-]

Any other resolutions which the proxy-holder is to propose or vote in favour of or against should be set out in numbered paragraphs in the space provided below Paragraph 1. If more room is required please use the other side of this form.

This form must be signed

Signature ______________________ **Date** ______________________

Name in CAPITAL LETTERS ______________________

Only to be completed if the creditor/member has not signed in person

Position with creditor/member or relationship to creditor/member or other authority for signature ______________________

Remember: there may be resolutions on the other side of this form.

Fourmat Publishing 27 & 28 St Albans Place Islington Green London N1 ONX

Insolvency Act 1986
Proxy (Winding up by the Court or Bankruptcy)

In the No of 19
[In Bankruptcy
Re **]**
[In the matter of
and in the matter of the Insolvency Act 1986]

Notes to help completion of the form

Notes	
Please give full name & address for communication	Name of creditor/contributory ______ Address ______ ______
Please insert name of person (who must be 18 or over) or the "Official Receiver". If you wish to provide for alternative proxy-holders in the circumstances that your first choice is unable to attend please state the name(s) of the alternatives as well.	Name of proxy-holder ______ 1 ______ ______ ______ 2 ______ ______ ______ 3 ______ ______ ______
Please delete words in brackets if the proxy-holder is only to vote as directed, ie he has no discretion.	I appoint the above person to be my/the creditor's/contributory's proxy-holder at the meeting of creditors/contributories to be held on ______, or at any adjournment of that meeting. The proxy-holder is to propose or vote as instructed below [and in respect of any resolution for which no specific instruction is given, may vote or abstain at his/her discretion].
Please complete paragraph 1 if you wish to nominate or vote for a specific person as trustee/liquidator Please delete words in brackets if the proxy-holder is only to vote as directed, ie he has no discretion Any other resolutions which the proxy-holder is to propose or vote in favour of or against should be set out in numbered paragraphs in the space provided below Paragraph 1. If more room is required please use the other side of this form.	**Voting instructions for resolutions** 1. For the appointment of ______ of ______ ______ as liquidator of the company/trustee of the bankrupt's estate. [in the event of a person named in paragraph 1 withdrawing or being eliminated from any vote for the appointment of a liquidator/trustee the proxy-holder may vote or abstain in any further ballot at his/her discretion]
This form must be signed	**Signature** ______ **Date** ______ **Name in CAPITAL LETTERS** ______
Only to be completed if the creditor/contributory has not signed in person	Position with creditor/contributory or relationship to creditor/contributory or other authority for signature ______ ______

Remember: there may be resolutions on the other side of this form.

In the

No of 19

[In Bankruptcy
Re]

[In the matter of
and in the matter of the Insolvency Act 1986]

Upon the application of [(a)]

And upon hearing

And upon reading the evidence

IT IS ORDERED that [(b)]

do attend on:

Date: ____________________

Time: ____________________ hours

Place: ____________________

to be examined on oath in the above matter

[(c)] [and to have and produce the documents specified below [(d)]

]

Dated: ____________________

Note: If you fail to comply with this order without reasonable excuse having been given to and accepted by the court, a warrant may be issued for you to be arrested and brought before the court for examination

(a) Insert full name, address and description of applicant (b) Insert full name, address and description of person to be examined (c) Delete as applicable (d) Insert details of documents to be produced

 Fourmat Publishing 27 & 28 St Albans Place Islington Green London N1 ONX

Forms under the Insolvency Regulations 1986
(SI 1986 No 1994)

Form 1: Liquidator/Trustee Receipts and Payments Account

In the
Re No of 19

Date	Voucher No	Receipts (nature & of whom received)	VAT	Total	Paid into bank	Date	Voucher No	Payments (nature & to whom paid)	VAT	Total	Drawn from bank

Form 2: Application to the Department of Trade and Industry for the issue of payable orders for the payment of dividend to the Trustee or Liquidator

In the
Re No of 19

In my records the sum of £ stands to the credit of the above estate with the Insolvency Services Account at the Bank of England. The sum of £ is required to pay the dividends as shown on the attached certified list of proofs and accordingly I apply for payable orders to be issued to me for distribution among the creditors whose proofs I have admitted for dividend.

The dividend is payable on

Date: ______________________________
Signed: ______________________________ [Trustee] [Liquidator]
Name of [trustee] [liquidator] [in BLOCK LETTERS]: ______________________________
Address to which payable orders should be sent: ______________________________
____

[In the High Court of Justice
Chancery Division
Companies Court]
[District Registry]
[In the County Court]

No of 19

The Insolvent Partnerships Order 1986
In the matter of

and in the matter of the Insolvency Act 1986

To [(a)] ______________________________

____

The petition of [(b)] ______________________________

____

____

____

1. I am the liquidator/trustee of [(c)] ______________________________

____

who is/was a member of[(d)] ______________________________

____

(hereinafter called "the partnership") [(e)]

2. The principal place of business of the partnership is at [(f)] ______________________________

____

3. [(g)]

4. In the circumstances the partnership should be wound up.
The petitioner therefore prays as follows:-
(1) that [(d)] ______________________________
may be wound up by the court under the provisions of the Insolvency Act 1986

OR (2) that such other order may be made as the court thinks fit.

Note: It is intended to serve this petition on the partnership [and] [(h)]

PTO

(a) Insert title of court (b) Insert full name and address of petitioner (c) Insert name of insolvent (d) Insert full name of partnership subject to petition (e) Insert the nature of the partnership's business (f) Insert address of principal place of business (g) Set out the grounds on which a winding-up order is sought (h) Add full name and address of any other person on whom it is intended to serve this petition

ENDORSEMENT

This petition against the partnership having been presented to the Court on ______________________________ will be heard at [(j)] Royal Courts of Justice, Strand, London WC2A 2LL] [[(k)] ______________________________ County Court______________________________]

[[(l)]______________________________ District Registry ______________________________]

on:

Date: ______________________________

Time: ______________________________

(or as soon thereafter as the petition can be heard)

The Solicitor to the petitioner is:

Name ______________________________

Address ______________________________

____

Telephone no ______________________________

Reference ______________________________

[Whose Agents are:

Name ______________________________

Address ______________________________

____

Telephone no ______________________________

Reference ______________________________]

(j) Delete as applicable
(k) Insert name and address of court
(l) Insert name and address of District Registry

 Fourmat Publishing 27 & 28 St Albans Place Islington Green London N1 ONX

The Insolvent Partnerships Order 1986
In the matter of

and in the matter of the Insolvency Act 1986

Warning

- This is an important document. This demand must be dealt with within 21 days of its service upon the partnership or a winding-up order could be made in respect of the partnership.
- **Please read the demand and the notes overleaf carefully**

Demand

To ____________________

Address ____________________

This demand is served by the member:

____

of (Address) ____________________

The member claims that the partnership owes the following debt which he has paid, other than out of money belonging to the partnership:

When incurred (1)	Description of debt (2)	Amount due as at the date of this demand (3)	Date of order, decree or judgment of court obtained by a member and steps that he has taken to enforce it (4)
	Amount of debt	£	

The member demands that the partnership do pay the above debt or secure or compound for it to his satisfaction

Signature ____________________

Name of signatory (BLOCK LETTERS) ____________________

Date ____________________

Position with or relationship to member ____________________

duly authorised ____________________

Address ____________________

Tel. no. ____________________

Reference No. ____________________

Notes:

- If signatory is a solicitor or other agent of the creditor the name of his/her firm should be given.
- The person making the demand must complete the whole of this page and Part A overleaf.

Part A

The person(s) to whom any communication regarding this demand should be addressed is

Name(s) ____________________

Address(es) ____________________

____

Tel No.(s) ____________________

How to comply with a written demand

To avoid insolvency proceedings being taken the debt set out on page 1 of this notice must be paid within the period of 21 days of service of the written demand. Alternatively, a settlement can be reached with the member. To do this the person named in Part A above must be informed immediately:

- of the security offered for the debt to the member's satisfaction; or
- of any terms available for settlement of the debt to the member's satisfaction.

If the debt is disputed in whole or in part contact the person named in Part A immediately.

REMEMBER! There are only 21 days from the date of service of this document before the member may present the winding-up petition.

 Fourmat Publishing 27 & 28 St Albans Place Islington Green London N1 ONX

The Insolvent Partnerships Order 1986
In the matter of

and in the matter of the Insolvency Act 1986

Warning

- This is an important document. This demand must be dealt with within 21 days of its service upon the partnership and its members or a winding-up order could be made in respect of the partnership and any corporate member, and a bankruptcy order against any individual member.
- **Please read the demand and the notes carefully**
- If you are in any doubt about your position you should seek advice immediately from a solicitor or your nearest Citizens Advice Bureau.
- There are additional notes overleaf

Demand

To________________________________

Address________________________________

____

This demand is served by the creditor:

____

of Address________________________________

____

The creditor claims that the partnership owes the following debt:

When incurred (1)	Description of debt (2)	Amount due as at the date of this demand (3)
	Amount of debt	£

The creditor demands that the partnership or a member do pay the above debt or secure or compound for it to the creditor's reasonable satisfaction

Signature________________________________

Name of signatory (BLOCK LETTERS) ________________

____

Date________________________________

Position with or relationship to creditor ________________

________________________________duly authorised

Address________________________________

____

Tel. no.________________________________

Reference No.________________________________

Notes for creditor

- If the creditor is entitled to the debt by way of assignment, details of the original creditor and any intermediary assignees should be given in part B on page 2.
- * If the amount of the debt includes interest, details should be given in column (2), including the grounds upon which interest is charged. The amount of interest must be shown separately in column (3)
- Any other charge accruing due from time to time may be claimed. The amount or rate of the charge must be identified and the grounds on which it is claimed must be stated.
- In either case the amount claimed must be limited to that which has accrued due at the date of the demand.
- If signatory is a solicitor or other agent of the creditor the name of his/her firm should be given.

Note: The person making the demand must complete the whole of this page and Parts A, B, C and D

Part A

The person(s) to whom any communication regarding this demand should be addressed is

Name(s)

Address(es)

Tel No.(s)

Part B

For completion if the creditor is entitled to the debt by way of assignment

	Name	*Date(s) of Assignment*
Original creditor		
Assignees		

Part C

It is intended that a demand in respect of the debt shown on page 1 will also be served on the following:

Part D Appropriate court

If this demand is not complied with within 21 days of service I intend to present winding-up and/or bankruptcy petitions against all the persons named in this demand to[a]

Any application by you to set aside this demand should be made to that court.

(a) Insert name and address of court

How to comply with a demand

To avoid insolvency proceedings being taken the debt set out on page 1 of this notice must be paid within the period of 21 days of service of the demand. Alternatively, a settlement can be reached with the creditor. To do this the person named in Part A above must be informed immediately:

- of the security offered for the debt to the creditor's satisfaction; or
- of any terms available for settlement of the debt to the creditor's satisfaction.

If the debt is disputed in whole or in part contact the person named in Part A immediately.

Note: Only applicable where demand served on an individual member of the partnership

If you consider that you have grounds to have this notice set aside or if you do not receive a satisfactory written reply from the person or persons (or one of the persons) named in Part A before the expiration of 18 days after the service you should:

- apply without delay to the appropriate court shown in Part D to have the notice set aside.

REMEMBER! There are only 21 days from the date of service of this document before the creditor may present the winding-up/bankruptcy petitions.

 Fourmat Publishing 27 & 28 St Albans Place Islington Green London N1 ONX

The Insolvent Partnerships Order 1986
[In the High Court of Justice
Chancery Division
Companies Court]

[District Registry]
[In the County Court]

No of 19

In the matter of

and in the matter of the Insolvency Act 1986

To [(a)] ______________________________

____

The petition of [(b)] ______________________________

____

____

____

1. [(c)] ______________________________

____

(hereinafter called "the partnership"), [(d)]
has carried on business in England and Wales in the period of 3 years ending with the day on which this petition is presented.

2. The principal place of business of the partnership is at [(e)] ______________________________

____

3. The partnership is justly and truly indebted to me [us] in the aggregate sum of £______________.

The above-mentioned debt is for a liquidated sum payable immediately.

On [(f)] ______________ a written demand was served upon the partnership by [(g)] ______________________________ in respect of the above-mentioned debt. To the best of my knowledge and belief the demand has not been complied with.

OR This petition is presented by all the members of the partnership.

4. The partnership is unable to pay its debts and in the circumstances the partnership should be wound up.

The petitioner therefore prays as follows:-

(1) that [(c)] ______________________________
may be wound up by the court under the provisions of the Insolvency Act 1986

OR (2) that such other order may be made as the court thinks fit.

PTO

Note 1: Petitions are also being presented against the following members of the partnership:

Name	Address	Type of Petition (winding-up or bankruptcy)	Date demand served

Note 2: It is intended to serve this petition on the partnership

ENDORSEMENT

This petition against the partnership having been presented to the Court on ______________________ will be heard at [(h)] Royal Courts of Justice, Strand, London WC2A 2LL] [(j) ______________________ County Court______________________]
[(k)______________________ District Registry
______________________]

on:

Date: ______________________

Time: ______________________

(or as soon thereafter as the petition can be heard)

The Solicitor to the petitioner is:

Name ______________________

Address ______________________

____

Telephone no ______________________

Reference ______________________

[Whose Agents are:

Name ______________________

Address ______________________

____

Telephone no ______________________

Reference ______________________]

(a) Insert title of court (b) Insert full name(s) and address(es) of petitioner(s) (c) Insert full name of partnership subject to petition (d) Insert the nature of the partnership's business (e) Insert address of principal place of business (f) Insert date of service (g) State manner of service of demand (h) Delete as applicable (i) Insert name and address of court (j) Insert name and address of District Registry

The Insolvent Partnerships Order 1986
[In the High Court of Justice
Chancery Division
Companies Court]
[District Registry]
[In the County Court]

No of 19

In the matter of

and in the matter of the Insolvency Act 1986

Petitions to wind up [(a)]

presented on [(b)]
by [(c)]

[(d)] [claiming to be a creditor of the partnership] will be heard at[(d)] [The Royal Courts of Justice, Strand, London WC2A 2LL] [______________________
County Court at ______________________]
[______________________ District Registry at ______________________
______________________]
on:
Date ______________________
Time ______________________
(or as soon thereafter as the petition can be heard)

Any person intending to appear on the hearing of the petition(s) (whether in support or opposition) must give notice of intention to do so to the petitioner or his/its solicitor in accordance with Rule 4.16 of the Insolvency Rules 1986 by 1600 hours on[(e)]

The petitioner's solicitor is[(f)]

Dated ______________________

Note: Details of individual members of the partnership against whom bankruptcy petitions are being presented in conjunction with the winding-up petition against the partnership should *not* be included in this advertisement.

(a) Insert full names of partnership and any corporate members, and partnership's principal place of business and nature of its business (b) Insert date (c) Insert name and address of petitioner (d) Delete as applicable (e) Insert date, which should be the business day before that appointed for the hearing (f) Where applicable insert name and address of solicitor

 Fourmat Publishing 27 & 28 St Albans Place Islington Green London N1 ONX

The Insolvent Partnerships Order 1986
[In the High Court of Justice
Chancery Division
Companies Court]
[District Registry]
[In the County Court]

No of 19

In the matter of

and in the matter of the Insolvency Act 1986

To [(a)] ______________________________

____

The petition of [(b)] ______________________________

____

1. [(c)] ______________________________
(hereinafter called "the company") was incorporated on [(d)] __________ under the Companies Act 19 _____

2. The registered office of the company is at [(e)] ______________________________
____

3. The nominal capital of the company is £ __________ divided into _______ shares of £ ________ each. The amount of the capital paid up or credited as paid up is £ __________

4. The principal objects for which the company was established are as follows:

and other objects stated in the memorandum of association of the company.

5. The subject of this petition is a member of [(f)] ______________________________ which has carried on business in England and Wales in the period of 3 years ending with [(g)] __________________, the day on which a winding-up petition was presented to this court against the partnership.

6. The partnership is justly and truly indebted to me [us] in the aggregate sum of £______________.
The above-mentioned debt is for a liquidated sum payable immediately.
On [(g)] ______________________ a demand was served upon the company and the partnership by [(h)] ______________________________
in respect of the above-mentioned debt. To the best of my knowledge and belief the demand has not been complied with.

OR A petition has been presented against the partnership by all its members and this petition is presented in conjunction with that petition.

7. The partnership is unable to pay its debts, [each member is willing for an insolvency order to be made against him] and in the circumstances the member should be wound up. The petitioner(s) therefore pray(s) as follows:
(1) that [(c)] ______________________________
may be wound up by the court under the provisions of the Insolvency Act 1986

OR (2) that such other order may be made as the court thinks fit.

PTO

Note 1: Petitions are also being presented against the following members of the partnership:

Name	Address	Type of Petition (winding-up or bankruptcy)	Date demand served

Note 2: It is intended to serve this petition on (c)

ENDORSEMENT

This petition against the partnership having been presented to the Court on ______________________ will be heard at (k) Royal Courts of Justice, Strand, London WC2A 2LL] [(l) ______________________ County Court______________________]

[(m)______________________ District Registry ______________________]

on Date: ______________________

Time: ______________________

(or as soon thereafter as the petition can be heard)

The Solicitor to the petitioner is:

Name ______________________

Address ______________________

____

Telephone no ______________________

Reference ______________________

[Whose Agents are:

Name ______________________

Address ______________________

Telephone no ______________________

Reference ______________________]

(a) Insert title of court (b) Insert full name(s) and address(es) of petitioner(s) (c) Insert full name of company subject to petition (d) Insert date of incorporation (delete if member is a partnership) (e) Insert address of registered office of company or principal place of business if member is a partnership (f) Insert full name of partnership against which winding-up petition has been presented to this court (g) Insert appropriate date (h) State manner of service of demand (k) Delete as applicable (l) Insert name and address of court (m) Insert name and address of District Registry

 Fourmat Publishing 27 & 28 St Albans Place Islington Green London N1 ONX

The Insolvent Partnerships Order 1986

In the

In Bankruptcy

No of 19

Re

I/We[(a)] ____

petition the court that a bankruptcy order may be made against [(b)] ________________

____

[also known as[(c)] ____]

[and carrying on business as[(d)] ________________________________]

[and lately residing at [(e)] ________________________________]

[and lately carrying on business as[(f)] ________________________________

____]

On the ground that:

(1) He is a member of[(g)] ________________________________ which has carried on business in England and Wales in the period of 3 years ending with[(h)] ________________________, the day on which a winding-up petition was presented to this court against the partnership.
The partnership is justly and truly indebted to me [us] in the aggregate sum of £________________.
The above-mentioned debt is for a liquidated sum payable immediately.
On [(h)] ________________________ a demand was served upon the member and the partnership by [(j)] ________________________________ in respect of the above-mentioned debt.
To the best of my knowledge and belief the demand has not been complied with and no application has been made to set it aside.

OR

(2) A petition has been presented against the partnership by all its members and this petition is presented in conjunction with that petition.

The partnership is unable to pay its debts, [each member is willing for an insolvency order to be made against him] and in the circumstances a bankruptcy order should be made against[(b)]

Note 1: Petitions are also being presented against the following members of the partnership:

Name	Address	Type of Petition (winding-up or bankruptcy)	Date demand served

Note 2: It is intended to serve this petition on [(b)]

* Signature ________________________________ *Date ________________________

* Only required where petition presented by member

PTO

ENDORSEMENT

This petition having been presented to the Court on ____________________

it is ordered that the petition shall be heard as follows:

Date: ____________________

Time: ____________________ ____________________

Place: ____________________

and you, the above-named[k] ____________________

are to take notice that if you intend to oppose the petition you must not later than 7 days before the day fixed for the hearing:

(i) file in court a notice in Form 6.19 of the Insolvency Rules 1986 specifying the grounds on which you object to the making of a bankruptcy order; and

(ii) send a copy of the notice to the petitioner or his solicitor.

The Solicitor to the petitioner is[l]:

Name ____________________

Address ____________________

____

Telephone no ____________________

Reference ____________________

[Whose Agents are:

Name ____________________

Address ____________________

____

Telephone no ____________________

Reference ____________________]

(a) Insert full name(s) and address(es) of petitioner(s) (b) Insert full name, place of residence and occupation (if any) of member (c) Insert in full any other name(s) by which the member is or has been known (d) Insert trading name (adding "with another or others", if this is so), business address and nature of business (e) Insert any other address(es) at which the member has resided at or after the time at which the petition debt of the partnership (g) was incurred (f) Give the same details as specified in note (d) above for any other business(es) which have been carried on at or after the time at which the petition debt of the partnership (g) was incurred (g) Insert name of partnership subject to winding-up petition (h) Insert appropriate date (j) State manner of service of demand (k) Insert name of member (l) Only to be completed where the petitioning creditor is represented by a solicitor

The Insolvent Partnerships Order 1986

In the

In Bankruptcy No of 19

Re

Details of members

(1) I [(a)]

(b)

[and carrying on /lately carrying on business as

]

(c)

AND

(2) I [(a)]

(b)

[and carrying on /lately carrying on business as

]

(c)

AND

* Continue with separate numbered paragraphs for each member

*(3) I [(a)]

(b)

(c)

PTO

being all members of[d]

("the partnership")
none of us being limited partners
(e)

and being unable to pay our debts, petition the court that bankruptcy orders be made against us and that the trustee of our estates wind up the partnership business and administer the partnership property.

Signature ________________________________ (member of partnership)

Date ________________________________

Note: This petition must be accompanied by an affidavit made by the partner who signs the petition showing that all the partners concur in the presentation of the petition

(a) Insert separately for each member their full name, any other names by which they are or have been known and their occupation. (b) Insert separately for each member their residential address (c) Excluding the partnership insert separately for each member the trading name, business address and nature of any business carried on at, or after the time, the partnership debts were incurred (d) Insert name of partnership (e) Insert trading name, business address and nature of partnership business subject to this petition.

 Fourmat Publishing 27 & 28 St Albans Place Islington Green London N1 ONX

The Administration of Insolvent Estates of Deceased Persons Order 1986

In the

In Bankruptcy No of 19

Re

I/We[(a)] ____________________

____

petition the court that an order be made for the administration of the insolvent estate in bankruptcy of the late [(b)] ____________________

____

____

____

[also known as[(c)] ____________________]
[and lately residing at [(d)] ____________________]
[and lately carrying on business as[(e)] ____________________]
____________________]

who died on[(f)] ____________________

and say as follows:

1. The deceased debtor for the greater part of six months immediately preceding the date of death [(g)] [resided at] [carried on business at] ____________________
____
____
within the district of this court[(h)].

2. The estate of the deceased debtor is justly and truly indebted to me/us in the aggregate sum of £[(i)] ____________________

3. The above-mentioned debt is for a liquidated sum payable[(j)] ____________________ and the estate of the deceased debtor is according to my/our information and belief insufficient to pay his debts.

4. I/We do not, nor does any person on my/our behalf, hold any security on the deceased's debtor's estate, or any part thereof, for the payment of the above-mentioned sum.

OR I/We hold security for the payment of[(k)] [part of] the above-mentioned sum. I/We will give up such security for the benefit of all the creditors in the event of an insolvency administration order being made. PTO

OR I/We hold security for the payment of part of the above-mentioned sum and I/we estimate the value of such security to be £ ____________. This petition is not made in respect of the secured part of my/our debt.

5. The Will of the deceased debtor was on[l] ____________________
proved by[m] ____________________

____

OR The letters of administration of his estate were on[n] ____________________
granted to[o] ____________________

____

ENDORSEMENT

This petition having been presented to the Court on ____________________

it is ordered that the petition shall be heard as follows:

Date: ____________________

Time: ____________________

Place: ____________________

and you[p] ____________________

____

are to take notice that if you intend to oppose the petition you must not later than 7 days before the day fixed for the hearing:

(i) file in court a notice specifying the grounds on which you object to the making of an insolvency administration order

(ii) send a copy of the notice to the petitioner or his solicitor

The solicitor to the petitioning creditor is[q]:

Name ____________________

Address ____________________

____

Telephone no ____________________

Reference ____________________

(a) Insert full name(s) and address(es) of petitioner(s) (b) Insert full name and former occupation of deceased debtor (c) Insert in full any other name(s) by which the deceased debtor was known (d) Insert any address(es) at which the deceased debtor has resided at or after the time the petition debt was incurred (e) Insert trading name (adding "with another or others" if this was so), business address(es) and nature of business(es) carried on by the deceased debtor at or after the time the petition debt was incurred (f) Insert date of death (g) Delete as applicable (h) Or as the case may be following the terms of Rule 6.9 (i) Please give the amount of debt(s), what they relate to and when they were incurred. Please show separately the amount or rate of any interest or other charge not previously notified to the deceased debtor and the reason why you are claiming it (j) State date payable or "immediately" if this is so (k) Delete as appropriate (l) Insert date Will proved (m) Insert full names and addresses of parties proving Will (n) Insert date letters of administration granted (o) Insert full names and addresses of parties letters of administration granted to (p) Insert full names and addresses of parties given notice (q) Only to be completed where the petitioning creditor is represented by a solicitor

The Administration of Insolvent Estates of Deceased Persons Order 1986

In the

In Bankruptcy No of 19

Re

I/We[a] ______________________________

____

petition the court that an order be made for the administration of the insolvent estate in bankruptcy of the late [b] ______________________________

____

____

____

[also known as[c] ______________________________]
[and lately residing at[d] ______________________________]
[and lately carrying on business as[e] ______________________________

______________________________]

and say as follows:

1. The deceased debtor for the greater part of six months immediately preceding the date of death [f] [resided at] [carried on business at] __________

   ____

   ____

   within the district of this court[g].
2. On [h] ______________ a voluntary arrangement proposed by the deceased debtor was approved by his creditors and I am[f] [a person who is for the time being bound by the said voluntary arrangement and[i] __________ ______________ is the supervisor] [i] [______________ ______________ the supervisor of the said voluntary arrangement].
3. The deceased debtor died on[j] ______________
4. The Will of the deceased debtor was on[k] ______________ proved by[l] ______________________________

   ____

OR The letters of administration of his estate were on[m] ______________ granted to[n] ______________________________

   ____

5. The estate of the deceased debtor is according to my/our information and belief insufficient to pay his debts

ENDORSEMENT

This petition having been presented to the Court on ____________________

it is ordered that the petition shall be heard as follows:

Date: ____________________

Time: ____________________

Place: ____________________

and you[o] ____________________

____

are to take notice that if you intend to oppose the petition you must not later than 7 days before the day fixed for the hearing:

(i) file in court a notice specifying the grounds on which you object to the making of an insolvency administration order

(ii) send a copy of the notice to the petitioner or his solicitor

The solicitor to the petitioning creditor is[p]:

Name ____________________

Address ____________________

____

Telephone no ____________________

Reference ____________________

(a) Insert full name(s) and address(es) of petitioner(s) (b) Insert full name and former occupation of deceased debtor (c) Insert in full any other name(s) by which the deceased debtor was known (d) Insert any address(es) at which the deceased debtor has resided at or after the time the petition debt was incurred (e) Insert trading name (adding "with another or others" if this was so), business address(es) and nature of business(es) carried on by the deceased debtor at or after the time the petition debt was incurred (f) Delete as applicable (g) Or as the case may be following the terms of Rule 6.9 (h) Insert date the deceased entered into voluntary arrangement (i) Insert name of supervisor (j) Insert date of death (k) Insert date Will proved (l) Insert full names and addresses of parties proving Will (m) Insert date letters of administration granted (n) Insert full names and addresses of parties letters of administration granted to (o) Insert full names and addresses of parties given notice (p) Only to be completed where the petitioning creditor is represented by a solicitor

The Administration of Insolvent Estates of Deceased Persons Order 1986

In the

In Bankruptcy

No of 19

Re

I [(a)] [the Offical Petitioner of________________________________]
or [I/We[(b)]]________________________________

____

petition the court that an order be made for the administration of the insolvent estate in bankruptcy of the late [(c)]________________________________

____

____

____

[also known as[(d)]________________________________]
[and lately residing at[(e)]________________________________]
[and lately carrying on business as[(f)]________________________________

________________________________]
who died on[(g)]________________________________
and say as follows:

1. A criminal bankruptcy order was made against the said[(c)] ________________

   ____

   at the[(h)] ________________________________court
   on[(i)] ________________________________
   and an office copy of the order is annexed to this petition.
2. The said order remains in force

OR The said order was amended by the Court of Appeal on[(i)]________________
and an office copy of the order of the Court of Appeal is annexed to this petition and the order as amended by the Court of Appeal remains in force.

3. According to the said criminal bankruptcy order the late[(c)] ________________

   ____

   is indebted to[(j)] ________________________________

   ____

   ____

   ____

   ____

   in the aggregate sum of[(k)] ________________________________
4. The Will of the deceased debtor was on[(l)] ________________________________
   proved by[(m)] ________________________________
   ________________________________PTO

OR The letters of administration of his estate were on(n) ______________________

granted to(o) ____

____

5. The estate of the deceased debtor is according to my/our information and belief insufficient to pay his debts

ENDORSEMENT

This petition having been presented to the Court on ______________

it is ordered that the petition shall be heard as follows:

Date: ____

Time: ____

Place: ____

and you(p) ____

____

are to take notice that if you intend to oppose the petition you must not later than 7 days before the day fixed for the hearing:

(i) file in court a notice specifying the grounds on which you object to the making of an insolvency administration order

(ii) send a copy of the notice to the petitioner or his solicitor

The solicitor to the petitioning creditor is(q):

Name ____

Address ____

____

Telephone no ____

Reference ____

(a) Delete as appropriate (b) Insert full name(s) and address(es) of petitioner(s) if other than the Official Petitioner (c) Insert full name and former occupation of deceased debtor (d) Insert in full any other name(s) by which the deceased debtor was known (e) Insert any address(es) at which the deceased debtor has resided at or after the time the petition debt was incurred (f) Insert trading name (adding "with another or others" if this was so), business address(es) and nature of business(es) carried on by the deceased debtor at or after the time the petition debt was incurred (g) Insert date of death (h) Insert name of court at which the criminal bankruptcy order was made (i) Insert date (j) Insert names and addresses of the persons specified in the order as having suffered loss or damage (k) State the amount of loss or damage suffered as specified in the order (l) Insert date Will proved (m) Insert full names and addresses of parties proving Will (n) Insert date letters of administration granted (o) Insert full names and addresses of parties letters of administration granted to (p) Insert full names and addresses of parties given notice (q) Only to be completed where the petitioning creditor is represented by a solicitor

The Administration of Insolvent Estates of Deceased Persons Order 1986

In the

In Bankruptcy No of 19

Re

Upon the petition of [(a)] ______________________________
dated[(b)] ______________________________
and numbered [(c)] ______________________________
and upon hearing ______________________________
____

and upon reading the evidence ______________________________
____

It is ordered that the estate of[(d)] ______________________________
formerly of [(e)] ______________________________
____
who died insolvent, be administered in bankruptcy and that the costs of this application be[(f)]

(a) Insert full name of petitioner (b) Insert date of petition (c) Insert court number of petition (d) Insert full name of deceased debtor (e) Insert residential address of deceased debtor at date of death (f) Terms of any order as to payment of costs of application

 Fourmat Publishing 27 & 28 St Albans Place Islington Green London N1 ONX

The Administration of Insolvent Estates of Deceased Persons Order 1986

In the

In Bankruptcy No of 19

Re

Proceedings for the administration of the estate of the late[(a)] ______________________

____

having been commenced in [(b)] ______________________

______________________ court

on[(c)] ______________________

And whereas the Court did on [(c)] ______________________

transfer such proceedings to this Court.

It is ordered that the estate of [(a)] ______________________

____

who died insolvent, be administered in bankruptcy.

(a) Insert full name of deceased debtor (b) Insert name of court in which proceedings commenced (c) Insert date

 Fourmat Publishing 27 & 28 St Albans Place Islington Green London N1 ONX

The Administration of Insolvent Estates of Deceased Persons Order 1986

In the

In Bankruptcy

No of 19

Re

I/We[a] __________

____

petition the court that an order be made for the administration of the insolvent estate in bankruptcy of the late [b] __________

____

____

____

[also known as[c] __________]
[and lately residing at[d] __________]
[and lately carrying on business as[e] __________

__________]

and say as follows:

1. [g] I am/We are the personal representative(s) of the deceased debtor and his Will was on [h] __________
   proved by [i] __________

   ____

OR that the letters of administration of his estate were on[j] __________
   granted to[k] __________

   ____

2. The deceased debtor for the greater part of six months immediately preceding the date of death [resided at] [carried on business at] __________

   ____

   within the district of this court [m].
3. The estate of the deceased debtor is according to my/our information and belief insufficient to pay his debts

(a) Insert full name(s) and address(es) of petitioner(s) (b) Insert full name and former occupation of deceased debtor (c) Insert in full any other name(s) by which the deceased debtor was known (d) Insert any address(es) at which the deceased debtor has resided at or after the time in which the outstanding liabilities were incurred (e) Insert trading name (adding "with another or others" if this was so), business address(es) and nature of business(es) carried on by the deceased debtor (f) Insert date of death (g) Delete as appropriate (h) Insert date Will proved (i) Insert full names and addresses of parties proving Will (j) Insert date letters of administration granted (k) Insert full names and addresses of parties letters of administration granted to (l) Delete as appropriate (m) Or as the case may be following the terms of Rule 6.9

 Fourmat Publishing 27 & 28 St Albans Place Islington Green London N1 ONX

The Administration of Insolvent Estates of Deceased Persons Order 1986

*In the

In Bankruptcy No of 19

Re

THE 'GUIDANCE NOTES' BOOKLET TELLS YOU HOW TO COMPLETE THIS FORM EASILY AND CORRECTLY

Show the financial position of the deceased debtor by completing all the pages of this form which will then be the Statement of Affairs

---

Affidavit

THIS AFFIDAVIT MUST BE SWORN BEFORE A SOLICITOR OR COMMISSIONER OF OATHS OR AN OFFICER OF THE COURT DULY AUTHORISED TO ADMINISTER OATHS WHEN YOU HAVE COMPLETED THE REST OF THIS FORM

I(a) ____

____

of(b) ____

____

Make oath and say that the several pages marked ______________________

are to the best of my knowledge and belief a full, true and complete statement of the affairs of the deceased debtor as at ______________________, the date of the insolvency administration/bankruptcy order.

Sworn at ____

Date ____

Signature(s) ____

Before me, ____

A Solicitor or Commissioner of Oaths or duly authorised officer

---

Before swearing the affidavit, the Solicitor, Commissioner or duly authorised officer is particularly requested to make sure that the full name, address and description of the deponent are stated, and to initial any crossings-out or other alterations in the printed form. A defect in the affidavit in any of the above respects will mean that it will be refused by the court, and will need to be re-sworn.

* These details will be the same as those shown at the top of the petition

(a) Insert your full name and occupation

(b) Insert your full address

IS ANYONE CLAIMING SOMETHING OF THE DECEASED DEBTOR'S TO CLEAR OR REDUCE THEIR CLAIM?

Tick Box
YES ☐ NO ☐

If 'YES" give details below

	Name of creditor	Address (with postcode)	Amount owed to creditor - £	What property is claimed and what is it worth?
1.				
2.				
3.				
4.				

Signature ______________________ Dated ______________________

B

1. Has the deceased debtor any creditors under hire-purchase or conditional sale agreements? If 'YES' name the creditors and give a description of the goods subject to each agreement and the amount owed

   Tick Box YES ☐ NO ☐

   ____

   ____

   ____

   ____

   ____

   ____

   ____

   ____

2. Has the deceased debtor any liability under leasing agreements? If 'YES' name the creditors and give details of the property leased

   YES ☐ NO ☐

   ____

   ____

   ____

   ____

   ____

   ____

   ____

3. Are any other creditors claiming title to goods that they supplied to the deceased debtor? If 'YES' name the creditor and give details of the goods claimed

   YES ☐ NO ☐

   ____

   ____

   ____

   ____

   ____

   ____

   ____

Signature ____________________ Dated ____________________

C

LIST THE REST OF THE CREDITORS HERE

1. No.	2. Name of creditor or claimant	3. Address (with postcode)	4. Creditor's claim at date of death £	5. Creditor's claim at date of insolvency administration bankruptcy order £

Signature ______________________ Dated ______________________

D

1. Did the deceased have any personal bank accounts, including joint accounts?
   If 'YES' state where they are and how much is in them now

   Tick Box
   YES ☐ NO ☐

2. Did the deceased have any business bank accounts, including joint accounts?
   If 'YES' state the names of the accounts, where they are and how much is in them now

   YES ☐ NO ☐

3. Did the deceased have any building society accounts, or an interest in one?
   If 'YES' state where they are and how much is in them now

   YES ☐ NO ☐

Signature ____________________ Dated ____________________

4. Are there any other savings? If 'YES' state the amounts and where they are

Tick Box
YES ☐ NO ☐

5. Did the deceased debtor have any interest in any life policies? If 'YES' state with whom they were effected, the policy numbers, and any value to the estate

YES ☐ NO ☐

6. Did the deceased debtor have an interest, of value, in any other policies or agreements? If 'YES' state with whom they were effected, the policy or agreement numbers and the value to the estate

YES ☐ NO ☐

Signature ____________________ Dated ____________________

E

List here any debts due to the estate

1. No.	2. Name of debtor	3. Address (with postcode)	4. Amount of debt £	5. Year debt incurred	6. Why has debt not yet been paid and what action has been taken to obtain payment	7. What evidence is there to confirm that the sum is owed	8. Amount now likely to be recovered £	9. Particulars of any securities held for debt

Signature ______________________ Dated ______________________

F

Property

NOW SHOW ANYTHING OF THE DECEASED DEBTOR'S WHICH MAY BE OF VALUE AND IS NOT SHOWN ON ANOTHER PAGE: £

a) Cash deposited with solicitor at ________

b) Cash in hand ________

c) Stock in trade at ________

d) Machinery at ________

e) Trade fixtures, fittings, utensils etc at ________

f) Farming stock at ________

g) Growing crops and tenant rights at ________

h) Housing furniture and effects at ________

i) Stocks and shares in ________

j) Any interests under WIlls etc ________

k) Motor vehicles (give details) ________

l) Bills of exchange, promissory notes etc available as assets ________

m) Other property, viz

____

£________

Signature ______________________ Dated ______________________

1. Is there any claim against the estate for funeral, testamentary and administration expenses? If 'YES' give details below

Tick Box
YES ☐ NO ☐

2. Did the deceased debtor have any assets when he died which are not now shown in this statement of affairs? If 'YES' list them below and state what has happened to them

YES ☐ NO ☐

Signature ________________ Dated ________________

H

Statement of the dealings and administration of the estate since the date of death

Receipts	£	£	Payments	£	£

Signature ______________________ Dated ______________________

Forms under the Deeds of Arrangement Rules 1925
(SR&O 1925 No 795)

Form 1: General title

In the Matter of a Deed of Arrangement between
of[(1)]
and his creditors, dated the day of 19
[(2)](and registered under the Deeds of Arrangement Act 1914, on the day of 19).
Trustee (AB) of

(1) Add description (2) Strike out words in brackets if deed has not already been registered

Form 2: Assent of creditor to deed

[Title]
I (*or* we), being a creditor (*or* creditors) of
for £ , hereby assent to the above-mentioned Deed of Arrangement.
Dated this day of 19 (CD)
Name, address and description of witness to creditor's signature

Form 3: Statutory declaration by trustee to be filed with Registrar as to assents of creditors

[Title]
I, of
being the trustee under the above-mentioned Deed of Arrangement, do solemnly and sincerely declare that the requisite majority in number and value of the creditors of the said , so far as the same are known to me, have assented to the said Deed of Arrangement, and I make this solemn declaration conscientiously believing the same to be true and by virtue of the provisions of the Statutory Declarations Act 1835.
Declared at
this day of 19
Before me, A Solicitor/Commissioner for Oaths

Form 4: Affidavit of execution by debtor

[Title]
I, of
make oath and say as follows:

1. The document hereto annexed marked "A" is a true copy of a Deed of [(a)] and of every Schedule or Inventory thereto annexed or therein referred to, and of every attestation of the execution thereof.
2. The Deed was executed on the day of 19 , by the debtor, at o'clock in the fore [after] noon. I was present when the debtor executed the said Deed, and saw him execute the same.
3. The said [(b)] resides at and is a
4. The place or places where the business of the said

is carried on is [*or* are] s follows: [c]

Sworn at

this day of 19

Before me, A Solicitor/Commissioner for Oaths

(a) State whether deed of assignment of property; deed of or agreement for a composition; a deed of inspectorship; a letter of licence, or an agreement to carry on or wind up debtor's business. (b) Insert name, residence and occupation of the debtor. (c) State also in what other names (if any) debtor carries on business.

Form 5: Affidavit of execution where deed is first executed by a creditor

[Title]

I, of

make oath and say as follows:

1. The Document hereto annexed marked "A" is a true copy of a Deed of [a] and of every Schedule or Inventory thereto annexed or therein referred to.
2. The Deed was first executed by [b] , a creditor (who resides at and is) on the day of 19 , at o'clock in the fore [after] noon. I was present when the said executed the said Deed and saw him execute the same.
3. The debtor [c] resides at , and is
4. The place or places where business of the said debtor is carried on is [*or* are] as follows: [d]

Sworn etc, as Form 4

(a) State whether deed of assignment of property; deed of or agreement for a composition; a deed of inspectorship; a letter of licence, or an agreement to carry on or wind up debtor's business. (b) Insert name, residence and occupation of creditor (c) Insert name, residence and occupation of debtor. (d) State also in what other names (if any) the debtor carries on business.

Form 6: Debtor's affidavit with schedule of creditors

[Title]

I, of

make oath and say as follows:

1. That on the day of 19 I executed a Deed of [a]
2. The total estimated amount of my property included under the Deed is £ and the net amount of my property included under the Deed after deducting £ , being the value [b] of securities held by creditors, and required to cover debts due to them, is £
3. The total estimated amount of my liabilities included under the Deed is £ , and the net amount of my liabilities included under the Deed after deducting £ being the [c] amount covered by securities held by creditors, is £ .
4. [d] The total amount of the composition payable thereunder is £ .
5. The names of my creditors under the Deed with their full postal addresses (so far as the same are known to me) and the amount of debt due to or claimed by each of such creditors are contained in the Schedule to this my Affidavit.

Sworn etc, as Form 4

(a) State whether deed of assignment of property; deed of or agreement for a composition; a deed of inspectorship; a letter of licence, or an agreement to carry on or wind up debtor's business. (b) The estimated surplus (if any) from securities held by creditors should not be deducted from the gross amount of property. (c) This amount must correspond with the amount of securities deducted above. No deduction should be made in respect of the unsecured balances of partially secured debts. (d) If there is no composition payable, strike this clause out.

Schedule

Names of Creditors	*Full Postal Addresses*	*Amount of debt due to or claimed by each creditor after deduction of value of securities held by the creditor*

Form 7: Form of register to be kept by Registrar

The prescribed form consists of column headings as follows:
No;
Name of Debtor;
Address;
Place or places where business carried on;
Description;
Title of firm or firms under which Debtor carried on business;
Names and address of trustee (if any);
Amount of property as estimated by Debtor (sub-divided into gross amount of property; value of securities given excluding any estimated surplus; net value of property);
Amount of liabilities as estimated by Debtor (sub-divided into gross amount of liabilities; amount of debts covered by securities; net amount of liabilities);
Date of Deed;
Date of Registration;
Date of declaration of assent by majority of creditors;
Security (including Date of certificate; Date of declaration of dispensation);
Avoidance of Deed (including date of order of court under s.11(2) of the Deeds of Arrangement Act 1914; date of notice by trustee under s.20);
Appointment of new trustee (including name and address of new trustee; by whom appointed; date of appointment);
Remarks

Form 8: Statutory declaration by trustee to be filed with Registrar that creditors have dispensed with his giving security

[Title]

I, of

being the trustee under the above-mentioned Deed of Arrangement, do solemnly and sincerely declare that the requisite majority in number and value of the creditors of , so far as the same are known to me, by resolution passed at a meeting convened by notice to all the creditors and duly held on the day of (or by writing addressed to me) dispensed with my giving the security directed to be given by section 11(1) of the Deeds of Arrangement Act 1914, and I make this solemn declaration *[etc as Form 3]*

Form 9: Security by trustee under s.11(1): form of bond

No:

Amount of guarantee £ Annual premium, £

Know All Men by these Presents, that we (trustee) and the (a guarantee society) (hereinafter called the said Society), are jointly and severally held and firmly bound to the Senior Registrar of the High Court of Justice in Bankruptcy (or Registrar of the County Court of holden at) in the sum of £ to be paid to the said Registrar, his successors and assigns, for which payment to be made I, the said , for myself, my heirs executors, and administrators, and we, the said Society for ourselves and our successors, jointly and severally bind ourselves firmly by these presents.

Sealed with our seals and dated this day of 19

Whereas on the day of 19 , of executed a Deed of Arrangement for the benefit of his (her or their) creditors, which was duly registered on the day of 19 .

And whereas the said (hereinafter called the said trustee) is the trustee of the aforesaid Deed of Arrangement. And whereas the estimated assets available for distribution among the unsecured creditors, as shown by the Affidavit filed on registration of the Deed, amount to the sum of £ . Now, therefore, the condition of this Bond or Obligation is such that if the said trustee shall administer the trust deed properly and account fully for the assets which come to his hands, and shall and do from time to time well and sufficiently perform and execute all and singular the duties required of him under the Deed of Arrangement of which he is trustee, and by any Statutes and Rules relating to such trusteeship, or if the said trustee shall fail therein and the said Society shall make good any loss or damage occasioned by any such default made on or after the date hereof to the estate of the said debtor to the extent of £ , this Obligation shall be void or otherwise shall remain in full force and virtue.

Provided always, and it is hereby agreed and declared, that this Bond is entered into by the said Society on the condition that the capital stock and funds for the time being of the said Society shall alone to liable to answer and make good all claims or demands in respect of this Bond, and that no director or other proprietor or holder of shares of the said Society shall in any manner be personally liable or subject to any claims or demands, by reason of such bond, beyond his or her particular share or shares of such capital stock and funds.

Provided always, and it is further agreed between the said trustee and the said Society, that the said trustee on ceasing to act as such trustee as aforesaid shall forthwith give notice thereof in writing to the said Society.

Provided always that the said trustee, his heirs, executors or administrators shall and will from time to time and at all times save, defend, and keep harmless the said Society and their successors and the capital stock, funds or property of the said Society from and against all loss or damage, costs and expenses which the said Society or the capital stock funds or property thereof shall or may or otherwise might at any time sustain or be put unto for or by reason or in consequence of the said Society having entered into the above written Bond for him and at his request.

And the said trustee hereby covenants that he will, on the day of of each successive year during the continuance of his administration of the estate, under the Deed, pay or cause to be paid to the said Society, the annual premium of £

In witness whereof the said trustee hath hereunto set his hand and seal, and the said Society have hereunto caused their seal to be affixed the day and year first above written.
Signed sealed and delivered by the said
In the presence of
The Seal of the said Society was hereunto affixed in the presence of

Form 10: Security by trustee: cover note
Bond No , 19 .
Mr , of , having this day effected a Guarantee for £ in favour of the Registrar of the Court, as trustee under a Deed of Arrangement executed by
on the terms and conditions contained in the Society's Bonds (according to the form prescribed under the Deeds of Arrangement Rules), a Bond will be prepared and delivered to the said Registrar within fourteen days of this date.

Manager of the said Society

Form 11: Certificate by registrar of the court that security has been given by trustee
[Title]
I hereby certify that Mr of , the trustee under the above-mentioned Deed of Arrangement, has given security to me in the sum of £ by Bond [*or* cover note] of the
Society for the due performance of his duties under the Deed pursuant to section 11(1) of the Deeds of Arrangement Act 1914.
Dated the day of 19
Registrar of the High Court or of the County Court of

Form 12: Order declaring deed void or appointing new trustee
Whereas is the trustee under the above-mentioned Deed of Arrangement and whereas it has been proved to the satisfaction of the Court that the said has failed to comply with the requirements of section 11(1) of the Deeds of Arrangement Act 1914.
Now, on the application of a creditor and upon hearing and upon reading this Court doth declare the said Deed of Arrangement to be void [or doth order that of be appointed trustee under the said Deed in place of the said but this Order shall not take effect unless the said shall give security as provided by section 11(1) of the Deeds of Arrangement Act 1914, within days after this day (*or as the Court may order with reference to security*)]

By the Court, Registrar

Form 13: Statement of accounts to be sent to creditors pursuant to Section 14

[Title]

Statement of trustee's accounts and of proceedings under the deed from .... 19.. to .... 19...

Receipts	£	*Payments*	£
Cash deposited by Debtor with solicitor for costs of deed		Law costs of preparation and registration of deed	
Cash at bank at date of deed		Law costs of solicitor to trustee	
Cash in hand at date of deed		Other law costs [3]	______
Book debts			
Stock in trade realised from sale by [1]		Accountant's charges	
		Auctioneer's and valuer's charges	
Machinery realised from sale by [1]		Trustee's remuneration	
Trade fixtures, fittings etc realised from sale by [1]		Possession	
		Incidental expenses	
Furniture realised from sale by [1]		Other costs and charges [3]	______
		Total costs and charges	
Surplus from securities in hands of creditors		Allowance to debtor	
		Payments to creditors, viz-	
Trading receipts		Rent from ..... to	
Other property, viz		Rates and taxes	
realised from sale by [1]	________	Salaries and wages	
Gross receipts		Other preferential payments, viz	
Less:		Dividends of .... in the £ on £	
Trading payments		Paid	
Payments to redeem securities, viz [2]		Unpaid	
		Other payments (if any)[3]	
Net realisations		Total	
Balance due to Trustee (if any)		*Balance in hand (if any)*	

(1) Insert gross proceeds of sale, and state how goods were sold, eg by auction, by valuation or as the case may be. (2) Here insert to whom payments made, nature of security redeemed and amount of each payment or annex schedule giving these particulars. (3) Insert particulars or annex schedule.

The total payments into the [4] Bank to the day of 19 were £ and the total payments out of the said Bank to the day of 19 were £

The amounts of the Assets and Liabilities at the time the Deed was executed as estimated by the debtor were:

Assets, after deducting £ the value of securities held by creditors and required to cover debts due to them £

Liabilities, after deducting £ , the amount covered by securities, £

The nature and value of the assets unrealised are[3]

The causes which delay the termination of the winding up of the estate are [3]

The estate will probably be completely wound up within

The following special circumstances affect the costs of realisation and the administration of the estate, viz (3)

Trustee; address; date.

(3) Insert particulars or annex schedule (4) Insert name of bank

[Form 14: Notice to creditors of deed of arrangement under s 24(1) repealed by the Insolvency Act 1985]

Form 15: Trustee's account of receipts and payments

[Title]

Trustee

Account of receipts and payments pursuant to section 13 of the Deeds of Arrangement Act 1914

RECEIPTS				PAYMENTS			
Date	*Of whom received*	*Nature of receipt*	*Amount*	*Date*	*To whom paid*	*Nature of payment*	*Amount*

Note: The outstanding estate consists of (*here set out particulars of any outstanding estate and the estimated value thereof*).

[Form 16 is a form of affidavit certifying trustee's account where the deed was executed before 1 April 1914]

Form 17: Affidavit verifying trustee's account

[Title]

I, of , the Trustee for the purposes of the above-mentioned Deed (*or* the person distributing the composition herein) make oath and say:

1. That * *the account hereunto annexed marked "B" contains a full and true account of my receipts and payments on account of the estate comprised in the said Deed* from the day of 19 to the day of 19 , inclusive, * *and that* I have not, nor has any other person by my order or for my use during such period, received or paid any moneys on account of the said estate * *other than and except the items mentioned and specified in the said account.*
2. That on the day of 19 , and the day of 19 I duly sent to each creditor of the said who has assented to the Deed a statement of accounts and proceedings as required by section 14 of the Deeds of Arrangement Act 1914.

[Sworn etc, as Form 4]

* If no receipts or payments, strike out the words in italics

Form 18: Trustee's trading account

[Title]

Accounts of receipts and payments in connection with the debtor's business, pursuant to Rule 33.

RECEIPTS	PAYMENTS
Date	Date

GH, Trustee

[To be inserted if the accounts have been audited by a committee of inspection:]
We have examined this account with the vouchers and find the same correct, and we are of opinion the expenditure has been proper.
Dated this day of 19
Committee of Inspection [or member of the Committee of Inspection]

Form 19: List of dividends or compositions
[Title]
I hereby certify that a dividend (*or* composition) of in the £ has been paid in the above matter and that the creditors whose names are set forth below are entitled to the amounts set opposite their respective names in the columns headed "amount of dividend (*or* composition)", and I further certify that the column headed "Unpaid" contains a full and complete list of all unpaid dividends or compositions.

Trustee

Dated the day of 19
To the Department of Trade & Industry

Surname	*Christian name*	*Amount of claim*	*Amount of dividend (or composition)*	
			Paid	*Unpaid*

Form 20: Affidavit verifying trustee's final account
[Title]
I, of , the Trustee for the purposes of the above-mentioned Deed (*or* the person distributing the composition herein) make oath and say:

1. That * *the account hereunto annexed marked "B" contains a full and true account of my receipts and payments on account of the estate comprised in the said Deed,* from the day of 19 to the date of swearing this my affidavit inclusive, * *and that* I have not, nor has any person by my order or for my use during such period, received or paid any moneys on account of the said estate * *other than and except the items mentioned and specified in the said account.*
2. † That all the property assigned under the Deed, or so much thereof as can probably be realised, has been realised and distributed according to the terms of the Deed, and that a dividend (or dividends) of in the £ has been paid as shown in the list hereunto annexed, marked "C".

or

2. †That the composition proposed under the Deed has been fully received and distributed as far as possible, as shown in the list hereunto annexed marked "C".
3. ¥ That on the day of 19 and the day of 19 , I duly sent to each creditor of the said who has assented to the Deed a statement of accounts and proceedings as required by section 14 of the Deeds of Arrangement Act 1914.

[Sworn etc as Form 4]

* If no receipts or payments, strike out the words in italics. † Strike out paragraph not applicable, or if neither paragraph is applicable, strike out both and add a special paragraph setting out the facts. ¥ Strike out paragraph 3 where deed executed before 1 April 1914.

Forms in administration order proceedings
(The County Court (Forms) Rules 1982, SI 1982 No 586)

N92: Request for administration order (CCR O.39, r.2(1))

In the	County Court
Between	Plaintiff
and	Defendant
	Case No:
	Request no:

I,
of
the above-named Defendant, state that a judgment was obtained against me in [the County Court] [the High Court of Justice Division] on the day of 19 , for the sum of £ and that I am unable to pay the amount forthwith*.
I owe the persons mentioned in the list below, including the plaintiff in this action, the sums given opposite their names, which do not total more than £5,000.
To the best of my knowledge I am not indebted to any other person whatsoever.
I request that an order may be made for the administration of my estate under Section 112 of the County Courts Act 1984, providing for the payment of my debts [in full] [to the extent of pence in the pound] by instalments of £ for every month.
* If the request was not made to the court in which judgment was obtained, a copy of the judgment must be produced.

List of Creditors

PLEASE COMPLETE USING BLACK INK

Name of creditor (& case no. in the case of a judgment debt). If known, give creditor's ref. no.	Address & description of creditor	Amount of debt £ p	Name & address of any other person liable for the debt	Particulars & estimated value of any security given in respect of the debt
	Total	£		

NOTE: The plaintiff's judgment debt must be inserted as well as all other debts. If any of the above creditors, in addition to the plaintiff, has sued the defendant in any Court, the summons or order in each case must be produced to the Registrar.

PLEASE ANSWER ALL THE FOLLOWING QUESTIONS USING BLOCK CAPITALS AND BLACK INK

1. Employment

(a) By whom are you employed? If you have more than one employer give answers in respect of each of them. If you are not employed, say so and give the name of your last employer, if any.
(b) Where are you employed?
(c) In what capacity are you employed?
(d) What is the address of your employer's Head Office if different from (b) above?
(e) What is your works number and/or pay reference? Works No:................ Pay Ref:................

2. Pay and income

(a) What is your pay before deductions? £ .... per week/month
(b) What overtime, bonuses, fees, allowances or commission do you receive (State whether on a regular basis or otherwise) £ .... per week/month
(c) Give details of deductions which are normally made from your pay £ .... per week/month
(d) Do you receive-
    (i) a pension? £ .... per week/month
    (ii) any state benefits? £ .... per week/month
    (iii) any other income? £ .... per week/month
(e) What is your usual take home pay? £ .... per week/month
(f) What contribution, if any, do other members of your family make to household expenses. Please give full details.

3. Liabilities

(a) What persons, if any, are financially dependent on you?
    (i) Living with you - please give details (including the ages of any dependent children)
    (ii) Not living with you: please give details including any maintenance payments you make to them
(b) What rent or mortgage instalments are you liable to pay? £ .... per week/month
(c) What rates are you liable to pay? £ .... per week/month
    What amount do you actually pay? £ .... per week/month
(d) If you have to pay under any other Court orders give details, including the name of the Court and Case No, the amount still owing and the instalments you are paying.
(e) What other regular payments have you to make?
(f) Have you any other liabilities which you would like the Court to take into account?

I,
aforesaid make oath and say that to the best of my knowledge, the names of all my creditors, and the debts due from me to them, are truly set forth in the above list of my creditors, and that the particulars contained in my request and the above statements are true.

Sworn at
in the
this day of
Before me,
Solicitor/Officer of a court, appointed by the judge to take affidavits

N93: List of creditors furnished under Attachment of Earnings Act 1971 (CCR O.39, r.2(3))

In the	County Court
Between	Plaintiff
and	Defendant
	Case No:
	Attachment application no:

I

of

the above-named defendant, state that I owe the persons mentioned in the list below, including the plaintiff in this action, the sums given opposite their names, which do not total more than £5,000. To the best of my knowledge I am not indebted to any other person whatsoever.

If an order is made for the administration of my estate, I request that it may provide for the payment of my debts [in full] [to the extent of pence in the pound] by instalments of £ per month.

* If the request was not made to the court in which judgment was obtained, a copy of the judgment must be produced.

List of Creditors

PLEASE COMPLETE USING BLACK INK

Name of creditor (& case no. in the case of a judgment debt). If known, give creditor's ref. no.	Address & description of creditor	Amount of debt £ p	Name & address of any other person liable for the debt	Particulars & estimated value of any security given in respect of the debt
	Total	£		

NOTE: The plaintiff's judgment debt must be inserted as well as all other debts. If any of the above creditors, in addition to the plaintiff, has sued the defendant in any Court, the summons or order in each case must be produced to the Registrar.

I,

aforesaid make oath and say that to the best of my knowledge, the names of all my creditors, and the debts due from me to them, are truly set forth in the above list of my creditors, and that the above particulars and statements are true.

Sworn etc as Form N92

N94: Administration order (CCR O.39, r.9)

In the County Court

Administration Order No:

IN THE MATTER OF an Administration Order against

IT IS ORDERED that the above-named debtor do pay the debts in the Schedule to this Order, and all other debts now due and afterwards proved under this Order in full [or to the extent of pence in the £] by instalments of £ for every month until this Order is complied with.

[AND IT IS ORDERED that the said Debtor do pay the said instalments into the office of this court the first of such payments to be made on or before the day of 19 .]

[AND IT IS DIRECTED that this order be subject to review after [or at intervals of].]

AND IT IS DIRECTED that of have the conduct of this Order.

Schedule of Debts

Name of creditor	Amount
Total	

To the Debtor
TAKE NOTICE that if you change your address you must at once give notice of your new address to the Chief Clerk of

N95: Order revoking, suspending or varying an administration order (CCR O.39 r.14(2))

In the County Court
Debtor

Administration Order No:
TO THE DEBTOR AND CREDITOR (State creditor's reference)
IT IS ORDERED that the Administration Order made against the above named Debtor on the be revoked [because] [unless]
OR be [suspended] [varied] provided that
Dated
Case No
Your ref: (State creditor's reference)
TO THE CREDITOR (Delete if inapplicable)
The Court has declared a dividend on the amount of money paid by the Debtor. Enclosed in a payable order for £

Index